EIGHTH EDITION

COLLEGE & CAREER SUCCESS

MARSHA FRALICK

Kendall Hunt
publishing company

Book Team

Chairman and Chief Executive Officer   Mark C. Falb
President and Chief Operating Officer   Chad M. Chandlee
Vice President, Higher Education   David L. Tart
Director of Publishing Partnerships   Paul B. Carty
Product/Development Supervisor   Lynne Rogers
Vice President, Operations   Timothy J. Beitzel
Senior Project Coordinator   Stefani DeMoss
Permissions Editor   Caroline Kieler
Cover Designer   Suzanne Millius

Cover images © Shutterstock, Inc.

www.kendallhunt.com
Send all inquiries to:
4050 Westmark Drive
Dubuque, IA 52004-1840

CONTENTS

PART II   College Success   139

I have always believed that education provides a means for accomplishing a person's dreams. I guess I learned that idea from my parents and teachers in high school. When I started college at the University of New Mexico, it was the beginning of a great adventure which was to last my lifetime. I can still recall being a college freshman. I had attended a small school in northern New Mexico, Pojoaque High School. I was a good student in high school and was motivated to succeed in college. As a freshman, I had career goals that were pretty unrealistic and changed from week to week. I thought about becoming the first woman president or maybe a diplomat. Since Nancy Drew was my heroine, I thought about being a spy or detective like Nancy Drew. Deciding on a major and career was a monumental task.

When I started at the University of New Mexico, I was soon overwhelmed. I did not know how to take notes, remember what I read, or manage my time. I remember that I was anxious and stressed out about taking tests. I worked and went to school during the day and tried to study at night. Sometimes I studied all night and then the next day forgot what I had studied. College was not fun, and I wished that someone had written a book on how to survive in college. I decided that I would figure out how to be successful and maybe someday write a book about it so that other people would not have to struggle as much as I did.

I learned how to survive and was very successful in college, completing my bachelor's, master's, and doctorate degrees. I enjoyed the college environment so much that I ended up being a college counselor and teacher. That was pretty far from being Nancy Drew, but it has been a career that I have found very satisfying. In 1978, the vice-president of newly opened Cuyamaca College in El Cajon, California, asked if I would design a college success course for the new college. I was excited to design a course that would help students to be successful in college. I was motivated because I believed in the value of education and remembered what it was like to be a new college student. Now it is 39 years later and I am still designing and teaching college success courses. Every semester that I teach, I learn more from students and continue to develop ideas for a college success course that makes a positive difference in students' lives. My experiences as a student and faculty member have helped me design a class with proven success. I have also done research on student success and designed this textbook based on my research findings.

What do students need to be successful? First of all, they need to know how to study. This includes being able to apply memory techniques, read effectively, listen to lectures, take notes, and prepare for exams. Without these skills, students may wrongly decide that they are not capable of doing college work. If students know these techniques and apply them, they can be confident in their abilities and reach their true potential. With confidence, they can begin to relax and meet the challenges of tests and term papers. They might even learn to like education.

Being able to study is not enough. Students need to know what to study, so having a career goal is important. I have observed that students choose their career goals for a variety of reasons. Just like I wanted to be Nancy Drew, some students choose their occupations based on some person that they admire. Some choose their career based on familiarity. They choose occupations that they have observed in their families or communities. Others choose a career by accident; they obtain whatever job is available. We now have a great deal of information on how to choose a satisfying career goal. The first step is personal assessment. What are the students' personality types, interests, multiple intelligences, and values? Once these are determined, what careers match these personal characteristics? What careers will be a good choice for the future? These are all questions that need to be answered in order to continue to study in college.

Managing time and money and setting goals are important. Like many other students, I had always worked while attending college. While getting my master's and doctorate degrees, I worked and had a family. I have felt the pressures of these many roles and learned how to manage them. Students can learn these important life skills to make the journey easier.

Learning how to speak and write well has been a great asset to me in college and in my career. These skills did not come easily. I remember getting papers back with so many red corrections that they looked like decorated Christmas trees. I learned from the mistakes and kept practicing. These are skills that all college students need to master early in their college careers.

One of the goals of a college education is to learn to think critically and creatively. The world is full of complex issues with no easy answers. We find solutions by working with others, questioning the status quo, looking at different alternatives, respecting the opinions of others, and constructing our own personal views. Through creative thinking, we can come up with ideas to solve problems in our careers and personal lives.

I had the advantage of growing up with two cultures and speaking two languages. This has given me an appreciation for different groups of people. Appreciating others and working with diverse groups of people are skills needed by everyone today because the world is becoming more diverse. If we have hope for being able to live peacefully in the world, we will need to understand and appreciate this diversity.

Probably the most important skill for success is that of positive thinking. I truly believe that we accomplish what we think we can do. We need to become aware of our thoughts, and when they are negative, we need to change them. I often ask students to notice their negative thoughts and then, as if making a new video, change their negative thoughts to positive thoughts. Positive thoughts are powerful influences on attitude and behavior.

What good does it do to attend college if students do not enjoy good health? I have resolved to emphasize achieving wellness and maintaining good health in all my college classes. In the new millennium, we are all supposed to live to be 100 years old. I collect stories about seniors who climb mountains, orbit the earth, write bestselling novels, and become famous artists. We can learn from them about how to live long, healthy, and productive lives.

Through the study of psychology, neuroscience, and education, we have discovered many ways to help people to be successful. I have briefly introduced these theories and the names of the psychologists who have done research in this area. It is not enough to know the theory or idea; it is necessary to know how to apply it. This book contains many exercises designed to assist students apply the material learned.

The sections titled "Keys to Success," located near the end of each chapter, are my personal philosophies of life developed from being in education for over 49 years. Although I still remember being a college freshman, that was a long time ago, and I have learned a lot since then. If I could survive in college, you can too. I wrote that book that I thought about many years ago. I hope that it makes your journey through college, your career, and your life a little easier.

Comprehensive
Topics include college, career, and lifelong success.

Includes Concepts from Positive Psychology
Concepts from positive psychology are used to help students:

- discover their strengths, interests, and values.
- build on their strengths.
- think positively about themselves and their future.
- clarify what happiness means and work toward attaining happiness in life.

Helps Students Assume Responsibility for Their Own Success
Topics include motivation, positive thinking, locus of control, mindset, future mindedness, hope, belief, persistence, grit, emotional intelligence, and learning positive behavior.

Incorporates The Latest Research in Psychology, Education, and Neuroscience
The suggested strategies in this textbook are all based on current research. The latest research in neuroscience is translated into practical strategies for memory and study skills.

Online Career Portfolio
The career material in the online portfolio helps students to make an informed choice of their college major and career. It includes the AchieveWORKS Personality assessment and the AchieveWORKS Intelligences assessment of multiple intelligences. The results of these assessments are linked to the O*Net database of careers for career exploration. It includes Indeed.com that helps students to find employment. The material in the online portfolio is supplemented by The Interest Profiler integrated into Chapter 3 that helps students to identify their vocational interests. The AchieveWORKS Learning and Productivity assessment is also part of the portfolio.

Helps Students Find Employment after Graduation
This textbook includes:

- information on career trends, the career decision-making process, educational planning, researching career information, and career outlook.
- updated job search strategies including the concept of online personal branding and using social media to find jobs.
- the basics of writing a resume and cover letter as well as interviewing tips.

Increasing Math Success
Since math is the gateway to high-paying careers and is a challenging requirement for graduation, this edition has expanded material on how to study math, take math notes, deal with math anxiety, and how to be successful on math tests.

Tools for Student Engagement

- Interactive activities within the text help students to practice the material learned.
- Frequent quizzes and answer keys within the chapters help students with reading comprehension and check understanding of key concepts.
- Journal entries help students think critically and apply what they have learned to their personal lives.
- Individual and group exercises are included at the end of each chapter.

Resources for Faculty and Students at College Success 1

The College Success 1 website at www.collegesuccess1.com has additional materials to accompany this text-book. Student resources include key ideas, Internet links related to each chapter, and Word documents for the journal entries. Resources for faculty include the **Instructor Manual** and **Faculty Resources** for teaching college success courses including over 500 pages of classroom exercises, handouts, video suggestions, Internet links to related material, and much more.

ACKNOWLEDGMENTS

I would like to give my sincere thanks to:

- My parents, Betty and Clarence Finley, who taught me the value of education,

- My seven brothers and sisters, who taught me to laugh at life,

- My children, Mark Fralick and Sara Corbett, who assisted with editing and shared their New Millennial perspective,

- Paul Delys, who provided love and encouragement and shared many of his ideas and materials for this book,

- The instructors of College and Career Success who tried out my material, gave valuable feedback, and shared their ideas,

- The many students who have taken my course over the years and shared their insights and experiences with me.

Used with permission. © Lifetouch Inc.

Dr. Marsha Fralick has been employed in the field of education for over 49 years, including 39 years of teaching college success courses. She has brought together research in psychology, education, neuroscience, health, and career development to provide students with strategies for college, career, and lifelong success. She has been recognized as an Outstanding First-Year Student Advocate by the National Resource Center for the First-Year Experience and Students in Transition for excellence in teaching, curriculum development, and leadership. Her college and career success materials are now used by community colleges and universities nationwide and in Canada. She has a doctorate from the University of Southern California with an emphasis in career counseling, a master's degree in counseling from the University of Redlands and a bachelor's degree in Spanish and English from Arizona State University.

PART I

Career Success

CHAPTER 1

Understanding Motivation

Learning Objectives

Read to answer these key questions:

- What do I want from college?

- What is the value of a college education?

- How do I choose my major and career?

- How can I motivate myself to be successful?

- How can I begin habits that lead to success?

- How can I be persistent in achieving my goal of a college education?

M ost students attend college with dreams of earning a college degree and improving their lives. Some students are there to explore interests and possibilities while others have more defined career goals. Although college students enter college with good intentions, about half of them (or less) graduate within 6 years.

Here are the graduation rates within 6 years for various types of colleges:[1]

- 50% of four-year public college students
- 60% of four-year private college students
- 26% of public two-year college students

Being successful in college and attaining your dreams begins with motivation. It provides the energy or drive to find your direction and reach your goals. It is easier to be motivated if you have chosen a major and career that matches your interests and personal strengths. Motivation can also be increased by having a positive mindset and exploring strategies to increase perseverance. Use the tools in this chapter to become one of the successful college students.

What Do I Want from College?

Succeeding in college requires time and effort. You will have to give up some of your time spent on leisure activities and working. You will give up some time spent with your friends and families. Making sacrifices and working hard are easier if you know what you want to achieve through your efforts. One of the first steps in motivating yourself to be successful in college is to have a clear and specific understanding of your reasons for attending college. Are you attending college as a way to obtain a satisfying career? Is financial security one of your goals? Will you feel more satisfied if you are living up to your potential? What are your hopes and dreams, and how will college help you to achieve your goals?

When you are having difficulties or doubts about your ability to finish your college education, remember your hopes and dreams and your plans for the future. It is a good idea to write these ideas down, think about them, and revise them from time to time.

What Is the Value of a College Education?

Many college students say that getting a satisfying job that pays well and achieving financial security are important motivators for attending college. As a result of the rising cost of higher education, students have started to question whether a college education is still a good investment. Recent analyses by the Federal Reserve Bank have shown that the benefits still outweigh the cost for both an associate's and a bachelor's degree. These degrees have a 15% return, which is considered a good investment.[2] By getting a degree, you can get a job that pays more per hour, work fewer hours to earn a living, and have more time for leisure activities. In addition, you can spend your time at work doing something that you enjoy. A report issued by the Census Bureau in 2016 listed the following education and income statistics for all races and both genders throughout the United States.[3] Lifetime income assumes that a person works 30 years before retirement.

Average Earnings Based on Education Level

Education	Yearly Income	Lifetime Income
High school graduate	35,984	1,079,520
Some college, no degree	39,312	1,179,360
Associate's degree	42,588	1,277,640
Bachelor's degree	60,112	1,803,360
Professional degree	90,740	2,722,200

© sergign/Shutterstock.com

Notice that income rises with educational level. Over a lifetime, a person with a bachelor's degree earns about 60% more than a high school graduate. Of course, these are average figures across the nation and some individuals earn higher or lower salaries. People fantasize about winning the lottery, but the reality is that the probability of winning the lottery is very low. In the long run, you have a better chance of increasing your income by going to college.

Let's do some further comparisons. A high-school graduate earns an average of $1,079,520 over a lifetime. A college graduate with a bachelor's degree earns $1,803,360 over a lifetime. A college graduate earns $723,840 more than a high-school graduate does over a lifetime. So how much is a college degree worth? It is worth $723,840 over a lifetime. Would you go to college and finish your degree if someone offered to pay you $723,840? Here are some more interesting figures we can derive from the above table:

Completing one college course is worth $18,096.
(723,840 divided by 40 courses in a bachelor's degree)

Going to class for one hour is worth $377.
($18,096 divided by 48 hours in a semester class)

Would you take a college course if someone offered you $18,096? Would you go to class today for one hour if someone offered you $377? Of course, if this sounds too good to be true, remember that you will receive these payments over a working lifetime of 30 years.

While college graduation does not guarantee employment, it increases your chances of finding a job. In 2016, high-school graduates had an unemployment rate of 5.2% as compared to college graduates who had an unemployment rate of 2.7%. Increase your chances of employment by continuing your education.

Employment and earnings are only some of the values of going to college. College helps develop your potential and increase your confidence, self-esteem, self-respect, and happiness. It increases your understanding of the world and prepares you to be an informed citizen.

Journal Entry #1

What are your dreams for the future? Write a paragraph about what you hope to accomplish by going to college.

© iQoncept/Shutterstock.com

Choosing a Major and Career

Having a definite major and career choice is a good motivation for completing your college education. It is difficult to put in the work necessary to be successful if you do not have a clear picture of your future career; however, three out of four college students are undecided about their major. For students who have chosen a major, 30 to 75 percent of a graduating class will change that major two or more times.[4] Unclear or indefinite career goals are some of the most significant factors that identify students at risk of dropping out of college.[5] Choosing an appropriate college major is one of the most difficult and important decisions that college students can make.

How can you choose the major that is best for you? The best way is to first understand yourself: become aware of your personality traits, interests, preferred lifestyle, values, gifts, and talents. The next step is to do career research to determine the career that best matches your personal characteristics. Then, plan your education to prepare for your career. By following these steps, you can find the major that is best for you and minimize the time you spend in college. This textbook helps you to move through the process of self-understanding and find the major and career that is the best match for you.

How to Be Motivated

There are many ways to be motivated to be successful in college and in your future career. Set the stage with a positive mindset, increase your perseverance, think positively about the future, and find something interesting in your studies. Apply some concepts from psychology including intrinsic motivation, locus of control, affiliation, achievement, and simply using a reward. We will examine each of these concepts in more detail. As you read through them, think about how you can apply them to your personal life.

Your Mindset Makes a Difference

Did you know that your mindset has a powerful effect on learning and college success? Mindset is related to your self-image as a learner. It affects the effort you put into your studies and how you deal with challenges and setbacks. A positive mindset can even make you smarter as you learn new material and exercise your brain. Scientists have identified a **growth mindset** that leads to success.[6] It includes the belief that

- Intelligence is increased as you learn new knowledge.
- Through practice and effort, skills can be improved.
- Learning and self-improvement continue over a lifetime.
- Challenges are a way to be tested and improve performance.
- Failure is an opportunity to learn.

© Aliwak/Shutterstock.com

- Constructive criticism improves performance.
- The success of others is an inspiration.

In contrast, the **fixed mindset** is an obstacle to success. It includes these beliefs:

- Intelligence is fixed at birth.
- Increased effort does not lead to success.
- There is a limit to what we can accomplish.
- Roadblocks or obstacles are an excuse to be absent.
- It is best to take on only easy tasks in which success is guaranteed.
- Constructive criticism is a personal attack.
- The success of others makes me look bad.
- Hard work is unpleasant.
- The amount of work needed to be successful is underestimated.

The good news is that you can learn to identify and change your mindset so that you can be successful in college, in your career, and in your personal life. If you believe that effort can produce rewards, you are on your way to success.

Activity: What is Your Mindset?

Circle the number that best describes your mindset.

	Strongly Agree	Agree	Disagree	Strongly Disagree
People are born with a certain amount of intelligence that cannot be changed.	0	1	2	3
I appreciate feedback on my performance and use it to improve my skills.	3	2	1	0
I avoid challenges and prefer to complete school work that is easy.	0	1	2	3
The more you learn, the more intelligent you become.	3	2	1	0
Completing challenging work is worth the effort because it gives me a sense of accomplishment.	3	2	1	0
When the work is difficult, I feel like I am not very smart.	0	1	2	3
When I receive a failing grade, I feel discouraged and feel like giving up.	0	1	2	3
When I receive a failing grade, I look at what I did wrong and try to do better next time.	3	2	1	0
I get angry when teachers or coaches tell me how to improve my performance.	0	1	2	3
The more work you put into learning a new skill, the better you will get at doing it.	3	2	1	0

Write your total points here: _____

25–30	You have a growth mindset that will help you to be successful in college.
20–24	You have many qualities of a positive mindset, but could benefit from thinking more positively about learning.
15–19	You have some qualities of a growth mindset, but would benefit from re-reading the information about growth mindset and thinking about how you can use this material to increase your success.
14 or less	Re-read the material on growth mindset and think about how you can apply it to improve your success in college.

Grit: A Powerful Tool for Student Success

Psychologists have found that one of the most important factors related to success in college is grit. What is grit? Grit is defined as a combination of perseverance and passion. Psychologist Angela Duckworth studied students who were successful at the United States Military Academy at West Point, one of the most selective colleges in the country.[7] Even though only the top students are admitted, 20% of these students drop out before graduation. Most of the dropouts leave during the first two months of college. What is the difference between those who are successful and those who drop out? **Those who are successful have a "never give up" attitude, or grit**. They are constantly tested with tasks that challenge their skills and are successful because they have grit, and not because of superior academic or athletic ability. The successful students can keep going through challenges and even failure.

Grit includes the element of passion, or the drive to constantly improve. Successful students have a goal or vision of the future and they strive to achieve it. Their goals are achievable because they match their interests and personal strengths. For this reason, having goals that match your personal strengths and interests is essential to your success. These goals give you the motivation and grit to continue when the going gets tough. Some of you have clear goals for the future while others are re-evaluating or beginning to work on them. The material in the following chapters helps you to think about your interests and personal strengths to set goals for the future and increase the motivation to complete your education.

What is more important, talent or grit? We have traditionally assumed that talent or intelligence is the key to success. In fact, there is a bias in society in which people assume that success is the result of talent. We look at successful people, admire their talent, and assume that their unusual talent made them successful. However, "our talent is one thing. What we do with it is quite another."[8] The most talented individuals are not always the most successful. The great philosopher Nietzsche proposed that we think of gifted individuals as people who worked hard to become geniuses.

How do famous people achieve excellence? Psychologists have studied famous musicians, athletes, scientists, and others to find out what makes them successful. Rather than talent, the characteristic connected to success is **effortful training.** Effortful training involves identifying a goal that challenges your skills, finding your weaknesses, and working to improve them one small step at a time. Life is easier if you can establish a habit or daily ritual of effortful practice. For example, you can make it a habit of exercising first thing in the morning. You can make a habit of studying at a certain time and place each day. If you are in the habit of doing something, you don't have to think about it; you just do it.

It is estimated that it takes about 10,000 hours to learn a complex skill.[9] The practice is often difficult and boring, but motivated individuals persist by keeping in mind what they want to accomplish. Here are some examples of effortful practice:

- Do you want to become an NBA superstar? Superstars such as Kobe Bryant, Lebron James, and James Hardin spend at least five hours a day for seven days a week practicing.[10]
- Do you want to be an all pro football player? Tom Brady spends 16 hours a day practicing, viewing films, and preparing for meetings before a Super Bowl game.[11]
- Do you want to become an Olympic gold medalist swimmer? Michael Phelps swims 50 miles a week. He also trains for five to 6 six hours a day for six days a week.[12]
- Do you want to become a world-famous violinist? Itzhak Perlman suggests that students spend from four to five hours of effortful practicing each day.[13]

These successful musicians and athletes have true grit and practice until their performance becomes a habit. The key idea is that learning complex skills is challenging, takes time, and is accomplished through effortful practice one small step at a time.

© Castleski/Shutterstock.com

How does grit apply to college students? To be successful in college, it is important to spend a significant amount of time on your studies. A common rule is to spend two hours a week for each unit enrolled. For example, a three-unit course would require three hours a week in class and six hours outside of class reading and studying. Of course, the time required varies with the difficulty of the subject and your prior knowledge. In math courses, students may need to spend 10 hours per week studying and practicing problems to be successful. Start spending time studying from the very beginning. Remember that most dropouts happen early in the semester as students quickly realize that they are too behind to catch up.

Most importantly, don't give up! It is important to understand that college is challenging and requires a great deal of effort to be successful. Because college is difficult, there may be times that you may struggle or even receive a failing grade. Maintain a positive attitude, spend more time on the subject, and ask for help. Seek out tutoring or see your college professor during office hours if you need extra help. Asking for help is not a sign of weakness. College professors generally respect students who are interested enough in their field of expertise to ask for help. Colleges set up programs such as tutoring to help students be successful.

Are there times when it is better to give up? Don't give up your important goals just because you think they are difficult. However, if you realize that the goals you have set for yourself do not match your interests, it is better to set new goals and follow a different path. Prioritize how you spend your time so that you are spending it on what is most important. If you realize that the time spent on your current goal is a distraction to accomplishing more important goals, then it is better to change directions. There may be times when you must take courses that you don't consider interesting to complete your long-term goal of a college degree. In this case, it is best to think about your long-term goal of graduating from college, be gritty, and persevere.

How can you develop grit? The good news is that grit is related to the growth mindset and can be learned. Here are three steps for learning grit:

1. The first step in learning grit is finding interest. Become aware of what you enjoy doing and follow your interests. Chapter 3 in this textbook helps you to explore your interests and values.

2. Invest your time in practice. Find your weaknesses and strive to improve them. Practice frequently and work one small step at a time.

3. Find your purpose. One of the most difficult questions you may ask yourself is, "What is my purpose in life?" To answer this important question, ask yourself why your work is important and how it will help others. Knowing about your purpose helps you to maintain interest, invest your time in practice, and become passionate about your work.[14]

Activity: How Gritty Are You?

	Strongly Agree	Agree	Disagree	Strongly Disagree
I have a "never give up" attitude.	3	2	1	0
I spend a significant amount of time studying each week.	3	2	1	0
A failing grade shows a lack of intelligence.	0	1	2	3
Failure is an opportunity to figure out what went wrong and fix it.	3	2	1	0
I believe that the most talented and intelligent people will become the most successful.	0	1	2	3
When work is challenging, I tend to get discouraged and lose interest.	0	1	2	3
I have a good awareness of my interests and what I enjoy doing.	3	2	1	0
I can write a statement about what is my purpose in life.	3	2	1	0
I have goals in life and spend my time on what is most important.	3	2	1	0
I would describe myself as a person who has grit.	3	2	1	0

Write your total points here: _____

25–30   Your grittiness will help you to be successful in college, careers, and life.
20–24   You have many qualities of a gritty person, but could benefit from thinking more about how to increase your grit.
15–19   You have some qualities of a gritty person, but would benefit from re-reading the information about grit and thinking about how you can use this material to increase your success.
14 or less   Re-read the material on grit and think about how you can apply it to improve your success in college.

Journal Entry #2

In how many units are you enrolled this term? Approximately how many hours per week will you have to study to be successful? Write five intention statements about improving your mindset and grit.

I am enrolled in ___ units. I will need to study approximately ___ hours per week to be successful. To improve my mindset and grit, I intend to . . .

Thinking Positively about the Future

Developing a growth mindset and grit both depend on positive thinking. You can motivate yourself to complete your education by thinking positively about the future. If you believe that your chances of graduating from college are good, you can be motivated to take the steps necessary to achieve your goals. Conversely, if you think that your chances of graduating are poor, it is difficult to motivate yourself to continue. The degree of optimism that you possess is greatly influenced by past experiences. For example, if you were a good student

© kentoh/Shutterstock.com

in the past, you are likely to be optimistic about the future. If you struggled with your education, you may have some negative experiences that you will need to overcome. Negative thoughts can often become a self-fulfilling prophecy: what we think becomes true.

How can you train yourself to think more optimistically? First, become aware of your thought patterns. Are they mostly negative or positive? If they are negative, make a conscious decision to change them to positive thoughts. Here is an example.

Pessimism

I failed the test. I guess I am just not college material. I feel really stupid. I just can't do this. College is too hard for me. My (teacher, father, mother, friend, boss) told me I would never make it. Maybe I should just drop out of college and do something else.

Optimism

I failed the test. Let's take a look at what went wrong, so I can do better next time. Did I study enough? Did I study the right material? Maybe I should take this a little slower. How can I get help so that I can understand? I plan to do better next time.

Can a person be too optimistic? In some circumstances, this is true. There is a difference between optimism and wishful thinking, for example. Wishful thinking does not include plans for accomplishing goals and can be a distraction from achieving them. Working toward unattainable goals can be exhausting and demoralizing, especially when the resources for attaining them are lacking. Goals must be realistic and achievable. Psychologists recommend that "people should be optimistic when the future can be changed by positive thinking, but not otherwise."[15] Using optimism requires some judgment about possible outcomes in the future.

There are some good reasons to think more positively. Psychologists have done long-term studies showing that people who use positive thinking have many benefits over a lifetime, including good health, longevity, happiness, perseverance, improved problem solving, and enhanced ability to learn. Optimism is also related to goal achievement. If you are optimistic and believe a goal is achievable, you are more likely to take the steps necessary to accomplish the goal. If you do not believe that a goal is achievable, you are likely to give up trying to achieve it. Being optimistic is closely related to being hopeful about the future. If you are hopeful about the future, you are likely to be more determined to reach your goals and to make plans for reaching them. Be optimistic about graduating from college, find the resources necessary to accomplish your goal, and start taking the steps to create your success.

> "Life is very interesting. In the end, some of your greatest pains become your greatest strengths."
> Drew Barrymore

> "There is nothing good or bad, but thinking makes it so."
> Shakespeare's Hamlet

Are you generally an optimist or pessimist about the future? Read the following items and rate your level of agreement or disagreement:

Rate the following items using this scale:

5   I definitely agree
4   I agree
3   I neither agree or disagree (neutral)
2   I disagree
1   I strongly disagree

_____   My chances of graduating from college are good.

_____   I am confident that I can overcome any obstacles to my success.

_____   Things generally turn out well for me.

_____   I believe that positive results will eventually come from most problem situations.

_____   If I work hard enough, I will eventually achieve my goals.

_____   Although I have faced some problems in the past, the future will be better.

_____   I expect that most things will go as planned.

_____   Good things will happen to me in the future.

_____   I am generally persistent in reaching my goals.

_____   I am good at finding solutions to the problems I face in life.

Add up your total points and multiply by two. My total points (× 2) are _____.

90–100   You are an excellent positive thinker.
80–89   You are a good positive thinker.
70–79   Sometimes you think positively, and sometimes not. Can you re-evaluate
                    your thinking?
60 and below   Work on positive thinking.

Journal Entry #3

Write five positive statements about your college education and your future.

> "No pessimist ever discovered the secrets of the stars, or sailed to an uncharted land, or opened a new doorway for the human spirit."
> Helen Keller

Find Something Interesting in Your Studies

Finding something interesting in your studies helps you to maintain a growth mindset and improve grit. If you can think positively about what you are studying, it makes the job easier and more satisfying. Begin your studies by finding something interesting in the course and your textbook. Contrast these two ideas:

I have to take economics. It is going to be difficult and boring. What do I need economics for anyway? I'll just need to get through it so I can get my degree.

I have to take economics. I wonder about the course content. I often hear about it on the news. How can I use this information in my future? What can I find that is interesting?

Make sure to attend the first class meeting. Remember that the professor is very knowledgeable about the subject and finds the content interesting and exciting. At the first class meeting, the professor will give you an overview of the course and should provide some motivation for studying the material in the course. Look at the course syllabus to find what the course is about and to begin to look for something that could be interesting or useful to you.

Skimming a textbook before you begin a course is a good way to find something interesting and to prepare for learning. Skimming will give you an organized preview of what's ahead. Here are the steps to skimming a new text:

1. **Quickly read the preface or introduction.** Read as if you were having a conversation with the author of the text. In the preface or introduction, you will find out how the author has organized the material, the key ideas, and his or her purpose in writing the text.

2. **Look at the major topics in the table of contents.** You can use the table of contents as a window into the book. It gives a quick outline of every topic in the text. As you read the table of contents, look for topics of special interest to you.

3. **Spend five to 15 minutes quickly looking over the book.** Turn the pages quickly, noticing boldfaced topics, pictures, and anything else that catches your attention. Again, look for important or interesting topics. Do not spend too much time on this step. If your textbook is online, skim through the website.

4. **What resources are included?** Is there an index, glossary of terms, answers to quiz questions, or solutions to math problems? These sections will be of use to you as you read. If your book is online, explore the website to find useful features and content.

Skimming a text or website before you begin to read has several important benefits. The first benefit is that it gets you started in the learning process. It is an easy and quick step that can help you avoid procrastination. It increases motivation by helping you notice items that have appeal to you. Previewing the content will help you to relax as you study and remember the information. Early in the course, this step will help you verify that you have chosen the correct course and that you have the prerequisites to be successful in the class.

> "A pessimist sees the difficulty in every opportunity; an optimist sees the opportunity in every difficulty."
> Winston Churchill

Avoid Multi-Tasking

Multi-tasking is trying to study while talking on the cell phone, checking social media, and thinking about something else. It is difficult to focus and be motivated if you are multi-tasking. It is a common myth that the brain can multi-task and pay attention to several inputs at once.

However, the brain cannot multi-task; it pays attention to one input at a time. Research shows the following:[16]

- A person who is interrupted takes 50% longer to complete a task.
- The interruptions results in 50% more errors.

A good example of the problems with multi-tasking is driving while talking on the phone. The brain constantly switches between paying attention to the phone and driving. If you are talking on a cell phone, you are half a second slower in stepping on the brake. At 70 mph, the car travels 51 feet in half a second. In addition, drivers miss 50% of the visual clues noticed by drivers who are not trying to multi-task. Driving while using a cell phone is like driving drunk.[17] While studying, cell phones and other distractions reduce productivity and increase the chance for errors. Focusing on one task at a time saves time, improves the quality of work, and improves motivation.

© Arson0618/Shutterstock.com

Intrinsic or Extrinsic Motivation

Intrinsic motivation comes from within. It means that you do an activity because you enjoy it or find personal meaning in it. With intrinsic motivation, the nature of the activity itself or the consequences of the activity motivate you. For example, let's say that I am interested in learning to play the piano. I am motivated to practice playing the piano because I like the sound of the piano and feel very satisfied when I can play music that I enjoy. I practice because I like to practice, not because I have to practice. When I get tired or frustrated, I work through it or put it aside and come back to it because I want to learn to play the piano well.

You can be intrinsically motivated to continue in college because you enjoy learning and find the college experience satisfying. Look for ways to enjoy college and to find some personal satisfaction in it. If you enjoy college, it becomes easier to do the work required to be successful. Think about what you say to yourself about college. If you are saying negative things such as "I don't want to be here," it will be difficult to continue.

Extrinsic motivation comes as a result of an external reward from someone else. Examples of extrinsic rewards are certificates, bonuses, money, praise, and recognition. Taking the piano example again, let's say that I want my child to play the piano. The child does not know if he or she would like to play the piano. I give the child a reward for practicing the piano. I could pay the child for practicing or give praise for doing a good job. There are two possible outcomes of the extrinsic reward. After a while, the child may gain skills and confidence and come to enjoy playing the piano. The extrinsic reward is no longer necessary because the child is now intrinsically motivated. Or the child may decide that he or she does not like to play the piano. The extrinsic reward is no longer effective in motivating the child to play the piano.

You can use extrinsic rewards to motivate yourself to be successful in college. Remind yourself of the payoff for getting a college degree: earning more money, having a satisfying career, being able to purchase a car and a house. Extrinsic rewards can be a first step in motivating yourself to attend college. With experience and achievement, you may come to like going to college and may become intrinsically motivated to continue your college education.

If you use intrinsic motivation to achieve your goal, you will be happier and more successful. If you do something like playing the piano because you enjoy it, you are more likely to spend the time necessary to practice to achieve your goal. If you view college as something that you enjoy and as valuable to you, it is easier to spend the time to do the required studying. When you get tired or frustrated, tell yourself that you are doing a good job (praise yourself) and think of the positive reasons that you want to get a college education.

Locus of Control

Being aware of the concept of locus of control is another way of understanding motivation. The word **locus** means place. The locus of control is where you place the responsibility for control over your life. In other words, who is in charge? If you place the responsibility on yourself and believe that you have control over your life, you have an internal locus of control. If you place the responsibility on others and think that luck or fate determines your future, you have an external locus of control. Some people use the internal and external locus of control in combination or favor one type in certain situations. If you favor an internal locus of control, you believe that to a great extent your actions determine your future. **Studies have shown that students who use an internal locus of control are likely to have higher achievement in college.**[18] The characteristics of students with internal and external locus of control are listed below.

Students with an internal locus of control:

- Believe that they are in control of their lives.
- Understand that grades are directly related to the amount of study invested.
- Are self-motivated.
- Learn from their mistakes by figuring out what went wrong and how to fix the problem.
- Think positively and try to make the best of each situation.
- Rely on themselves to find something interesting in the class and learn the material.

Students with an external locus of control:

- Believe that their lives are largely a result of luck, fate, or chance.
- Think that teachers give grades rather than students earning grades.
- Rely on external motivation from teachers or others.
- Look for someone to blame when they make a mistake.
- Think negatively and believe they are victims of circumstance.
- Rely on the teacher to make the class interesting and to teach the material.

> "Ability is what you're capable of doing. Motivation determines what you do. Attitude determines how well you do it."
> Lou Holtz

ACTIVITY

Internal or External Locus of Control

Decide whether the statement represents an internal or external locus of control and put a checkmark in the appropriate column.

Internal	External	
_____	_____	1. Much of what happens to us is due to fate, chance, or luck.
_____	_____	2. Grades depend on how much work you put into it.
_____	_____	3. If I do badly on the test, it is usually because the teacher is unfair.
_____	_____	4. If I do badly on the test, it is because I didn't study or didn't understand the material.
_____	_____	5. I often get blamed for things that are not my fault.
_____	_____	6. I try to make the best of the situation.
_____	_____	7. It is impossible to get a good grade if you have a bad instructor.
_____	_____	8. I can be successful through hard work.

(Continued)

Internal	External	
_____	_____	9. If the teacher is not there telling me what to do, I have a hard time doing my work.
_____	_____	10. I can motivate myself to study.
_____	_____	11. If the teacher is boring, I probably won't do well in class.
_____	_____	12. I can find something interesting about each class.
_____	_____	13. When bad things are going to happen, there is not much you can do about it.
_____	_____	14. I create my own destiny.
_____	_____	15. Teachers should motivate the students to study.
_____	_____	16. I have a lot of choice about what happens in my life.

As you probably noticed, the even-numbered statements represent internal locus of control. The odd-numbered statements represent external locus of control. Remember that students with an internal locus of control have a greater chance of success in college. It is important to see yourself as responsible for your own success and achievement and to believe that with effort you can achieve your goals.

> "I am a great believer in luck, and I find that the harder I work, the more I have of it."
> Thomas Jefferson

Other Ways to Improve Motivation

Here are some additional ideas for improving your motivation and success:

- Participate in extra-curricular activities. When you join a club, participate in athletics, or involve yourself in student government, you gain new friends and develop a sense of belonging. You also get to explore some of your interests and gain future employment skills.
- Some students are achievement motivated, especially students interested in business, sales, law, engineering, or architecture. Strive to be the best that you can be so that you can be proud of your accomplishments.
- If a behavior is followed by a reward, it is likely to be increased. Do your studying first and follow it with a reward such as watching TV, playing your favorite video game, using social media, participating in athletics, or enjoying your favorite music. Just remember to do the work first and then follow it by a reward. If you have the reward first, you will not get around to studying.

© Andy Dean/Shutterstock.com

Motivation, Part I

1. The following statement is an example of grit:

    a. I have a "never give up" attitude.
    b. I believe that the most talented people are the most successful in life.
    c. I think that a failing grade shows a lack of intelligence

2. You can increase your motivation for studying by

    a. taking the required courses.
    b. reminding yourself that you have to do it.
    c. finding something interesting in your studies.

3. Intrinsic motivation

    a. comes from within.
    b. is the result of an external reward.
    c. involves higher pay or recognition for a job well done.

4. To be successful in college, it is best to use

    a. an external locus of control.
    b. extrinsic motivation.
    c. intrinsic motivation.

5. A person who is multitasking:

    a. Uses time efficiently.
    b. Takes 50% longer to complete a task.
    c. Minimizes errors.

How did you do on the quiz? Check your answers: 1. a, 2. c, 3. a, 4. c, 5. b

Journal Entry #4

Write a paragraph with at least three ideas about how you can motivate yourself to be successful in college. Include any of these ideas: mindset, grit, positive thinking, finding interest, concentration, attention, intrinsic motivation, locus of control, affiliation, achievement, and using rewards.

Success Is a Habit

We establish habits by taking small actions each day. Through repetition, these individual actions become habits. I once visited the Golden Gate Bridge in San Francisco and saw a cross section of the cable used to support the bridge. It was made of small metal strands twisted with other strands; then those cables were twisted together to make a stronger cable. Habits are a lot like cables. We start with one small action, and each successive action makes the habit stronger. Have you ever stopped to think that success can be a habit? We all have learned patterns of behavior that either help us to be successful or interfere with our success. With some effort and some basic understanding of behavior modification, you can choose to establish some new behaviors that lead to success or to get rid of behaviors that interfere with it.

Eight Steps to Change a Habit

You can establish new habits that lead to your success. Once a habit is established, it can become a pattern of behavior that you do not need to think about very much. For example, new students often need to get into the habit of studying. Following is an outline of steps that can be helpful to establish new behaviors.

1. **State the problem.** What new habit would you like to start? What are your roadblocks or obstacles? What bad habit would you like to change? Be truthful about it. This is sometimes the most difficult step. Here are two different examples:
   - I need to study to be successful in college. I am not in the habit of studying. I easily get distracted by work, family, friends, and other things I need to do. At the end of the day, I am too tired to study.
   - I need to improve my diet. I am overweight. I eat too much fast food and am not careful about what I eat. I have no time for exercise.

2. **Change one small behavior at a time.** If you think about climbing a mountain, the task can seem overwhelming. However, you can take the first step. If you can change one small behavior, you can gain the confidence to change another. For example:
   - I plan to study at least two hours each day on Mondays through Fridays.
   - I plan to eat more fruits and vegetables each day.

State the behavior you would like to change. Make it small.

3. **State in a positive way the behavior you wish to establish.** For example, instead of the negative statements "I will not waste my time" or "I will not eat junk food," say, "I plan to study each day" or "I plan to eat fruits and vegetables each day."

4. **Count the behavior.** How often do you do this behavior? If you are trying to establish a pattern of studying, write down how much time you spend studying each day. If you are trying to improve your diet, write down everything that you eat each day. Sometimes just getting an awareness of your habit is enough to begin to make some changes.

5. **Picture in your mind the actions you might take.** For example:
   - I picture myself finding time to study in the library. I see myself walking to the library. I can see myself in the library studying.
   - I see myself in the grocery store buying fruits and vegetables. I see myself packing these fruits and vegetables in my lunch. I see myself putting these foods in a place where I will notice them.

6. **Practice the behavior for 10 days.** In 10 days, you can get started on a new pattern of behavior. Once you have started, keep practicing the behavior for about a month to firmly establish your new pattern of behavior. The first three days are the most difficult.

If you fail, don't give up. Just realize that you are human and keep trying for 10 days. Think positively that you can be successful. Write a journal entry or note on your calendar about what you have accomplished each day.

7. **Find a reward for your behavior.** Remember that we tend to repeat behaviors that are rewarded. Find rewards that do not involve too many calories, don't cost too much money, and don't involve alcohol or drugs. Also, rewards are most effective if they directly follow the behavior you wish to reinforce.

8. **Ask yourself,** "What am I going to do to maintain the change?" In the long run, the new behavior has to become part of your lifestyle.

Ten Habits of Successful College Students

Starting your college education will require you to establish some new habits to be successful.

1. Attend class.

College lectures supplement the material in the text, so it is important to attend class. Many college instructors will drop you if you miss three hours of class. After three absences, most students do not return to class. If your class is online, log in frequently.

2. Read the textbook.

Start early and read a little at a time. If you have a text with 400 pages, read 25 pages a week rather than trying to read it all at once.

3. Have an educational plan.

Counselors or advisors can assist you in making an educational plan so that you take the right classes and accomplish your educational goal as soon as possible.

4. Use college services.

Colleges offer valuable free services that help you to be successful. Take advantage of tutoring, counseling, health services, financial aid, the learning resources center (library) and many other services.

5. Get to know the faculty.

You can get to know the faculty by asking questions in class or meeting with your instructors during office hours. Your instructors can provide extra assistance and write letters of recommendation for scholarships, future employment, or graduate school.

6. Don't work too much.

Research has shown that full-time students should have no more than 20 hours of outside employment a week to be successful in college. If you have to work more than 20 hours a week, reduce your college load. If you are working 40 hours a week or more, take only one or two classes.

7. Take one step at a time.

If you are anxious about going to college, remember that each class you attend takes you another step toward your goal. If you take too many classes, especially in the beginning, you may become overwhelmed.

8. Have a goal for the future.

Know why you are in college and what you hope to accomplish. What career will you have in the future? Imagine your future lifestyle.

9. Visualize your success.

See yourself walking across the stage and receiving your college diploma. See yourself working at a job you enjoy.

10. Ask questions if you don't understand.

Asking questions not only helps you to find the answers, but it shows you are motivated to be successful.

Motivation, Part II

1. When you participate in student activities in campus such as athletics, student government, or a club, you will be

    a. distracted from your studies.
    b. using affiliation motivation.
    c. decreasing your chances of success in college.

2. If the behavior is followed by a reward

    a. it is likely to be increased.
    b. it is likely to be decreased.
    c. there will probably be no effect.

3. For rewards to be effective, they must occur

    a. before the behavior.
    b. immediately after the behavior.
    c. either before or after the behavior.

4. If you plan to increase time spent studying, the following statement is most likely to help you to achieve your goal.

    a. I will increase the time I spend studying.
    b. I plan to study for at least two hours each day on Mondays through Fridays.
    c. I will study for five hours on Monday to prepare for the test on Tuesday.

5. To change a habit,

    a. set high goals.
    b. focus on negative behavior.
    c. begin with a concrete behavior that can be counted.

How did you do on the quiz? Check your answers: 1. b, 2. a, 3. b, 4. b, 5. c

KEYS TO SUCCESS

Persistence

There is an old saying that persistence will get you almost anything eventually. This saying applies to your success in life as well as in college. The first two to six weeks of college are a critical time in which many students drop out. Realize that college is a new experience and that you will face new challenges and growth experiences. Make plans to persist, especially in the first few weeks. Get to know a college counselor or advisor. These professionals can help you to get started in the right classes and answer any questions you might have. It is important to make a connection with a counselor or faculty member so that you feel comfortable in college and have the resources to obtain needed help. Plan to enroll on time so that you do not have to register late. It is crucial to attend the first class. In the first class, the professor explains the class requirements and expectations and sets the tone for the class. You may even get dropped from the class if you are not there on the first day. Get into the habit of studying right away. Make studying a habit that you start immediately at the beginning of the semester or quarter. If you can make it through the first six weeks, it is likely that you can finish the semester and complete your college education.

It has been said that 90 percent of success is just showing up. Any faculty member will tell you that the number one reason for students dropping out of college is lack of attendance. They know that when students miss three classes in a row, they are not likely to return. Even very capable students who miss class may find that they are lost when they come back. Many students are simply afraid to return. Classes such as math and foreign languages are sequential, and it is very difficult to make up work after an absence. One of the most important ways you can be successful is to make a habit of consistently showing up for class.

You will also need commitment to be successful. Commitment is a promise to yourself to follow through with something. In athletics, it is not necessarily the one with the best physical skills who makes the best athlete. Commitment and practice make a great athlete. Commitment means doing whatever is necessary to succeed. Like the good athlete, make a commitment to accomplishing your goals. Spend the time necessary to be successful in your studies.

When you face difficulties, persistence and commitment are especially important. History is full of famous people who contributed to society through persistence and commitment. Consider the following facts about Abraham Lincoln, for example.

- Failed in business at age 21.
- Was defeated in a legislative race at age 22.
- Failed again in business at age 24.
- Overcame the death of his sweetheart at age 26.
- Had a nervous breakdown at age 27.
- Lost a congressional race at age 34.
- Lost a congressional race at age 36.

- Lost a senatorial race at age 45.
- Failed in an effort to become vice president at age 47.
- Lost a senatorial race at age 49.
- Was elected president of the United States at age 52.[19]

© Gustavo Frazao/Shutterstock.com

The goal of getting a college education may seem like a mountain that is difficult to climb. Break it into smaller steps that you can accomplish. See your college counselor or advisor, register for classes, attend the first class, read the first chapter, do the first assignment, and you will be on the road to your success. Then continue to break tasks into small, achievable steps and continue from one step to the next. And remember, persistence will get you almost anything eventually.

Journal Entry #5

What will you do if you are tempted to drop out of college? What steps can you take to be persistent in achieving your college goals? Are there times when it is best to change goals rather than to be persistent if your efforts are not working? Write a paragraph about how you will be persistent in reaching your college goals.

© Lyudmyla Kharlamova/
Shutterstock.com

College Success 1

The College Success 1 website is continually updated with supplementary material for each chapter including Word documents of the journal entries, classroom activities, handouts, videos, links to related materials, and much more. See http://www.collegesuccess1.com/.

Notes

1. Moneybox: A Blog about Business and Economics, "America's Awful College Dropout Rates, in Four Charts," retrieved from http://www.slate.com/blogs/moneybox/2014/11/19/u_s_college_dropouts_rates_explained_in_4_charts.html, July 2017.

2. Federal Reserve Bank of New York, "Do the Benefits of College Still Outweigh the Costs?," *Current Issues in Economics and Finance* 20, no. 3, 2014. Available at www.newyorkfed.org/research/current-issues

3. U.S Census Bureau, "Earnings and Unemployment by Educational Attainment 2016," retrieved from http://www.bls.gov/emp/ep_chart_001.htm

4. W. Lewallen, "The Impact of Being Undecided on College Persistence," *Journal of College Student Development* 34 (1993): 103–112.

5. Marsha Fralick, "College Success: A Study of Positive and Negative Attrition," *Community College Review* 20 (1993): 29–36.

6. Terry Doyle and Todd Zakrajsek, The New Science of Learning (Sterling, Virginia: Stylus), 85–87.

7. Angela Duckworth, *Grit: The Power of Passion and Perseverance* (New York: Simon & Schuster, 2016).

8. Ibid., 14.

9. Ibid., 29.

10. Retrieved from https://www.quora.com/How-many-hours-a-week-does-an-NBA-player-work-during-the-season, July 2017.

11. Retrieved http://patriotswire.usatoday.com/2017/02/02/behind-tom-bradys-preparation-for-super-bowl-li/, July 2017.

12. Retrieved from https://www.muscleprodigy.com/michael-phelps-workout-and-diet/, July 2017.

13. Retrieved from http://www.thestrad.com/violinist-itzhak-perlman-talks-about-practice/, July 2017.

14. Duckworth, p. 91.

15. Christopher Peterson, *A Primer in Positive Psychology* (New York: Oxford University Press, 2006), 127.

16. John Medina, Brain Rules (Seattle: Pear Press, 2008), 87.

17. Ibid., 87.

18. M.J. Findley and H.M. Cooper, "Locus of Control and Academic Achievement: A Literature Review," *Journal of Personality and Social Psychology* 44 (1983): 419–427.

19. Anthony Robbins, Unlimited Power (New York: Ballantine Books, 1986), 73.

Begin with Self-Assessment

Name _____ Date _____

A good way to begin your success in college is to assess your present skills to determine your strengths and areas that need improvement. Complete the following assessment to get an overview of the topics presented in the textbook and to measure your present skills.

Measure Your Success

The following statements represent major topics included in the textbook. Read the following statements and rate how true they are for you at the present time. At the end of the course, you will have the opportunity to complete this assessment again to measure your progress.

© Kenishirotie/Shutterstock.com

5 Definitely true
4 Mostly true
3 Somewhat true
2 Seldom true
1 Never true

_____ I am motivated to be successful in college.

_____ I know the value of a college education.

_____ I know how to establish successful patterns of behavior.

_____ I avoid multi-tasking while studying.

_____ I am attending college to accomplish my own personal goals.

_____ I believe to a great extent that my actions determine my future.

_____ I am persistent in achieving my goals.

_____ **Total points for Motivation**

_____ I can describe my personality type.

_____ I can list careers that match my personality type.

_____ I can describe my personal strengths and talents based on my personality type.

_____ I understand how my personality type affects how I manage my time and money.

_____ I know what college majors are most in demand.

_____ I am confident that I have chosen the best major for myself.

_____ Courses related to my major are interesting and exciting to me.

_____ **Total points for Personality and Major**

_____ I understand the concept of multiple intelligences.

_____ I can list my multiple intelligences and matching careers.

_____ I can describe my vocational interests.

_____ I can list my top values.

_____ My personal values generally guide my actions.

_____ I can balance work, study, and leisure activities.

_____ I know the steps in making a good career decision.

_____ **Total points for Multiple Intelligences, Interests, and Values**

_____ I understand how current employment trends will affect my future.

_____ I know what work skills will be most important for the 21st century.

_____ I have an educational plan that matches my academic and career goals.

_____ I know how to use job outlook in planning my career.

_____ I have a good resume.

_____ I know how to interview for a job

_____ I know how to use up-to-date job search strategies to find a job.

_____ **Total points for Career and Education**

_____ I have a list or mental picture of my lifetime goals.

_____ I know what I would like to accomplish in the next four years.

_____ I spend my time on activities that help me accomplish my lifetime goals.

_____ I effectively use priorities in managing my time.

_____ I can balance study, work, and recreation time.

_____ I generally avoid procrastination on important tasks.

_____ I am good at managing my money.

_____ **Total points for Managing Time and Money**

_____ I understand the difference between short-term and long-term memory.

_____ I use effective study techniques for storing information in long-term memory.

_____ I can apply memory techniques to remember what I am studying.

_____ I know how to minimize forgetting.

_____ I know how to use mnemonics and other memory tricks.

_____ I know how to keep my brain healthy throughout life.

_____ I use positive thinking to be successful in my studies.

_____ **Total points for Brain Science and Memory**

_____ I understand the latest findings in brain science and can apply them to studying.

_____ I use a reading study system based on memory strategies.

_____ I am familiar with e-learning strategies for reading and learning online.

_____ I know how to effectively mark my textbook.

_____ I understand how math is different from studying other subjects.

_____ I have the math study skills needed to be successful in my math courses.

_____ I take responsibility for my own success in college and in life.

_____ **Total points for Brain Science and Study Skills**

_____ I know how to listen for the main points in a college lecture.

_____ I am familiar with note-taking systems for college lectures.

_____ I know how to review my lecture notes.

_____ I feel comfortable with writing.

_____ I know the steps in writing a college term paper.

_____ I know how to prepare a speech.

_____ I am comfortable with public speaking.

_____ **Total points for Taking Notes, Writing, and Speaking**

_____ I know how to adequately prepare for a test.

_____ I can predict the questions that are likely to be on the test.

_____ I know how to deal with test anxiety.

_____ I am successful on math exams.

_____ I know how to make a reasonable guess if I am uncertain about the answer.

_____ I am confident of my ability to take objective tests.

_____ I can write a good essay answer.

_____ **Total points for Test Taking**

_____ I understand how my personality affects my communication style.

_____ I know how to be a good listener.

_____ I can use some basic techniques for good communication.

_____ I can identify some barriers to effective communication.

_____ I know how to deal with conflict.

_____ I feel confident about making new friends in college and on the job.

_____ I am generally a good communicator.

_____ **Total points for Communication and Relationships**

_____ I have the skills to analyze data, generate alternatives, and solve problems.

_____ I can identify fallacies in reasoning.

_____ I can apply the steps of critical thinking to analyze a complex issue.

_____ I am willing to consider different points of view.

_____ I can use brainstorming to generate a variety of ideas.

_____ I am good at visualization and creative imagination.

_____ I am generally curious about the world and can spot problems and opportunities.

_____ **Total points for Critical and Creative Thinking**

_____ I understand the basics of good nutrition.

_____ I understand how to maintain my ideal body weight.

_____ I exercise regularly.

_____ I avoid addictions to smoking, alcohol, and drugs.

_____ I protect myself from sexually transmitted diseases.

_____ I generally get enough sleep.

_____ I am good at managing stress.

_____ **Total points for Health**

_____ I understand the concept of diversity and know why it is important.

_____ I understand the basics of communicating with a person from a different culture.

_____ I understand how the global economy will affect my future career.

_____ I understand how the concept of the electronic village will affect my future.

_____ I am familiar with the basic vocabulary of diversity.

_____ I try to avoid stereotypes when dealing with others who are different than me.

_____ I try to understand and appreciate those who are different from me.

_____ **Total points for Diversity**

_____ I expect good things to happen in the future and work to make them happen.

_____ Despite challenges, I always remain hopeful about the future.

_____ I have self-confidence.

_____ I use positive self-talk and affirmations.

_____ I have a visual picture of my future success.

_____ I have a clear idea of what happiness means to me.

_____ I usually practice positive thinking.

_____ **Total points for Future**

_____ I am confident of my ability to succeed in college.

_____ I am confident that my choice of a major is the best one for me.

_____ **Total additional points**

Total your points:

_____ Motivation

_____ Personality and Major

_____ Multiple Intelligences, Interests, and Values

_____ Career and Education

_____ Managing Time and Money

_____ Brain Science and Memory

_____ Brain Science and Study Skills

_____ Taking Notes, Writing, and Speaking

_____ Test Taking

_____ Communication and Relationships

_____ Critical and Creative Thinking

_____ Health

_____ Diversity

_____ Future

_____ Additional Points

_____ **Grand total points**

If you scored

450–500 You are very confident of your skills for success in college. Maybe you do not need this class?

400–449 You have good skills for success in college. You can always improve.

350–399 You have average skills for success in college. You will definitely benefit from taking this course.

Below 350 You need some help to survive in college. You are in the right place to begin.

Use these scores to complete the Success Wheel that follows this assessment. Note that the additional points are not used in the chart.

Success Wheel

Name _____ Date _____

Use your scores from the Measure Your Success assessment to complete the following Success Wheel. Use different colored markers to shade in each section of the wheel.

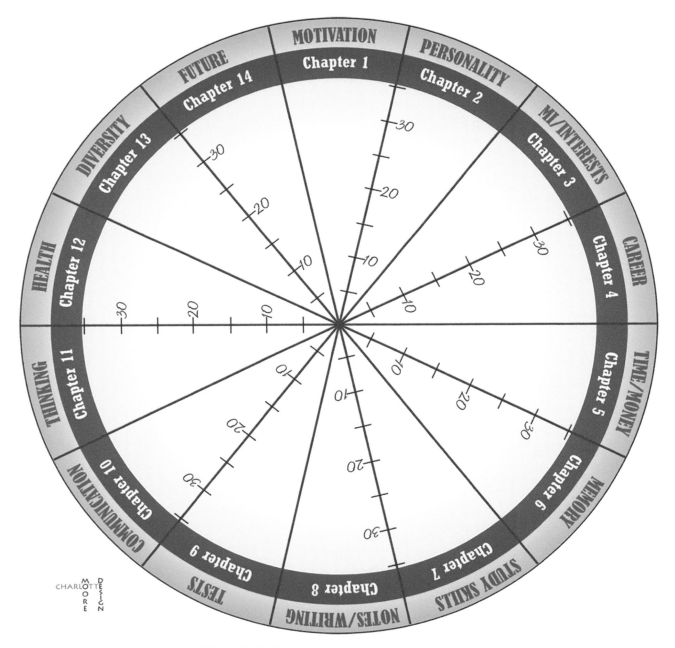

Courtesy of Charlotte Moore. © Kendall Hunt Publishing Company.

1. What are your best areas?

2. What are areas that need improvement?

What Do I Want from College?

Name _____ Date _____

Read the following list and place checkmarks next to your reasons for attending college. Think about why you are attending college and add your own personal reasons to the list.

_____ 1. To have financial security

_____ 2. To find a satisfying career

_____ 3. To explore possibilities provided by college

_____ 4. To expand my options

_____ 5. To become an educated person

_____ 6. To figure out what I want to do with my life

_____ 7. To develop my potential

_____ 8. To become a role model for my children

_____ 9. To make my parents happy

_____ 10. To respect myself

_____ 11. To feel good about myself

_____ 12. To see if I can do it

_____ 13. To meet interesting people

_____ 14. To have something to do and prevent boredom

_____ 15. To become the best I can be

_____ 16. To have better job opportunities

_____ 17. To have no regrets later on

_____ 18. To prepare for a good job or profession

_____ 19. To have job security

_____ 20. To gain confidence in myself

_____ 21. To get a degree

_____ 22. To gain a greater understanding of the world

_____ 23. To have fun

_____ **24.** To understand myself

_____ **25.** To learn how to think

_____ **26.** To enjoy what I do for a living

_____ **27.** To reach my potential

_____ **28.** Because my parents want me to get a degree

_____ **29.** For my own personal satisfaction

_____ **30.** To make a difference in other people's lives

_____ **31.** To have a position of power

_____ **32.** To have respect

_____ **33.** To have prestige

_____ **34.** To have time and money for travel

_____ **35.** To acquire knowledge

_____ **36.** _____

_____ **37.** _____

What are your top six reasons for attending college? You may include reasons not listed above. If you are tempted to give up on your college education, read this list and think about the reasons you have listed below.

1. _____   **4.** _____

2. _____   **5.** _____

3. _____   **6.** _____

Roadblocks and Pathways to Success

Name _____   Date _____

© IQoncept/Shutterstock.com

Students come to college with a dream of making a better future for themselves. What is your dream? Your instructor may have you share your ideas with other students in the course.

Place a checkmark next to any item that could be a roadblock to your success in college.

_____ Too much work   _____ Family obligations   _____ Lack of study skills

_____ Financial difficulties   _____ Social life   _____ Using time wisely

_____ Lack of confidence   _____ Computer games   _____ Speaking in class

_____ Difficulty with reading   _____ Social media   _____ Negative thinking

_____ Difficulty with writing   _____ Phone use and texting   _____ Lack of motivation

_____ Difficulty with math   _____ Lack of career goals   _____ Learning disabilities

_____ Difficulty with tests   _____ Dislike of homework   _____ Lack of persistence

_____ Difficulty with memory   _____ Dislike of school   _____ Health problems

List any other roadblocks in addition to the items checked above:

What are your top three roadblocks?

1. _____

2. _____

3. _____

Spend 5 minutes skimming through the table of contents in your textbook and looking quickly through the chapters to find ideas that will help you overcome any roadblocks to your success. List 5 topics from the textbook that can help you to be successful in college.

1. _____

2. _____

3. _____

4. _____

5. _____

What are other resources that can help you to overcome your roadblocks? (tutoring, financial aid, advising, family support, self-motivation)

Your instructor will help the class brainstorm ideas for overcoming roadblocks. What is your plan for overcoming the roadblocks to achieve your hopes and dreams for the future?

Textbook Skimming

Name _____ Date _____

Use this text or any new text to answer the following questions. Challenge yourself to do this exercise quickly. Remember that a textbook survey should take no longer than five to 15 minutes. Try to complete this exercise in 15 minutes to allow time for writing. Notice the time when you start and finish.

1. Write two key ideas found in the introduction or preface to the book.

2. Looking at the table of contents, list the first five main ideas covered in the text.

3. Write down five interesting topics that you found in the book.

4. What did you find at the back of the book (e.g., index, glossary, appendixes)?

5. How long did it take you to do this exercise? _____

6. Briefly, what did you think of this textbook skimming exercise?

CHAPTER 2

Exploring Your Personality and Major

Learning Objectives

Read to answer these key questions:

- What is my personality type?

- How is personality type related to choice of a major and career?

- What careers and majors should I consider based on my personality type?

- What are some other factors in choosing a major?

- What is my preferred work environment?

- How does my personality type affect decision making, time management, money management, learning, and meeting the professor's expectations?

- What are my passions in life?

To assure your success in college, it is important to choose the major that is best for you. If you choose a major and career that match your personality, interests, aptitudes, and values, you will enjoy your studies and excel in your work. It was Picasso who said that you know you enjoy your work when you do not notice the time passing by. If you can become interested in your work and studies, you are on your way to developing passion and joy in your life. If you can get up each morning and enjoy the work that you do (at least on most days), you will surely have one of the keys to happiness.

Choose a Major That Matches Your Gifts and Talents

The first step in choosing the major that is right for you is to understand your personality type. Psychologists have developed useful theories of personality that can help you understand how personality type relates to the choice of major and career. The personality theory used in this textbook is derived from the work of Swiss psychologist Carl Jung (1875–1961). Jung believed that we are born with a predisposition for certain personality preferences and that healthy development is based on the lifelong nurturing of inborn preferences rather than trying to change a person to become something different. Each personality type has gifts and talents that can be nurtured over a lifetime.

While assessments are not exact predictors of your future major and career, they provide useful information that will get you started on the path of career exploration and finding the college major that is best suited to you. Knowledge of your personality and the personalities of others is not only valuable in understanding yourself, but also in appreciating how others are different. This understanding of self and others will empower you to communicate and work effectively with others. Complete the AchieveWORKS Personality assessment that is included with this textbook before you begin this chapter. (See the inside front cover for further information.)

© Andril Kondiuk/Shutterstock.com

Understanding Personality Types

Just as no two fingerprints or snowflakes are exactly alike, each person is a different and unique individual. Even with this uniqueness, however, we can make some general statements about personality. When we make generalizations, we are talking about averages. These averages can provide useful information about ourselves and other people, but it is important to remember that no individual is exactly described by the average. As you read through the following descriptions of personality types, keep in mind that we are talking about generalizations or beginning points for discussion and thoughtful analysis.

As you read through your personality description from the AchieveWORKS Personality assessment and the information in this text, **focus on your personal strengths and talents.** Building on these personal strengths has several important benefits. It increases self-esteem and self-confidence, which contribute to your success and enjoyment of life. Building on your strengths provides the energy and motivation required to put in the effort needed to accomplish any worthwhile task. The assessment also identifies some of your possible weaknesses or "blind spots." Just be aware of these blind spots so that they do not interfere with your success. Being aware of your blind spots can even be used to your advantage. For example, some personality types thrive by working with people. A career that involves much public contact is a good match for this personality type, whereas choosing a career where public contact is limited can lead to job dissatisfaction. Knowing about your personality type can help you make the right decisions to maximize your potential.

Personality type has four dimensions:

1. Extraversion or Introversion

2. Sensing or Intuition

3. Thinking or Feeling

4. Judging or Perceiving

These dimensions of personality will be defined and examined in more depth in the sections that follow.

Extraversion or Introversion

The dimension of extraversion or introversion defines how we interact with the world and how our energy flows. In the general school population, 75 percent of students are usually extraverts and 25 percent are introverts.

> *Extraverts (E) focus their energy on the world outside themselves. They enjoy interaction with others and get to know a lot of different people. They enjoy and are usually good at communication. They are energized by social interaction and prefer being active. These types are often described as talkative and social.*

> *Introverts (I) focus their energy on the world inside of themselves. They enjoy spending time alone to think about the world in order to understand it. Introverts prefer more limited social contacts, choosing smaller groups or one-on-one relationships. These types are often described as quiet or reserved.*

We all use the introvert and extravert modes while functioning in our daily lives. Whether a person is an extravert or an introvert is a matter of preference, like being left- or right-handed. We can use our nondominant hand, but it is not as comfortable as using our dominant hand. We are usually more skillful in using the dominant hand. For example, introverts can learn to function well in social situations, but later may need some peace and quiet to recharge. On the other hand, social contact energizes the extravert.

One personality type is not better than the other: it is just different. Being an extravert is not better than being an introvert. Each type has unique gifts and talents that can be used in different occupations. An extravert might enjoy working in an occupation with lots of public contact, such as being a receptionist or handling public relations. An introvert might enjoy being an accountant or writer. However, as with all of the personality dimensions, a person may have traits of both types.

Introverts and Extraverts

The list below describes some qualities of introverts and extraverts. **For each pair of items**, quickly choose the phrase that describes you best and highlight or place a checkmark next to it. Remember that one type is not better than another. You may also find that you are a combination type and act like an introvert in some situations and an extravert in others. Each type has gifts and talents that can be used in choosing the best major and career for you. To get an estimate of your preference, notice which column has the most checkmarks.

Introvert (I)

_____ Energized by having quiet time alone

_____ Tend to think first and talk later

_____ Tend to think things through quietly

_____ Tend to respond slowly, after thinking

_____ Avoid being the center of attention

_____ Difficult to get to know, private

_____ Have a few close friends

_____ Prefer quiet for concentration

_____ Listen more than talk

_____ View telephone calls as a distraction

_____ Talk to a few people at parties

_____ Share special occasions with one or a few people

_____ Prefer to study alone

_____ Prefer the library to be quiet

_____ Described as quiet or reserved

_____ Work systematically

Extravert (E)

_____ Energized by social interaction

_____ Tend to talk first and think later

_____ Tend to think out loud

_____ Tend to respond quickly, before thinking

_____ Like to be the center of attention

_____ Easy to get to know, outgoing

_____ Have many friends, know lots of people

_____ Can read or talk with background noise

_____ Talk more than listen

_____ View telephone calls as a welcome break

_____ Talk to many different people at parties

_____ Share special occasions with large groups

_____ Prefer to study with others in a group

_____ Talk with others in the library

_____ Described as talkative or friendly

_____ Work through trial and error

Here are some qualities that describe the ideal work environment. Again, as you **read through each pair of items**, place a checkmark next to the work environment that you prefer.

Introvert (I)

_____ Work alone or with individuals

_____ Quiet for concentration

_____ Communication one-on-one

_____ Work in small groups

_____ Focus on one project until complete

_____ Work without interruption

_____ **Total** (from both charts above)

Extravert (E)

_____ Much public contact

_____ High-energy environment

_____ Present ideas to a group

_____ Work as part of a team

_____ Variety and action

_____ Talk to others

_____ **Total** (from both charts above)

Do these results agree with your personality assessment on the AchieveWORKS Personality assessment? If your results are the same, this is a good indication that your results are useful and accurate. Are there some differences with the results obtained from your personality assessment? If your results are different, this provides an opportunity for further reflection about your personality type. Here are a couple of reasons why your results may be different.

1. You may be a combination type with varying degrees of preference for each type.

2. You may have chosen your personality type on the AchieveWORKS Personality assessment based on what you think is best rather than what you truly are. Students sometimes do this because of the myth that there are good and bad personality types. It is important to remember that each personality type has strengths and weaknesses. By identifying strengths, you can build on them by choosing the right major and career. By being aware of weaknesses, you can come up with strategies to compensate for them to be successful.

Look at the total number of checkmarks for extravert and introvert on the two above charts. Do you lean toward being an introvert or an extravert? Remember that one type is not better than the other and each has unique gifts and talents. On the chart below, place an X on the line to indicate how much you prefer introversion or extraversion. If you selected most of the introvert traits, place your X somewhere on the left side. If you selected most of the extravert traits, place your X somewhere on the right side. If you are equally introverted and extraverted, place your X in the middle.

Introvert _____ Extravert

Do you generally prefer introversion or extraversion? In the box below, write **I** for introversion or **E** for extraversion. If there is a tie between **E** and **I**, write **I**.

Notice that it is possible to be a combination type. At times you might prefer to act like an introvert, and at other times you might prefer to act like an extravert. It is beneficial to be able to balance these traits. However, for combination types, it is more difficult to select specific occupations that match this type

Journal Entry #1

Look at the results from AchieveWORKS Personality assessment and your own self-assessment above. Are you an introvert or an extravert or a combination of these two types? Can you give examples of how it affects your social life, school, or work? Write a paragraph about this preference.

Sensing or Intuition

The dimension of sensing or intuition describes how we take in information. In the general school population, 70 percent of students are usually sensing types and 30 percent are intuitive types.

Sensing (S) persons prefer to use the senses to take in information (what they see, hear, taste, touch, smell). They focus on "what is" and trust information that is concrete and observable. They learn through experience.

Intuitive (N) persons rely on instincts and focus on "what could be." While we all use our five senses to perceive the world, intuitive people are interested in relationships, possibilities, meanings, and implications. They value inspiration and trust their "sixth sense" or hunches. (Intuitive is designated as N so it is not confused with I for Introvert.)

We all use both of these modes in our daily lives, but we usually have a preference for one mode or the other. Again, there is no best preference. Each type has special skills that can be applied to the job market. For example, you would probably want your tax preparer to be a sensing type who focuses on concrete information and fills out your tax form correctly. An inventor or artist would probably be an intuitive type.

Sensing and Intuitive

Here are some qualities of sensing and intuitive persons. As you **read through each pair of items**, quickly highlight or place a checkmark next to the item that usually describes yourself.

Sensing (S)	INtuitive (N)
_____ Trust what is certain and concrete	_____ Trust inspiration and inference
_____ Prefer specific answers to questions	_____ Prefer general answers that leave room for interpretation
_____ Like new ideas if they have practical applications (if you can use them)	_____ Like new ideas for their own sake (you don't need a practical use for them)
_____ Value realism and common sense	_____ Value imagination and innovation
_____ Think about things one at a time and step by step	_____ Think about many ideas at once as they come to you
_____ Like to improve and use skills learned before	_____ Like to learn new skills and get bored using the same skills
_____ More focused on the present	_____ More focused on the future
_____ Concentrate on what you are doing	_____ Wonder what is next
_____ Do something	_____ Think about doing something
_____ See tangible results	_____ Focus on possibilities
_____ If it isn't broken, don't fix it	_____ There is always a better way to do it

Sensing (S)	INtuitive (N)
_____ Prefer working with facts and figures	_____ Prefer working with ideas and theories
_____ Focus on reality	_____ Use fantasy
_____ Seeing is believing	_____ Anything is possible
_____ Tend to be specific and literal (say what you mean)	_____ Tend to be general and figurative (use comparisons and analogies)
_____ See what is here and now	_____ See the big picture

Here are some qualities that describe the ideal work environment. Again, as you **read through each pair of items**, place a checkmark next to the work environment that you prefer.

Sensing (S)	INtuitive (N)
_____ Use and practice skills	_____ Learn new skills
_____ Work with known facts	_____ Explore new ideas and approaches
_____ See measurable results	_____ Work with theories
_____ Focus on practical benefits	_____ Use imagination and be original
_____ Learn through experience	_____ Freedom to follow your inspiration
_____ Pleasant environment	_____ Challenging environment
_____ Use standard procedures	_____ Invent new products and procedures
_____ Work step-by-step	_____ Work in bursts of energy
_____ Do accurate work	_____ Find creative solutions
_____ **Total** (from both charts above)	_____ **Total** (from both charts above)

Look at the two charts above and see whether you tend to be more sensing or intuitive. One preference is not better than another: it is just different. On the chart below, place an X on the line to indicate your preference for sensing or intuitive. Again, notice that it is possible to be a combination type with both sensing and intuitive preferences.

Sensing _____|_____Intuitive

Do you generally prefer sensing or intuition? In the box below, write **S** for sensing or **N** for intuitive. If there is a tie between **S** and **N**, write **N**.

[ ]

Journal Entry #2

Look at the results from AchieveWORKS Personality assessment and your own self-assessment above. Are you a sensing, intuitive, or combination type? Can you give examples of how it affects your social life, school, or work? Write a paragraph about this preference.

Thinking or Feeling

The dimension of thinking or feeling defines how we prefer to make decisions. In the general school population, 60 percent of males are thinking types and 40 percent are feeling types. For females, 60 percent are feeling types and 40 percent are thinking types.

Thinking (T) individuals make decisions based on logic. They are objective and analytical. They look at all the evidence and reach an impersonal conclusion. They are concerned with what they think is right.

Feeling (F) individuals make decisions based on what is important to them and matches their personal values. They are concerned about what they feel is right.

We all use logic and have feelings and emotions that play a part in decision making. However, the thinking person prefers to make decisions based on logic, and the feeling person prefers to make decisions according to what is important to self and others. This is one category in which men and women often differ. Most women are feeling types, and most men are logical types. When men and women are arguing, you might hear the following:

Man: "I think that . . ."

Woman: "I feel that . . ."

By understanding these differences, it is possible to improve communication and understanding. Be careful with generalizations, since 40 percent of men and women would not fit this pattern.

When thinking about careers, a thinking type would make a good judge or computer programmer. A feeling type would probably make a good social worker or kindergarten teacher.

ACTIVITY

Thinking and Feeling

The following chart shows some qualities of thinking and feeling types. As you **read through each pair of items**, quickly highlight or place a checkmark next to the items that usually describe yourself.

Thinking (T)	Feeling (F)
_____ Apply impersonal analysis to problems	_____ Consider the effect on others
_____ Value logic and justice	_____ Value empathy and harmony
_____ Fairness is important	_____ There are exceptions to every rule
_____ Truth is more important than tact	_____ Tact is more important than truth
_____ Motivated by achievement and accomplishment	_____ Motivated by being appreciated by others
_____ Feelings are valid if they are logical	_____ Feelings are valid whether they make sense or not
_____ Good decisions are logical	_____ Good decisions take others' feelings into account

Thinking (T)	Feeling (F)
_____ Described as cool, calm, and objective	_____ Described as caring and emotional
_____ Love can be analyzed	_____ Love cannot be analyzed
_____ Firm-minded	_____ Gentle-hearted
_____ More important to be right	_____ More important to be liked
_____ Remember numbers and figures	_____ Remember faces and names
_____ Prefer clarity	_____ Prefer harmony
_____ Find flaws and critique	_____ Look for the good and compliment
_____ Prefer firmness	_____ Prefer persuasion

Here are some qualities that describe the ideal work environment. As you **read through each pair of items**, place a checkmark next to the items that usually describe the work environment that you prefer.

Thinking (T)	Feeling (F)
_____ Maintain business environment	_____ Maintain close personal relationships
_____ Work with people I respect	_____ Work in a friendly, relaxed environment
_____ Be treated fairly	_____ Be able to express personal values
_____ Fair evaluations	_____ Appreciation for good work
_____ Solve problems	_____ Make a personal contribution
_____ Challenging work	_____ Harmonious work situation
_____ Use logic and analysis	_____ Help others
_____ **Total** (from both charts above)	_____ **Total** (from both charts above)

While we all use thinking and feeling, what is your preferred type? Look at the charts above and notice whether you are more the thinking or feeling type. One is not better than the other. On the chart below, place an X on the line to indicate how much you prefer thinking or feeling.

Thinking _____|_____ Feeling

Do you generally prefer thinking or feeling? In the box below, write **T** for thinking or **F** for feeling. If there is a tie between **T** and **F**, write **F**.

```
┌─────┐
│     │
│     │
└─────┘
```

Journal Entry #3

Look at the results from AchieveWORKS Personality assessment and your own self-assessment above. Are you a thinking, feeling, or combination type? Can you give examples of how it affects your social life, school, or work? Write a paragraph about this preference.

Judging or Perceiving

The dimension of judging or perceiving refers to how we deal with the external world. In other words, do we prefer the world to be structured or unstructured? In the general school population, the percentage of each of these types is approximately equal.

*Judging (J) types like to live in a structured, orderly, and planned way. They are happy when their lives are structured and matters are settled. They like to have control over their lives. **Judging does not mean to judge others.** Think of this type as being orderly and organized.*

*Perceptive (P) types like to live in a spontaneous and flexible way. They are happy when their lives are open to possibilities. They try to understand life rather than control it. **Think of this type as spontaneous and flexible.***

Since these types have very opposite ways of looking at the world, there is a great deal of potential for conflict between them unless there is an appreciation for the gifts and talents of both. In any situation, we can benefit from people who represent these very different points of view. For example, in a business situation, the judging type would be good at managing the money, while the perceptive type would be good at helping the business to adapt to a changing marketplace. It is good to be open to all the possibilities and to be flexible, as well as to have some structure and organization.

Judging and Perceptive

As you **read through each pair of items**, quickly highlight or place a checkmark next to the items that generally describe yourself.

Judging (J)	Perceptive (P)
_____ Happy when the decisions are made and finished	_____ Happy when the options are left open; something better may come along
_____ Work first, play later	_____ Play first, do the work later
_____ It is important to be on time	_____ Time is relative
_____ Time flies	_____ Time is elastic
_____ Feel comfortable with routine	_____ Dislike routine
_____ Generally keep things in order	_____ Prefer creative disorder
_____ Set goals and work toward them	_____ Change goals as new opportunities arise
_____ Emphasize completing the task	_____ Emphasize how the task is done
_____ Like to finish projects	_____ Like to start projects
_____ Meet deadlines	_____ What deadline?
_____ Like to know what I am getting into	_____ Like new possibilities and situations
_____ Relax when things are organized	_____ Relax when necessary
_____ Follow a routine	_____ Explore the unknown
_____ Focused	_____ Easily distracted
_____ Work steadily	_____ Work in spurts of energy

Here are some qualities that describe the ideal work environment. Again, as you **read through each pair of items**, place a checkmark next to the work environment that you prefer.

Judging (J)	Perceptive (P)
_____ Follow a schedule	_____ Be spontaneous
_____ Clear directions	_____ Minimal rules and structure
_____ Organized work	_____ Flexibility
_____ Logical order	_____ Many changes
_____ Control my job	_____ Respond to emergencies
_____ Stability and security	_____ Take risks and be adventurous
_____ Work on one project until done	_____ Juggle many projects
_____ Steady work	_____ Variety and action
_____ Satisfying work	_____ Fun and excitement
_____ Like having high responsibility	_____ Like having interesting work
_____ Accomplish goals on time	_____ Work at my own pace
_____ Clear and concrete assignments	_____ Minimal supervision
_____ **Total** (from both charts above)	_____ **Total** (from both charts above)

Look at the charts above and notice whether you are more the judging type (orderly and organized) or the perceptive type (spontaneous and flexible). We need the qualities of both types to be successful and deal with the rapid changes in today's world. On the chart below, place an X on the line to indicate how much you prefer judging or perceiving.

Judging _____|_____ Perceptive

Do you generally have judging or perceptive traits? In the box below, write **J** for judging or **P** for perceptive. If there is a tie between **J** and **P**, write **P**.

Journal Entry #4

Look at the results from AchieveWORKS Personality assessment and your own self-assessment above. Are you a judging, perceptive, or combination type? Can you give examples of how it affects your social life, school, or work? Write a paragraph about this preference.

"Knowing thyself is the height of wisdom."
Socrates

Summarize Your Results

Look at your results above and summarize them on this composite chart. Notice that we are all unique, according to where the Xs fall on the scale.

Extravert (E) _____|_____ Introvert (I)

Sensing (S) _____|_____ Intuitive (N)

Thinking (T) _____|_____ Feeling (F)

Judging (J) _____|_____ Perceptive (P)

Write the letters representing each of your preferences: _____

The above letters represent your estimated personality type based on your understanding and knowledge of self. It is a good idea to confirm that this type is correct for you by completing the online AchieveWORKS Personality assessment.

© Gustavo Frazao/Shutterstock.com

Personality Types

Test what you have learned by selecting the correct answer to the following questions.

1. A person who is energized by social interaction is a/an:

   a. introvert
   b. extravert
   c. feeling type

2. A person who is quiet and reserved is a/an:

   a. introvert
   b. extravert
   c. perceptive type

3. A person who relies on experience and trusts information that is concrete and observable is a/an:

   a. judging type
   b. sensing type
   c. perceptive type

4. A person who focuses on "what could be" is a/an:

   a. perceptive type
   b. thinking type
   c. intuitive type

5. A person who makes decisions based on logic is a/an:

   a. thinker
   b. perceiver
   c. sensor

6. A person who makes decisions based on personal values is a/an:

   a. feeling type
   b. thinking type
   c. judging type

7. The perceptive type:

   a. has extrasensory perception
   b. likes to live life in a spontaneous and flexible way
   c. always considers feelings before making a decision

8. The judging type likes to:

   a. judge others
   b. use logic
   c. live in a structured and orderly way

9. Personality assessments are an exact predictor of your best major and career.

   a. true
   b. false

10. Some personality types are better than others.

    a. true
    b. false

How did you do on the quiz? Check your answers: 1. b, 2. a, 3. b, 4. c, 5. a, 6. a, 7. b, 8. c, 9. b, 10. b

Personality and Career Choice

While it is not possible to predict exactly your career and college major by knowing your personality type, it can help provide opportunities for exploration. The AchieveWORKS personality assessment links your personality type with suggested matching careers in the O*Net career database continually updated by the U.S. Department of Labor. You can find additional information at the College Success 1 website: http://www.collegesuccess1.com/careers.html. This page includes a description of each type, general occupations to consider, specific job titles, and suggested college majors.

© iQoncept/Shutterstock.com

Personality and Preferred Work Environment

Knowing your personality type will help you to understand your preferred work environment and provide some insights into selecting the major and career that you would enjoy. Selecting the work environment that matches your personal preferences helps you to be energized on the job and to minimize stress. Understanding other types will help you to work effectively with co-workers. As you read this section, think about your ideal work environment and how others are different.

Extraverts are career generalists who use their skills in a variety of ways. They like variety and action in a work environment that provides the opportunity for social interaction. Extraverts communicate well and meet people easily. They like to talk while working and are interested in other people and what they are doing. They enjoy variety on the job and like to perform their work in different settings. They learn new tasks by talking with others and trying out new ideas. Extraverts are energized by working as part of a team, leading others in achieving goals, and having opportunities to communicate with others.

Introverts are career specialists who develop in-depth skills. The introvert likes quiet for concentration and likes to focus on a work task until it is completed. They need time to think before taking action. This type often chooses to work alone or with one other person and prefers written communication such as emails to oral communication or presentations. They learn new tasks by reading and reflecting and using mental practice. Introverts are energized when they can work in a quiet environment with few interruptions. They are stressed when they have to work in a noisy environment and do not have time alone to concentrate on a project.

The **sensing** type is realistic and practical and likes to develop standard ways of doing the job and following a routine. They are observant and interested in facts and finding the truth. They keep accurate track of details, make lists, and are good at doing precise work. This type learns from personal experience and the experience of others. They use their experience to move up the job ladder. Sensing types are energized when they are doing practical work with tangible outcomes where they are required to organize facts and details, use common sense, and focus on one project at a time. They are stressed when they have to deal with frequent or unexpected change.

The **intuitive** type likes to work on challenging and complex problems where they can follow their inspirations to find creative solutions. They like change and finding new ways of doing work. This type focuses on the whole picture rather than the details. The intuitive type is an initiator, promoter, and inventor of ideas. They enjoy learning a new skill more than using it. They often change careers to follow their creative inspirations. Intuitive types are energized by working in an environment where they can use creative insight, imagination, originality, and individual initiative. They are stressed when they have to deal with too many details or have little opportunity for creativity.

The **thinking** type likes to use logical analysis in making decisions. They are objective and rational and treat others fairly. They want logical reasons before accepting any new ideas. They follow policy and are often firm-minded and critical, especially when dealing with illogic in others. They easily learn facts, theories, and principles. They are interested in careers with money, prestige, or influence. Thinking types are energized when they are respected for their expertise and recognized for a job well done. They enjoy working with others who are competent and efficient. They become stressed when they work with people they consider to be illogical, unfair, incompetent, or overly emotional.

© cristovao/Shutterstock.com

The **feeling** type likes harmony and the support of co-workers. They are personal, enjoy warm relationships, and relate well to most people. Feeling types know their personal values and apply them consistently. They enjoy doing work that provides a service to people and often do work that requires them to understand and analyze their own emotions and those of others. They prefer a friendly work environment and like to learn with others. They enjoy careers in which they can make a contribution to humanity. Feeling types are energized by working in a friendly, congenial, and supportive work environment. They are stressed when there is conflict in the work environment, especially when working with controlling or demanding people.

The **judging** type likes a work environment that is structured, settled, and organized. They prefer work assignments that are clear and definite. The judging type makes lists and plans to get the job done on time. They make quick decisions and like to have the work finished. They are good at doing purposeful and exacting work. They prefer to learn only the essentials that are necessary to do the job. This type carefully plans their career path. Judging types are energized by working in a predictable and orderly environment with clear responsibilities and deadlines. They become stressed when the work environment becomes disorganized or unpredictable.

The **perceptive** type likes to be spontaneous and go with the flow. They are comfortable in handling the unplanned or unexpected in the work environment. They prefer to be flexible in their work and feel restricted by structures and schedules. They are good at handling work which requires change and adaptation. They are tolerant and have a "live and let live" attitude toward others. Decisions are often postponed because this type wants to know all there is to know and explore all the options before making a decision. This type is often a career changer who takes advantage of new job openings and opportunities for change. Perceptive types are energized when the work environment is flexible and they can relax and control their own time. They are stressed when they have to meet deadlines or work under excessive rules and regulations.

> "True greatness is starting where you are, using what you have, and doing what you can."
>
> Arthur Ashe

More on Personality Type

Personality and Decision Making

Your personality type affects how you think and how you make decisions. Knowing your decision-making style will help you make good decisions about your career and personal life as well as work with others in creative problem solving. Each

© Stephen Coburn/Shutterstock. com

personality type views the decision-making process in a different way. Ideally, a variety of types would be involved in making a decision so that the strengths of each type could be utilized. As you read through the following descriptions, think about your personality type and how you make decisions as well as how others are different.

The **introvert** thinks up ideas and reflects on the problem before acting. The **extravert** acts as the communicator in the decision-making process. Once the decision is made, they take action and implement the decision. The **intuitive** type develops theories and uses intuition to come up with ingenious solutions to the problem. The **sensing** type applies personal experience to the decision-making process and focuses on solutions that are practical and realistic.

The thinking and feeling dimensions of personality are the most important factors in determining how a decision is made. Of course, people use both thinking and feeling in the decision-making process, but tend to prefer or trust either thinking or feeling. Those who prefer **thinking** use cause-and-effect reasoning and solve problems with logic. They use objective and impersonal criteria and include all the consequences of alternative solutions in the decision-making process. They are interested in finding out what is true and what is false. They use laws and principles to treat everyone fairly. Once a decision is made, they are firm-minded, since the decision was based on logic. This type is often critical of those who do not use logic in the decision-making process. The **feeling** type considers human values and motives in the decision-making process (whether they are logical or not) and values harmony and maintaining good relationships. They consider carefully how much they care about each of the alternatives and how they will affect other people. They are interested in making a decision that is agreeable to all parties. Feeling types are tactful and skillful in dealing with people.

It is often asked if thinking types have feelings. They do have feelings, but use them as a criterion to be factored into the decision-making process. Thinking types are more comfortable when feelings are controlled and often think that feeling types are too emotional. Thinking types may have difficulties when they apply logic in a situation where a feeling response is needed, such as in dealing with a spouse. Thinking types need to know that people are important in making decisions. Feeling types need to know that behavior will have logical consequences and that they may need to keep emotions more controlled to work effectively with thinking types.

Judging and **perceptive** types have opposite decision-making strategies. The judging type is very methodical and cautious in making decisions. Once they have gone through the decision-making steps, they like to make decisions quickly so that they can have closure and finish the project. The perceptive type is an adventurer who wants to look at all the possibilities before making a decision. They are open-minded and curious and often resist closure to look at more options.

If a combination of types collaborates on a decision, it is more likely that the decision will be a good one that takes into account creative possibilities, practicality, logical consequences, and human values.

Personality and Time Management

How we manage our time is not just a result of personal habits: it is also a reflection of our personality type. Probably the dimension of personality type most connected to time management is the judging or perceptive trait. **Judging** types like to have things under control and live in a planned and orderly manner. **Perceptive** types prefer more spontaneity and flexibility. Understanding the differences between these two types will help you to better understand yourself and others.

Judging types are naturally good at time management. They often use schedules as a tool for time management and organization. Judging types plan their time and work steadily to accomplish goals. They are good at meeting deadlines and often put off relaxation, recreation, and fun. They relax after projects are completed. If they have too many projects, they find it difficult to find time for recreation. Since judging types like to have projects under control, there is a danger that projects will be completed too quickly and that quality will suffer. Judging types may need to slow down and take the time to do quality work. They may also need to make relaxation and recreation a priority.

Perceptive types are more open-ended and prefer to be spontaneous. They take time to relax, have fun, and participate in recreation. In working on a project, perceptive types want to brainstorm all the possibilities and are not too concerned about finishing projects. This type procrastinates when the time comes to make a final decision and finish a project. There is always more information to gather and more possibilities to explore. Perceptive types are easily distracted and may move from project to project. They may have several jobs going at once. These types need to try to focus on a few projects at a time in order to complete them. Perceptive types need to work on becoming more organized so that projects can be completed on time.

Research has shown that students who are judging types are more likely to have a higher grade point average in the first semester.[1] It has also been found that the greater the preference for intuition, introversion, and judgment, the better the grade point average.[2] Why is this true? Many college professors are intuitive types that use intuition and creative ideas. The college environment requires quiet time for reading and studying, which is one of the preferences of introverts. Academic environments require structure, organization, and completion of assignments. To be successful in an academic environment requires adaptation by some personality types. Extroverts need to spend more quiet time reading and studying. Sensing types need to gain an understanding of intuitive types. Perceptive types need to use organization to complete assignments on time.

© STILLFX/Shutterstock.com

Personality and Money

Does your personality type affect how you deal with money? Otto Kroeger and Janet Thuesen make some interesting observations about how different personality types deal with money.

- **Judging types (orderly and organized).** These types excel at financial planning and money management. They file their tax forms early and pay their bills on time.

- **Perceptive types (spontaneous and flexible).** These types adapt to change and are more creative. Perceivers, especially intuitive perceivers, tend to freak out as the April 15 tax deadline approaches and as bills become due.

- **Feeling types (make decisions based on feelings).** These types are not very money-conscious. They believe that money should be used to serve humanity. They are often attracted to low-paying jobs that serve others.[3]

In studying stockbrokers, these same authors note that ISTJs (introvert, sensing, thinking, and judging types) are the most conservative investors, earning a small but reliable return on investments. The ESTPs (extravert, sensing, thinking, perceptive types) and ENTPs (extravert, intuitive, thinking, perceptive types) take the biggest risks and earn the greatest returns.[4]

Personality and Learning Strategies

Knowing about your personality type can help you to choose learning strategies that work for you.

© Monkey Business Images/Shutterstock.com

- **Extraverts** enjoy interactions with others and like to get to know other people. They learn best by discussing what they have learned with others. Form a study group. Be careful that excess socialization does not distract you from getting your studying done.

- **Introverts** are more quiet and reserved. They enjoy spending time alone to think about what they are studying. Study in the library. Be careful about missing out on the opportunities to share ideas with others.

- **Sensing** types focus on the senses (what they can see, hear, taste, touch, and smell.) These types are good at mastering the facts and details. Improve learning by first focusing on the big picture or broad outline and then the details will be easier to remember.

- **Intuitive** types focus on the big picture and may miss the details. Ask yourself, "What is the main point?" To improve learning, begin by looking at the big picture or broader outline and then organize the facts and details under the main ideas so you can recall them.

- **Thinking** types are good at logic. Make a personal connection with the material by asking yourself, "What do I think of these ideas?" Discuss or debate your ideas with others while remembering to respect their ideas.

- **Feeling** types are motivated by finding personal meaning in their studies. Ask yourself, "How is this material related to my life and what is important to me?" Look for a supportive environment or study group.

- **Judging** types are good at organizing the material to be learned and working steadily to accomplish their goals. Organize the material to be learned into manageable chunks to aid in recall.

- **Perceptive** types are spontaneous, flexible, adaptable, and open to new information. Pay attention to organizing your work and meeting deadlines to improve success in college and on the job. Be careful not to overextend yourself by working on too many projects at once.

Understanding Your Professor's Personality

© Alexander Raths/Shutterstock.com

Different personality types have different expectations of teachers.

- Extraverts want faculty who encourage class discussion.
- Introverts want faculty who give clear lectures.
- Sensing types want faculty who give clear and specific assignments.
- Intuitive types want faculty who encourage independent thinking.
- Thinking types want faculty who make logical presentations.
- Feeling types want faculty who establish personal rapport with students.
- Judging types want faculty to be organized.
- Perceptive types want faculty to be entertaining and inspiring.

College students and faculty often have different personality types. In summary,

College faculty tend to be	College students tend to be
Introverted	Extraverted
Intuitive	Sensing
Judging	Perceptive

Of course, the above is not always true, but there is a good probability that you will have college professors who are very different from you. What can you do if you and your professor have different personality types? First, try to understand the professor's personality. This has been called "psyching out the professor." You can usually tell the professor's personality type on the first day of class by examining class materials and observing his or her manner of presentation. If you understand the professor's personality type, you will know what to expect. Next, try to appreciate what the professor has to offer. You may need to adapt your expectations to be successful. For example, if you are an introvert, make an effort to participate in class discussions. If you are a perceptive type, be careful to meet the due dates of your assignments.

Journal Entry #5

Write a paragraph about how your personality type influences any of the following: preferred work environment, decision making, time management, money management, learning, and meeting the expectations of your professor.

Other Factors in Choosing a Major

> "Choose a job you love, and you will never have to work a day in your life."
> Confucius

Choosing your college major is one of the most difficult and important decisions you will make during your college years. After assessing personality type, students often come up with many different options for a major and career. The next chapter will help you think about your multiple intelligences, interests, values, and preferred lifestyle. This information will help narrow down your choices.

Once you have completed a thorough self-assessment, you may still have several majors to consider. At this point, it is important to do some research on the outlook for a selected career in the future and the pay you would receive. Sometimes students are disappointed after graduation when they find there are few job opportunities in their chosen career field. Sometimes students graduate and cannot find jobs with the salary they had hoped to earn. It is important to think about the opportunities you will have in the future. If you have several options for a career you would enjoy, you may want to consider seriously the career that has the best outlook and pay.

According to the Bureau of Labor Statistics, fields with the best outlook include health care, computers, and the new "green jobs" related to preserving the environment. The top-paying careers all require math skills and include the science, engineering, computer science, health care, and business fields. Only 4% of college graduates choose the engineering and computer science fields. Since there are fewer students in these majors, the salaries are higher. If you have a talent or interest in math, you can develop this skill and use it in high-paying careers.

© Maryna Pleshkun/Shutterstock.com

Some Majors with the Highest Earnings for Bachelor's Degrees 2017*[5]

Notice that the majors with the highest earnings require math, science, and/or business.

College Major	Beginning Median Salary	Mid-Career Median Salary
Petroleum Engineering	96,700	172,000
Actuarial Science	60,800	119,000
Chemical Engineering	69,800	119,000
Computer Science & Engineering	71,200	116,000
Nuclear Engineering	68,500	116,000
Electrical and Computer Engineering	68,100	114,000
Aeronautical Engineering	63,000	113,000
Physics & Mathematics	56,200	111,000
Government	49,600	105,000
Biomedical Engineering	62,700	104,000
Physician Assistant Studies	85,200	103,000
Finance & Real Estate	59,500	101,000
Economics	53,900	100,000

*Includes bachelor's degrees only. Excludes medicine, law, and careers requiring advanced degrees.

Other Common Majors and Earnings*[6]

Accounting and Finance	52,800	86,400
Business and Marketing	45,800	85,300
Advertising	41,400	79,800
Geology	44,800	79,800
Architecture	45,100	79,300
Biological Sciences	42,900	79,200
Fashion Design	41,400	77,700
History and Political Science	44,500	76,000
Entrepreneurship	48,000	74,600
English Literature	41,100	74,300
Foreign Languages	42,500	74,200
Business Administration	46,100	72,400
Communication	42,100	72,300
Forestry	41,500	67,400
Multimedia & Web Design	42,300	66,500
Film, Video & Media Studies	39,600	66,300
Music Performance	39,900	65,000
Criminal Justice	39,000	63,900
Art History	40,800	63,300
Hotel & Restaurant Management	50,500	62,700

(continued)

Art & Design	39,500	62,600
Liberal Arts	39,100	62,300
Psychology	38,300	62,100
Secondary Education	40,200	61,400
Humanities	40,900	57,200
Elementary Education	34,700	48,900

* Includes bachelor's degrees only. Excludes medicine, law, and careers requiring advanced degrees.

© Anson0618/Shutterstock.com

Most Meaningful College Majors*[7]

Money is often not the most important consideration in choosing a major. These careers were determined to be the most meaningful with the potential for changing the world.

College Major	Beginning Salary	Mid-Career Median Salary
Medical Laboratory Science	47,900	61,500
Pastoral Ministry	32,800	36,300
Physical Therapy	60,000	86,600
Practical Nursing	45,300	58,100
Physician Assistant Studies	85,200	103,000
Diagnostic Medical Sonography	57,700	71,100
Exercise Physiology	38,400	60,300
Nursing	57,500	74,100
Respiratory Therapy	46,200	62,900
Therapeutic Recreation	35,200	47,700
Community Health Education	37,200	55,200
Dietetics	44,300	60,500
Dental Hygiene	65,400	74,900
Environmental Health & Safety	51,200	89,800
Foods and Nutrition	40,900	58,700
Health	35,700	60,700
Social Work	33,800	46,700
Child Development	32,000	42,500

*Based on an extensive survey by Payscale.com asking college graduates with a bachelor's degree, "Does your work make the world a better place to live?"

Every career counselor can tell stories about students who ask, "What is the career that makes the most money? That's the career I want!" However, if you choose a career based on money alone, you might find it difficult and uninteresting for a lifetime of work. You might even find yourself retraining later in life for a job that you really enjoy. Remember that the first step is to figure out who you are and what you like. Then look at career outlook and opportunity. If you find your passion in a career that is in demand and pays well, you will probably be very happy with your career choice. If you find your passion in a career that offers few jobs and does not pay well, you will have to use your ingenuity to find a job and make a living. Many students happily make this informed choice and find a way to make it work.

© iQoncept/Shutterstock.com

KEYS TO SUCCESS

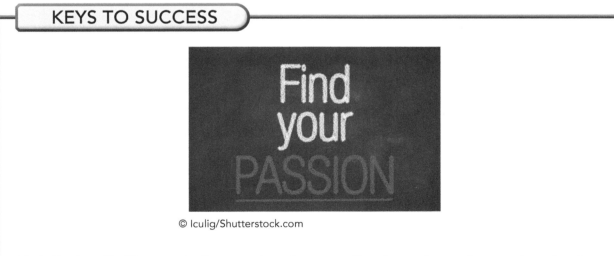

© lculig/Shutterstock.com

Mark Twain said, "The secret of success is making your vocation your vacation." Find what you like to do. Better yet, find your passion. If you can find your passion, it is easy to invest the time and effort necessary to be successful.

How do you know when you have found your passion? You have found your passion when you are doing an activity and you do not notice that the time is passing. The great painter Picasso often talked about how quickly time passed while

(Continued)

he was painting. He said, "When I work, I relax; doing nothing or entertaining visitors makes me tired." Whether you are an artist, an athlete, a scientist, or a business entrepreneur, passion provides the energy needed to be successful. It helps you to grow and create. When you are using your talents to grow and create, you can find meaning and happiness in your life. Finding your passion can help you to be grittier too.

Psychologist Martin Seligman has written a book entitled *Authentic Happiness,* in which he writes about three types of work orientation: a job, a career, and a calling.[8] A job is what you do for the paycheck at the end of the week. Many college students have jobs to earn money for college. A career has deeper personal meaning. It involves achievement, prestige, and power. A calling is defined as "a passionate commitment to work for its own sake."[9] When you have found your calling, the job itself is the reward. He notes that people who have found their calling are consistently happier than those who have a job or even a career. One of the ways that you know you have found your calling is when you are in the state of "flow." The state of "flow" is defined as "complete absorption in an activity whose challenges mesh perfectly with your abilities."[10] People who experience "flow" are happier and more productive. They do not spend their days looking forward to Friday. Understanding your personal strengths is the beginning step to finding your calling.

Seligman adds that any job can become a calling if you use your personal strengths to do the best possible job. He cited a study of hospital cleaners. Although some viewed their job as drudgery, others viewed the job as a calling. They believed that they helped patients get better by working efficiently and anticipating the needs of doctors and nurses. They rearranged furniture and decorated walls to help patients feel better. They found their calling by applying their personal talents to their jobs. As a result, their jobs became a calling.

Sometimes we wait around for passion to find us. That probably won't happen. The first step in finding your passion is to know yourself. Then find an occupation in which you can use your talents. You may be able to find your passion by looking at your present job and finding a creative way to do it based on your special talents. It has been said that there are no dead-end jobs, just people who cannot see the possibilities. Begin your search for passion by looking at your personal strengths and how you can apply them in the job market. If the job that you have now is not your passion, see what you can learn from it and then use your skills to find a career where you are more likely to find your passion.

> "Success is not the key to happiness; happiness is the key to success. If you love what you are doing, you will be successful."
> Anonymous

© Lyudmyla Kharlamova/ Shutterstock.com

College Success 1

The College Success 1 website is continually updated with supplementary material for each chapter including Word documents of the journal entries, classroom activities, handouts, videos, links to related materials, and much more. See http://www.collegesuccess1.com/.

Notes

1. Judith Provost and Scott Anchors, eds., *Applications of the Myers-Briggs Type Indicator In Higher Education* (Palo Alto, CA: Consulting Psychologists Press, 1991), 51.

2. Ibid., 49.

3. Otto Kroeger and Janet Thuesen, *Type Talk: The 16 Personality Types That Determine How We Live, Love and Work* (New York: Dell, 1989), 204.

4. Ibid.

5. Payscale, "College Salary Report 2016–17," from http://www.payscale.com/college-salary-report, accessed July 2017.

6. Ibid.

7. Ibid.

8. Martin Seligman, Authentic Happiness (Free Press, 2002).

9. Martin Seligman, as reported by Geoffrey Cowley, "The Science of Happiness," *Newsweek*, September 16, 2002, 49.

10. Ibid.

Personality Preferences

Name _____ Date _____

Use the textbook and personality assessment to think about your personality type. Place an X on the scale to show your degree of preference for each dimension of personality.

Introvert _____|_____ Extravert

Sensing _____|_____ INtuitive

Thinking _____|_____ Feeling

Judging _____|_____ Perceptive

Write a key word or phrase to describe each preference.

Introvert

Extravert

Sensing

INtuitive

Thinking

Feeling

Judging

Perceptive

What careers are suggested by your personality assessment?

Was the personality assessment accurate and useful to you?

Talkers and Listeners

Name _____ Date _____

In the classroom, talkers (extroverts) volunteer to speak and do so frequently. Listeners (introverts) are people who prefer to stay quiet and rarely join in on the discussions. Even though you may prefer talking or listening, it is best to develop both of these skills. Decide whether you are generally a talker or a listener and answer the following questions. Your instructor may want to do this as a group activity in the classroom.

Talkers

1. What made me a talker?

2. How can I develop my listening skills?

3. How can I help listeners talk more?

Listeners

1. What made me a listener?

2. How can I develop my talking skills?

3. How can I help talkers listen more?

Name _____ Date _____

Read the chapter on personality before commenting on these scenarios. Keep in mind the theory that we are all born with certain personality types and there are no good or bad types. Each type has gifts and talents that can be used to be a successful and happy person. Relate your comments to the concepts in this chapter. Your instructor may have you do this exercise as a group activity in class.

Scenario 1 (Sensing vs. Intuitive): Julie is a preschool teacher. She assigns her class to draw a picture of a bicycle. Students share their pictures with the class. One of the students has drawn a bicycle with wings. Another student laughs at the drawing and says, "Bicycles don't have wings!" How should the teacher handle this situation?

Scenario 2 (Thinking vs. Feeling): John has the almost perfect girlfriend. She is beautiful, intelligent, and fun to be with. She only has one flaw: John thinks that she is too emotional and wishes she could be a little more rational. When his girlfriend tries to talk to him about emotional issues, he analyzes her problems and proposes a logical solution. His girlfriend doesn't like the solutions that John proposes. Should John find a new girlfriend?

Scenario 3 (Introvert vs. Extravert): Mary is the mother of two children, ages five (daughter) and eight (son). The five-year-old is very social and especially enjoys birthday parties. At the last party, she invited 24 girls and they all showed up at the party. Everyone had a great time. The eight-year-old is very quiet and spends his time reading, doing artwork, building models, and hanging out with his one best friend. Mary is concerned that her son does not have very many friends. She decides to have a birthday party for her son also. The only problem is that he cannot come up with a list of children to invite to the party. What should Mary do?

Scenario 4 (Judging vs. Perceptive): Jerry and Jennifer have just been married, and they love each other very much. Jennifer likes to keep the house neat and orderly and likes to plan out activities so that there are no surprises. Jerry likes creative disorder. He leaves his things all over the house. He often comes up with creative ideas for having fun. How can Jerry and Jennifer keep their good relationship going?

CHAPTER 3

Exploring Multiple Intelligences, Interests, and Values

Learning Objectives

Read to answer these key questions:

- What kinds of intelligence do I have?

- How can I match my career to my personal strengths?

- What is emotional intelligence and how can I use it to increase personal and career success?

- What are my interests?

- What careers match my interests?

- What lifestyle do I prefer?

- What do I value the most?

- How can I put my values into action?

- How can I make good decisions about my future?

B ecoming aware of your multiple intelligences, interests, and values will enhance self-understanding, increase positive thinking about your abilities, and help you to make good decisions about your college major and future career. If you can match your career with your abilities, interests, and values, you will be more intrinsically motivated to excel in it.

Exploring Multiple Intelligences

In 1904, the French psychologist Alfred Binet developed the IQ test, which provided a single score to measure intelligence. This once widely used and accepted test came into question because it measured the intelligence of students in a particular culture. In different cultures, the test was less valid. As an alternative to traditional IQ tests, Harvard professor Howard Gardner developed the theory of multiple intelligences. He looked at intelligence in a broader and more inclusive way than people had done in the past.

Howard Gardner[1] observed famous musicians, artists, athletes, scientists, inventors, naturalists, and philosophers who were recognized contributors to society to formulate a more meaningful definition of intelligence. **He defined intelligence as the human ability to solve problems or design or compose something valued in at least one culture.** His

© VLADGRIN/Shutterstock.com

definition broadens the scope of human potential. He identified nine different intelligences: musical, interpersonal, logical–mathematical, spatial, bodily–kinesthetic, linguistic, intrapersonal, naturalist, and existential. He selected these intelligences because they are all represented by an area in the brain and are valued in different cultures. His theory helps us to realize that there are many different kinds of talents and to think more positively about our abilities. To assess your multiple intelligences, take the AchieveWORKS Intelligences assessment using the access code on the inside front cover of your textbook.

These intelligences are measured by looking at performance in activities associated with each intelligence. A key idea in this theory is that most people can develop all of their intelligences and become relatively competent in each area. Another key idea is that these intelligences work together in complex ways to make us unique. For example, an athlete uses bodily–kinesthetic intelligence to run, kick, or jump. They use spatial intelligence to keep their eye on the ball and hit it. They also need linguistic and interpersonal skills to be good member of a team.

Developing intelligences is a product of three factors:

1. Biological endowment based on heredity and genetics

2. Personal life history

3. Cultural and historical background[2]

For example, Wolfgang Amadeus Mozart was born with musical talent (biological endowment). Members of his family were musicians who encouraged Mozart in music (personal life history). Mozart lived in Europe during a time when music flourished and wealthy patrons were willing to pay composers (cultural and historical background).

Each individual's life history contains **crystallizers** that promote the development of the intelligences and **paralyzers** that inhibit the development of the intelligences. These crystallizers and paralyzers often take place in early childhood. For example, Einstein was given a magnetic compass when he was four years old. He became so interested in the compass that he started on his journey of exploring the universe. An example of a paralyzer is being embarrassed or feeling humiliated about your math skills in elementary school so that you begin to lose confidence in your ability to do math. Paralyzers involve shame, guilt, fear, and anger and prevent intelligence from being developed.

"I have no special talent. I am only passionately curious."

Albert Einstein

Describing Your Multiple Intelligences

Below are some definitions and examples of the different intelligences. As you read each section, think positively about your intelligence in this area. Highlight or place a checkmark in front of each item that is true for you.

Musical

Musical intelligence involves hearing and remembering musical patterns and manipulating patterns in music. Some occupations connected with this intelligence include musician, performer, composer, and music critic. Place a checkmark next to each skill that you possess in this area.

_____ I enjoy singing, humming, or whistling.

_____ One of my interests is playing recorded music.

_____ I have collections of recorded music.

_____ I play or used to play a musical instrument.

_____ I can play the drums or tap out rhythms.

_____ I appreciate music.

_____ Music affects how I feel.

_____ I enjoy having music on while working or studying.

_____ I can clap my hands and keep time to music.

_____ I can tell when a musical note is off key.

_____ I remember melodies and the words to songs.

_____ I have participated in a band, chorus, or other musical group.

Look at the items you have checked above and summarize your musical intelligence.

_____

_____

_____

Interpersonal

Interpersonal intelligence is defined as understanding people. Occupations connected with this intelligence involve working with people and helping them, as in education or health care. Place a checkmark next to each skill that you possess in this area.

_____ I enjoy being around people.

_____ I am sensitive to other people's feelings.

_____ I am a good listener.

_____ I understand how others feel.

_____ I have many friends.

(Continued)

_____ I enjoy parties and social gatherings.

_____ I enjoy participating in groups.

_____ I can get people to cooperate and work together.

_____ I am involved in clubs or community activities.

_____ People come to me for advice.

_____ I am a peacemaker.

_____ I enjoy helping others.

Look at the items you have checked above and summarize your interpersonal intelligence.

_____

_____

_____

Logical-Mathematical

Logical-mathematical intelligence involves understanding abstract principles and manipulating numbers, quantities, and operations. Some examples of occupations associated with logical-mathematical intelligence are mathematician, tax accountant, scientist, and computer programmer. Place a checkmark next to each skill that you possess. Keep an open mind. People usually either love or hate this area.

_____ I can do arithmetic problems quickly.

_____ I enjoy math.

_____ I enjoy doing puzzles.

_____ I enjoy working with computers.

_____ I am interested in computer programming.

_____ I enjoy science classes.

_____ I enjoy doing the experiments in lab science courses.

_____ I can look at information and outline it easily.

_____ I understand charts and diagrams.

_____ I enjoy playing chess or checkers.

_____ I use logic to solve problems.

_____ I can organize things and keep them in order.

Look at the items you have checked above and summarize your logical-mathematical intelligence.

_____

_____

_____

Spatial

Spatial intelligence involves the ability to manipulate objects in space. For example, a baseball player uses spatial intelligence to hit a ball. Occupations associated with spatial intelligence include pilot, painter, sculptor, architect, inventor, and surgeon. This intelligence is often used in athletics, the arts, or the sciences. Place a checkmark next to each skill that you possess in this area.

_____ I can appreciate a good photograph or piece of art.

_____ I think in pictures and images.

_____ I can use visualization to remember.

_____ I can easily read maps, charts, and diagrams.

_____ I participate in artistic activities (art, drawing, painting, photography).

_____ I know which way is north, south, east, and west.

_____ I can put things together.

_____ I enjoy jigsaw puzzles or mazes.

_____ I enjoy seeing movies, slides, or photographs.

_____ I can appreciate good design.

_____ I enjoy using telescopes, microscopes, or binoculars.

_____ I understand color, line, shape, and form.

Look at the items you have checked above and summarize your spatial intelligence.

_____

_____

_____

Bodily-Kinesthetic

Bodily-kinesthetic intelligence is defined as being able to use your body to solve problems. People with bodily-kinesthetic intelligence make or invent objects or perform. They learn by doing, touching, and handling. Occupations connected to this type of intelligence include athlete, performer (dancer, actor), craftsperson, sculptor, mechanic, and surgeon. Place a checkmark next to each skill that you possess in this area.

_____ I am good at using my hands.

_____ I have good coordination and balance.

_____ I learn best by moving around and touching things.

_____ I participate in physical activities or sports.

_____ I learn new sports easily.

_____ I enjoy watching sports events.

_____ I am skilled in a craft such as woodworking, sewing, art, or fixing machines.

_____ I have good manual dexterity.

_____ I find it difficult to sit still for a long time.

_____ I prefer to be up and moving.

_____ I am good at dancing and remember dance steps easily.

_____ It was easy for me to learn to ride a bike or skateboard.

(Continued)

Look at the items you checked above and describe your bodily-kinesthetic intelligence.

_____

_____

_____

Linguistic

People with linguistic intelligence are good with language and words. They have good reading, writing, and speaking skills. Linguistic intelligence is an asset in any occupation. Specific related careers include writing, education, and politics. Place a checkmark next to each skill that you possess in this area.

_____ I am a good writer.

_____ I am a good reader.

_____ I enjoy word games and crossword puzzles.

_____ I can tell jokes and stories.

_____ I am good at explaining.

_____ I can remember names, places, facts, and trivia.

_____ I'm generally good at spelling.

_____ I have a good vocabulary.

_____ I read for fun and relaxation.

_____ I am good at memorizing.

_____ I enjoy group discussions.

_____ I have a journal or diary.

Look at the items you have checked above and summarize your linguistic intelligence.

_____

_____

_____

Intrapersonal

Intrapersonal intelligence is the ability to understand yourself and how to best use your natural talents and abilities. Examples of careers associated with this intelligence include novelist, psychologist, or being self-employed. Place a checkmark next to each skill that you possess in this area.

_____ I understand and accept my strengths and weaknesses.

_____ I am very independent.

_____ I am self-motivated.

_____ I have definite opinions on controversial issues.

_____ I enjoy quiet time alone to pursue a hobby or work on a project.

_____ I am self-confident.

_____ I can work independently.

_____ I can help others with self-understanding.

_____ I appreciate quiet time for concentration.

_____ I am aware of my own feelings and sensitive to others.

_____ I am self-directed.

_____ I enjoy reflecting on ideas and concepts.

Look at the items you have checked above and summarize your intrapersonal intelligence.

_____

_____

_____

Naturalist

The naturalist is able to recognize, classify, and analyze plants, animals, and cultural artifacts. Occupations associated with this intelligence include botanist, horticulturist, biologist, archeologist, and environmental occupations. Place a checkmark next to each skill you possess in this area.

_____ I know the names of minerals, plants, trees, and animals.

_____ I think it is important to preserve our natural environment.

_____ I enjoy taking classes in the natural sciences such as biology.

_____ I enjoy the outdoors.

_____ I take care of flowers, plants, trees, or animals.

_____ I am interested in archeology or geology.

_____ I would enjoy a career involved in protecting the environment.

_____ I have or used to have a collection of rocks, shells, or insects.

_____ I belong to organizations interested in protecting the environment.

_____ I think it is important to protect endangered species.

_____ I enjoy camping or hiking.

_____ I appreciate natural beauty.

Look at the items you have checked above and describe your naturalist intelligence.

_____

_____

_____

Existential

Existential intelligence is the capacity to ask profound questions about the meaning of life and death. This intelligence is the cornerstone of art, religion, and philosophy. Related occupations include minister, philosopher, psychologist, and artist. Place a checkmark next to each skill that you possess in this area.

_____ I often think about the meaning and purpose of life.

_____ I have strong personal beliefs and convictions.

(Continued)

_____ I enjoy thinking about abstract theories.

_____ I have considered being a philosopher, scientist, theologian, or artist.

_____ I often read books that are philosophical or imaginative.

_____ I enjoy reading science fiction.

_____ I like to work independently.

_____ I like to search for meaning in my studies.

_____ I wonder if there are other intelligent life forms in the universe.

Look at the items you have checked above and describe your existential intelligence.

_____

_____

_____

Journal Entry #1

Look at the items you have checked above. What are your highest intelligences? How do your results compare with your results from the AchieveWORKS Intelligences assessment?

Build on Your Strengths

Consider your personal strengths when deciding on a career. People in each of the multiple intelligence areas have different strengths:

- Musical strengths include listening to music, singing, playing a musical instrument, keeping a beat, and recognizing musical patterns. People with this intelligence are "musical smart."

- Interpersonal strengths include communication skills, social skills, helping others, understanding other's feelings, and the ability to resolve conflicts. People with this intelligence are "people smart."

- Logical-mathematical strengths include math aptitude, interest in science, problem-solving skills, and logical thinking. People with this intelligence are "number/reasoning smart."

- Spatial strengths include visualization, understanding puzzles, navigation, visual arts, reading, and writing. People with this intelligence are "picture smart."

- Bodily-kinesthetic strengths include hand and eye coordination, athletics, dance, drama, cooking, sculpting, and learning by doing. People with this intelligence are "body smart."

- Linguistic strengths include good reading, writing, vocabulary, and spelling skills; good communication skills; being a good listener; having a good memory; and learning new languages easily. People with this intelligence are "word smart."

- Intrapersonal strengths include good self-awareness. They are aware of their feelings and emotions and are often independent and self-motivated to achieve. People with this intelligence are "self-smart."
- Naturalist strengths include exploring and preserving the environment and are very aware of natural surroundings. People with this intelligence are "nature smart."
- Existential strengths include reflecting on important questions about the universe, the purpose of life, and religious beliefs. People with this intelligence are "curiosity smart."

ACTIVITY

© iQoncept/Shutterstock.com

Some Careers and Multiple Intelligences

Circle any careers that seem interesting to you		
Musical	**Interpersonal**	**Logical–Mathematical**
disc jockey	cruise director	engineer
music teacher	mediator	accountant
music retailer	human resources	computer analyst
music therapist	dental hygienist	physician
recording engineer	nurse	detective
singer	psychologist	researcher
song writer	social worker	scientist
speech pathologist	administrator	computer programmer
music librarian	marketer	database designer
choir director	religious leader	physicist
music critic	teacher	auditor
music lawyer	counselor	economist
Spatial	**Bodily-Kinesthetic**	**Linguistic**
architect	athlete	journalist
artist	carpenter	writer
film animator	craftsperson	editor
mechanic	mechanic	attorney
pilot	jeweler	curator
webmaster	computer game designer	newscaster
interior decorator	firefighter	politician
graphic artist	forest ranger	speech pathologist
sculptor	physical therapist	translator
surveyor	personal trainer	comedian
urban planner	surgeon	historian
photographer	recreation specialist	librarian
		marketing consultant

(Continued)

Intrapersonal	Naturalist	Existential
career counselor	park ranger	counselor
wellness counselor	dog trainer	psychologist
therapist	landscaper	psychiatrist
criminologist	meteorologist	social worker
intelligence officer	veterinarian	minister
entrepreneur	animal health technician	philosopher
psychologist	ecologist	artist
researcher	nature photographer	scientist
actor	wilderness guide	researcher
artist	anthropologist	motivational speaker
philosopher	environmental lawyer	human resources
writer	water conservationist	writer

Using Emotional Intelligence in Your Personal Life and Career

Emotional intelligence is related to interpersonal and intrapersonal intelligences. It is the ability to recognize, control, and evaluate your own emotions while realizing how they affect people around you. Emotional intelligence affects career and personal success because it is related to the ability to build good relationships, communicate, work as part of a team, concentrate, remember, make decisions, deal with stress, overcome challenges, deal with conflict, and empathize with others. Research has shown emotional intelligence can predict career success and that workers with high emotional intelligence are more likely to end up in leadership positions in which workers are happy with their jobs.

The premise of emotional intelligence is that you can be more successful if you are aware of your own emotions as well as the emotions of others. There are two aspects of emotional intelligence:

- Understanding yourself, your goals, intentions, responses, and behavior.
- Understanding others and their feelings.

Daniel Goleman has identified the five most important characteristics of emotional intelligence:[3]

1. **Self-Awareness**

   People with high emotional intelligence are aware of their emotions including strengths and weaknesses.

2. **Self-Regulation**

   This involves the ability to control emotions and impulses. Being impulsive can lead to careless decisions like attending a party the night before a final exam. Characteristics of self-regulation include comfort with change, integrity, and the ability to say no.

3. **Motivation**

   People with high emotional intelligence can defer immediate results for long-term success. For example, investing your time in education can lead to future career opportunities and income.

4. Empathy

Empathy is the ability to understand the needs and viewpoints of others around you and avoiding stereotypes. It involves good listening skills that enhance personal relationships.

5. Social Skills

People with good social skills are good team players and willing to help others to be successful.

You can enhance your personal and career success by developing your emotional intelligence. Here are some tips for developing good relationships in your personal life and on the job.

- Be empathetic when working with others by trying to put yourself in their place to understand different perspectives and points of view. Don't be quick to jump to conclusions or stereotype others.
- Think about how your actions affect others. Always treat others as you would like to be treated.
- Be open-minded and intellectually curious. Consider the opinions of others in a positive manner. Be willing to examine and change your mind-set.
- Give others credit for accomplishments in their personal life and in the workplace. When speaking about your own accomplishments, confidently state what you accomplished without trying to seek too much attention.
- Evaluate your own strengths and weaknesses. Focus on your strengths, but be aware of the weaknesses and work to improve them. The personality assessment in the previous chapter helps you to understand your personal strengths and weaknesses.
- Work on stress management by finding some stress reduction techniques that work for you. In stressful situations, it is helpful to remain calm and in control. Seek workable solutions without blaming others. Your college health services office often provides workshops on stress management. There is also additional material in this textbook on stress management.
- Take a college course to improve verbal as well as nonverbal communication. When talking with others, focus on what they are saying rather than what you are going to say next. Learn how to make "I statements" that effectively communicate your thoughts without blaming others. Become aware of nonverbal communication which adds a significant dimension to communication.
- Use humor to help you deal with challenges. Humor helps you to keep things in perspective, deal with differences, relax, and come up with creative solutions.
- Deal with conflicts in a way that builds trust. Focus on win-win solutions that allow both parties to have their needs met.
- Take responsibility for your actions. Admit when you make mistakes and work to improve the situation in the future.
- Use critical thinking to analyze the pros and cons of the situation.
- Be goal oriented and focus on the task and the steps needed to achieve your goals.
- Be optimistic. Optimism leads to greater opportunities and results in better personal relationships.

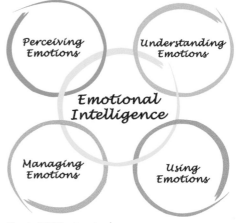

© arka38/Shutterstock.com

Journal Entry #2

Comment on your emotional intelligence and how you can use it to be successful in your personal life and your career.

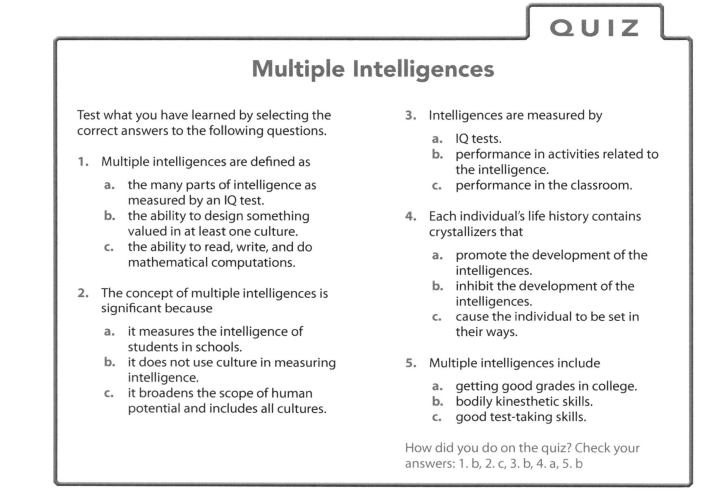

QUIZ

Multiple Intelligences

Test what you have learned by selecting the correct answers to the following questions.

1. Multiple intelligences are defined as

    a. the many parts of intelligence as measured by an IQ test.
    b. the ability to design something valued in at least one culture.
    c. the ability to read, write, and do mathematical computations.

2. The concept of multiple intelligences is significant because

    a. it measures the intelligence of students in schools.
    b. it does not use culture in measuring intelligence.
    c. it broadens the scope of human potential and includes all cultures.

3. Intelligences are measured by

    a. IQ tests.
    b. performance in activities related to the intelligence.
    c. performance in the classroom.

4. Each individual's life history contains crystallizers that

    a. promote the development of the intelligences.
    b. inhibit the development of the intelligences.
    c. cause the individual to be set in their ways.

5. Multiple intelligences include

    a. getting good grades in college.
    b. bodily kinesthetic skills.
    c. good test-taking skills.

How did you do on the quiz? Check your answers: 1. b, 2. c, 3. b, 4. a, 5. b

"The best years of your life are the ones in which you decide your problems are your own. You do not blame them on your mother, the ecology, or the president. You realize that you control your own destiny."

Albert Ellis

Exploring Your Interests

Interests are simply what a person likes to do. As interests are developed, they can become a passion. Research shows that students who choose a major that matches their interests are more likely to earn high grades and finish their degrees.[4] It is difficult to be gritty if you are not interested in what you are doing. After college, people are more satisfied with their jobs if it matches their interests. If you like your job, both your job performance and life satisfaction increase.

How do you learn about your interests? Interests are a result of many factors, including personality, family life, values, and interaction with the environment. Part of developing an interest is trying new things and sticking with them for a while to find out if they match your interests. Participating in extracurricular activities, volunteering, internships, and working part time while in college can help you to explore your interests. One barrier to discovering your interests is unrealistic expectations. Often students are expecting the perfect job; however, every job has enjoyable aspects and aspects you don't like.

Another way to explore your interests is through vocational interest assessments. By studying people who are satisfied with their careers, psychologists have been able to help people choose careers based on their interests. The U.S. Department of Labor has developed the O*Net Interest Profiler, which helps to identify your career interests.[5] The O*Net Interest Profiler is compatible with Holland's Theory of Vocational Personality. This is one of the most widely accepted approaches to vocational choice. According to the theory, there are six vocational personality types. These six types and their accompanying definitions are presented below. As you read through each description, think about your own interests.

> **Holland's Basic Categories of Career Interests**
> - Realistic
> - Investigative
> - Artistic
> - Social
> - Enterprising
> - Conventional

Realistic

People with **realistic** interests like work activities that include practical, hands-on problems and solutions. They enjoy dealing with plants, animals, and real-world materials like wood, tools, and machinery. They enjoy outside work. Often people with realistic interests do not like occupations that mainly involve doing paperwork or working closely with others.

Investigative

People with **investigative** interests like work activities that have to do with ideas and thinking more than with physical activity. They like to search for facts and figure out problems mentally rather than to persuade or lead people.

Artistic

People with **artistic** interests like work activities that deal with the artistic side of things, such as forms, designs, and patterns. They like self-expression in their work. They prefer settings where work can be done without following a clear set of rules.

Social

People with **social** interests like work activities that assist others and promote learning and personal development. They prefer to communicate more than to work with objects, machines, or data. They like to teach, give advice, help, or otherwise be of service to people.

Enterprising

People with **enterprising** interests like work activities that have to do with starting up and carrying out projects, especially business ventures. They like persuading and leading people and making decisions. They like taking risks for profit. These people prefer action rather than thought.

Conventional

People with **conventional** interests like work activities that follow set procedures and routines. They prefer working with data and detail rather than with ideas. They prefer work in which there are precise standards rather than work in which you have to judge things by yourself. These people like working where the lines of authority are clear.

According to Holland, most individuals can be described by one or more of these six personality types, frequently summarized as R-I-A-S-E-C (the first letter of each personality type). Additionally, the theory proposes that there are six corresponding work environments (or occupational groups), and that people seek out work environments that match their personality types. The better the match individuals make, the more satisfied they will be with their jobs.[6]

Holland arranged these interests on a hexagon that shows the relationship of the interests to one another. He notes that most people are not just one type, but rather a combination of types. Types that are close to each other on the hexagon are likely to have interests in common. For example, a person who is social is likely to have some artistic interests and some enterprising interests. Interests on opposite points of the hexagon are very different. For example, artistic and conventional types are opposites. Artistic types prefer freedom to be creative; conventional types prefer structure and order. The figure that follows illustrates the relationship between interest areas.[7]

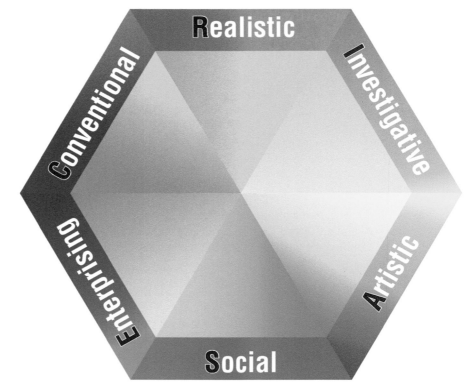

Figure 3.1 Relationships between interest areas.
© Kendall Hunt Publishing Company

The Interest Profiler[8]

Place a checkmark next to the items in each list that you might **like to do**. Keep a positive attitude when thinking about your interests. You do not need to know how to do these activities or have the opportunity to do them to select items that you might like to do in the future. Also, be careful not to select an activity just because it is likely to produce higher income. You can earn higher income by increasing your skills and education in these areas. For example, if you would like to build a brick walkway, you could work in construction, or with more education, become a civil engineer. Just indicate what you would enjoy doing. Remember that this is not a test and that there are no right or wrong answers to the questions. The goal is for you to learn more about your personal career interests and related occupations.

When you are finished with each section, tally the number of checkmarks in each area. Sample job titles for each area of interest are included. Underline any jobs that appeal to you. You can also match your interests to over 900 occupations listed at O*Net Online (https://www.onetonline.org/find/descriptor/browse/Interests/). This site includes information on specific occupations, including work tasks; tools and technology; knowledge, skills, and abilities required; work activities and work context; level of education required; work styles; work values; and wages and employment information.

Realistic (R)

I would like to:

_____ Build kitchen cabinets

_____ Guard money in an armored car

_____ Operate a dairy farm

_____ Lay brick or tile

_____ Monitor a machine on an assembly line

_____ Repair household appliances

_____ Drive a taxi cab

_____ Install flooring in houses

_____ Raise fish in a fish hatchery

_____ Build a brick walkway

_____ Assemble electronic parts

_____ Drive a truck to deliver packages to offices and homes

_____ Paint houses

_____ Enforce fish and game laws

_____ Operate a grinding machine in a factory

_____ Work on an offshore oil-drilling rig

_____ Perform lawn care services

_____ Assemble products in a factory

_____ Catch fish as a member of a fishing crew

_____ Refinish furniture

_____ Fix a broken faucet

_____ Do cleaning or maintenance work

_____ Maintain the grounds of a park

_____ Operate a machine on a production line

_____ Spray trees to prevent the spread of harmful insects

_____ Test the quality of parts before shipment

_____ Operate a motorboat to carry passengers

_____ Repair and install locks

_____ Set up and operate machines to make products

_____ Put out forest fires

R =

(Continued)

Matching Job Titles for Realistic Interests[9]

Construction worker, building contractor, cook, landscaper, housekeeper, janitor, firefighter, hazardous materials removal worker, security guard, truck driver, automotive mechanic, cardiovascular technologist, civil engineer, commercial pilot, computer support specialist, plumber, police officer, chemical engineer, fish and game warden, surveyor, archaeologist, athletic trainer, dentist, veterinarian

Investigative (I)

I would like to:

_____ Study space travel

_____ Make a map of the bottom of an ocean

_____ Study the history of past civilizations

_____ Study animal behavior

_____ Develop a new medicine

_____ Plan a research study

_____ Study ways to reduce water pollution

_____ Develop a new medical treatment or procedure

_____ Determine the infection rate of a new disease

_____ Study rocks and minerals

_____ Diagnose and treat sick animals

_____ Study the personalities of world leaders

_____ Conduct chemical experiments

_____ Conduct biological research

_____ Study the population growth of a city

_____ Study whales and other types of marine life

_____ Investigate crimes

_____ Study the movement of planets

_____ Examine blood samples using a microscope

_____ Investigate the cause of a fire

_____ Study the structure of the human body

_____ Develop psychological profiles of criminals

_____ Develop a way to better predict the weather

_____ Work in a biology lab

_____ Invent a replacement for sugar

_____ Study genetics

_____ Study the governments of different countries

_____ Do research on plants or animals

_____ Do laboratory tests to identify diseases

_____ Study weather conditions

I =

Matching Job Titles for Investigative Interests

Electronic engineering technician, emergency medical technician, fire investigator, paralegal, police detective, engineer (aerospace, biomedical, chemical, electrical, computer, environmental, or industrial), chemist, computer systems analyst, geoscientist, market research analyst, anesthesiologist, biochemist, biophysicist, clinical psychologist, dietician, physician, microbiologist, pharmacist, psychiatrist, surgeon, veterinarian, science teacher, college professor

Artistic (A)

I would like to:

_____ Conduct a symphony orchestra

_____ Write stories or articles for magazines

_____ Direct a play

_____ Create dance routines for a show

_____ Write books or plays

_____ Play a musical instrument

_____ Perform comedy routines in front of an audience

_____ Perform as an extra in movies, plays, or television shows

_____ Write reviews of books or plays

_____ Compose or arrange music

_____ Act in a movie

_____ Dance in a Broadway show

_____ Draw pictures

_____ Sing professionally

_____ Perform stunts for a movie or television show

_____ Create special effects for movies

_____ Conduct a musical choir

_____ Act in a play

_____ Paint sets for plays

_____ Audition singers and musicians for a musical show

_____ Design sets for plays

_____ Announce a radio show

_____ Write scripts for movies or television shows

_____ Write a song

_____ Perform jazz or tap dance

_____ Direct a movie

_____ Sing in a band

_____ Design artwork for magazines

_____ Edit movies

_____ Pose for a photographer

$$A =$$

Matching Job Titles for Artistic Interests

Model, actor, fine artist, floral designer, singer, tile setter, architectural drafter, architect, dancer, fashion designer, film and video editor, hairdresser, makeup artist, museum technician, music composer, photographer, self-enrichment education teacher, art director, broadcast news analyst, choreographer, editor, graphic designer, landscape architect, creative writer, public relations specialist, teacher (of art, drama, or music)

Social (S)

I would like to:

_____ Teach an individual an exercise routine

_____ Perform nursing duties in a hospital

_____ Give CPR to someone who has stopped breathing

_____ Help people with personal or emotional problems

_____ Teach children how to read

_____ Work with mentally disabled children

_____ Teach an elementary school class

_____ Give career guidance to people

_____ Supervise the activities of children at a camp

_____ Help people with family-related problems

_____ Perform rehabilitation therapy

_____ Do volunteer work at a nonprofit organization

_____ Help elderly people with their daily activities

_____ Teach children how to play sports

_____ Help disabled people improve their daily living skills

_____ Teach sign language to people with hearing disabilities

_____ Help people who have problems with drugs or alcohol

_____ Help conduct a group therapy session

_____ Help families care for ill relatives

(Continued)

_____ Provide massage therapy to people

_____ Plan exercises for disabled patients

_____ Counsel people who have a life-threatening illness

_____ Teach disabled people work and living skills

_____ Organize activities at a recreational facility

_____ Take care of children at a day care center

_____ Organize field trips for disabled people

_____ Assist doctors in treating patients

_____ Work with juveniles on probation

_____ Provide physical therapy to people recovering from injuries

_____ Teach a high school class

S =

Matching Job Titles for Social Interests

Host, hostess, bartender, lifeguard, food server, child care worker, home health aide, occupational therapist, occupational therapist aide, personal and home care aide, physical therapist, physical therapist aide, veterinary assistant, dental hygienist, fitness trainer, medical assistant, nanny, teacher (preschool, kindergarten, elementary, middle, or high school), registered nurse, respiratory therapist, self-enrichment education teacher, tour guide, mediator, educational administrator, health educator, park naturalist, probation officer, recreation worker, chiropractor, clergy, counseling psychologist, social worker, substance abuse counselor, physician assistant, speech and language pathologist

Enterprising (E)

I would like to:

_____ Buy and sell stocks and bonds

_____ Manage a retail store

_____ Sell telephone and other communication equipment

_____ Operate a beauty salon or barber shop

_____ Sell merchandise over the telephone

_____ Run a stand that sells newspapers and magazines

_____ Give a presentation about a product you are selling

_____ Buy and sell land

_____ Sell compact discs at a music store

_____ Run a toy store

_____ Manage the operations of a hotel

_____ Sell houses

_____ Sell candy and popcorn at sports events

_____ Manage a supermarket

_____ Manage a department within a large company

_____ Sell a soft drink product line to stores and restaurants

_____ Sell refreshments at a movie theater

_____ Sell hair-care products to stores and salons

_____ Start your own business

_____ Negotiate business contracts

_____ Represent a client in a lawsuit

_____ Negotiate contracts for professional athletes

_____ Be responsible for the operation of a company

_____ Market a new line of clothing

_____ Sell newspaper advertisements

_____ Sell merchandise at a department store

_____ Sell automobiles

_____ Manage a clothing store

_____ Sell restaurant franchises to individuals

_____ Sell computer equipment to a store

E =

Matching Job Titles for Enterprising Interests

Cashier, food worker, customer service representative, sales worker, supervisor, gaming dealer, inspector, retail sales clerk, chef, food service manager, operations manager, real estate broker, realtor, sheriff, wholesale or retail buyer, advertiser, appraiser, construction manager, criminal investigator, financial manager, insurance sales agent, meeting and convention planner, personal financial advisor, sales engineer, judge, lawyer, business or political science teacher, educational administrator, librarian, medical health manager, treasurer, controller

Conventional (C)

I would like to:

_____ Develop a spreadsheet using computer software

_____ Proofread records or forms

_____ Use a computer program to generate customer bills

_____ Schedule conferences for an organization

_____ Keep accounts payable/receivable for an office

_____ Load computer software into a large computer network

_____ Transfer funds between banks using a computer

_____ Organize and schedule office meetings

_____ Use a word processor to edit and format documents

_____ Operate a calculator

_____ Direct or transfer phone calls for a large organization

_____ Perform office filing tasks

_____ Compute and record statistical and other numerical data

_____ Generate the monthly payroll checks for an office

_____ Take notes during a meeting

_____ Keep shipping and receiving records

_____ Calculate the wages of employees

_____ Assist senior-level accountants in performing bookkeeping tasks

_____ Type labels for envelopes and packages

_____ Inventory supplies using a handheld computer

_____ Develop an office filing system

_____ Keep records of financial transactions for an organization

_____ Record information from customers applying for charge accounts

_____ Photocopy letters and reports

_____ Record rent payments

_____ Enter information into a database

_____ Keep inventory records

_____ Maintain employee records

_____ Stamp, sort, and distribute mail for an organization

_____ Handle customers' bank transactions

C =

Matching Job Titles for Conventional Interests

Cashier, cook, janitor, landscaping worker, resort desk clerk, medical records technician, medical secretary, bookkeeping and accounting clerk, dental assistant, drafter, loan officer, paralegal, pharmacy technician, purchasing agent, accountant, auditor, budget analyst, city and regional planner, computer security specialist, cost estimator, credit analyst, database administrator, environmental compliance inspector, financial analyst, geophysical data technician, librarian, proofreader, computer science teacher, pharmacist, statistician, treasurer

(Continued)

Summing Up Your Results

Put the number of checkmarks from each section of the Interest Profiler on the lines that follow:

_____ **R**ealistic   _____ **S**ocial

_____ **I**nvestigative   _____ **E**nterprising

_____ **A**rtistic   _____ **C**onventional

What are your top three areas of interest? (Realistic, Investigative, Artistic, Social, Enterprising, Conventional?)

1. _____

2. _____

3. _____

Journal Entry #3

List your top three areas of interest from the Interest Profiler above (realistic, investigative, social, enterprising, or conventional). Go to https://www.onetonline.org/find/descriptor/browse/Interests/ and click on your highest interests to find matching careers. List one matching career and briefly describe the education required, salary, and projected growth for the career. Here is an easy outline:

My top three interests on the Interest Profiler are . . .

One career that matches my interests is . . .

The education required is . . .

The median salary is . . .

Interests and Lifestyle

Our occupational interests determine what we study and the kinds of occupations we choose. While study and work form the basis of our lifestyle, there are other important components. What we choose to do for fun and relaxation helps us to be refreshed and keeps life interesting. Another component of a balanced lifestyle is time spent with friends and family. It is important to choose work that allows you to have the resources and time to lead a balanced lifestyle with all of these components. A balanced lifestyle has been described as a triangle with work and study forming the base, leisure and recreation forming one side, and kinship and friendship forming the other side.

Give some thought to the kind of lifestyle you prefer. Think about balancing your work, leisure, and social activities.

Figure 3.2 Lifestyle Triangle.

© The Lifestyle Triangle adapted from NTL Institute, "Urban Middle-Class Lifestyles in Transition," by Paula Jean Miller and Gideon Sjoberg, *Journal of Applied Behavior Science 9* (1973), nos. 2/3: 149.

Using Values to Make Important Life Decisions

Values are what we think is important and what we feel is right and good. Our values tell the world who we are. They help us to determine which goals are more valuable than others and to spend time on what is most important. Our values make us different and unique individuals. We often take pride in our values by displaying them on bumper stickers, tee shirts, and tattoos.

Values come from many sources, including our parents, friends, the media, our religious background, our culture, society, and the historical time in which we live. Knowing our values helps to make good decisions about work and life. For example, consider a situation in which a person is offered a high-paying job that involves a high degree of responsibility and stress. If the person values challenge and excitement and views stress as a motivator, the chances are that it would be a good decision to take the job. If the person values peace of mind and has a difficult time coping with stress, it might be better to forgo the higher income and maintain quality of life. Making decisions consistent with our values is one of the keys to happiness and success.

Researchers studied values in 70 different countries around the world and found 10 values rated as important around the world.[10] As you read the list, think about your own personal values.

> "Try not to be a man of success, but rather to become a man of value."
> Albert Einstein

The 10 Most Important Values around the World

- **Achievement**: personal success
- **Benevolence**: concern about the welfare of others
- **Conformity**: acting within social norms
- **Hedonism**: personal gratification and pleasure
- **Power**: status and prestige
- **Security**: safety, harmony, law, and order
- **Self-direction**: independent thought and action
- **Stimulation**: excitement, novelty, and challenge
- **Tradition**: respect for cultural or religious customs
- **Universalism**: understanding and appreciating all people and nature

ACTIVITY

Values Checklist

Assessing Your Personal Values

Use the following checklist to begin to think about what values are important to you.
Place a checkmark next to any value that is important to you. There are no right or wrong answers. If you think of other values that are important to you, add them to the bottom of the list.

_____ Having financial security

_____ Making a contribution to humankind

_____ Being a good parent

_____ Being honest

_____ Acquiring wealth

_____ Being a wise person

_____ Becoming an educated person

_____ Believing in a higher power (God)

_____ Preserving civil rights

_____ Never being bored

_____ Enjoying life and having fun

_____ Making something out of my life

_____ Being an ethical person

_____ Feeling safe and secure

_____ Having a good marriage

_____ Having good friends

_____ Having social status

_____ Being patriotic

_____ Having power

_____ Having good morals

_____ Being creative

_____ Having control over my life

_____ Growing and developing

_____ Feeling competent

_____ Feeling relaxed

_____ Having good family relationships

_____ Preserving the environment

_____ Having the respect of others

_____ Becoming famous

_____ Happiness

_____ Freedom and independence

_____ Common sense

_____ Having pride in my culture

_____ Doing community service

_____ Achieving my goals in life

_____ Having adventures

_____ Having leisure time

_____ Having good health

_____ Being loyal

_____ Having a sense of accomplishment

_____ Participating in church activities

_____ Being physically fit

_____ Helping others

_____ Being a good person

_____ Having time to myself

_____ Loving and being loved

_____ Being physically attractive

_____ Achieving something important

_____ Accepting who I am

_____ Appreciating natural beauty

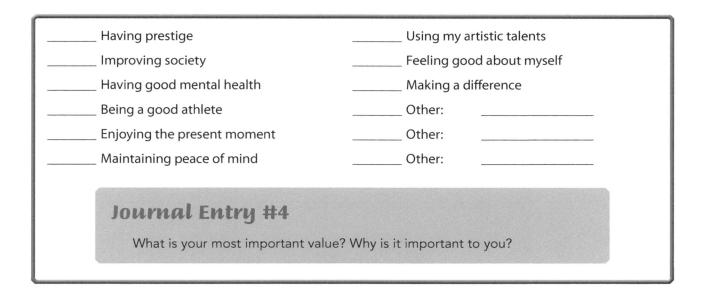

_____ Having prestige	_____ Using my artistic talents
_____ Improving society	_____ Feeling good about myself
_____ Having good mental health	_____ Making a difference
_____ Being a good athlete	_____ Other: _____
_____ Enjoying the present moment	_____ Other: _____
_____ Maintaining peace of mind	_____ Other: _____

Journal Entry #4

What is your most important value? Why is it important to you?

Making Good Decisions

© Anastasia vish/Shutterstock.com

Knowing how to make a good decision about your career and important life events is very important to your future, as this short poem by J. Wooden sums up:

> *There is a choice you have to make, In everything you do*
>
> *And you must always keep in mind, The choice you make, makes you.*[11]

Sometimes people end up in a career because they simply seized an opportunity for employment. A good job becomes available and they happen to be in the right place at the right time. Sometimes people end up in a career because it is familiar to them, because it is a job held by a member of the family or a friend in the community. Sometimes people end up in a career because of economic necessity. The job pays well and they need the money. These careers are the result of chance circumstances. Sometimes they turn out well, and sometimes they turn out miserably.

Whether you are male or female, married or single, you will spend a great deal of your life working. By doing some careful thinking and planning about your career, you can improve your chances of success and happiness. Use the following steps to do some careful decision making about your career. Although you are the person who needs to make the decision about a career, you can get help from your college career center or your college counselor or advisor.

Steps in Making a Career Decision

1. **Begin with self-assessment.**
   - What is your personality type?
   - What are your interests?
   - What are your talents, gifts, and strengths?

- What are your values?
- What lifestyle do you prefer?

2. **Explore your options.**
   - What careers match your personal characteristics?

3. **Research your career options.**
   - Read the job description.
   - Investigate the career outlook.
   - What is the salary?
   - What training and education is required?
   - Speak with an advisor, counselor, or person involved in the career that interests you.
   - Choose a career or general career area that matches your personal characteristics.

4. **Plan your education to match your career goal.**
   - Try out courses in your area of interest.
   - Start your general education if you need more time to decide on a major.
   - Try an internship or part-time job in your area of interest.

5. **Make a commitment to take action and follow through with your plan.**

6. **Evaluate.**
   - Do you like the courses you are taking?
   - Are you doing well in the courses?
   - Continue research if necessary.

7. **Refine your plan.**
   - Make your plan more specific to aim for a particular career.
   - Select the college major that is best for you.

8. **Change your plan if it is not working.**
   - Go back to the self-assessment step.

> "Find a job you like and add five days to every week".
> H. Jackson Browne

Making a Planful Decision

For important decisions, it is advantageous to use what is called a planful decision. The planful decision is made after carefully weighing the consequences and the pros and cons of the different alternatives. The planful decision-making strategy is particularly useful for important decisions such as

- What will be my major?
- What career should I choose?
- Whom should I marry?

The steps in a planful decision-making process:

1. **State the problem.** When we become aware of a problem, the first step is to state the problem in the simplest way possible. Just stating the problem will help you to clarify the issues.

2. **Consider your values.** What is important to you? What are your hopes and dreams? By keeping your values in mind, you are more likely to make a decision that will make you happy.

3. **What are your talents?** What special skills do you have? How can you make a decision that utilizes these skills?

4. **Gather information.** What information can you find that would be helpful in solving the problem? Look for ideas. Ask other people. Do some research. Gathering information can give you insight into alternatives or possible solutions to the problem.

5. **Generate alternatives.** Based on the information you have gathered, identify some possible solutions to the problem.

6. **Evaluate the pros and cons of each alternative.** List the alternatives and think about the pros and cons of each one. In thinking about the pros and cons, consider your values and talents as well as your future goals.

7. **Select the best alternative.** Choose the alternative that is the best match for your values and helps you to achieve your goals.

8. **Take action.** You put your decision into practice when you take some action on it. Get started!

> "The most difficult thing is to decide to act. The rest is tenacity."
> Amelia Earhart

KEYS TO SUCCESS

Act on Your Values

Values are what are most important to you; they are your highest principles. They provide the road map to your success and happiness. You will face important turning points along life's journey. Should I go to college? What will be my major? What career will I have? Whom should I marry? What job should I take? Where shall I live? You can find good answers to these questions by being aware of your values and using them to make decisions and guide your actions. If your decisions follow your values, you can get what you want out of life.

The first step is knowing your values. You may need some time to think about your values and change them if they are not right for you. What values were you taught as a child? What values do you want to keep as an adult? Look around at people that you admire. What are their values? What values have you learned from your religion? Are these values important to you? Ask your friends about their values and share yours. Revise and rethink your values periodically. Make sure your values are your own and not necessarily values that someone has told you were important. When you begin to think about values, you can come up with many things that are important. The key is to find out which values are most important. In this way, when you are faced with a choice, you will not be confused. You will know what is most important to you.

> "The great aim of education is not knowledge, but action."
> Herbert Spencer

Knowing about values is not enough. It is important to act consistently with your values and to follow them. For example, if people value health but continue to smoke, they are saying one thing but doing another. If they value family but spend all of their time at work, they are not acting consistently with their values. As a result, they might find that their family is gone and they have lost something that is really valuable.

Use your actions to question or reaffirm your values. Do you really value your health and family? If so, take action to preserve your good health and spend time with your family. It is necessary to periodically look at your patterns of behavior. Do you act out of habit or do you act according to what is important to you? Habits might need to be changed to get what you value most out of life.

In times of doubt and difficulty, your values can keep you going. If you truly value getting a college education, you can put in the effort to accomplish your goal. When you have doubts about whether you can be successful, examine your values again and remind yourself of why you are doing what you are doing. For example, if you value being an independent business entrepreneur, you will put in the effort to be successful. If you value being a good parent, you will find the patience and develop the skill to succeed. Reminding yourself of your values can help you to continue your commitment to accomplishing your goals.

By knowing your values and following them, you have a powerful tool for making decisions, taking action, and motivating yourself to be successful.

Values

Test what you have learned by selecting the correct answers to the following questions.

1. Values are

    a. what we find interesting.
    b. what we find important.
    c. what we find entertaining.

2. Holland described interests as realistic, investigative, artistic, social, enterprising, and conventional. He arranged these interests in a _____ to show the relationship of the interests to one another.

    a. table
    b. list
    c. hexagon

3. The following is an important step in making a career decision:

    a. Persevere with your plan even if it is not working.
    b. Limit your options so you are not confused.
    c. Investigate the career outlook.

4. Acting on your values means:

    a. Acting consistently with your values
    b. Creating a job search plan
    c. Deciding on your most important value

5. Knowing what we value helps us to make good

    a. wages.
    b. decisions.
    c. expenditures.

How did you do on the quiz? Check your answers: 1. b, 2. c, 3. c, 4. a, 5. b

---

Journal Entry #5

Write down your most important value. Write an intention statement about how you plan to act on this value. For example, my most important value is to maintain my good health. I intend to act on this value by eating right and exercising.

© Lyudmyla Kharlamova/
Shutterstock.com

College Success 1

The College Success 1 website is continually updated with supplementary material for each chapter including Word documents of the journal entries, classroom activities, handouts, videos, links to related materials, and much more. See http://www.collegesuccess1.com/.

Notes

1. Howard Gardner, *Intelligence Reframed: Multiple Intelligences for the Twenty-First Century* (Boulder, CO: Basic Books, 1999).

2. Thomas Armstrong, *Multiple Intelligences in the Classroom* (Alexandria, VA: Association for Curriculum Development, 1994).

3. "Emotional Intelligence in Career Planning," available at https://www1.cfnc.org, accessed August 2013.

4. Angela Duckworth, Grit: The Power of Passion and Perseverance (New York: Simon & Schuster, 2016) p. 98.

5. U.S. Department of Labor, "O*Net Interest Profiler User's Guide," available at http://onetcenter.org

6. John L. Holland, *Making Vocational Choices: A Theory of Vocational Personalities and Work Environments* (2nd Ed.), (Englewood Cliffs, NJ: Prentice-Hall, 1985).

7. U.S. Department of Labor, "O*Net Interest Profiler User's Guide."

8. Adapted from U.S. Department of Labor, "O*Net Interest Profiler."

9. Job titles in this section is from http://wwwonetonline.org/find/descriptor/browse/Interests/

10. Christopher Peterson, *A Primer in Positive Psychology* (New York: Oxford University Pres, 2006) pp. 181–182.

11. Quoted in Rob Gilbert, ed., *Bits and Pieces*, November 4, 1999.

Multiple Intelligences Matching Quiz

Name _____   Date _____

Directions: Match the person with the intelligence at the right:

_____Michael Jordan

_____Aristotle

_____Martin Luther King, Jr.

_____Sigmund Freud

_____William Shakespeare

_____Albert Einstein

_____William James "will.i.am"

_____Charles Darwin

_____George Lucas

A   Musical: hearing and remembering musical patterns

B   Interpersonal: understanding other people

C   Mathematical: working with numbers

D   Spatial: manipulating objects in space

E   Bodily–Kinesthetic: using your body

F   Linguistic: using language

G   Intrapersonal: understanding yourself

H   Naturalist: understanding the environment

I   Existential: pondering the meaning of life and our place in the universe

Work with other students in a group to give examples of other famous person's in these categories.

Musical

Interpersonal

Mathematical

Spatial

Bodily–Kinesthetic

Linguistic

Intrapersonal

Naturalist

Existential

Crystallizers and Paralyzers

Name _____ Date _____

Complete the "Describing Your Multiple Intelligences" activity in this chapter before doing this exercise.

Each individual's life history contains **crystallizers** that promote the development of intelligences. Look at your highest scores on the multiple intelligences activity. List your highest scores below. Write down at least two crystallizers you experienced that may have helped you to develop these intelligences. For example, you may have been praised for your athletic skills and developed your bodily-kinesthetic intelligence.

My highest scores:

Crystallizers:

Each individual's life history also contains paralyzers that inhibit the development of intelligences. Look at your lowest scores on the multiple intelligences activity. Write down two paralyzers that may have discouraged you from developing this intelligence. For example, maybe you had a bad experience with math in elementary or middle school. Paralyzers often involve shame, guilt, fear, or anger.

My lowest scores:

Paralyzers:

How can you overcome some of your paralyzers if they are interfering with your success?

Are there some scores that you need to improve to accomplish your career and educational goals?

Based on the above analysis, write a discovery statement about what you have learned. I discovered that I . . . .

Summing Up Values

Name _____ Date _____

Look at the "Values Checklist" you completed in this chapter. Choose the 10 values most important to you and list them here.

_____   _____

_____   _____

_____   _____

_____   _____

_____   _____

Next, pick out the value that is most important and label it 1. Label your second most important value 2, and so on, until you have picked out your top five values.

1. My most important value is _____.
    Why?

2. My second most important value is _____.
    Why?

3. My third most important value is _____.
    Why?

4. My fourth most important value is _____.
   Why?

5. My fifth most important value is _____.
   Why?

The Planful Decision Strategy

Name _____   Date _____

Read the following scenario describing a college student in a problem situation. Then, answer the questions that follow to practice the planful decision strategy. You may want to do this as a group activity with other students in the class.

Rhonda is an 18-year-old student who is trying to decide on her major. She was a good student in high school, earning a 3.4 grade point average. Her best subjects were English and American history. She struggled with math and science but still earned good grades in these subjects. While in high school, she enjoyed being on the debate team and organizing the African American Club. This club was active in writing letters to the editor and became involved in supporting a local candidate for city council.

Rhonda is considering majoring in political science and has dreams of eventually going to law school. Rhonda likes being politically involved and advocating for different social causes. The highlight of her life in high school was when she organized students to speak to the city council about installing a traffic light in front of the school after a student was killed trying to cross the street. The light was installed during her senior year.

Rhonda's family has always been supportive, and she values her family life and the close relationships in the family. She comes from a middle-income family that is struggling to pay for her college education. Getting a bachelor's degree in political science and going to law school would take seven years and be very expensive. There is no law school in town, so Rhonda would have to move away from home to attend school.

Rhonda's parents have suggested that she consider becoming a nurse and attending the local nursing college. Rhonda could finish a bachelor's degree in nursing in four years and could begin working part-time as a nurse's aide in a short time. A cousin in the family became a nurse and found a job easily and is now earning a good income. The cousin arranged for Rhonda to volunteer this summer at the hospital where she works. Rhonda enjoys helping people at the hospital. Rhonda is trying to decide on her major. What should she do?

1. State the problem.

2. Describe Rhonda's values, hopes, and dreams.

3. What special talents, interests, or values does she have?

4. What further information would be helpful to Rhonda in making her decision?

5. What are the alternatives and pros and cons of each choice? Write these in the box on the back of this page.

Alternative 1	
Pros:	Cons:

Alternative 2	
Pros:	Cons:

Alternative 3 (be creative!)	
Pros:	Cons:

6. Only Rhonda can choose what is best for her. If you were Rhonda, what would you do and why? Use a separate piece of paper, if necessary, to write your answer.

CHAPTER 4

Planning Your Career and Education

Learning Objectives

Read to answer these key questions:

- What are some employment trends for the future?

- What are work skills necessary for success in the twenty-first century?

- How do I research a career?

- How do I plan my education?

- What are some new job search strategies?

- What is a dangerous opportunity?

It is always easier to get where you are going if you have a road map or a plan. To start the journey, it is helpful to know about yourself, including your personality, interests, talents, and values. Once you have this picture, you will need to know about the world of work and job trends that will affect your future employment opportunities. Next, you will need to make decisions about which road to follow. Then, you will need to plan your education to reach your destination. Finally, you will need some job-seeking skills such a writing a resume and cover letter, using social media to market yourself online, and preparing for a successful interview.

© Kiselev Andrey Valerevich/Shutterstock.com

Keep Your Eyes on the Future

The world is changing quickly, and these changes will affect your future career. To assure your future career success, you will need to become aware of career trends and observe how they change over time so that you can adjust your career plans accordingly. For example, recently a school was established for training bank tellers. The school quickly went out of business and the students demanded their money back because they were not able to get jobs. A careful observer of career trends would have noticed that bank tellers are being replaced by automatic teller machines (ATMs) and would not have started a school for training bank tellers. Students observant of career trends would not have paid money for the training. It is probably a good idea for bank tellers to look ahead and plan a new career direction.

How can you find out about career trends that may affect you in the future? Become a careful observer by reading about current events. Good sources of information include:

- Your local newspaper, especially the business section
- News programs
- Current magazines
- Government statistics and publications
- The Internet

When thinking about future trends, use your critical thinking skills. Sometimes trends change quickly or interact in different ways. For example, since we are using email to a great extent today, it might seem that mail carriers would not be as much in demand in the future. However, since people are buying more goods over the Internet, there has been an increased demand for mail carriers and other delivery services.

Develop the habit of looking at what is happening to see if you can identify trends that may affect your future.

Usually trends get started as a way to meet the following needs:[1]

- To save money
- To reduce cost
- To do things faster
- To make things easier to use
- To improve safety and reliability
- To lessen the impact on the environment

The following are some trends to watch that may affect your future career. As you read about each trend, think about how it could affect you.

Baby Boomers, Generation X, the Millennials and the New Generation Z

About every 20 years, sociologists begin to describe a new generation with similar characteristics based on shared historical experiences. Each generation has different opportunities and challenges in the workplace.

The Baby Boomers were born following World War II between 1946 and 1964. Four out of every 10 adults today are in this Baby Boom Generation.[2] Because there are so many aging Baby Boomers, the average age of Americans is increasing. Life expectancy is also increasing. In 2016 the projected life expectancy is 76.3 for men and 81.2 for women.[3] In the new millennium, many more people will live to be 100 years old or more! Think about the implications of an older population. Older people need such things as health care, recreation, travel, and financial planning. Occupations related to these needs are likely to be in demand now and in the future.

Those born between 1965 and 1977 are often referred to as Generation X. They are sometimes called the "baby bust" generation because fewer babies were born during this period than in the previous generations. There is much in the media about this generation having to pay higher taxes and Social Security payments to support the large number of aging Baby Boomers. Some say that this generation will not enjoy the prosperity of the Baby Boomers. Those who left college in the early nineties faced a recession and the worst job market since World War II.[4] Many left college in debt and returned home to live with their parents. Because of a lack of employment opportunities, many in this generation became entrepreneurs, starting new companies at a faster rate than previous generations.

Jane Bryant Quinn notes that in spite of economic challenges, Generation Xers have a lot going for them:[5]

- They have record-high levels of education, which correlate with higher income and lower unemployment.
- Generation Xers are computer literate, and those who use computers on the job earn 10 to 15 percent more than those who don't.
- This group often has a good work ethic valued by employers. However, they value a balanced lifestyle with time for outside interests and family.
- As Baby Boomers retire, more job opportunities are created for this group.
- Unlike the Baby Boomers, this generation was born into a more integrated and more diverse society. They are better able than previous generations to adapt to diversity in society and the workplace.

Those in the New Millennial Generation were born between 1977 and 1995. This generation is sometimes called Generation Y or the Echo Boomers, since they are the children of the Baby Boomers.[6] This new generation of approximately 60 million is three times larger than Generation X and will eventually exceed the number of Baby Boomers.

Millennials are more ethnically diverse than previous generations with 34 percent ethnic minorities. One in four lives with a single parent; three in four have working mothers. Most of them started using computers before they were five years old. Marketing researchers describe this new generation as "technologically adept, info-savvy, a cyber-generation, the clickeratti."[7] They are the connected generation, accustomed to cell phones, chatting on the Internet, and listening to downloaded music.

Young people in the Millennial Generation share a different historical perspective from the Baby Boom Generation. Baby Boomers remember the Vietnam War and the assassinations of President John F. Kennedy and Martin Luther King. For Millennials, school shootings such as Columbine and acts of terrorism such as the Oklahoma City bombing and the 9–11 attack on New York City stand out as important events. The Millennial Generation will see their main problems as dealing with violence, easy access to weapons, and the threat of terrorism.

Neil Howe and William Strauss paint a very positive picture of this new generation in their book *Millennials Rising: The Next Great Generation*:

- Millennials will rebel by tearing down old institutions that do not work and building new and better institutions. The authors predict that this will be the can-do generation filled with technology planners, community shapers, institution builders, and world leaders.
- Surveys show that this generation describes themselves as happy, confident, and positive.
- They are cooperative team players.
- They generally accept authority and respect their parents' values.
- They follow rules. The rates of homicides, violent crime, abortion, and teen pregnancy are decreasing rapidly.
- The use of alcohol, drugs, and tobacco is decreasing.
- Millennials have a fascination with and mastery of new technology.
- Their most important values are individuality and uniqueness.[8]

© Vaju Ariel/Shutterstock.com

In the past, new generations emerged about every twenty years. However, because of rapid social change, generations are now being defined in shorter time periods. **A new generation born since 1995 is currently emerging.** Various names for this generation have been proposed such as Generation Z, Generation Wii, the iGeneration, Gen Tech, Digital Natives, Net Gen, and the Plurals.[9] These names reflect this generation's fascination and ease of using technology as well as their increasing diversity. This is a large generation with one in four Americans under 18 years old.[10]

This generation has been affected by historical events such as the election of President Obama (the first biracial president), events surrounding 9/11, wars in Iraq and Afghanistan, the tsunami and nuclear meltdown in Japan, school violence, and economic recession. They are referred to as digital natives since they have always lived in a world with the Internet, smart phones, and other devices.

Some characteristic of this new generation include:[11]

- This is the last generation with a Caucasian majority. Only 55% of this generation is Caucasian as compared to 72% of Baby Boomers. In 2019, less than 50% of births will be Caucasian.

- They are more positive than older Americans about becoming an ethnically diverse society and more likely to have friends from different racial, ethnic, and religious groups.

- There is a continuing decline in two-parent households with only two out of three people from two parent households. Increased same sex marriage is changing the definition of family.

- Women are more likely to get a college degree and hold 51% of managerial and professional jobs. As a result, gender roles are blending with men assuming more familial responsibilities.

- It is an age of "girl power." Girls ages 8–15 care more about their grades than boys and have more expectations of receiving a college degree and having work that changes the world.

- Technology will continue to influence this group as in the New Millennial Generation. Use of technology will transform the way that people communicate and purchase goods. People will communicate with shorter and more immediate communications such as texting and Twitter. More purchases will be made on the Internet.

- This generation hopes to use technology as a tool to change the world.

It is predicted that the world of work for both the Millennials and Generation Z will be dramatically different. Previous generations anticipated having a lifetime career. By the year 2020, many jobs will probably be short-term contracts. This arrangement will provide cost savings and efficiency for employers and flexibility for employees to start or stop work to take vacations, train for new jobs, or meet family responsibilities. One in five people will be self-employed. Retirement will be postponed as people look forward to living longer and healthier lives.[12]

Journal Entry #1

Describe your generation (Baby Boomer, Generation X, New Millennial or Generation Z.) What are your best qualities and challenges?

Developments Affecting Future Careers

Jobs of the future will continue to be influenced by changes in our society and economy. These new developments will affect the job market for the future:[13]

We are evolving into a service, technology, and information society. Fewer people are working in agriculture and manufacturing. Futurists note that we are moving toward a service economy based on high technology, rapid communications, biotechnology for use in agriculture and medicine, health care, and sales of merchandise.[14] Service areas with increasing numbers of jobs include health care and social assistance; professional, scientific, and technical services; education services; accommodation and food services; government; retail trade; transportation and warehousing; finance and insurance; arts, entertainment, and recreation; wholesale trade; real estate, rental, and leasing; and information management.

There will be an increased need for education. Constant change in society and innovation in technology will require lifelong learning on the job. Education will take place in a variety of forms: community college courses, training on the job, private training sessions, and learning on your own. Those who do not keep up with the new technology will find that their skills quickly become obsolete. Those who do keep up will find their skills in demand. Higher education is linked to greater earnings and increased employment opportunities.

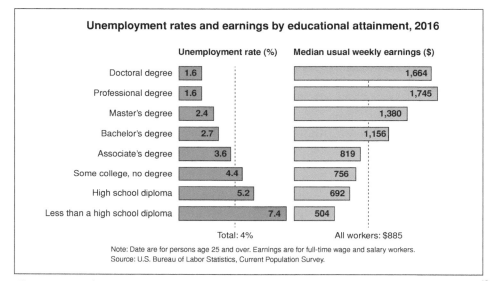

Figure 4.1 Education Pays, Unemployment rate and median weekly earnings, 2014.[15]

There will be increased opportunities for Stem (science, technology, engineering, and math) jobs. These jobs will grow 17% by 2020. These occupations jobs include many of the highest paying jobs.

Beware of job outsourcing. To reduce costs and improve profits, many jobs in technology, manufacturing, and service are being outsourced to countries such as India, China, and Taiwan, where well-educated, English-speaking workers are being used to do these jobs. For example, programmers in India can produce software at only 10% of the cost of these services in the United States. Jobs that are currently being outsources include accounting, payroll clerks, customer service, data entry, assembly line workers, industrial engineering, machine operators, computer-assisted design (CAD) technicians, purchasing managers, textile workers, software developers, and technical support. Jobs that are most likely to be outsourced are[16]

- Repetitive jobs, such as accounting,
- Well-defined jobs, such as customer service,
- Small manageable projects, such as software development,
- Jobs in which proximity to the customer is not important, such as technical support.

Jobs that are least likely to be outsourced include

- Jobs with ambiguity, such as top management jobs,
- Unpredictable jobs, such as troubleshooters,
- Jobs that require understanding of the culture, such as marketing,
- Joss that require close proximity to the customer, such as auto repair,
- Jobs requiring a high degree of innovation and creativity, such as product design,
- Jobs in entertainment, music, art, and design.

To protect yourself from outsourcing,

- Strive to be the best in the field.
- Be creative and innovative.
- Avoid repetitive jobs that do not require proximity to the customer.
- Choose a career where the demand is so high that it won't matter if some are outsourced.
- Consider a job in the skilled trades: carpenters, plumbers, electricians, hair stylists, construction workers, auto mechanics, and dental hygienists will always be in demand.

Globalization is changing the job market. Multinational corporations will locate their companies based on the availability of workers and the cost of labor. This trend will reduce the cost of goods and services but will change the nature of the job market. While this trend has resulted in outsourcing, there are increasing numbers of jobs in the United States requiring workers who speak different languages and understand how to do business in other countries.

Nontraditional jobs are increasing. Unlike traditional workers, nontraditional workers do not have full-time, year-round jobs with health and retirement benefits. Employers are moving toward using nontraditional workers, including multiple job holders, contingent and part-time workers, independent contractors, and temporary workers. Nearly four out of five employers use nontraditional workers to help them become more efficient, prevent layoffs, and access workers with special skills. There are advantages and disadvantages to this arrangement. Nontraditional workers have no benefits and risk unemployment. However, this arrangement can provide workers with a flexible work schedule in which they work during some periods and pursue other interests or gain new skills when not working.

© Mathias Rosenthal/Shutterstock.com

Automation will continue to reduce repetitive jobs in every industry. Increasingly sophisticated robots will be used to decrease the cost of goods and services. Engineers and technicians will be needed to design and maintain these robots.

There is a mismatch between workers and available jobs. It is often difficult for companies to fill jobs requiring highly skilled technical and scientific workers. These workers are often hired in other countries and use technology to work remotely.

More companies will use teleworking. Teleworking involves using smart phones to do some work at home. Currently, about 40% of workers use their smart phones to do some work at home. As a result, there will be increased flexibility of work hours and more people will work remotely using smart devices. There will be increased demand for application designers and designers for smart devices.

E-commerce is changing the way we do business. E-commerce is the purchasing of goods, services, and information over the Internet. More people are using e-commerce because of convenience, selection, cost savings, and ease of shopping. Online sales are a growing part of the market, increasing 10–20% a year for the past several years. By 2017, the web will account for 10% of retail sales, and approximately 43% of sales are influenced by online research.[17] There are more career opportunities in related fields such as computer graphics, web design, online marketing, and package delivery services.

Business will increase virtual collaboration. Workers are increasingly using Skype and other collaboration software to work with others.

New media literacy will become an essential skill for most new jobs. Workers who do not keep up with new media will quickly find their skills obsolete.

Career Trends for 2020

The good news is that over 20 million new jobs will be created by 2020, which represents a 14% annual growth rate. Approximately 60% of the competitive, high-demand, and high-paying jobs will require at least a bachelor's degree. Majors most in demand include accounting, engineering, computer science, business, and economics. However, most college students are majoring in history, education, and social science, which are lower in demand. Here are some specific areas where there will be increasing demand in the future.[18]

Data analysis. Companies are increasingly using data for market research. Opportunities exist for those who can find and analyze data.

Mental health. After being neglected for a long time, people are beginning to understand the importance of mental health for safety and the enjoyment of life. Current health-care insurance includes mental health coverage that will result in increased demand for services.

Technology-related jobs will continue to increase. Information and technology workers are now the largest group of workers in the United States. The Bureau of Labor Statistics reports that two million technology-related jobs will be created by 2018. Jobs in computer systems design and related services are expected to increase by 34% by 2018.[19]

Careers in **information technology** include the design, development, and support of computers, software, hardware, and networks. Some newer jobs in this area include animation for video games, film, videos, setting up websites, and Internet security. Jobs that will grow faster than the average include computer network administrators, data communications analysts, web developers, and App designers. Some new fields include data loss prevention, online security, and risk management. Computer science degrees are especially marketable when combined with traditional majors such as finance, accounting, or marketing. [20]

Radiation and laser technologies will provide new technical careers in the future. It has been said that lasers will be as important to the 21st century as electricity was for the 20th century. New uses for lasers are being found in medicine, energy, industry, computers, communications, entertainment, and outer space. The use of lasers is creating new jobs and causing others to become obsolete. For example, many welders are being replaced by laser technicians, who have significantly higher earnings. New jobs will open for people who purchase, install, and maintain lasers.

Careers in fiber optics and telecommunications are among the top new emerging fields in the 21st century. Fiber optics are thin glass fibers that transmit light. This new technology may soon make copper wire obsolete. One of the most important uses of fiber optics is to speed up delivery of data over the Internet and to improve telecommunications. It is also widely used in medical instruments, including laser surgery.

Artificial intelligence has interesting possibilities for the future. It enables computers to recognize patterns, improve from experience, make inferences, and approximate human thought. Artificial intelligence will be increasingly used in robots and smart machines. Two recent examples are IPhone's Siri, which uses voice recognition software to search the Internet, and Google's development of the self-driving car.

Research. There will be high demand for people with advanced degrees in engineering, chemistry, math, biology, biotechnology, and other sciences who will be the innovators in technology, medicine, and manufacturing.

Biology. Future historians may describe the 21st century as the biology century because of all the developments in this area. One of the most important developments is the Human Genome Project, which has identified the genes in human DNA, the carrier of genetic material. This research has resulted in new careers in biotechnology and biomedical technology.

Biotechnology will become increasingly important as a way to combat disease, develop new surgical procedures and devices, increase food production, reduce pollution, improve recycling, and provide new tools for law enforcement. Biotechnology includes genomic profiling, biomedical engineering, new pharmaceuticals, genetic engineering, and DNA identification. In the future, biotechnology may be used to find cures for diabetes, arthritis, Alzheimer's disease, and heart disease.

The field of **biomedical engineering,** which involves developing and testing health-care innovations, is expected to grow by 72% by 2018.[21] Biomedical technology is the field in which bionic implants are being developed for the human body. Scientists are working on the development of artificial limbs and organs including eyes, ears, hearts, and kidneys. A promising new development in this field is brain and computer interfaces. Scientists recently implanted a computer chip into the brain of a quadriplegic, enabling him to control a computer and television with his mind.[22] Biotechnology also develops new diagnostic test equipment and surgical tools.

Veterinary medicine. The demand for veterinarians is expected to increase by 35% because of the demand for pet products and health. However, it is interesting to note that there will be 35 times as many jobs for nurses as for veterinarians.[23]

Health-care occupations will add the most new jobs between 2012 and 2022 and registered nurses will see the most job growth.[24] This trend is being driven by an aging

© zhang kan/Shutterstock.com

population, increased longevity, health-care reform, and new developments in the pharmaceutical and medical fields. Demand will be especially high for dentists, nurses, physician specialists, optometrists, physical therapists, audiologists, pharmacists, athletic trainers, and elder-care providers. Because of increasing health-care costs, many of the jobs done by doctors, nurses, dentists, or physical therapists are now being done by physician's assistants, dental assistants, physical therapy aides, and home health aides. Health-care workers will increasingly use technology to do their work. For example, a new occupation is nursing informatics, which combines traditional nursing skills with computer and information science. Health care will be continually connected to technology such as in the biomedical engineering field.

Environmental science. There will be increased demand for limited resources requiring new technology to conserve water, control pollution, manage global warming, and produce food.

Green jobs are occupations dealing with the efficient use of energy, finding renewable sources of energy, and preserving the environment.

As fossil fuels are depleted, the world is facing a major transformation in how energy is generated and used. Sustainability, wind turbines, solar panels, farmer's markets, biofuels, and wind energy are just some of the ways to transition to a post-fossil fuel world. Jobs in this field include engineers who design new technology, consultants to audit energy needs, and technicians who install and maintain systems. Here are some titles of green jobs: environmental lawyer, environmental technician, sustainability consultant, sustainability project director, green architect, green building project manager, marine biologist, environmental technician, energy efficiency specialist, organic farmer, compliance manager, product engineer, wind energy engineer, and solar engineer.

Finance. Money management has become increasingly complex and important requiring professionals who understand finance, investments, and taxes.

Business. Today's business managers need to understand increased competition, the global economy, and must stay up-to-date with the latest forms of communication and social media. The median salaries in this category range from 70,000 to 80,000 and beyond making this occupation a good choice for those interested in higher incomes. Jobs with fast growth include market research analysts, marketing specialists, personal financial advisers, and health-care managers.

Entrepreneurship and small business. An important trend for the new millennium is the increase in entrepreneurship, which means starting your own business. Small

© Kheng Guan Toh/Shutterstock.com

businesses that can find innovative ways of meeting customer needs will be in demand for the future. A growing number of entrepreneurs operate their small businesses from home, taking advantage of telecommuting and the Internet to communicate with customers. While being an entrepreneur has some risks involved, there are many benefits, such as flexible scheduling, being your own boss, taking charge of your destiny, and greater potential for future income if your company is successful. You won't have to worry about being outsourced either.

Teaching. As the current generation of Baby Boomers retires, there will be increased jobs for educators who will serve the children of the New Millennial generation.

The effect of terrorism and the need for security. Fear of terrorism has changed attitudes that will affect career trends for years to come. Terrorist attacks have created an atmosphere of uncertainty that has had a negative effect on the economy and has increased unemployment. People are choosing to stay in the safety of their homes, offices, cars, and gated communities. Since people are spending more time at home, they spend more money making their homes comfortable. As a result, construction, home remodeling, and sales of entertainment systems are increasing.

Another result of terrorism is the shift toward occupations that provide value to society and in which people can search for personal satisfaction. More people volunteer their time to help others and are considering careers in education, social work, and medical occupations. When people are forced to relocate because of unemployment, they are considering moving to smaller towns that have a sense of community and a feeling of safety.

As the world population continues to grow, there is continued conflict over resources and ideologies and an increased need for security and safety. Law enforcement, intelligence, forensics, international relations, foreign affairs, and security administration careers will be in demand.

Careers with a Good Outlook for the Future

Jobs That Will Always Be in Demand[25]	2016 Best Jobs Rankings[26]	Top 10 Jobs for the Next Decade and Beyond[27]
Teachers	App Developer	Computer Programmer
Lawyers	Nurse Practitioner	Day Care Provider
Engineers	Information Security Analyst	Elder Care Specialist
Doctors	Computer Systems Analyst	Employment Specialist
Law Enforcement	Physical Therapist	Environmental Engineer
Accountants	Market Research Analyst	Home Health Aide
Food Preparers and Servers	Medical Sonographer	Management Consultant
	Dental Hygienist	Networking Specialist
	Operations Research Analyst	Physician's Assistant
	Health Services Manager	Social Services Coordinator

Journal Entry #2

Do a quick review of the developments affecting future careers and career trends for 2020. Write one paragraph about how any of these trends might affect your future.

Top Jobs for the Future[28]

Based on current career trends, here are some jobs that should be in high demand for the next 10 years.

Field of Employment	Job Titles
Business	Marketing Manager, Security and Financial Service, Internet Marketing Specialist, Advertising Executive, Buyer, Sales Person, Real Estate Agent, Business Development Manager, Marketing Researcher, Recruiter
Education	Teacher, Teacher's Aide, Adult Education Instructor, Math and Science Teacher
Entertainment	Dancer, Producer, Director, Actor, Content Creator, Musician, Artist, Commercial Artist, Writer, Technical Writer, Newspaper Reporter, News Anchor Person
Health	Emergency Medical Technician, Surgeon, Chiropractor, Dental Hygienist, Registered Nurse, Medical Assistant, Therapist, Respiratory Therapist, Home Health Aide, Primary Care Physician, Medical Lab Technician, Radiology Technician, Physical Therapist, Dental Assistant, Nurse's Aide
Information Technology	Computer Systems Analyst, Computer Engineer, Web Specialist, Network Support Technician, Java Programmer, Information Technology Manager, Web Developer, Database Administrator, Network Engineer
Law/Law Enforcement	Correction Officer, Law Officer, Anti-Terrorist Specialist, Security Guard, Tax/Estate Attorney, Intellectual Property Attorney
Services	Veterinarian, Social Worker, Hair Stylist, Telephone Repair Technician, Aircraft Mechanic, Guidance Counselor, Occupational Therapist, Child Care Assistant, Baker, Landscape Architect, Pest Controller, Chef, Caterer, Food Server
Sports	Athlete, Coach, Umpire, Physical Trainer
Technology	Electrical Engineer, Biological Scientist, Electronic Technician, CAD Operator, Product Designer, Sales Engineer, Applications Engineer, Product Marketing Engineer, Technical Support Manager, Product Development Manager
Trades	Carpenter, Plumber, Electrician
Travel/Transportation	Package Delivery Person, Flight Attendant, Hotel/Restaurant Manager, Taxi Driver, Chauffeur, Driver

QUIZ

Career Trends of the Future

Test what you have learned by selecting the correct answers to the following questions:

1. Students in Generation Z are
   a. limited by technology.
   b. more likely to have a lifetime career.
   c. more likely to appreciate ethnic diversity.

2. Use of the Internet will result in
   a. increased e-commerce.
   b. increased use of conventional stores.
   c. decreased mail delivery.

3. The largest group of workers in the United States is in
   a. manufacturing.
   b. information technology.
   c. agriculture.

4. Jobs unlikely to be outsourced include
   a. jobs that require close proximity to the customer.
   b. computer programming jobs.
   c. customer service jobs.

5. Future historians will describe the 21st century as the
   a. art and entertainment century.
   b. biology century.
   c. industrial development century.

How did you do on the quiz? Check your answers: 1. c, 2. a, 3. b, 4. a, 5. b

Work Skills for the 21st Century

Because of rapid changes in technology, college students of today may be preparing for jobs that do not exist right now. After graduation, many college students find employment that is not even related to their college majors. One researcher found that 48 percent of college graduates find employment in fields not related to their college majors.[29] More important than one's college major are the general skills learned in college that prepare students for the future.

To define skills needed in the future workplace, the U.S. Secretary of Labor created the Secretary's Commission on Achieving Necessary Skills (SCANS). Based on interviews with employers and educators, the members of the commission outlined foundation skills and workplace competencies needed to succeed in the workplace in the 21st century.[30] The following skills apply to all occupations in all fields and will help you to become a successful employee, regardless of your major. As you read through these skills, think about your competency in these areas.

Foundation Skills

Basic Skills

- Reading
- Writing
- Basic arithmetic
- Higher-level mathematics
- Listening
- Speaking

© iQoncept/Shutterstock.com

Thinking Skills

- Creative thinking
- Decision making
- Problem solving
- Mental visualization
- Knowing how to learn
- Reasoning

Personal Qualities

- Responsibility
- Self-esteem
- Sociability
- Self-management
- Integrity/honesty

© VLADGRIN/Shutterstock.com

Workplace Competencies

The following are some workplace competencies required to be successful in all well-paying jobs. The successful employee:

- can manage resources such as time, money, materials, and human resources;
- has good interpersonal skills and can participate as a member of a team, teach others, serve clients and customers, exercise leadership, negotiate workable solutions, and work with diverse individuals;
- can learn new information on the job and use computers to acquire, organize, analyze, and communicate information;
- works within the system, monitors and corrects performance, and improves the system as needed;
- uses technology to produce the desired results.

Because the workplace is changing, these skills may be more important than the background acquired through a college major. Work to develop these skills and you will be prepared for whatever lies ahead.

How to Research Your Career

After you have assessed your personality, interests, values, and talents, the next step is to learn about the world of work. If you can match your personal strengths to the world of work, you can find work that is interesting and you can excel in it. To learn about the world of work, you will need to research possible careers. This includes reading career descriptions and investigating career outlooks, salaries, and educational requirements.

Career Descriptions

The career description tells you about the nature of the work, working conditions, employment, training, qualifications, advancement, job outlook, earnings, and related occupations. The two best sources of job descriptions are the *Occupational Outlook Handbook* and *Occupational Outlook Quarterly*. The *Handbook*, published by the Bureau of Labor Statistics, is like an encyclopedia of careers. You can search alphabetically by career or by career cluster.

The *Occupational Outlook Quarterly* is a periodical with up-to-date articles on new and emerging occupations, training opportunities, salary trends, and new studies from the Bureau of Labor Statistics. You can find these resources in a public or school library, at a college career center, or on the *College Success Website* at http://www.collegesuccess1.com/Links9Career.htm.

© iQoncept/Shutterstock.com

Career Outlook

It is especially important to know about the career outlook of an occupation you are considering. Career outlook includes salary and availability of employment. How much does the occupation pay? Will the occupation exist in the future, and will there be employment opportunities? Of course, you will want to prepare yourself for careers that pay well and have future employment opportunities.

You can find information about career outlooks in the sources listed above, current periodicals, and materials from the Bureau of Labor Statistics. The following table, for example, lists the fastest-growing occupations, occupations with the highest salaries, and occupations with the largest job growth. Information from the Bureau of Labor Statistics is also available online.

Employment Projections 2008–2018[31]

10 Fastest-Growing Occupations	10 Industries with the Largest Wage and Salary Employment Growth	10 Occupations with the Largest Numerical Job Growth
Biomedical engineers	Management, scientific, technical	Registered nurses
Network systems and data communications analysts	Physicians	Home health aides
Home health aides	Computer systems design and related	Customer service representatives
Personal and home care aides	General merchandise stores	Food preparation workers
Financial examiners	Employment services	Personal and home care aides
Medical scientists	Local government	Retail salespersons
Physician assistants	Home health care services	Office clerks
Skin care specialists	Services for elderly and disabled	Accountants and auditors
Biochemists and biophysicists	Nursing care facilities	Nursing aides, orderlies
Athletic trainers	Full-service restaurants	Postsecondary teachers

Planning Your Education

Once you have assessed your personal characteristics and researched your career options, it is important to plan your education. If you have a plan, you will be able to finish your education more quickly and avoid taking unnecessary classes. You can begin work on your educational plan by following the steps below. After you have done some work on your plan, visit your college counselor or advisor to make sure that your plan is appropriate.

ACTIVITY

Steps in Planning Your Education

_____ 1. **Take your college entrance or assessment tests before you apply to colleges.** Most colleges require the Scholastic Aptitude Test (SAT) or their own local placement tests in order for you to be admitted. You can find information about these tests at your high school or college counseling center or online at http://www.ets.org/ or http://cbweb1.collegeboard.org/index.html. If you are attending a community college, check the college website, admissions office, or counseling office to see what placement exams are required.

_____ 2. **Take English the first semester, and continue each semester until your English requirement is complete.** English courses provide the foundation for further college study. Your SAT or college placement test will determine what level of English you need to take. As a general rule, community colleges require one semester of college-level English. Four-year colleges and universities generally require two semesters or three quarters of college-level English. If your placement scores are low, you may be required to take review courses first.

_____ 3. **Start your math classes early, preferably in the first semester or quarter.** Many high-paying careers require a long series of math classes, particularly those in the sciences, engineering, and business. If you delay taking math courses until later, you may limit your career options and extend your time in college. Take the required math courses each semester until you have

(Continued)

finished your requirements. Having a gap between math courses will make future courses more difficult.

_____ 4. **Take the required general education courses.** Find out what your college requires for general education and put these classes on your plan. You will find this information in the college catalog. Be careful to select the correct general education plan. At community colleges, there are different plans for transfer and associate's degree students. At a university, there may be different plans for different colleges within the university. Check with a college counselor or advisor to make sure you have the correct plan.

_____ 5. **Prepare for your major.** Consult your college catalog to see what courses are required for your major. If you are undecided on a major, take the general education courses and start working on a decision about your major. If you are interested in the sciences or engineering, start work on math in the first semester. Start on your major requirements as soon as possible so that you do not delay your graduation.

_____ 6. **Check prerequisites.** A prerequisite is a course that is required before taking a higher-level course. The college catalog lists courses offered and includes prerequisites. Most colleges will not let you register for a course for which you do not have the prerequisite. It is also difficult to succeed in an advanced course without taking the prerequisite first.

_____ 7. **Make an educational plan.** The educational plan includes all the courses you will need to graduate. Again, use the college catalog as your guide.

_____ 8. **Check your plan.** See your college counselor or advisor to check your plan. He or she can save you from taking classes that you do not need and help you to graduate in the minimum amount of time.

Finding Employment

After investing your time in achieving a college education, you will need some additional skills to get a job. Having a good resume and cover letter, marketing yourself online and knowing how to successfully interview for a job will help you to obtain your dream job.

Get Started with a Resume and Cover Letter

Your resume is important in establishing a good first impression and provides the basic content for job seeking social media sites such as LinkedIn and Facebook. A resume is a snapshot of your education and experience. It is generally one page in length. You will need a resume to apply for scholarships, part-time jobs, or find a position after you graduate. Start with a file of information you can use to create your resume. Keep your resume on file in your computer or on your flash drive so that you can revise it or post it online as needed.

A resume includes the following basic components:

- Contact information: your name, address, telephone number, and e-mail address
- A brief statement of your career objective
- A summary of your education:
  - Names and locations of schools
  - Dates of attendance
  - Diplomas or degrees received

"Think not of yourself as the architect of your career but as the sculptor. Expect to have a lot of hard hammering, chiseling, scraping and polishing."

B.C. Forbes

"The nearest to perfection that most people come is when filling out an employment application."

Source unknown

© NAN728/Shutterstock.com

- A summary of your work and/or volunteer experience
- If you have little directly related work experience, a list of courses you have taken that would help the employer understand your skills for employment
- Special skills, honors, awards, or achievements
- References (people who can recommend you for a job or scholarship)

There is no one best way to write a resume, but here are some helpful tips:

- Begin your resume with your contact information. Make sure that your email is professional. Consider creating a new email for job seeking purposes. Your email should include your first and last name.
- In the job history section, include brief statements about job tasks including what you did to make your company better. It is helpful to look for key words in the job announcement and make sure these key words are in your resume.
- List your present or most recent job first and work back chronologically.
- If you are just graduating from college and have little work experience, put the education section first along with related coursework.
- Keep in mind that the average resume gets read in 10 seconds. Make sure your resume is organized and brief. Bold those ideas that you want to highlight.
- Do not include personal information or photos.
- Carefully proofread your resume to make sure it has no errors. It is a good idea to have someone else review it also.
- Store your resume on your computer so that you can update it regularly and have it available to post online.

It is easy to upload your content to resume templates online. Here are some resume template sites:

Choose your template from a variety of examples and then create or upload your content. http://www.myperfectresume.com/

This site has 114 templates depending on your experience and career. You can upload your current resume into a suggested template and add their suggested improvements. http://www.resume-now.com/

Create a resume and set up a resume webpage. http://www.jobwinningresume.com/

Tips for Writing a Resume

- Write clearly
- Be brief
- Be neat
- Be honest
- Have letters of reference
- Use good-quality paper
- Post resume online

Ask for a letter of reference from your current supervisor at work or someone in a position to recommend you, such as a college professor or community member. Ask the person to address the letter "To Whom It May Concern" so that you can use the letter many times. If the person is on LinkedIn, ask him or her for an endorsement. The person recommending you should comment on your work habits, skills, and personal qualities. If appropriate, offer to write the letter yourself and then the person can edit it or send it as is. This often helps people who would like to recommend you, but are very busy. If you wait until you graduate to obtain letters of reference, potential recommenders may no longer be there or may not remember who you are. Always ask if you can use a person's name as a reference. When you are applying for a job and references are requested, phone the persons who have agreed to recommend you and let them know to expect a call.

While most resumes are shared online, if you need a printed copy, print your resume so that it looks professional. Use a good-quality white, tan, or gray paper. It is a good idea to take a printed copy of your resume to an interview.

© Alexander Iotzov/Shutterstock.com

When you respond to job announcements, you may be asked to send a cover letter with your resume attached. Address your letter to a specific person at the company or organization and spell the name correctly. You can call the personnel office to obtain this information. The purpose of the cover letter is to state your interest in the job, highlight your qualifications, and get the employer to read your resume and call you for an interview. The cover letter should be brief and to the point. Include the following items:

- State the job you are interested in and how you heard about the opening.
- Briefly state how your education and experience would be assets to the company.
- Ask for an interview and tell the employer how you can be contacted.
- Attach your resume.
- Your cover letter is the first contact you have with the employer. Make it neat and free from errors. Use spell check and grammar check, read it over again, and have someone else check it for you.

Select templates and view samples of cover letters online at http://www.cover-letter-now.com/

Establishing Your Personal Brand Online

Personal branding is the process by which we market ourselves to others. It is an important concept that has been used to sell products and services. Through the use of social media, you can use this concept to market your strengths to potential employers and to find a satisfying career. Throughout this textbook you have been challenged to become more aware of these personal strengths which can be used to create your own personal brand. Here are the steps for establishing your personal brand and marketing yourself:

© Maksim Kabakou/Shutterstock.com

Define Your Brand

The first step in marketing yourself is to define your personal brand. What are your passions, goals, and personal strengths and how can they be used in the job market? Review the assessments in this textbook and write a brief description of your personal brand along with a brief job title. A few examples of a personal brand include financial expert, entrepreneur, educator, consultant, engineer, and personal trainer.

Manage Your Online Presence

Most employers do online searches to find employees and to find information on job candidates before the interview. Make sure that your online presence is a professional one that you would want an employer to see. Make sure that your email address is a professional one or consider setting up an account for job seeking. Google your name and see what information a potential employer can find about you. Take a look at your online sites and make sure that the content is appropriate. Some online content may make it difficult to be hired including:

- photos or references to drug or alcohol use or abuse.
- discriminatory comments on race, religion, or gender.
- negative comments about previous employers.
- poor communication skills.

When using Facebook, manage your privacy settings so that no one can see your list of friends since you can be judged by the company you keep and you have no control over what your friends post. To keep your friends private, specify that no one can tag you in a Facebook photo without your authorization. Be careful about what you put on your front page, since it is the most visible page.

Set Up a Nameplate Website

Take control of your online presence by setting up a nameplate website which defines who you are and directs potential employers to your media sites. Good sites for setting up this nameplate include about.me, zerply.com, and sites.google.com. On these sites, you can

> "Everyone should find something they love doing. Then work isn't work. It's a part of themselves. Of who they are."
>
> Paul Mcauley

upload your photo, include your biography, list your education, describe your work experience, and provide links to LinkedIn or Facebook.

© Andresr/Shutterstock.com

Using Online Tools

At the present time, LinkedIn and Facebook are the most commonly used sites used by employers to research job candidates. Invest some of your time setting up accounts at these sites.

LinkedIn

LinkedIn is a directory of professionals and companies used for job searching, networking, and hiring. Many employers use LinkedIn profiles to search for potential employees. This profile is similar to a resume and includes your education and job experience. Make sure that your profile is complete and well written since it represents who you are online. Since recruiting software is used to search through profiles, use key words in your resume that relate to your desired job. Key words include job requirements, experience, software competencies, education, and previous employers. To find key words, take a look at job listings in your area of interest and expertise and include the words in your profile. It is helpful to include recommendations and endorsements which you can request from other contacts on LinkedIn. Personalize your profile by uploading a photo. Use a current photo and dress appropriately for the type of job you are seeking.

LinkedIn is also a job search tool in which you can search for and apply for jobs within the site. The job listings page allows you to search for jobs by location, industry, company, job function, level or position, employer, or key words. The site can also be used for networking. As you link to others, they can refer you to jobs open at their site. Maintaining a large network is job security because you can use it for job advancement or to find a new job in the future. You can join groups of other professionals in your area of expertise to receive notices about job openings in your area of interest. Use the status update function to let your contacts know that you are looking for a job.

When you find a specific job listing in which you are interested, you will have the option to apply within LinkedIn or you will be directed to the company website where you will need to create an account. The site also provides company profiles to help you to find the job that best matches your qualifications and help you with information useful for interviewing.

Facebook

Facebook is a social network that can be useful in finding a job. The first step in using your Facebook account to find a job is to clean up your profile to make sure that it does not contain any detrimental content. The next step is to post a status update letting your friends know that you are looking for a job and ask if they know about any job openings.

© PromesaArtStudio/Shutterstock.com

Use Facebook as a marketing tool. Post samples or links to your work online. If you are a photographer, post some of your photos online. If you are a writer, post links to material you have written. Keep your materials up to date so that prospective employers can see your best and most recent work. If your chosen company has a public Facebook page, you can show your passion, knowledge, and interest for your dream job by participating in discussion boards that can showcase your expertise. You can "like" the company on Facebook and receive news, information, and job openings from them. You can join or create groups on Facebook to discuss your area of interest. In this way, you may be considered for a job before it is posted.

Use Facebook's Marketplace app to search for jobs. Just click on Jobs in Marketplace and enter the job in which you are interested. It contains information about job openings and links to sites with job applications. Facebook also has an app called Social Jobs that allows you to search for jobs.

> "We do not go to work only to earn an income, but to find meaning in our lives. What we do is a large part of what we are."
> Alan Ryan

Journal Entry #3

What steps can you take to establish or improve your personal brand?

> "Many of life's failures are people who do not realize how close they were to success when they gave up."
> Thomas Edison

The Job Interview

Knowing how to be successful in an interview will help you to get the job that you want. Here are some ideas for being prepared and making a good impression.

- **Learn about the job.** Before the interview, it is important to research both the company and the job. This research will help you in two ways: you will know if the job is really the one you want, and you will have information that will help you to succeed at the interview. If you have taken the time to learn about the company before the interview, you will make a good impression and show that you are really interested in the job. Here are some ways that you can find this information:
  - Your college or public library may have a profile describing the company and the products it produces. This profile may include the size of the company and the company mission or philosophy.

Tips for a Successful
Job Interview

- Learn about job
- Understand criteria of
  interview
- Make a good
  impression
- Anticipate interview
  questions
- Send thank-you note

- Do you know someone who works for the company? Do any members of your family, friends, or teachers know someone who works for the company? If so, you can find out valuable information about the company.
- The personnel office often has informational brochures that describe the employer.
- Visit the company website on the Internet.

- **Understand the criteria used in an interview.** The interviewer represents the company and is looking for the best person to fill the job. It is your job to show the interviewer that you will do a good job. Of course you are interested in salary and benefits, but in order to get hired you must first convince the interviewer that you have something to offer the company. Focus on what you can offer the company based on your education and experience and what you have learned about the company. You may be able to obtain information on salary and benefits from the personnel office before the interview.

  Interviewers look for candidates who show the enthusiasm and commitment necessary to do a good job. They are interested in hiring someone who can work as part of a team. Think about your education and experience and be prepared to describe your skills and give examples of how you have been successful on the job. Give a realistic and honest description of your work.

- **Make a good impression.** Here are some suggestions for making a good impression:
  - Dress appropriately for the interview. Look at how the employees of the company dress and then dress a little better. Of course, your attire will vary with the type of job you are seeking. You will dress differently if you are interviewing for a position as manager of a surf shop or an entry-level job in an engineering firm. Wear a conservative dark-colored or neutral suit for most professional positions. Do not wear too much jewelry, and hide excess body piercings (unless you are applying at a piercing shop). Cover any tattoos if they are not appropriate for the workplace.
  - Relax during the interview. You can relax by preparing in advance. Research the company, practice interview questions, and visualize yourself in the interview room feeling confident about the interview.
  - When you enter the interview room, smile, introduce yourself, and shake hands with the interviewer. If your hands are cold and clammy, go to the restroom before the interview and run warm water over your hands or rub them together.
  - Maintain eye contact with the interviewer and sit up straight. Poor posture or leaning back in your chair could be seen as a lack of confidence or interest in the job.

Making a Good
Impression

- Dress appropriately
- Relax
- Prepare in advance
- Smile
- Shake hands
- Introduce yourself
- Maintain eye contact
- Sit up straight

"Was the interview too early for you?"
© Cartoonresource/Shutterstock.com

- **Anticipate the interview questions.** Listen carefully to the interview questions. Ask for clarification of any question you do not understand. Answer the questions concisely and honestly. It helps to anticipate the questions that are likely to be asked and think about your answers in advance. Generally, be prepared to talk about yourself, your goals, and your reasons for applying for the job. Following are some questions that are typically asked in interviews and some suggestions for answering them:

1. **What can you tell us about yourself?** Think about the job requirements, and remember that the interviewer is looking for someone who will do a good job for the company. Talk about your education and experience as they relate to the job. You can put in interesting facts about your life and your hobbies, but keep your answers brief. This question is generally an icebreaker that helps the interviewer get a general picture of you and help you relax.

2. **Why do you want this job? Why should I hire you?** Think about the research you did on this company and several ways that you could benefit the company. A good answer might be, "I have always been good at technical skills and engineering. I am interested in putting these technical skills into practice in your company." A not-so-good answer would be, "I'm interested in making a lot of money and need health insurance."

3. **Why are you leaving your present job?** Instead of saying that the boss was horrible and the working conditions were intolerable (even if this was the case), think of some positive reasons for leaving, such as:

   - I am looking for a job that provides challenge and an opportunity for growth.

   - I received my degree and am looking for a job where I can use my education.

   - I had a part-time job to help me through school. I have graduated and am looking for a career.

   - I moved (or the company downsized or went out of business).

   Be careful about discussing problems on your previous job. The interviewers might assume that you were the cause of the problems or that you could not get along with other people.

4. **What are your strengths and weaknesses?** Think about your strengths in relation to the job requirements, and be prepared to talk about them during the interview. When asked about your weaknesses, smile and try to turn them into strengths. For example, if you are an introvert, you might say that you are quiet and like to concentrate on your work, but you make an effort to communicate with others on the job. If you are an extrovert, say that you enjoy talking and working with others, but you are good at time management and get the job done on time. If you are a perfectionist, say that you like to do an excellent job, but you know the importance of meeting deadlines, so you do the best you can in the time available.

5. **Tell us about a difficulty or problem that you solved on the job.** Think about some problem that you successfully solved on the job and describe how you did it. Focus on what you accomplished. If the problem was one that dealt with other people, do not focus on blaming or complaining. Focus on your desire to work things out and work well with everyone.

6. **Tell us about one of your achievements on the job.** Give examples of projects you have done on the job that have turned out well and projects that gave you a sense of pride and accomplishment.

Tips for Answering Questions

- Listen carefully
- Ask for clarification
- Answer concisely and honestly

7. **What do you like best about your work? What do you like least?** Think about these questions in advance and use the question about what you like best to highlight your skills for the job. For the question about what you like the least, be honest but express your willingness to do the job that is required.

8. **Are there any questions that you would like to ask?** Based on your research on the company, think of some specific questions that show your interest in the company. A good question might be, "Tell me about your company's plans for the future." A not-so-good question would be, "How much vacation do I get?"

9. **Write a thank-you note.** After the interview, write a thank-you note and express your interest in the job. It makes a good impression and causes the interviewer to think about you again.

Journal Entry #4

A friend is looking for a job. What advice would you give him or her about the resume and job interview?

QUIZ

Employment Skills

1. Career outlook refers to

   a. whether the job is done inside or outside.
   b. the salary and availability of employment.
   c. realistic careers.

2. In planning your education,

   a. you can delay taking English courses.
   b. start your math classes early.
   c. complete general education before you begin your major.

3. A resume is generally _____ page(s) in length.

   a. one
   b. two
   c. four

4. The cover letter

   a. contains a brief statement of how your qualifications would be an asset to the company.
   b. includes a detailed list of your education and experience.
   c. does not include a request for an interview.

5. Personal branding refers to

   a. wearing name brand clothing.
   b. the design of your resume.
   c. using social media to market yourself online.

How did you do on the quiz? Check your answers: 1. b, 2. b, 3. a, 4. a, 5. c

Life Is a Dangerous Opportunity

Even though we may do our best in planning our career and education, life does not always turn out as planned. Unexpected events happen, putting our life in crisis. The crisis might be loss of employment, divorce, illness, or death of a loved one. How we deal with the crisis events in our lives can have a great impact on our current well-being and the future.

The Chinese word for crisis has two characters: one character represents danger and the other represents opportunity. Every crisis has the danger of loss of something important and the resulting emotions of frustration, sorrow, and grief. But every crisis also has an opportunity. Sometimes it is difficult to see the opportunity because we are overwhelmed by the danger. A crisis, however, can provide an impetus for change and growth. A crisis forces us to look inside ourselves to find capabilities that have always been there, although we did not know it. If life goes too smoothly, there is no motivation to change. If we get too comfortable, we stop growing. There is no testing of our capabilities. We stay in the same patterns.

To find the opportunity in a crisis, focus on what is possible in the situation. Every adversity has the seed of a greater benefit or possibility. Expect things to work out well. Expect success. To deal with negative emotions, consider that feelings are not simply a result of what happens to us, but of our interpretation of events. If we focus on the danger, we cannot see the possibilities.

As a practical application, consider the example of someone who has just lost a job. John had worked as a construction worker for nearly 10 years when he injured his back. His doctor told him that he would no longer be able to do physical labor. John was 30 years old and had two children and large house and truck payments. He was having difficulty finding a job that paid as well as his construction job, and was suffering from many negative emotions resulting from his loss of employment.

John decided that he would have to use his brain rather than his back. As soon as he was up and moving, he started taking some general education courses at the local college. He assessed his skills and identified his strengths. He was a good father and communicated well with his children. He had wanted to go to college, but got married early and started to work in construction instead. John decided that he would really enjoy being a marriage and family counselor. It would mean getting a bachelor's and a master's degree, which would take five or more years.

John began to search for a way to accomplish this new goal. He first tackled the financial problems. He investigated vocational rehabilitation, veteran's benefits, financial aid, and scholarships. He sold his house and his truck. His wife took a part-time job. He worked out a careful budget. He began to work toward his new goal with a high degree of motivation and self-satisfaction. He had found a new opportunity.

© Shutter_M/Shutterstock.com

"When written in Chinese, the word 'crisis' is composed of two characters; one represents danger and the other represents opportunity."

John F. Kennedy

Journal Entry #5

At times in life, you may face a crisis or setback which causes an unexpected change in plans. If you think positively about the situation, you can think of some new opportunities for the future. This situation is called a dangerous opportunity. Describe a dangerous opportunity you have faced in your life. What were the dangers and what opportunities did you find?

"Life is not about waiting for the storms to pass . . . it's about learning how to dance in the rain."
Vivian Greene

© Lyudmyla Kharlamova/
Shutterstock.com

College Success 1

The College Success 1 website is continually updated with supplementary material for each chapter including Word documents of the journal entries, classroom activities, handouts, videos, links to related materials, and much more. See http://www.collegesuccess1.com/.

Notes

1. Michael T. Robinson, "Top Jobs for the Future," from www.careerplanner.com, 2004.

2. Gail Sheehy, *New Passages* (New York: Random House, 1995), 34.

3. U.S. National Center for Health Statistics, "Health, United States, 2016," retrieved from https://www.cdc.gov/nchs/data/hus/hus16.pdf#015, July 2017

4. Jeff Giles, "Generalization X," *Newsweek,* June 6, 1994.

5. Jane Bryant Quinn, "The Luck of the Xers, Comeback Kids: Young People Will Live Better Than They Think," *Newsweek,* 6 June 1994, 66–67.

6. Ellen Neuborne, http://www.businessweek.com, 1999.

7. Claudia Smith Brison, http://www.thestate.com, 14 July 2002.

8. Neil Howe and William Strauss, *Millennials Rising: The Next Great Generation* (New York: Vintage Books, 2000).

9. *USA Today*, "After Gen X, Millennials, What Should Next Generation Be?" by Bruce Horovitz, May 24, 2012.

10. US Census Bureau, "State and County QuickFacts 2012", http://quickfacts.census.gov/qfd/states/00000.html

11. "The First Generation of the Twenty First Century, an Introduction to the Pluralist Generation" by Magid Generational Strategies, April 30, 2012 from http://magid.com/sites/default/files/pdf/MagidPluralistGenerationWhitepaper.pdf

12. Neuborne, www.businessweek.com, 1999.

13. "Where Will Jobs be in 2020?," from http://www.careerprofiles.info/jobs-of-2020.html, 2015.

14. John Naisbitt, Patricia Aburdeen, and Walter Kiechel III, "How We Will Work in the Year 2000," *Fortune*, 17 May 1993, 41–52.

15. U.S. Bureau of Labor Statistics Employment Projections, "Unemployment Rates and Earnings by Educational Attainment," 2016, retrieved from https://www.bls.gov/emp/ep_chart_001.htm, July 2107.

16. "Tomorrow's Best Careers," from http://www.future-trends.com, 2004.

17. "U.S. Online Sales to Reach $370 billion by 2017" by Forrester Research, March 13, 2013, accessed from www.forrester.com.

18. "7 Trends for the Future of Work to 2020," from http://www.staff.com/blog/7-trends-for-the-future-of-work-to-2020/, 2015.

19. "Where Will You (and Your Kids) Work in 2020 and Beyond?," from http://www.beinkandescent.com/articles/956/Where+will+you+work+in+2020, 2015.

20. Ibid.

21. U.S. Bureau of Labor Statistics, "Overview of the 2008-18 Projections."

22. Roxanne Khamsi, "Paralyzed Man Sends E-Mail by Thought," News@Nature.com, October 13, 2004.

23. "Career Trends: The Essential Skills You'll Need for the Jobs of the Next Five Years," from http://www.workopolis.com/content/advice/article/career-trending-where-the-jobs-will-be-through-2020-and-beyond/, 2015.

24. Ibid.

25. Bureau of Labor Statistics, "Employment Projections: 2012-2022 Summary," from http://www.bls.gov/news.release/ecopro.nr0.htm.

26. Kiplinger, "2016 Best Jobs Rankings," retrieved from http://www.kiplinger.com/slideshow/business/T012-S001-best-jobs-for-the-future-2017/index.html, July 2017.

27. WorldWideLearn, "Top Jobs and Career Trends," retrieved from http://www.worldwidelearn.com/online-education-guide/top-ten-job-trends.htm, July, 2017.

28. Michael T. Robinson, "Top Jobs for the Future," CareerPlanner.com, 2008.

29. T.J. Grites, "Being 'Undecided' Could Be the Best Decision They Could Make," *School Counselor* 29 (1981): 41-46.

30. Secretary's Commission on Achieving Necessary Skills (SCANS), *Learning a Living: A Blueprint for High Performance* (Washington, DC: U.S. Department of Labor, 1991).

31. U.S. Bureau of Labor Statistics, "Overview of the 2008-18 Projections."

Sara Student
222 College Avenue
San Diego, CA 92019
(619) 123-4567

June 20, 2018

Mr. John Smith
Director of Human Resources
Future Technology Company
111 Technology Way
La Jolla, CA 92111

Dear Mr. Smith:

At our college job fair last week, I enjoyed speaking with you about some new engineering jobs available at Future Technology Company. As you suggested, I am sending my resume. I am interested in your opening for an electrical engineer. Is there anything else I need to do to apply for this position?

While at UCSD, I gained experience in laboratory projects, writing scientific reports, and preparing technical presentations. Some engineering projects that I completed relate to work done at your company:

- Constructed a programmable robot with motor and sensors
- Worked with a group of students on the design of a satellite communications system
- Completed lab projects on innovative fiber-optic fabrication techniques
- Proposed a design for a prosthetic device to help the visually impaired

For my senior design project, I used my knowledge of digital signal processing and systems integration to design and construct a voice modulator. This project involved applying theory to hardware and understanding information processing as well as the relation of a computer to its controlled devices.

I am excited about the possibility of continuing work in this field and would enjoy the opportunity to discuss my qualifications in more detail. I am available for an interview at your convenience. I look forward to hearing from you.

Sincerely,

Sara Student

Encl.: Resume

Sara Student
222 College Avenue; San Diego, CA 92019
(619) 123-4567
saraengineer@aol.com

OBJECTIVE	Electrical Engineer

HIGHLIGHTS

Recent degree in Electrical Engineering
Specialized coursework in electromagnetism, photonics and lasers, biomedical imaging devices, and experimental techniques

EDUCATION

B.S., Electrical Engineering, University of California, San Diego, CA, 2017
A.S. with Honors, Cuyamaca College, El Cajon, CA, 2015

KEY RELATED COURSES

- **Circuits and systems:** solving network equations, Laplace transforms, practical robotics development
- **Electromagnetism:** Maxwell's equations, wave guides and transmission, electromagnetic properties of circuits and materials
- **Experimental techniques:** built and programmed a voice processor; studied transducers, computer architecture, and interfacing; applied integrated construction techniques
- **Photonics and lasers:** laser stability and design, holography, optical information processing, pattern recognition, electro-optic modulation, fiber optics
- **Biomedical imaging devices:** microscopy, x-rays, and neural imaging; designed an optical prosthesis
- **Quantum physics:** uncertainty principle, wave equation and spin, particle models, scattering theory and radiation

SKILLS

Computer Skills: PSpice, Matlab, Java, DSP, Assembly Language, Unix, Windows, Microsoft Word, Excel, and PowerPoint
Technical Skills: Microprocessors, circuits, optical components, oscilloscope, function generator, photovoltaics, signal processing, typing, SQUID testing
Personal Skills: Leadership, good people skills, organized, responsible, creative, motivated, hardworking, good writing skills

EMPLOYMENT

Intern, Quantum Design, La Jolla, CA, Summer 2015
Computer Lab Assistant, UCSD, La Jolla, CA, 2016–2017
Teacher's Aide, Cuyamaca College, El Cajon, CA, 2013–2015
Volunteer, Habitat for Humanity, Tijuana, Mexico, 2013–2015

INTERESTS

Optics, computing, programming, physics, electronic music, sampling, marine biology, and scuba diving

ACHIEVEMENTS

Advanced Placement Scholar
Dean's List, Phi Theta Kappa Honor Society
Provost's Honors List

Resume Worksheet for Your Ideal Career

Name _____ Date _____

Use this worksheet to prepare a resume similar to the sample on the previous page. Assume that you have graduated from college and are applying for your ideal career.

1. What is the specific job title of your ideal job?

2. What are two or three qualifications you possess that would especially qualify you for this job? These qualifications can be listed under Highlights on your resume.

3. List your degree or degrees, major, and dates of completion.

4. List five courses you will take to prepare for your ideal career. For each course, list some key components that would catch the interest of your potential employer. Use a college catalog to complete this section.

5. List the skills you would need in each of these areas.

Computer skills:

Technical or other job-related skills:

Personal skills related to your job objective:

6. List employment that would prepare you for your ideal job. Consider internships or part-time employment.

7. What are your interests?

8. What special achievements or awards do you have?

Interview Worksheet

Name _____ Date _____

Answer the following questions to prepare for the interview for your ideal job. If you do not know what your ideal job is, pretend that you are interviewing for any professional job. You may want to practice these questions with a classmate.

1. What can you tell us about yourself?

2. Why are you leaving your present job?

3. What are your strengths and weaknesses?

4. Tell us about a difficulty or problem that you solved on the job.

5. Tell us about one of your achievements on the job.

6. What do you like best about your work? What do you like least?

7. Are there any questions that you would like to ask?

Rate Your Skills for Success in the Workplace

Name _____ Date _____

Read each statement relating to skills needed for success in the workplace. Use the following scale to rate your competencies:

5 = Excellent   **4** = Very good   **3** = Average   **2** = Needs improvement   **1** = Need to develop

_____ 1. I have good reading skills. I can locate information I need to read and understand and interpret it. I can pick out the main idea and judge the accuracy of the information.

_____ 2. I have good writing skills. I can communicate thoughts, ideas, and information in writing. I know how to edit and revise my writing and use correct spelling, punctuation, and grammar.

_____ 3. I am good at arithmetic. I can perform basic computations using whole numbers and percentages. I can make reasonable estimates without a calculator and can read tables, graphs, and charts.

_____ 4. I am good at mathematics. I can use a variety of mathematical techniques including statistics to predict the occurrence of events.

_____ 5. I am good at speaking. I can organize my ideas and participate in discussions and group presentations. I speak clearly and am a good listener. I ask questions to obtain feedback when needed.

_____ 6. I am a creative thinker. I can come up with new ideas and unusual connections. I can imagine new possibilities and combine ideas in new ways.

_____ 7. I make good decisions. I can specify goals and constraints, generate alternatives, consider risks, and evaluate alternatives.

_____ 8. I am good at solving problems. I can see when a problem exists, identify the reasons for the problem, and devise a plan of action for solving the problem.

_____ 9. I am good at mental visualization. I can see things in my mind's eye. Examples include building a project from a blueprint or imagining the taste of a recipe from reading it.

_____ 10. I know how to learn new information. I am aware of my learning style and can use learning strategies to obtain new knowledge.

_____ 11. I am good at reasoning. I can use logic to draw conclusions and apply rules and principles to new situations.

_____ 12. I am a responsible person. I work toward accomplishing goals, set high standards, and pay attention to details. I usually accomplish tasks on time.

_____ 13. I have high self-esteem. I believe in my self-worth and maintain a positive view of myself.

_____ 14. I am sociable, understanding, friendly, adaptable, polite, and relate well to others.

_____ 15. I am good at self-management. I know my background, skills, and abilities and set realistic goals for myself. I monitor my progress toward completing my goals and complete them.

_____ 16. I practice integrity and honesty. I recognize when I am faced with a decision that involves ethics and choose ethical behavior.

_____ 17. I am good at managing my time. I set goals, prioritize, and follow schedules to complete tasks on time.

_____ 18. I manage money well. I know how to use and prepare a budget and keep records, making adjustments when necessary.

_____ 19. I can manage material and resources. I can store and distribute materials, supplies, parts, equipment, space, or products.

_____ 20. I can participate as a member of a team. I can work cooperatively with others and contribute to group efforts.

_____ 21. I can teach others. I can help others to learn needed knowledge and skills.

_____ 22. I can exercise leadership. I know how to communicate, encourage, persuade, and motivate individuals.

_____ 23. I am a good negotiator. I can work toward an agreement and resolve divergent interests.

_____ 24. I can work with men and women from a variety of ethnic, social, or educational backgrounds.

_____ 25. I can acquire and evaluate information. I can identify a need for information and find the information I need.

_____ 26. I can organize and maintain information. I can find written or computerized information.

_____ 27. I can use computers to process information.

_____ 28. I have an understanding of social, organizational, and technological systems and can operate effectively in these systems.

_____ 29. I can improve the design of a system to improve the quality of products and services.

_____ 30. I can use machines and computers to accomplish the desired task.

_____ Total

Score your skills for success in the workplace.

150–121	Excellent
120–91	Very good
90–61	Average
Below 60	Need improvement

From the previous list of workplace skills, make a list of five of your strong points. What do you do well?

From the list of workplace skills, make a list of areas you need to improve.

PART II

College Success

CHAPTER 5

Managing Time and Money

Learning Objectives

Read to answer these key questions:

- What are my lifetime goals?

- How can I manage my time to accomplish my goals?

- How much time do I need for study and work?

- How can I make an effective schedule?

- What are some time management tricks?

- How can I deal with procrastination?

- How can I manage my money to accomplish my financial goals?

- What are some ways to save money?

- How can I pay for my education?

- How can I use priorities to manage my time?

College and career success requires that you manage both time and money. You will need time to study and money to pay for your education. Begin to think about time management by asking yourself, "What is my purpose in life?" This may be one of the most difficult questions you will ever answer. Start by thinking about your interests and what matters most to you. Think about how your work will affect your life, your family, and ultimately how it will affect your community, and the world around you. Think about how you want your life to be five, ten, or fifteen years from now. Developing a vision for the future helps you to become more motivated and passionate about your work. It also helps you to prioritize and spend your time doing what is most important to accomplish your goals. Having a purpose helps you to be grittier too. This chapter provides some useful techniques for managing time and money so you can accomplish the goals you have set for yourself.

What Are My Lifetime Goals?

Setting goals helps you to establish what is important and provides direction for your life. Goals help you to focus your energy on what you want to accomplish. Goals are a promise to yourself to improve your life. Setting goals can help you turn your dreams into reality. Steven Scott, in his book *A Millionaire's Notebook,* lays out five steps in this process:

1. Dream or visualize.
2. Convert the dream into goals.
3. Convert your goals into tasks.
4. Convert your task into steps.
5. Take your first step, and then the next.[1]

As you begin to think about your personal goals in life, make your goals specific and concrete. Rather than saying, "I want to be rich," make your goal something that you can break into specific steps. You might want to start learning about money management or begin a savings plan. Rather than setting a goal for happiness, think about what brings you happiness. If you want to live a long and healthy life, think about the health habits that will help you to accomplish your goal. You will need to break your goals down into specific tasks to be able to accomplish them.

GOAL SETTING

Specific
Measurable
Achievable
Realistic
Timely

© winui/Shutterstock.com

Here are some criteria for successful goal setting:

1. **Is it specific and measurable?** Can it be counted or observed? The most common goal mentioned by students is happiness in life. What is happiness, and how will you know when you have achieved it? Is happiness a career you enjoy, owning your own home, or a travel destination?

2. **Is it achievable?** Do you have the skills, abilities, and resources to accomplish this goal? If not, are you willing to spend the time to develop the skills, abilities, and resources needed to achieve this goal?

3. **Is it realistic?** Do you believe that you can achieve it? Are you positive and optimistic about this goal?

4. **Is it timely?** When will you finish this goal? Set a date to accomplish your goal.

5. **What steps do you need to take to begin?** Are you willing to take action to start working on it?

6. **Do you want to do it?** Is this a goal you are choosing because it provides personal satisfaction, rather than meeting a requirement or expectation of someone else?

7. **Are you motivated to achieve it?** What are your rewards for achieving it?

8. **Does the goal match your values?** Is it important to you?

> "A goal is a dream with a deadline."
> Napoleon Hill

Journal Entry #1

Write a paragraph about your lifetime goals. Use any of these questions to guide your thinking:

- What is your career goal? If you do not know what your career goal is, describe your preferred work environment. Would your ideal career require a college degree?
- What are your family goals? Are you interested in marriage and family? What would be your important family values?
- What are your social goals (friends, community, and recreation)?
- When you are older and look back on your life, what are the three most important life goals that you want to have accomplished?

A Goal or a Fantasy?

One of the best questions ever asked in my class was, "What is the difference between a goal and a fantasy?" As you look at your list of lifetime goals, are some of these items goals or fantasies? Think about this question as you read the following scenario:

When Linda was a college student, she was walking through the parking lot, noticed a beautiful red sports car, and decided that it would become a lifetime goal for her to own a similar car one day. However, with college expenses and her part-time job, it was not possible to buy the car. She would have to be content with the used car that her dad had given her so that she could drive to college. Years passed by, and Linda now has a good job, a home, and a family. She is reading a magazine and sees a picture of a similar red sports car. She cuts out this picture and tapes it to the refrigerator. After it has been on the refrigerator for several months, her children ask her why the picture is on the refrigerator. Linda replies, "I just like to dream about owning this car." One day, as Linda is driving past a car dealership, she sees the red sports car on display and stops in for a test drive. To her surprise, she decides that she does not like driving the car. It doesn't fit her lifestyle, either. She enjoys outdoor activities that would require a larger car. Buying a second car would be costly and reduce the amount of money that the family could spend on vacations. She decides that vacations are more important than owning the sports car. Linda goes home and removes the picture of the red sports car from the refrigerator.

© Natursports/Shutterstock.com

There are many differences between a goal and a fantasy. A fantasy is a dream that may or may not become a reality. A goal is something that we actually plan to achieve. Sometimes we begin with a fantasy and later it becomes a goal. A fantasy can become a goal if steps are taken to achieve it. In the preceding example, the sports car is a fantasy until Linda actually takes the car for a test drive. After driving the car, she decides that she really does not want it. The fantasy is sometimes better than the reality. Goals and fantasies change over a lifetime. We set goals, try them out, and change them as we grow and mature and find out what is most important in life. Knowing what we think is important, and what we value most, helps us make good decisions about lifetime goals.

What is the difference between a goal and a fantasy? **A goal is something that requires action.** Ask yourself if you are willing to take action on the goals you have set for yourself. Begin to take action by thinking about the steps needed to accomplish the goal. Then take the first step and continue. Change your goals if they are no longer important to you.

> "Vision without action is a daydream. Action without vision is a nightmare."
> Japanese Proverb

> "In life, as in football, you won't go far unless you know where the goalposts are."
> Arnold Glasgow

Journal Entry #2

Write a paragraph about how you will accomplish one of your important lifetime goals. Start your paragraph by stating an important goal from the previous journal entry. What is the first step in accomplishing this goal? Next, list some additional steps needed to accomplish it. How can you motivate yourself to begin taking these steps?

For example:

One of my important lifetime goals is _____. The first step in accomplishing this goal is . . . Some additional steps are . . . I can motivate myself to accomplish this goal by . . .

The ABCs of Time Management

Using the **ABCs of time management** is a way of thinking about priorities. Priorities are what you think is important. An **A priority** is a task that relates to your lifetime goal. For example, if my goal is to earn a college degree, studying becomes an A priority. This activity would become one of the most important tasks that I could accomplish today. If my goal is to be healthy, an A priority would be to exercise and plan a healthy diet. If my goal is to have a good family life, an A priority would be to spend time with family members. Knowing about your lifetime goals and spending time on those items that are most important to you will help you to accomplish the goals that you have set for yourself. If you do not spend time on your goals, you may want to look at them again and decide which ones are fantasies that you do not really value or want to accomplish.

A **B priority** is an activity that you have to do, but that is not directly related to your lifetime goal. Examples of B priorities might be getting out of bed, taking a shower, buying groceries, paying bills, or getting gas for the car. These activities are less important, but still are necessary for survival. If I do not put gas in the car, I cannot even get to school or work. If I do not pay the bills, I will soon have financial difficulties. While we often cannot postpone these activities in order to accomplish lifetime goals, we can learn efficient time management techniques to accomplish these tasks quickly.

A **C priority** is something that I can postpone until later with no harmful effect. For example, I could wait until tomorrow or another day to wash my car, do the laundry, buy groceries, or organize my desk. As these items are postponed, however, they can move up the list to a B priority. If I cannot see out of my car window or have no clean clothes to wear, it is time to move these tasks up on my list of priorities. I can wait until I have finished studying to use my cell phone, social media, or video games.

Have you ever been a victim of "**C fever**"? This is an illness in which we do the C activities first and do not get around to doing the A activities that are connected to lifetime goals. Tasks required to accomplish lifetime goals are often ones that are more difficult, challenge our abilities, and take some time to accomplish. These tasks are often more difficult than the B or C activities. The C activities can fill our time and exhaust the energy we need to accomplish the A activities. An example of C fever is the student who cleans the desk, checks the cell phone, starts a video game, or checks Facebook or other social media before studying. C fever is doing the endless tasks that keep us from accomplishing goals that are really important to us. Why do we fall victim to C fever? C activities are often fun or easy and give us a sense of accomplishment. We can see immediate progress without too much effort. I can wash my car and get a sense of accomplishment and satisfaction in my shiny clean car. The task is easy and does not challenge my intellectual capabilities.

© iQoncept/Shutterstock.com

Setting Priorities

To see how the ABCs of time management work, read the profile of Justin, a typical college student, below.

Justin is a 19-year-old college student who plans to major in physical therapy. He is athletic and values his good health. He cares about people and likes helping others. He has a part-time job working as an assistant in the gym, where he monitors proper use of the weightlifting machines. Justin is also a member of the soccer team and practices with the team every afternoon.

Here is a list of activities that Justin would like to do today. Label each task as follows:

A if it relates to Justin's lifetime goals
B if it is something necessary to do
C if it is something that could be done tomorrow or later

_____ Get up, shower, get dressed

_____ Eat breakfast

_____ Go to work

_____ Go to class

_____ Visit with friends between classes

_____ Buy a new battery for his watch

_____ Go shopping for new gym shoes

_____ Attend soccer practice

_____ Do weightlifting exercises

_____ Study for biology test that is tomorrow

_____ Meet friends for pizza at lunch

_____ Call girlfriend

_____ Eat dinner

_____ Unpack gear from weekend camping trip

_____ Watch football game on TV

_____ Play video games

_____ Do math homework

While Justin is the only one who can decide how to spend his time, he can take some steps toward accomplishing his lifetime goal of being healthy by eating properly, exercising, and going to soccer practice. He can become a physical therapist by studying for the biology test and doing his math homework. He can gain valuable experience related to physical therapy by working in the gym. He cares about people and likes to maintain good relationships with others. Any tasks related to these goals are high-priority A activities.

What other activities are necessary B activities? He certainly needs to get up, shower, and get dressed. What are the C activities that could be postponed until tomorrow or later? Again, Justin needs to decide. Maybe he could postpone shopping for a new watch battery and gym shoes until the weekend. He would have to decide how much time to spend visiting with friends, watching TV, or playing video games. Since he likes these activities, he could use them as rewards for studying for the biology test and doing his math homework.

How to Estimate Study and Work Time

Students are often surprised at the amount of time necessary for study to be successful in college. A general rule is that you need to study two hours for every hour spent in a college class. A typical weekly schedule of a full-time student would look like this:

Typical College Schedule

> 15 hours of attending class
> +30 hours of reading, studying, and preparation
> 45 hours total

A full-time job involves working 40 hours a week. A full-time college student spends 45 hours or more attending classes and studying. Some students will need more than 45 hours a week if they are taking lab classes, need help with study and learning skills, or are taking a heavy course load.

Some students try to work full-time and go to school full-time. While some are successful, this schedule is extremely difficult.

The Nearly Impossible Schedule

> 15 hours attending class
> 30 hours studying
> +40 hours working
> 85 hours total

This schedule is the equivalent of having two full-time jobs! Working full-time makes it very difficult to find the time necessary to study for classes. Lack of study causes students to do poorly on exams and to doubt their abilities. Such a schedule causes stress and fatigue that make studying difficult. Increased stress can also lead to problems with personal relationships and emotional problems. These are all things that lead to dropping out of college.

Many students today work and go to college. Working during college can provide some valuable experience that will help you to find a job when you finish college. Working can teach you to manage your time efficiently and give you a feeling of independence and control over your own future. Many people need to work to pay for their education. A general guideline is to work no more than 20 hours a week if you plan to attend college full-time. Here is a workable schedule.

Part-Time Work Schedule

> 12 hours attending class
> 24 hours studying
> +20 hours working
> 56 hours total

A commitment of 56 hours a week is like having a full-time job and a part-time job. While this schedule takes extra energy and commitment, many students are successful with it. Notice that the course load is reduced to 12 hours. This schedule involves taking one less class per semester. The class missed can be made up in summer school, or the time needed to graduate can be extended. Many students take five years to earn the bachelor's degree because they work part-time. It is better to take longer to graduate than to give up because of frustration and drop out of college. If you must work full-time, consider reducing your course load to one or two courses. You will gradually reach your goal of a college degree.

> "The key is not to prioritize what's on the schedule, but to schedule your priorities."
>
> Stephen Covey

> "When you do the things you have to do when you have to do them, the day will come when you can do the things you want to do when you want to do them."
>
> Zig Ziglar

Part-Time Student Schedule

6 hours attending class
12 hours studying
+40 hours working
58 hours total

Add up the number of hours you are attending classes, double this figure for study time, and add to it your work time, as in the above examples. How many hours of commitment do you have? Can you be successful with your current level of commitment to school, work, and study?

To begin managing your schedule, use the weekly calendar located at the end of this chapter to write in your scheduled activities such as work, class times, and athletics.

Schedule Your Success

What Is Your Chronotype?

It is interesting that scientists describe different time preferences or chronotypes as larks, owls, or hummingbirds.[2] Understanding your chronotype is important in scheduling your learning at a time when you can learn most efficiently and use the rest of the time for less important tasks.

- Larks like to get up and go to bed early. They are most alert during the day with productivity peaking about two hours before noon. If you are a lark or morning person, schedule your classes and study time for the morning.
- Owls prefer to get up and go to bed late. They are most productive around 6 pm. If you are an owl or evening person, schedule your classes and study time for later in the day or evening.
- Humming birds are combination types that tend to be more like larks or owls, or somewhere in between.

Another way to describe time of day preference is your prime time. Use your prime time for studying and you will accomplish more in less time.

Researchers have found that night owls often have lower GPAs because they are frequently sleep deprived. Did you know that sleep deprivation can reduce your intelligence, cause weight gain, and accelerate the aging process? Healthy 30-year-olds who slept for only four hours a night for six days had the body chemistry of a 60-year-old.[3] Loss of sleep interferes with attention, memory, mathematical skills, logical reasoning, and manual dexterity. If you are a night owl, consider changing your sleeping pattern to make sure you get enough sleep. This change will be helpful in your career after college. Here are some suggestions for getting more sleep:

Avoid

- Staying up all night or late in the night to study.
- Alcohol, nicotine, exercise, or food late in the evening. Note that alcohol initially makes you sleepy, but it interferes with sleep later in the night.

Do this

- Relax before bedtime by reading a good book or listening to soft music.
- Have a regular pattern of sleep. Go to bed at the same time each evening and get up at the same time each morning.
- Get some exercise every day so that you feel tired at night.

Using a Schedule

If you have not used a schedule in the past, consider trying a schedule for a couple of weeks to see if it is helpful in completing tasks and working toward your lifetime goals. There are several advantages to using a schedule:

- It gets you started on your work.
- It helps you avoid procrastination.
- It relieves pressure because you have things under control.
- It frees the mind of details.
- It helps you find time to study.
- It eliminates the panic caused by doing things at the last minute.
- It helps you find time for recreation and exercise.

Once you have made a master schedule that includes classes, work, and other activities, you will see that you have some blanks that provide opportunities for using your time productively. Here are some ideas for making the most of your schedule:

1. Fill in your study times. Use the time immediately before class for previewing and the time immediately after class for reviewing. Remember that you need to study two hours or more for each hour spent in a college class.

© Caroline Eibl/Shutterstock.com

2. Break large projects such as a term paper or studying for a test into small tasks and begin early. Double your time estimates for completion of the project. Larger projects often take longer than you think. If you finish early, use the extra time for something fun.

3. Set priorities. Make sure you include activities related to your lifetime goals.

4. Allow time for sleep and meals. It is easier to study if you are well rested and have good eating habits.

5. Schedule your time in manageable blocks of an hour or two. Having every moment scheduled leads to frustration when plans change.

6. Leave some time unscheduled to use as a shock absorber. You will need unscheduled time to relax and to deal with unexpected events.

7. Leave time for recreation, exercise, and fun.

See the weekly study schedule form at the end of this chapter.

If You Dislike Schedules

© iQoncept/Shutterstock.com

Some personality types like more freedom and do not like the structure that a schedule provides. There are alternatives for those who do not like to use a schedule. Here are some additional ideas.

1. A simple and fast way to organize your time is to use a to-do list. Take an index card or small piece of paper and simply write a list of what you need to do during the day. You can prioritize the list by putting an A or star by the most important items. Cross items off the list as you accomplish them. A list helps you focus on what is important and serves as a reminder not to forget certain tasks.

2. Another idea is to use monthly or yearly calendars to write down important events, tasks, and deadlines. Use these calendars to note the first day of school, when important assignments are due, vacations, and final exams. Place the calendars in a place where they are easily seen.

3. Use this simple question to keep you on track, "What is the best use of my time right now?"[4] This question works well if you keep in mind your goals and priorities.

4. Use reminders and sticky notes to keep on track and to remind yourself of what needs to be done each day. Place the notes in a place where you will see them, such as your computer, the bathroom mirror, or the dashboard of your car.

5. Some families use their refrigerators as time management devices. Use the refrigerator to post your calendars, reminders, goals, tasks, and to-do lists. You will see these reminders every time you open the refrigerator.

6. Invent your own unique ideas for managing time. Anything will work if it helps to accomplish your goals.

Manage Your Time with a Web Application

There are thousands of new web applications available to organize your life. You can use a web application on your phone, laptop, computer, or other mobile device to:

- Create a to-do list or schedule.
- Send reminders when assignments are due.
- Organize your calendar and plan your tasks.
- Organize your study time and plan assignments.
- Avoid procrastination.
- Create a virtual assistant to keep you organized.

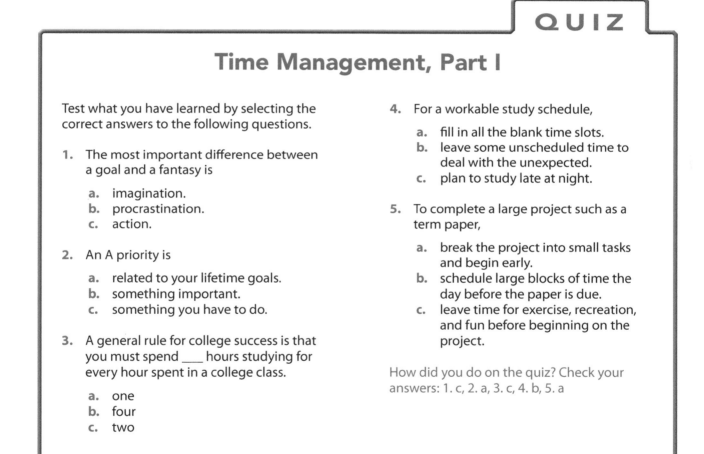

QUIZ

Time Management, Part I

Test what you have learned by selecting the correct answers to the following questions.

1. The most important difference between a goal and a fantasy is

   a. imagination.
   b. procrastination.
   c. action.

2. An A priority is

   a. related to your lifetime goals.
   b. something important.
   c. something you have to do.

3. A general rule for college success is that you must spend ___ hours studying for every hour spent in a college class.

   a. one
   b. four
   c. two

4. For a workable study schedule,

   a. fill in all the blank time slots.
   b. leave some unscheduled time to deal with the unexpected.
   c. plan to study late at night.

5. To complete a large project such as a term paper,

   a. break the project into small tasks and begin early.
   b. schedule large blocks of time the day before the paper is due.
   c. leave time for exercise, recreation, and fun before beginning on the project.

How did you do on the quiz? Check your answers: 1. c, 2. a, 3. c, 4. b, 5. a

Time Management Tricks

Life is full of demands for work, study, family, friends, and recreation. Time management tricks can help you get started on the important tasks and make the most of your time. Try the following techniques when you are feeling frustrated and overwhelmed.

Divide and Conquer

When large tasks seem overwhelming, think of the small tasks needed to complete the project and start on the first step. For example, suppose you have to write a term paper. You have to take out a paper and pencil, log onto your computer, brainstorm some ideas, go to the library to find information, think about your main ideas, and write the first sentence. Each of these steps is manageable. It's looking at the entire project that can be intimidating.

I once set out hiking on a mountain trail. When I got to the top of the mountain and looked down, I enjoyed a spectacular view and was amazed at how high I had climbed. If I had thought about how high the mountain was, I might not have attempted the hike. I climbed the mountain by taking it one step at a time. That's the secret to completing any large project: break it into small, manageable parts, then take the first step and keep going.

Learning a small part at a time is also easy and helps with motivation for learning. While in college, carry around some material that you need to study. Take advantage of five or ten minutes of time to study a small part of your material. In this way you make good use of your time and enhance memory by using distributed practice. Don't wait until you have large blocks of uninterrupted study time to begin your studies. You may not have the luxury of large blocks of time, or you may want to spend that time in other ways.

© iQoncept/Shutterstock.com

Do the First Small Step

The most difficult step in completing any project is the first step. If you have a challenging project to do, think of a small first step and complete that small step. Make the first step something that you can accomplish easily and in a short amount of time. Give yourself permission to stop after the first step. However, you may find that you are motivated to continue with the project. If you have a term paper to write, think about some small step you can take to get started. Log onto your computer and look at the blank screen. Start writing some ideas. Type the topic into a computer search engine and see what information is available. Go to the library and see what is available on your topic. If you can find some interesting ideas, you can motivate yourself to begin the project. Once you have started the project, it is easier to continue.

The 80/20 Rule

Alan Lakein is noted for many useful time management techniques. One that I have used over the years is the 80/20 rule. Lakein says, "If all items are arranged in order of value, 80 percent of the value would come from only 20 percent of the items, while the remaining 20 percent of the value would come from 80 percent of the items."[5] For example, if you have a list of ten items to do, two of the items on the list are more important than the others. If you were to do only the two most important items, you would have accomplished 80 percent of the value. If you are short on time, see if you can choose the 20 percent of the tasks that are the most valuable. Lakein noted that the 80/20 rule applies to many situations in life:

- 80 percent of file usage is in 20 percent of the files.
- 80 percent of dinners repeat 20 percent of the recipes.
- 80 percent of the washing is done on the 20 percent of the clothes worn most frequently.
- 80 percent of the dirt is on the 20 percent of the floor used most often.

Think about how the 80/20 rule applies in your life. It is another way of thinking about priorities and figuring out which of the tasks are C priorities. This prioritizing is especially important if you are short on time. The 80/20 rule helps you to focus on what is most important.

Aim for Excellence, Not Perfection

Are you satisfied with your work only if it is done perfectly? Do you put off a project because you cannot do it perfectly? Aiming for perfection in all tasks causes anxiety and procrastination. There are times when perfection is not necessary. Dave Ellis calls this time management technique "It Ain't No Piano."[6] If a construction worker bends a nail in the framing of a house, it does not matter. The construction worker simply puts in another nail. After all, "it ain't no piano." It is another matter if you are building a fine cabinet or finishing a piano. Perfection is more important in these circumstances. We need to ask: Is the task important enough to invest the time needed for perfection? A final term paper needs to be as perfect as we can make it. A rough draft is like the frame of a house that does not need to be perfect.

In aiming for excellence rather than perfection, challenge yourself to use perspective to see the big picture. How important is the project and how perfect does it need to be? Could your time be better invested accomplishing other tasks? This technique requires flexibility and the ability to change with different situations. Do not give up if you cannot complete a project perfectly. Do the best that you can in the time available. In some situations, if life is too hectic, you may need to settle for completing the project and getting it in on time rather than doing it perfectly. With this idea in mind, you may be able to relax and still achieve excellence.

Make Learning Fun by Finding a Reward

Time management is not about restriction, self-control, and deprivation. If it is done correctly, time can be managed to get more out of life and to have fun while doing it. Remember that behavior is likely to increase if followed by a reward. Think about activities that you find rewarding. In our time management example with Justin who wants to be a physical therapist, he could use many tasks as rewards for completing his studies. He could meet friends for pizza,

© carmen2011/Shutterstock.com

call his girlfriend, play video games, or watch TV. The key idea is to do the studying first and then reward the behavior. Maybe Justin will not be able to do all of the activities we have mentioned as possible rewards, but he could choose what he enjoys most.

Studying first and then rewarding yourself leads to peace of mind and the ability to focus on tasks at hand. While Justin is out having pizza with his friends, he does not have to worry about work that he has not done. While Justin is studying, he does not have to feel that he is being deprived of having pizza with friends. In this way, he can focus on studying while he is studying and focus on having a good time while relaxing with his friends. It is not a good idea to think about having pizza with friends while studying or to think about studying while having pizza with friends. When you work, focus on your work and get it done. When you play, enjoy playing without having to think about work.

Take a Break

If you are overwhelmed with the task at hand, sometimes it is best to just take a break. If you're stuck on a computer program or a math problem, take a break and do

"Don't say you don't have enough time. You have exactly the same number of hours per day that were given to Helen Keller, Pasteur, Michelangelo, Mother Teresa, Leonardo da Vinci, Thomas Jefferson, and Albert Einstein."

H. Jackson Browne

© NorGal/Shutterstock.com

something else. As a general rule, take a break of 10 minutes for each hour of study. During the break, do something totally different. It is a good idea to get up and move around. Get up and pet your cat or dog, observe your goldfish, or shoot a few baskets. If time is really at a premium, use your break time to accomplish other important tasks. Put your clothes in the dryer, empty the dishwasher, or pay a bill.

Learn to Say No Sometimes

Learn to say no to tasks that you do not have time to do. Follow your statement with the reasons for saying no: you are going to college and need time to study. Most people will understand this answer and respect it. You may need to say no to yourself as well. Maybe you cannot go out on Wednesday night if you have a class early on Thursday morning. Maybe the best use of your time right now is to turn off the TV or get off the Internet and study for tomorrow's test. You are investing your time in your future.

Dealing with Time Bandits

Time bandits are the many things that keep us from spending time on the things we think are important. Another word for a time bandit is a time waster. In college, it is tempting to do many things other than studying. We are all victims of different kinds of bandits.

ACTIVITY

Put a checkmark next to the items that waste your time. Add your own personal time wasters at the end of the list.

_____ TV	_____ Procrastination	_____ Sleeping in
_____ Other electronic devices	_____ Household chores	_____ Shopping
_____ Daydreaming	_____ Roommates	_____ Being easily distracted
_____ Social media	_____ Video games	_____ Studying at a bad time
_____ Saying yes when you mean no	_____ Partying	_____ Reading magazines
_____ Friends	_____ Children	_____ Studying in a distracting place
_____ Internet	_____ Cell phone	
_____ Social time	_____ Waiting time	_____ Movies
_____ Family	_____ Girlfriend, boyfriend, spouse	_____ Commuting time (travel)

List some of your personal time bandits here.

_____

_____

Here are some ideas for keeping time bandits under control:

- **Schedule time for other people.** Friends and family are important, so we do not want to get rid of them! Discuss your goal of a college education with your friends and family. People who care about you will respect your goals. You may need to use a Do Not Disturb sign at times. If you are a parent, remember that you are a role model for your children. If they see you studying, they are more likely to value their own education. Plan to spend quality time with your children and the people who are important to you. Make sure they understand that you care about them.

- **Remember the rewards.** Many of the time bandits listed above make good rewards for completing your work. Put the time bandits to work for you by studying first and then enjoying a reward. Enjoy the TV, Internet, cell phone, video games, or socializing with friends after you have finished your studies. Aim for a balance of work, study, and leisure time.

- **Remind yourself about your priorities.** When time bandits attack, remind yourself of why you are in college. Think about your personal goals for the future. Remember that college is not forever. By doing well in college, you will finish in the shortest time possible.

- **Use a schedule.** Using a schedule or a to-do list is helpful in keeping you on track. Make sure you have some slack time in your schedule to handle unexpected phone calls and deal with the unplanned events that happen in life. If you cannot stick to your schedule, just get back on track as soon as you can.

Journal Entry #3

Write a paragraph about how you will manage your time to accomplish your goal of a college education. Use any of these questions to guide your thinking:

- What are your priorities?
- How will you balance school, work, and family/friends?
- What are some time management tools you plan to use?
- How can you deal with time bandits?

Dealing with Procrastination

Procrastination means putting off things until later. We all use delaying tactics at times. Procrastination that is habitual, however, can be self-destructive. Understanding some possible reasons for procrastination can help you use time more effectively and be more successful in accomplishing goals.

Why Do We Procrastinate?

There are many psychological reasons for procrastinating. Just becoming aware of these may help you deal with procrastination. If you have serious difficulty managing your time for psychological reasons, visit the counseling center at your college or university. Do you recognize any of these reasons for procrastination in yourself or others?

© bloomua/
Shutterstock.com

- **Fear of failure.** Sometimes we procrastinate because we are afraid of failing. We see our performance as related to how much ability we have and how worthwhile we are as human beings. We may procrastinate in our college studies because of doubts about our ability to do the work. Success, however, comes from trying and learning from mistakes. There is a popular saying: falling down is not failure, but failing to get up or not even trying is failure.

- **Fear of success.** Most students are surprised to find out that one of the reasons for procrastination is fear of success. Success in college means moving on with your life, getting a job, leaving a familiar situation, accepting increased responsibility, and sometimes leaving friends behind. None of these tasks is easy. An example of fear of success is not taking the last step required to be successful. Students sometimes do not take the last class needed to graduate. Some good students do not show up for the final exam or do not turn in a major project. If you ever find yourself procrastinating on an important last step, ask yourself if you are afraid of success and what lies ahead in your future.

- **Perfectionism.** Some people who procrastinate do not realize that they are perfectionists. Perfectionists expect more from themselves than is realistic and more than others expect of themselves. There is often no other choice than to procrastinate because perfectionism is usually unattainable. Perfectionism generates anxiety that further hinders performance. Perfectionists need to understand that perfection is seldom possible. They need to set time limits on projects and do their best within those time limits.

- **Need for excitement.** Some students can only be motivated by waiting until the last minute to begin a project. These students are excited and motivated by playing a game of "Beat the Clock." They like living on the edge and the adrenaline rush of responding to a crisis. Playing this game provides motivation, but it does not leave enough time to achieve the best results. Inevitably, things happen at the last minute to make the game even more exciting and dangerous: the printer breaks, the computer crashes, the student gets ill, the car breaks down, or the dog eats the homework. These students need to start projects earlier to improve their chances of success. It is best to seek excitement elsewhere, in sports or other competitive activities.

- **Excellence without effort.** In this scenario, students believe that they are truly outstanding and can achieve success without effort. These students think that they can go to college without attending classes or reading the text. They believe that they can pass the test without studying. They often do not succeed in college the first semester, which puts them at risk of dropping out of school. They often return to college later and improve their performance by putting in the effort required.

- **Loss of control.** Some students fear loss of control over their lives and procrastinate to gain control. An example is students who attend college because others (such as parents) want them to attend. Procrastination becomes a way of gaining control over the situation by saying, "You can't make me do this." They attend college but accomplish nothing. Parents can support and encourage education, but students need to choose their own goals in life and attend college because it is an important personal goal.

Tips for Dealing with Procrastination

When you find yourself procrastinating on a certain task, think about the consequences. Will the procrastination lead to failing an exam or getting a low grade? Think about the rewards of doing the task. If you do well, you can take pride in yourself and celebrate your success. How will you feel when the task is completed? Will you be able to enjoy your leisure time without guilt about not doing your work? How does the task help you to achieve your lifetime goals?

Maybe the procrastination is a warning sign that you need to reconsider lifetime goals and change them to better suit your needs.

Procrastination Scenario

George is a college student who is on academic probation for having low grades. He is required to make a plan for improving his grades in order to remain in college. George tells the counselor that he is making poor grades because of his procrastination. He is an accounting major and puts off doing homework because he dislikes it and does not find it interesting. The counselor asks George why he had chosen accounting as a major. He replies that accounting is a major that is in demand and has a good salary. The counselor suggests that George consider a major that he would enjoy more. After some consideration, George changes his major to psychology. He becomes more interested in college studies and is able to raise his grades to stay in college.

Most of the time, you will reap benefits by avoiding procrastination and completing the task at hand. Jane Burka and Lenora Yuen suggest the following steps to deal with procrastination:

1. Select a goal.

2. Visualize your progress.

3. Be careful not to sabotage yourself.

4. Stick to a time limit.

5. Don't wait until you feel like it.

6. Follow through. Watch out for excuses and focus on one step at a time.

7. Reward yourself after you have made some progress.

8. Be flexible about your goal.

9. Remember that it does not have to be perfect.[7]

© iQoncept/Shutterstock.com

Time Management, Part II

Test what you have learned by selecting the correct answers to the following questions.

1. To get started on a challenging project,

   a. think of a small first step and complete it.
   b. wait until you have plenty of time to begin.
   c. wait until you are well rested and relaxed.

2. If you are completing a to-do list of 10 items, the 80/20 rule states that

   a. 80% of the value comes from completing most of the items on the list.
   b. 80% of the value comes from completing two of the most important items.
   c. 80% of the value comes from completing half of the items on the list.

3. It is suggested that students aim for

   a. perfection.
   b. excellence.
   c. passing.

4. Sometimes students procrastinate because of

   a. fear of failure.
   b. fear of success.
   c. all of the above.

5. Playing the game "Beat the Clock" when doing a term paper results in

   a. increased motivation and success.
   b. greater excitement and quality work.
   c. increased motivation and risk.

How did you do on the quiz? Check your answers: 1. a, 2. b, 3. b, 4. c, 5. c

Journal Entry #4

Write a paragraph about how you will avoid procrastination. Consider these ideas when thinking about procrastination: fear of failure, fear of success, perfectionism, need for excitement, excellence without effort, and loss of control. How will you complete your assignments on time?

Managing Your Money

To be successful in college and in life, you will need to manage not only time, but money. One of the top reasons that students drop out of college is that they cannot pay for their education or that they have to work so much that they do not have time for school. Take a look at your lifetime goals. Most students have a goal related to money, such as becoming financially secure or becoming wealthy. If financial security or wealth is one of your goals, you will need to begin to take some action to accomplish that goal. If you don't take action on a goal, it is merely a fantasy.

© ARENA Creative/Shutterstock.com

How to Become a Millionaire

Save regularly. Frances Leonard, author of *Time Is Money,* cites some statistics on how much money you need to save to become a millionaire.[8] You can retire with a million dollars by age 68 by saving the following amounts of money at various ages. These figures assume a 10 percent return on your investment.

At age 22, save $87 per month

At age 26, save $130 per month

At age 30, save $194 per month

At age 35, save $324 a month

Notice that the younger you start saving, the less money is required to reach the million-dollar goal. (And keep in mind that even a million dollars may not be enough money to save for retirement.) How can you start saving money when you are a student struggling to pay for college? The answer is to practice money management techniques and to begin a savings habit, even if the money you save is a small amount to buy your books for next semester. When you get that first good job, save 10 percent of the money. If you are serious about becoming financially secure, learn about investments such as real estate, stocks and bonds, and mutual funds. Learning how to save and invest your money can pay big dividends in the future.

Managing Your Money

- Monitor your spending
- Prepare a budget
- Beware of credit and interest
- Watch spending leaks

Budgeting: The Key to Money Management

Money management begins with looking at your attitude toward money. Pay attention to how you spend your money so that you can accomplish your financial goals such as getting a college education, buying a house or car, or saving for the future. One of the most important things that you can do to manage your money and begin saving is to use a budget. A budget helps you become aware of how you spend your money and will help your make a plan for the future. It is important to control your money, rather than letting your money control you.

Monitor how you spend your money. The first step in establishing a workable budget is to monitor how you are actually spending your money at the present time. For one month, keep a list of purchases with the date and amount of money spent for each. You can do this on a sheet of paper, on your calendar, on index cards, or on a money management application for your phone. If you write checks for items, include the checks written as part of your money monitor. At the end of the month, group your purchases in categories such as food, gas, entertainment, and credit card payments, and add them up. Doing this will yield some surprising results. For example, you may not be aware of just how much it costs to eat at a fast-food restaurant or to buy lunch or coffee every day.

© koya979/ Shutterstock.com

Prepare a budget. One of the best tools for managing your money is a budget. At the end of this chapter, you will find a simple budget sheet that you can use as a college student. After you finish college, update your budget and continue to use it. Follow these three steps to make a budget:

1. Write down your income for the month.

2. List your expenses. Include tuition, books, supplies, rent, phone, utilities (gas, electric, water, cable TV, Internet), car payments, car insurance, car maintenance (oil, repairs), parking fees, food, personal grooming, clothes, entertainment, savings, credit card payments, loan payments, and other bills. Use your money monitor to discover how you are spending your money and include categories that are unique to you.

3. Subtract your total expenses from your total income. You cannot spend more than you have. Make adjustments as needed.

Beware of credit and interest. College students are often tempted to use credit cards to pay for college expenses. This type of borrowing is costly and difficult to repay. It is easy to pull out a plastic credit card and buy items that you need and want. Credit card companies earn a great deal of money from credit cards. Jane Bryant Quinn gives an example of the cost of credit cards.[9] She says that if you owe $3,000 at 18 percent interest and pay the minimum payment of $60 per month, it will take you 30 years and 10 months to get out of debt! Borrowing the $3,000 would cost about $22,320 over this time! If you use a credit card, make sure you can pay it off in one to three months. It is good to have a credit card in order to establish credit and to use in an emergency.

Watch those spending leaks. We all have spending problem areas. Often we spend small amounts of money each day that add up to large spending leaks over time. For example, if you spend $3 on coffee each weekday for a year, this adds up to $780 a year! If you eat lunch out each weekday and spend $8 for lunch, this adds up to $2,080 a year. Here are some common areas for spending leaks:

- Fast food and restaurants
- Entertainment and vacations
- Clothing
- Miscellaneous cash
- Gifts

© Andrey Armyagov/Shutterstock.com

Need More Money?

You may be tempted to work more hours to balance your budget. Remember that to be a full-time college student, it is recommended that you work no more than 20 hours per week. If you work more than 20 hours per week, you will probably need to decrease your course load. Before increasing your work hours, see if there is a way you can decrease your monthly expenses. Can you make your lunch instead of eating out? Can you get by without a car? Is the item you are purchasing a necessity, or do you just want to have it? These choices are yours.

1. **Check out financial aid.** All students can qualify for some type of financial aid. Visit the Financial Aid Office at your college for assistance. Depending on your income level, you may qualify for one or more of the following forms of aid.

    - **Loans.** A loan must be paid back. The interest rate and terms vary according to your financial need. With some loans, the federal government pays the interest while you are in school.

> "Money is, in some respects, like fire; it is a very excellent servant, but a terrible master."
> P. T. Barnum

> "Empty pockets never held anyone back. Only empty heads and empty hearts can do that."
> Norman Vincent Peale

- **Grants.** A grant does not need to be repaid. There are both state and federal grants based on need.
- **Work/study.** You may qualify for a federally subsidized job depending on your financial need. These jobs are often on campus and provide valuable work experience for the future.

The first step in applying for financial aid is to fill out the Free Application for Federal Student Aid (FAFSA). This form determines your eligibility for financial aid. You can obtain this form from your college's financial aid office or over the Internet at https://fafsa.ed.gov/

Here are some other financial aid resources that you can obtain from your financial aid office or over the Internet.

- **Federal Student Aid Resources.** This site provides resources on preparing for college, applying for aid, online tools, and other resources: https://studentaid.ed.gov/sa/resources.
- **How to apply for financial aid.** Learn how to apply for federal financial aid and scholarships at www.finaid.org.

2. **Apply for a scholarship.** Applying for a scholarship is like having a part-time job, only the pay is often better, the hours are flexible, and you can be your own boss. For this part-time job, you will need to research scholarship opportunities and fill out applications. There are multitudes of scholarships available, and sometimes no one even applies for them. Some students do not apply for scholarships because they think that high grades and financial need are required. While many scholarships are based on grades and financial need, many are not. Any person or organization can offer a scholarship for any reason they want. For example, scholarships can be based on hobbies, parent's occupation, religious background, military service, and personal interests, to name a few.

There are several ways to research a scholarship. As a first step, visit the financial aid office on your college campus. This office is staffed with persons knowledgeable about researching and applying for scholarships. Organizations or persons wishing to fund scholarships often contact this office to advertise opportunities.

You can also research scholarships through your public or college library. Ask the reference librarian for assistance. You can use the Internet to research scholarships as well. Use any search engine such as Google.com and simply type in the keyword scholarships. The following websites index thousands of scholarships:

- The Federal Student Aid Scholarship site is located at https://studentaid.ed.gov/sa/types/grants-scholarships/finding-scholarships
- fastweb.com
- http://www.scholarships.com/
- collegenet.com/mach25
- studentscholarshipsearch.com
- collegeboard.com/paying

To apply for scholarships, start a file of useful material usually included in scholarship applications. You can use this same information to apply for many scholarships.

- Three current letters of recommendation
- A statement of your personal goals
- A statement of your financial need
- Copies of your transcripts
- Copies of any scholarship applications you have filled out

Be aware of scholarship scams. You do not need to pay money to apply for a scholarship. No one can guarantee that you will receive a scholarship. Use your college scholarship office and your own resources to research and apply for scholarships.

© mangostock/Shutterstock.com

The Best Ideas for Becoming Financially Secure

Financial planners provide the following ideas as the best ways to build wealth and independence.[10] If you have financial security as your goal, plan to do the following:

1. **Use a simple budget to track income and expenses.** Do not spend more than you earn.

2. **Have a financial plan.** Include goals such as saving for retirement, purchasing a home, paying for college, or taking vacations.

3. **Save 10 percent of your income.** As a college student, you may not be able to save this much, but plan to do it as soon as you get your first good-paying job. If you cannot save 10 percent, save something to get in the habit of saving. Save to pay for your tuition and books.

4. **Don't take on too much debt.** Be especially careful about credit cards and consumer debt. Credit card companies often visit college campuses and offer high-interest credit cards to students. It is important to have a credit card, but pay off the balance each month. Consider student loans instead of paying college fees by credit card.

5. **Don't procrastinate.** The earlier you take these steps toward financial security, the better.

Tips for Managing Your Money

Keeping these guidelines in mind can help you to manage your money.

- Don't let friends pressure you into spending too much money. If you can't afford something, learn to say no.
- Keep your checking account balanced or use online banking so you will know how much money you have.
- Don't lend money to friends. If your friends cannot manage their money, your loan will not help them.
- Use comparison shopping to find the best prices on the products that you buy.
- Get a part-time job while in college. You will earn money and gain valuable job experience.
- Don't use shopping as a recreational activity. When you visit the mall, you will find things you never knew you needed and will wind up spending more money than intended.
- Make a budget and follow it. This is the best way to achieve your financial goals.

Do What Is Important First

The most important thing you can do to manage time and money is to spend it on what is most important. Manage time and money to help you live the life you want. How can you do this? Author Stephen Covey wrote a book titled *The Seven Habits of Highly Effective People.* One of the habits is "Put first things first." Covey suggests that in time management, the "challenge is not to manage our time but to manage ourselves."[11]

How can you manage yourself? Our first thoughts in answering this question often involve suggestions about willpower, restriction, and self-control. Schedules and budgets are seen as instruments for self-control. It seems that the human spirit resists attempts at control, even when we aim to control ourselves. Often the response to control is rebellion. With time and money management, we may not follow a schedule or budget. A better approach to begin managing yourself is to know your values. What is important in your life? Do you have a clear mental picture of what is important? Can you describe your values and make a list of what is important to you? With your values and goals in mind, you can begin to manage both your time and your money.

When you have given some thought to your values, you can begin to set goals. When you have established goals for your life, you can begin to think in terms of what is most important and establish your priorities. Knowing your values is essential in making decisions about how to invest your time and money. Schedules and budgets are merely tools for helping you accomplish what you have decided is important. Time and money management is not about restriction and control, but about making decisions regarding what is important in your life. If you know what is important, you can find the strength to say no to activities and expenditures that are less important.

As a counselor, I have the pleasure of working with many students who have recently explored and discovered their values and are highly motivated to succeed. They are willing to do what is important first. I recently worked with a young couple who came to enroll in college. They brought their young baby with them. The new father was interested in environmental engineering. He told me that in high school, he never saw a reason for school and did just the minimum needed to get by. He was working as a construction laborer and making a living, but did not see a future in the occupation. He had observed an environmental engineer who worked for the company and decided that was what he wanted for his future. As he looked at his new son, he told me that he needed to have a better future for himself and his family.

He and his wife decided to do what was important first. They were willing to make the sacrifice to attend school and invest the time needed to be successful. The father planned to work during the day and go to school at night. Later, he would go to school full-time and get a part-time job in the evening. His wife was willing to get a part-time job also, and they would share in taking care of the baby. They were willing to manage their money carefully to accomplish their goals. As they left, they added that their son would be going to college as well.

How do you get the energy to work all day, go to school at night, and raise a family? You can't do it by practicing self-control. You find the energy by having a clear idea of what you want in your life and focusing your time and resources on the goal. Finding what you want to do with your life is not easy either. Many times people find what they want to do when some significant event happens in their lives.

Begin to think about what you want out of life. Make a list of your important values and write down your lifetime goals. Don't forget about the people who are important to you, and include them in your priorities. Then you will be able to do what is important first.

> "Fathers send their sons to college either because they went to college or because they didn't."
>
> L. L. Henderson

Journal Entry #5

What is your plan for managing your money? Consider these ideas when thinking about your plan: monitoring how you spend your money, using a budget, applying for financial aid and scholarships, saving money, and spending money wisely.

College Success 1

The College Success 1 website is continually updated with supplementary material for each chapter including Word documents of the journal entries, classroom activities, handouts, videos, links to related materials, and much more. See http://www.collegesuccess1.com/.

© Lyudmyla Kharlamova/
Shutterstock.com

Notes

1. Steven K. Scott, *A millionaire's Notebook,* quoted in Rob Gilbert, Editor, Bits & Pieces, November 4, 1999, 15.

2. John Medina, *Brain Rules,* (Seattle: Pear Press, 2008), 157.

3. Ibid, pp. 162–163.

4. Alan Lakein, *How to Get Control of Your Time and Your life* (New York: Peter H. Wyden, 1973).

5. Ibid., 70–71.

6. Dave Ellis, *Becoming a Master Student* (Boston: Houghton Mifflin, 1998).

7. Jane Burka and Lenora Yuen, *Procrastination* (Reading, MA: Addison-Wesley, 1983).

8. Francis Leonard, *Time is Money* (Addison-Wesley), cited in the San Diego Union Tribune, October 14, 1995.

9. Jane Bryant Quinn, "Money Watch," *Good Housekeeping*, November 1996, 80.

10. Robert Hanley, "Breaking Bad Habits," *San Diego Union Tribune*, September 7, 1992.

11. Stephen R. Covey, *The Seven Habits of Highly Effective People* (New York: Simon and Schuster, 1990), 150.

My Lifetime Goals: Brainstorming Activity

Name _____ Date _____

1. Think about the goals that you would like to accomplish in your life. At the end of your life, you do not want to say, "I wish I would have _____." Set a timer for five minutes and write whatever comes to mind about what you would like to do and accomplish over your lifetime. Include goals in these areas: career, personal relationships, travel, and financial security or any area that is important to you. Write down all your ideas. The goal is to generate as many ideas as possible in five minutes. You can reflect on which ones are most important later. You may want to do this as part of a group activity in your class.

Look over the ideas you wrote above and highlight or underline the goals that are most important to you.

2. Ask yourself what you would like to accomplish in the next five years. Think about where you want to be in college, what you want to do in your career, and what you want to do in your personal life. Set a timer and write whatever comes to mind in five minutes. The goal is to write down as many ideas as possible.

Again, look over the ideas you wrote and highlight or underline the ideas that are most important to you.

3. What goals would you like to accomplish in the next year? What are some steps that you can begin now to accomplish your lifetime goals? Consider work, study, leisure, and social goals. Set your timer for five minutes and write down your goals for the next year.

Review what you wrote and highlight or underline the ideas that are most important to you. When writing your goals, include fun activities as well as taking care of others.

Looking at the items that you have highlighted or underlined, make a list of your lifetime goals using the form that follows. Make sure your goals are specific enough so that you can break them into steps you can achieve.

My Lifetime Goals

Name _____ Date _____

Using the ideas that you brainstormed in the previous exercise, make a list of your lifetime goals. Make sure your goals are specific and concrete. Begin with goals that you would like to accomplish over a lifetime. In the second section, think about the goals you can accomplish over the next one to three years.

Long-Term Goals (lifetime goals)

Short-Term Goals (one to three years)

What are some steps you can take now to accomplish intermediate and long-term goals?

Successful Goal Setting

Name _____   Date _____

Look at your list of lifetime goals. Which one is most important? Write the goal here:

Answer these questions about the goal you have listed above.

1. What skills, abilities, and resources do you have to achieve this goal? What skills, abilities, and resources will you need to develop to achieve this goal?

2. Do you believe you can achieve it? Write a brief positive statement about achieving this goal.

3. State your goal in specific terms that can be observed or counted. Rewrite your goal if necessary.

4. Write a brief statement about how this goal will give you personal satisfaction.

5. How will you motivate yourself to achieve this goal?

6. What are your personal values that match this goal?

7. List some steps that you will take to accomplish this goal.

8. When will you finish this goal?

9. What roadblocks will make this goal difficult to achieve?

10. How will you deal with these roadblocks?

Weekly College Schedule

Name _____ Date _____

Copy the following schedule to use in future weeks or design your own schedule. Fill in this schedule and try to follow it for at least one week. First, fill in scheduled commitments (classes, work, activities). Next, fill in the time you need for studying. Put in some tasks related to your lifetime goals. Leave some blank time as a shock absorber to handle unexpected activities.

Time	Monday	Tuesday	Wednesday	Thursday	Friday	Saturday	Sunday
7 A.M.							
8							
9							
10							
11							
Noon							
1 P.M.							
2							
3							
4							
5							
6							
7							
8							
9							
10							
11							

Weekly To-Do Chart

Name _____   Date _____

Using a to-do list is an easy way to remind yourself of important priorities each day. This chart is divided into three areas representing types of tasks that college students need to balance: academic, personal, and social.

Weekly To-Do List

	Monday	Tuesday	Wednesday	Thursday	Friday
Academic					
Personal					
Social					

Study Schedule Analysis

Name _____ Date _____

Before completing this analysis, use the schedule form to create a master schedule. A master schedule blocks out class and work times as well as any regularly scheduled activities. Looking at the remaining time, write in your planned study times. It is recommended that you have two hours of study time for each hour in class. For example, a three-unit class would require six hours of study time. A student with 12 units would require 24 hours of study time. You may need more or fewer hours, depending on your study skills, reading skills, and difficulty of courses.

1. How many units are you enrolled in?

2. How many hours of planned study time do you have?

3. How many hours do you work each week?

4. How many hours do you spend in relaxation/social activities?

5. Do you have time planned for exercise?

6. Do you get enough sleep?

7. What are some of your time bandits (things that take up your time and make it difficult to accomplish your goals)?

Write a few discovery statements about how you use your time.

8. Are you spending enough time to earn the grades you want to achieve? Do you need to spend more time studying to become successful?

9. Does your work schedule allow you enough time to study?

10. How can you deal with your time bandits?

11. How can you use your time more effectively to achieve your goals?

Name _____   Date _____

Before you complete this budget, monitor your expenses for one month. Write down all expenditures and then divide them into categories that have meaning for you. Then complete the following budget and try to follow it for at least two months. Do this exercise on your own, since it is likely to contain private information.

College Student Monthly Budget

Monthly income for _____ (month)

Income from job _____

Money from home _____   **Total Income** [   ]

Financial aid _____

Other _____

Budgeted Monthly Expenses:	**Actual Monthly Expenses:**
Total Budgeted [ ]	**Total Actual**

Total Income [   ]   **Minus Total Budgeted** [   ]   **Equals** [   ]

CHAPTER 6

Using Brain Science to Improve Memory

Learning Objectives

Read to answer these key questions:

- How does the memory work?

- How can I improve my memory?

- Why do I forget?

- What are some practical memory techniques based on brain science?

- What are some memory tricks?

- How can I optimize my brain power?

- Why is positive thinking important for improving memory and studying?

L earning how to improve your memory and remember what you are studying will be great assets in college, on the job, and in your personal life. This chapter translates the latest findings in brain science into some practical techniques for improving memory.

Improving Your Memory

Memory: Short Term Versus Long Term

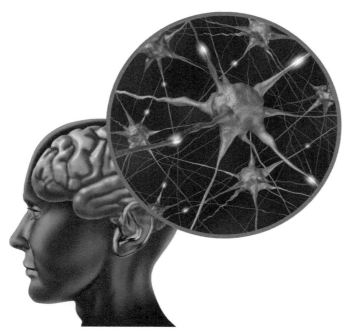

© Lightspring/Shutterstock.com

Effective studying in college involves transferring learning from short-term to long-term memory. Short-term memory is often called the working memory, which is a temporary space or desktop used to process information. The short-term memory has limited capacity and duration. If information is not transferred to long-term memory, it quickly disappears.

Through repetition or rehearsal, information is transferred to long-term memory, which has a higher capacity and duration. For example, if you just read your textbook, the information is stored in short-term memory and quickly disappears. Storing material in long-term memory is like making a trail through the jungle. The more the trail is used, the easier it is to follow and the more distinct it becomes. Learning requires effort; the more you practice or rehearse the more you learn.[1]

It is necessary to use some study strategies that involve repeating or reviewing the material to transfer the information to long-term memory available for passing tests and for later success in your career. To be most effective, this rehearsal or repetition must be done immediately and then at spaced intervals over time. Waiting to study just before a test by using intense marathon study sessions is not effective in transferring the material to long-term memory and is not very enjoyable either.

Forgetting

It was previously thought that once information was stored in long-term memory, it was there forever. However, scientists have found that our memories are often inaccurate and become distorted over time. Forgetting allows us to prioritize events. We forget items that are not important for our survival.

Examining the following lists of items frequently forgotten or remembered can give us insight into why forgetting occurs and how to minimize it.

We frequently forget these things:

- Names of people, places, or things

- Numbers and dates

- What we have barely learned

- Material we do not fully understand

- What we try to remember when embarrassed, frustrated, tired, or ill

- Material we have learned by cramming

- Ideas or theories that conflict with our beliefs

  We tend to remember these things:

- Pleasant experiences

- Material that is important to us

- What we have put an effort into learning

- What we have reviewed or thought through often

- Material that is interesting to us

- Muscular skills such as riding a bike

- What we had an important reason to remember

- Items we discuss with others

- Material that we understand

- Frequently used information

© Edyta Pawlowska/Shutterstock.com

To improve memory, you must first fully understand the material. Then convince your-self that the material you are learning is important and find something interesting about it. If you approach your studies with a positive attitude, it is easier to recall what you are studying. It is helpful if you can think about the material and discuss it with others. The critical step is putting in the effort to review the material you have learned so that it is transferred to long-term memory.

Minimizing Forgetting

Herman Ebbinghaus (1850–1909), a German psychologist and pioneer in research on forgetting, described a curve of forgetting.[2] He invented nonsense syllables such as WUX, CAZ, BIJ, and ZOL. He chose these nonsense syllables so that there would be no meaning, associations, or organizations that could affect the memory of the words. He would learn these lists of words and measure forgetting over time. The following is a chart of time and forgetting of nonsense syllables.

"Just as iron rusts from disuse, even so does inaction spoil the intellect."
Leonardo da Vinci

Time	Percent Forgotten
After 20 minutes	47
After 1 day	62
After 2 days	69
After 15 days	75
After 31 days	78

We can draw three interesting conclusions from examining these figures. First, **most of the forgetting occurs within the first 20 minutes**. Immediate review, or at least review during the first 20 minutes, would prevent most of the forgetting. Second, forgetting slows down over time. The third conclusion is that forgetting is significant after 31 days. Fortunately, we do not need to memorize nonsense syllables. We can use meaning, associations, organization, and proper review to minimize forgetting.

Review is important in transferring information from short-term to long-term memory. You can also minimize forgetting over time through the proper use of review.[3] Let's assume that you spend 45 minutes studying and learning something new. The optimum schedule for review would look like this:

After 10 minutes	Review for 5 minutes
After 1 day	Review for 5 minutes
After 1 week	Review for 3 minutes
After 1 month	Review for 3 minutes
After 6 months	Review for 3 minutes

Journal Entry #1

Review the material on memory and forgetting. How can you use this information to improve your studying in college?

Practical Memory Techniques Based on Brain Science

Remember that recitation or rehearsal of information is crucial in transferring information to long-term memory. Based on current research on brain science and psychology, here are some additional practical suggestions for improving memory.[4]

Think Positively about Learning

Positive emotions such as interest, joy, amusement, contentment, and relaxation optimize learning and memory. These positive emotions increase openness to new information as well as improve attention, memory, and verbal fluency. For greater success and achievement, it is important to think positively about learning. Rather than viewing learning as stressful or an unpleasant obligation, view it as a new and interesting adventure, and it can be easier and more rewarding.

Develop an Interest

We tend to remember what interests us. People often have phenomenal memories when it comes to sports, automobiles, music, stamp collecting, or anything they consider fun or pursue as a hobby. Find something interesting in your college studies. If you are not interested in what you are studying, look for something interesting or even pretend that you are interested and then reward yourself by doing something enjoyable.

Motivation and attitude have a significant impact on memory. Being highly motivated and approaching your studies with a positive attitude will help you to find something interesting and make it easier to remember. In addition, the more you learn about a topic, the more interesting it becomes. Often we judge a subject as boring because we know nothing about it.

Memorization Tips
• Meaningful organization
• Visualization
• Recitation
• Develop an interest
• See the big picture first
• Intend to remember
• Learn small amounts frequently
• Basic background
• Relax

© Zurijeta/Shutterstock.com

Another way to make something interesting is to look for personal meaning. How can I use this information in my future career? Does the information relate to my personal experience in some way? How can I use this information? What is the importance of this information? And finally, is this information likely to be on the test?

See the Big Picture First

Imagine looking at a painting one inch at a time. It would be difficult to understand or appreciate a painting in this way. College students often approach reading a textbook in the same way. They focus on the small details without first understanding the main points. By focusing on the details without looking at the main points, it is easy to get lost. The first step in reading is to skim the chapter headings to form a mental outline of what you will be learning. Then read for detail.

Meaningful Organization

Another powerful memory technique is imposing your own form of personal organization on the material you are trying to remember. Psychologists have even suggested that your intelligence quotient (IQ) may be related to how well you have organized material you learned in the past. When learning new material, cluster facts and ideas into categories that are meaningful to you. Think of the mind as a file cabinet or a computer. Major topics are like folders in which we file detailed information. When we need to find the information, we think of the major topic and look in the folder to find the details. If we put all our papers into the file drawer without organization, it is difficult to find the information we need. Highlight or underline key ideas to focus on the main points and organize what you are learning.

The Magical Number 7 Theory

Grouping together or chunking bits of information together can make remembering easier. George Miller of the Harvard University found that the optimum number of chunks or bits of information that we can hold in short-term memory is five to nine.[5] It is much easier to remember material that is grouped in chunks of seven or less. You can find many examples of groups of seven used to enhance memory. There are seven digits in a phone number, seven days of the week, and seven numbers in your driver's license and license plate. There are also seven dwarfs, seven deadly sins, and Seven Wonders of the World!

Does this mean that we should try to remember only seven or less ideas in studying a textbook chapter? No, it is most efficient to identify seven or fewer key ideas and then cluster less important ideas under major headings. In this way, you can remember the key ideas in the chapter you are studying along with the details. The critical thinking required by this process also helps in remembering ideas and information.

Magical Number Seven

Remember George Miller's Magical Number Seven Theory? It is more efficient to limit the number of categories to seven or less, although you can have subcategories. Examine the following list of words.

goat	horse	cow
carrot	cat	lettuce
banana	tomato	pig
celery	orange	peas
cherry	apple	strawberry

Look at the list for one minute. Then look away from the list and write down all the words you can recall. Record the number of words you remembered: _____

Note that the following lists are divided into categories: animals, crops, and tropical fruits.

animals	**crops**	**tropical fruits**
lion	wheat	banana
giraffe	beans	kiwi
kangaroo	corn	mango
coyote	hay	guava
bear	oats	orange

Look at the above list for one minute. Then look away from the list and write down the words you recall. Record the number of words you remembered: _____

You probably remembered more from the second list because the list is organized into categories. Notice that there are only five words in each category. Remember that it is easier to remember lists with seven items or less. If these words have some meaning for you, it is easier to remember them. A farmer from the Midwest would probably have an easier time remembering the crops. A person from Hawaii would probably remember the list of tropical fruits. We also tend to remember unusual items and the first and last items on the list. If you need to memorize a list, pay more attention to the mundane items and the items in the middle of the list.

Visualization

One of the most powerful memory techniques is visualization. If you can read the words and accompany them with pictures, you are using your brain in the most efficient way. Advertisers use pictures as powerful influences to motivate you to purchase their products. You can use the same power of visualization to enhance your studying. While you are studying history, picture what life would be like in that time period. In engineering, make pictures in your mind or on paper to illustrate scientific principles. Challenge yourself to see the pictures along with the words. Add movement to your pictures, as in a video. During a test, relax and recall the pictures.

© scyther5/Shutterstock.com

Intend to Remember

Tell yourself that you are going to remember. If you think you won't remember, you won't remember. This step also relates to positive thinking and self-confidence and will take some practice to apply. Once you have told yourself to remember, apply some of the above techniques such as organizing, visualizing, and reciting. If you intend to remember, you will pay attention, make an effort to understand, and use memory techniques to strengthen your memory.

One practical technique that involves intent to remember is the memory jogger. This involves doing something unusual to jog or trigger your memory. If you want to be sure to remember your books, place your car keys on the books. Since you cannot go anywhere without your keys, you will find them and remember the books too. Another application is putting your watch on your right hand to remember to do something. When you look at your left hand and notice that the watch is not there, the surprise will jog your memory for the item you wish to recall. You can be creative with this technique and come up with your own memory joggers.

> To learn something new, it is helpful if you
> - Are motivated.
> - Find it interesting.
> - Think it is valuable.
> - Pay attention to it.
> - Practice or repeat it.

Elaboration

Just as decorations or stories can be made more elaborate, learning can be made more elaborate too. The more you add details, connect the information, or make it personally meaningful, the easier it is to learn. Here are some ways to elaborate:[6]

- Write it in your own words. Look for personal meaning.

- Make a silly song or rhyme with the material.

- Rewrite your notes.

- Use flash cards to quiz yourself.

- Make a mind map.

- Underline the important points in the text and make notes in the margin about important points.

- Discuss the information with others.

- Study with a scented candle.

- Use multisensory learning including audio, visual, tactile, kinesthetic, and olfactory strategies.

- Associate the material learned to something you already know. How does the information match your experiences?

Distribute the Practice

Learning small amounts of material and reviewing frequently are more effective than a marathon study session. One research study showed that a task that took 30 minutes to learn in one day could be learned in 22 minutes if spread over two days. This is almost a 30 percent increase in efficiency.[7]

If you have a list of vocabulary words or formulas to learn, break the material into small parts and frequently review each part for a short period of time. Consider putting these facts or figures on index cards to carry with you in your purse or pocket. Use small amounts of time to quickly review the cards. This technique works well because it prevents fatigue and helps to keep motivation high. One exception to the distributed practice rule is creative work such as writing a paper or doing an art project, where a longer time period is needed for creative inspiration and immediate follow-through.

A learning technique for distributed practice is summed up in the acronym **SAFMEDS**, which stands for Say All Fast for one Minute Each Day and Shuffle.[7] With this technique, you can easily and quickly learn 100 or more facts. To use this technique, prepare flash cards that contain the material to be learned (vocabulary, foreign language words, numbers, dates, places, names, formulas). For example, if you are learning Spanish, place the Spanish word on one side of the card and the English word on the other side. Just writing out the flash cards is an aid to learning and is often sufficient for learning the material. Once the cards are prepared, *say* the Spanish word and see if you can remember what it means in English. Look at the back of the card to see if your answer is correct. Do this with *all* of the cards as *fast* as you can for *one minute each day*. Then *shuffle* the cards and repeat the process the next day.

It is important that you do this activity quickly. Don't worry if you do not know the answer. Just flip each card over, quickly look at the answer, and put the cards that you missed into a separate pile. At the end of the minute, count the number of cards you answered correctly. You can learn even faster if you take the stack of cards you missed and practice them quickly one more time. Shuffling the cards helps you to remember the actual meanings of the words, instead of just the order in which they appear. In the case of the Spanish cards, turn the cards over and say each English word to see if you can remember the equivalent word in Spanish. Each day, the number of correct answers will increase, and you will have a concrete measure of your learning. Consider this activity as a fun and fast-moving game to challenge yourself.

Create a Basic Background

You remember information by connecting it to things you already know. The more you know, the easier it is to make connections that make remembering easier. You will even find that it is easier to remember material toward the end of a college class because you have established a basic background at the beginning of the semester. With this in mind, freshman-level courses will be the most difficult in college because they form the basic background for your college education. College does become easier as you establish this basic background and practice effective study techniques.

You can enhance your basic background by reading a variety of books. Making reading a habit also enhances vocabulary, writing, and spelling. College provides many opportunities for expanding your reading horizons and areas of basic knowledge.

Stress and Emotions

Memory and learning are affected by stress and emotions. Moderate stress can be turned into motivation. For example, if you are moderately stressed over an exam, you may be more motivated to study for it. However, severe or chronic stress, along with the feeling that you have no control over it, results in a reduced ability to learn. If you are overly stressed, both short- and long-term memories are decreased as well as your ability to process language and do math.

Fear and stress are closely related. Fear causes us to run away from threatening or dangerous situations or to avoid them. Fear is one of the most powerful causes of academic failure. If you are fearful or doubt your ability to succeed in college, seek help from your counselor or advisor and use services such as tutoring to increase your self-confidence and minimize fear.

Relax While Studying

The brain works much better when it is relaxed. As you become more confident in your study techniques, you can become more relaxed. Here are some suggestions to help you relax during study time.

- Use distributed practice to take away some of the pressure of learning; take breaks between periods of learning. Give yourself time to absorb the material.

- Plan ahead so that you do not have to cram. Waiting until the last minute to study produces anxiety that is counterproductive.

- If you are anxious, try a physical activity or relaxation exercise before study sessions. For example, imagine a warm, relaxing light beginning at the feet and moving slowly up the body to the top of the head. Feel each part of the body relax as the light makes contact with it. Take a few deep breaths and focus on your breathing.

- If you are feeling frustrated, it is often a good idea to stop and come back to your studies later. You may gain insight into your studies while you are more relaxed and doing something else. You can often benefit from a fresh perspective.

Journal Entry #2

Review the memory techniques explained in this chapter. List and briefly explain at least three techniques and give examples of how you can use them.

Using Mnemonics and Other Memory Tricks

© Lightspring/Shutterstock.com

Memory tricks can be used to enhance your memory. These memory tricks include acrostics, acronyms, peg systems, and loci systems. These systems are called *mnemonics*, from the Greek word *mneme* which means "to remember."

Mnemonic devices are very effective. A research study by Gerald R. Miller found that students who used mnemonic devices improved their test scores by up to 77 percent.[8] Mnemonics are effective because they help to organize material. They have been used throughout history, in part as a way to entertain people with amazing memory feats.

Mnemonics are best used for memorizing facts. They are not helpful for understanding or thinking critically about the information. Be sure to memorize your mnemonics carefully and review them right before exam time. Forgetting the mnemonic or a part of it can cause major problems.

Acrostics

Acrostics are creative rhymes, songs, poems, or sentences that help us to remember. Maybe you previously learned some of these in school.

- Continents: Eat an Aspirin after a Nighttime Snack (Europe, Antarctica, Asia, Africa, Australia, North America, South America)

- Directions of the compass: Never Eat Sour Watermelons (North, East, South, West)
- Geological ages: Practically Every Old Man Plays Poker Regularly (Paleocene, Eocene, Oligocene, Miocene, Pliocene, Pleistocene, Recent)
- Guitar Strings: Eat All Dead Gophers Before Easter (E, A, D, G, B, E)
- Oceans: I Am a Person (Indian, Arctic, Atlantic, Pacific)
- Metric system in order: King Henry Drinks Much Dark Chocolate Milk (Kilometer, hectometer, decameter, meter, decimeter, centimeter, millimeter
- Notes on the treble clef in music: Every Good Boy Does Fine (E, G, B, D, F)
- Classification in biology: Kings Play Cards on Fairly Good Soft Velvet (Kingdom, Phylum, Class, Order, Family, Genus, Species, Variety)
- Order of operations in algebra: Please Excuse My Dear Aunt Sally (Parenthesis, Exponents, Multiplication, Division, Addition, and Subtraction)

An effective way to invent your own acrostics is to first identify key ideas you need to remember, underline these key words or write them down as a list, and think of a word that starts with the first letter of each idea you want to remember. Rearrange the words if necessary to form a sentence. The more unusual the sentence, the easier it is to remember.

In addition to acrostics, there are many other creative memory aids:

- Days in each month: Thirty days hath September, April, June, and November. All the rest have 31, except February which has 28 until leap year gives it 29.
- Spelling rules: *i* before *e* except after *c*, or when sounding like *a* as in neighbor and weigh.
- Numbers: Can I remember the reciprocal? To remember the reciprocal of pi, count the letters in each word of the question above. The reciprocal of pi = .3 1 8 3 10

Mnemonics become more powerful when used with visualization. For example, if you are trying to remember the planets, use a mnemonic and then visualize Saturn as a hula-hoop dancer to remember that it has rings. Jupiter could be a king with a number of maids to represent its moons.

Acronyms

Acronyms are commonly used as shortcuts in our language. The military is especially fond of using acronyms. For example, NASA is the acronym for the National Aeronautics and Space Administration. You can invent your own acronyms as a memory trick. Here are some common ones that students have used:

- The colors of the spectrum: Roy G. Biv (red, orange, yellow, green, blue, indigo, violet)
- The Great Lakes: HOMES (Huron, Ontario, Michigan, Erie, Superior)
- The stages of cell division in biology: IPMAT (interphase, prophase, metaphase, and telophase)

To make your own acronym, list the items you wish to remember. Use the first letter of each word to make a new word. The word you make can be an actual word or an invented word.

Peg Systems

Peg systems start with numbers, typically 1 to 100. Each number is associated with an object. The object chosen to represent each number can be based on rhyme or on a logical association. The objects are memorized and used with a mental picture to recall a list.

There are entertainers who can have the audience call out a list of 100 objects and then repeat all of the objects through use of a peg system. Here is an example of a commonly used peg system based on rhyme:

One	Bun	Six	Sticks
Two	Shoe	Seven	Heaven
Three	Tree	Eight	Gate
Four	Door	Nine	Wine
Five	Hive	Ten	Hen

For example, if I want to remember a grocery list consisting of milk, eggs, carrots, and butter, I would make associations between the peg and the item I want to remember. The more unusual the association is, the better. I would start by making a visual connection between *bun*, my peg word, and *milk*, the first item on the list. I could picture dipping a bun into a glass of milk for a snack. Next I would make a connection between *shoe* and *eggs*. I could picture eggs being broken into my shoe as a joke. Next I would picture a *tree* with orange *carrots* hanging from it and then a *door* with *butter* dripping from the doorknob. The technique works because of the organization provided by the pegs and the power of visualization and association.

There are many variations of the peg system. One variation is using the letters of the alphabet instead of numbers. Another variation is to visualize objects and put them in a stack, one on top of the other, until you have a great tottering tower, like a totem pole telling a story. Still another variation is to use your body or your car as a peg system. Using our example of the grocery list above, visualize balancing the milk on your head, carrying eggs in your hands, having carrots tied around your waist and smearing butter on your feet. Remember that the more unusual the pictures, the easier they are to remember.

Loci Systems

Loci or location systems use a series of familiar places to aid the memory. The Roman orators often used this system to remember the outline of a speech. For example, the speaker might connect the entry of a house with the introduction, the living room with the first main point, and each part of the speech with a different room. Again, this technique works through organization and visualization.

Another example of using a loci system to remember a speech or dramatic production is to imagine a long hallway. Mentally draw a picture of each topic or section you need to remember, and then hang each picture on the wall. As you are giving your speech or acting out your part in the play, visualize walking down the hallway and looking at the pictures on the wall to remind yourself of the next topic. For multiple topics, you can place signs over several hallway entrances labeling the contents of each hallway.

Visual Clues

Visual clues are helpful memory devices. To remember your books, place them in front of the door so you will see them on your way to school. To remember to take your finished homework to school, put it in your car when you are done. To remember to fill a prescription, put the empty bottle on the front seat of your car. Tie a bright ribbon on your backpack to remind you to attend a meeting with your study group. When parking your car in the mall, look around and notice landmarks such as nearby stores or row numbers. When you enter a large department store, notice the items that are near the door you entered. Are you worried that you left the iron on? Tie a ribbon around the handle of the iron each time you turn it off or unplug it. To find out if you have all the items you need to go skiing, visualize yourself on the ski slope wearing all those items.

Say It Aloud

You can enhance memory by repeating aloud the items you are trying to remember. For example, if you want to remember where you hid your diamond ring, say it aloud a few times. Then reinforce the memory by making a visual picture of where you have hidden it. You can also make a rhyme or song to remember something. Commercials use this technique all the time to try to get you to remember a product and purchase it.

Have a Routine

Do you have a difficult time trying to remember where you left your keys, wallet, or purse? Having a routine can greatly simplify your life and help you to remember. As you enter your house, hang your keys on a hook each time. Decide where you will place your wallet or purse and put it in the same place each time. When I leave for work, I have a mental checklist with four items: keys, purse, glasses, and cell phone.

Write It Down

One of the easiest and most effective memory techniques is to simply write something down. Make a grocery list or to-do list, send yourself an email, or tape a note to your bathroom mirror or the dashboard of your car.

Remembering Names

Many people have difficulty remembering names of other people in social or business situations. The reason we have difficulty in remembering names is that we do not take the time to store the name properly in our memories. When we first meet someone, we are often distracted or thinking about ourselves. We are trying to remember our own names or wondering what impression we are making on the other person.

To remember a name, first make sure you have heard the name correctly. If you have not heard the name, there is no way you can remember it. Ask the person to repeat his or her name or check to see if you have heard it correctly. Immediately use the name. For example, say "It is nice to meet you, *Nancy*." If you can mentally repeat the name about five times, you have a good chance of remembering it. You can improve the chances of remembering the name if you can make an association. For example, you might think, "She looks like my daughter's friend Nancy." Some people remember names by making a rhyme such as "fancy Nancy."

Journal Entry #3

Review the material on using mnemonics and other memory tricks. List and explain at least three techniques that you find useful.

Memory Techniques

Test what you have learned by circling the letters of the correct answers to the following questions.

1. An effective memory technique is

    a. focusing on the details first.
    b. focusing on the main ideas first.
    c. realizing that learning in college is an unpleasant obligation.

2. Chunking information together can make learning easier. The optimum number of chunks which can be easily recalled is

    a. 10
    b. 20
    c. 7

3. To learn something new, it is helpful if you

    a. are interested in it.
    b. learn it right before the test.
    c. read it at least one time.

4. A mnemonic is

    a. a memory chip implanted in the brain to help you remember.
    b. a Greek word that means "repetition."
    c. an acrostic or acronym.

5. To remember names

    a. make sure you have heard the name correctly and repeat it.
    b. focus on the introduction and making a good impression.
    c. avoid saying the name aloud.

How did you do on the quiz? Check your answers: 1.b, 2.c, 3.a, 4.c, 5.a

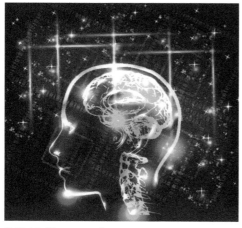

© Hubis/Shutterstock.com

Optimize Your Brain Power

The health of the body is connected to the health of your brain and your ability to learn. Specifically, brain health and optimal learning are affected by exercise, sleep, nutrition, hydration, stress, caffeine, alcohol, and drugs.[10]

Do aerobic exercise. The brain needs oxygen to function and exercise improves the flow of oxygen to the brain. Researchers have found that the human brain can grow new nerve cells by putting subjects on a three-month aerobic workout regimen. It is interesting to note that these new nerve cells can be generated at any age and are important in reversing the aging process. Exercise lowers your chance of getting Alzheimer's disease by 60%.[11] Exercise produces chemicals in the brain that help you to be alert, motivated, and pay attention. It has a positive effect on long-term memory, reasoning, and problem solving. For optimum health and learning, it is important to exercise the body as well as the mind. How much is needed? It is recommended that you do 30 minutes of aerobic exercise four to five times a week.

Sleep to remember. During sleep, we organize and consolidate learning from the previous day. It is important for transferring the information from short-term to long-term memory. During sleep, memories are sorted and stored according to their importance to you. One powerful learning strategy is to review the material you want to remember just before going to sleep. If sleep does not occur or is interrupted, it is more difficult to remember what has been studied the previous day. Lack of sleep negatively affects attention, memory, logical reasoning, mathematical skills, and manual dexterity. Scientists have found that lack of sleep decreases mental abilities:[12]

- There is a 30% decline in mental abilities after missing one night of sleep.
- There is a 60% decline in mental abilities after missing two nights of sleep.
- When sleep is restricted to six hours or less for five nights, mental abilities also decline 60%.

How much sleep do you need for optimum memory? It is recommended that adults have between 7.5 and 9 hours of sleep each night. The last two hours between 5.5 hours and 7.5 hours are the most important since it is during this time that rapid eye movement (REM) sleep occurs that the memories from the day are reviewed and stored in long-term memory. During sleep, the short-term memory is cleared out leaving space for new learning to occur. After the proper amount of sleep, you are able to remember more accurately and with less stress and anxiety.

Good nutrition and water are important. The brain learns easier if it is well hydrated and has the energy from good nutrition including whole grains, fruits, and vegetables. Low-fat diets have been shown to improve mental performance.

Remember to relax. Chronic stress, which we do not feel we can control, interferes with both short- and long-term memory. Studies have shown that adults performed 50% worse on cognitive tests as compared to adults with low stress.[13]

Drink caffeine in moderation. Caffeine can make you feel stressed, making it difficult to think.

Don't smoke, abuse alcohol, or use drugs. Smoking blocks the carotid artery that supplies blood to the brain. Alcohol and drugs kill brain cells and change brain chemistry.

Use safety gear. Wear a seat belt when driving and a helmet when biking, boarding, or skating to reduce head injuries.

Keep active. Do puzzles, play a musical instrument, take something apart and fix it, draw or paint, dance, make friends with interesting people, read challenging books, or take a college course.

Journal Entry #4

What is your plan for keeping your brain healthy throughout life? Include some of these ideas: keeping mentally active, exercise, getting enough sleep, nutrition, drinking water, relaxation, avoiding addictions, and using safety gear.

Positive Thinking

You can improve your memory as well as your life by using positive thinking. Positive thinking involves two aspects: thinking about yourself and thinking about the world around you. When you think positively about yourself, you develop confidence in your abilities and become more capable of whatever you are attempting to do. When you think positively about the world around you, you look for possibilities and find interest in what you are doing.

Golfer Arnold Palmer has won many trophies but places high value on a plaque on his wall with a poem by C.W. Longenecker:

> If you think you are beaten, you are.
> If you think you dare not, you don't.
> If you like to win but think you can't,
> It's almost certain that you won't.
> Life's battles don't always go
> To the stronger woman or man,
> But sooner or later, those who win
> Are those who think they can.[14]

Success in athletics, school, or any other endeavor begins with positive thinking. To remember anything, first, you have to believe that you can remember. Trust in your abilities. Then apply memory techniques to help you to remember.

If you think that you cannot remember, you will not even try.

The second part of positive thinking involves thinking about the world around you. If you can convince yourself that the world and your college studies are full of interesting possibilities, you can start on a journey of adventure to discover new ideas. For example, it is easier to remember what you read if you find the subject interesting. If the topic is interesting, you will learn more about it. The more you learn about a topic, the more interesting it becomes, and you are well on your way in your journey of discovery. If you tell yourself that the task is boring, you will struggle and find the task difficult. You will also find it difficult to continue.

To find something interesting, look for personal meaning. How can I use this information? Does it relate to something I know? Will this information be useful in my future career? Why is this information important? Write down your personal goals and remind yourself of your purpose for attending college. You are not just completing an assignment: you are on a path to discovery.

To be successful in college, start with the belief that you can be successful. Anticipate that the journey will be interesting, challenging, and full of possibilities. Enjoy the journey!

© Anson0618/Shutterstock.com

College Success 1

© Lyudmyla Kharlamova/
Shutterstock.com

The College Success 1 website is continually updated with supplementary material for each chapter including Word documents of the journal entries, classroom activities, handouts, videos, links to related materials, and much more. See http://www.collegesuccess1.com/.

Notes

1. Terry Doyle and Todd Zakrajsek, *The New Science of Learning, How to Learn in Harmony with Your Brain*, (Sterling, VA: Stylus, 2013), 6–7.

2. Colin Rose, *Accelerated Learning*, (New York: Dell Publishing, 1985), 33–36.

3. Ibid., 50–51.

4. Doyle and Zakrajsek, *The New Science of Learning, How to Learn in Harmony with Your Brain*, 77.

5. G.A. Miller, "The Magical Number Seven, Plus or Minus Two: Some Limits on Our Capacity for Processing Invformation," *Psychological Review* 63 (March 1956): 81–97.

6. Doyle and Zakrajsek, *The New Science of Learning, How to Learn in Harmony with Your Brain*, 49–50.

7. Adapted from Paul Chance, *Learning and Behavior* (Pacific Grove, CA: Brooks/Cole, 1979), 301.

8. Walter Pauk, *How to Study in College* (Boston: Houghton Mifflin, 1989), 108.

9. Colin Rose, *Accelerated Learning* (New York: Dell Publishing, 1985), 33–36.

10. John Medina, *Brain Rules: 12 Principles for Surviving and Thriving at Work, Home, and School*, (Seattle, WA: Pear Press, 2008).

11. Ibid., p. 16.

12. Ibid., p. 162.

13. Ibid., p. 178.

14. Rob Gilbert, ed., *Bits and Pieces* (Fairfield, NJ: The Economics Press, 1998), Vol. R, No. 40, p. 12.

Scenarios

Name _____ Date _____

Review the main ideas on improving memory and reading. Based on these ideas, how would you be successful in the following situations? You may want to do this as a group activity in your class.

1. You just read the assigned chapter in economics and cannot remember what you read. It went in one ear and out the other.

2. In your anatomy and physiology class, you are required to remember the scientific names for 100 different muscles in the body.

3. You signed up for a philosophy class because it meets general education requirements. You are not interested in the class at all.

4. You have a midterm in your literature class and have to read 400 pages in one month.

5. You must take American history to graduate from college. You think that history is boring.

6. You have been introduced to an important business contact and would like to remember his/her name.

7. You are enrolled in an algebra class. You continually remind yourself that you have never been good at math. You don't think that you will pass this class.

8. You have noticed that your grandmother is becoming very forgetful. You want to do whatever is possible to keep your mind healthy as you age.

Memory Test

Name _____ Date _____

Part 1. Your professor will read a list of 15 items. Do not write them down. After listening to this list, see how many you can remember and write them here.

1.	6.	11.
2.	7.	12.
3.	8.	13.
4.	9.	14.
5.	10.	15.

After your professor has given you the answers, write the number of words you remembered: _____

Part 2. Your professor will discuss memory techniques that you can use to improve your test scores and then will read another list. Again, do not write the words down, but try to apply the recommended techniques. Write as many words as you can remember.

1.	6.	11.
2.	7.	12.
3.	8.	13.
4.	9.	14.
5.	10.	15.

How many words did you remember this time? _____

Practice with Mnemonics

Name _____ Date _____

Join with a group of students in your class to invent some acrostics and acronyms.

Acrostics

Acrostics are creative rhymes, songs, poems, or sentences that help us to remember. To write an acrostic, think of a word that starts with the same letter as each idea you want to remember. Sometimes you can rearrange the words if necessary to form a sentence. At other times, it is necessary to keep the words in order. The more unusual the sentence, the easier it is to remember.

> **Example:** Classification in biology: Kings Play Cards on Fairly Good Soft Velvet (Kingdom, Phylum, Class, Order, Family, Genus, Species, Variety)

Create an acrostic for the planets in the solar system. Keep the words in the same order as the planets from closest to the sun to farthest from the sun.

> Mercury, Venus, Earth, Mars, Jupiter, Saturn, Uranus, Neptune, Pluto (now a dwarf planet)

_____

_____

_____

Acronyms

To make your own acronym, list the items you wish to remember. Use the first letter of each word to make a new word. The new word you invented can be an actual word or an invented word.

> **Example:** The Great Lakes: HOMES (Huron, Ontario, Michigan, Erie, and Superior)

The following are the excretory organs of the body. Make an acronym to remember them. Rearrange the words if necessary.

> intestines, liver, lungs, kidneys, skin

_____

_____

_____

Write down any acrostics or acronyms that you know. Share them with your group.

CHAPTER 7

Using Brain Science to Improve Study Skills

Learning Objectives

Read to answer these key questions:

- What are some learning strategies based on brain science?

- How can I apply memory techniques to reading?

- What is a reading system for college texts?

- What are some reading strategies for different subjects?

- What are some e-learning strategies?

- What are the best ways to study math?

- How can I create my success in college, careers, and life?

© VLADGRIN/Shutterstock.com

Learning how to learn is not only important in college but also in your future career. The world is in a constant state of change requiring continued learning on the job. Learning strategies based on current research in neuroscience, psychology, and education can make studying easier, more effective, and more productive. This chapter explores some key ideas that can make you an efficient lifelong learner. Apply these memory strategies to improve study skills, make reading more effective, and increase your success in math.

Neuroscience and Practical Learning Strategies

Recent discoveries in neuroscience can be translated into practical and efficient learning strategies for students. Neuroscientists have shown that learning can be increased by **using and integrating all the senses**, not just the preferred ones. This process is called **multi-sensory integration**. It is important to emphasize that multi-sensory integration is based on current research and is different from traditional learning style theory.

Learning is optimized when more senses are used when trying to remember what we are studying. Researchers note that "it is likely that the human brain has evolved to develop, learn, and operate optimally in multi-sensory environments."[1]

The senses work together as a team to optimize learning by encoding the information into the brain in the form of long-term memories. Sensory inputs include

- **Visual:** learning through reading, observing, or seeing things.
- **Auditory:** learning through listening and talking.
- **Tactile:** learning through touching the material or using a "hands-on approach."
- **Kinesthetic:** learning through movement as in learning to ride a bicycle.
- **Olfactory:** learning by smell.
- **Gustatory:** learning through taste.

The AchieveWORKS Learning and Productivity assessment located in your career portfolio offers suggestions on how to make your learning easier and more productive.

Use all of your senses to help you to remember. For example, when studying Spanish, motivate yourself to learn by watching videos of Spanish speaking countries, listen to the words and say them out loud, use flash cards you can touch to practice the vocabulary, imagine the smell of Mexican food, eat some salsa and chips, and if possible, travel to a Spanish speaking country where you can practice the language.

Are there differences between the left brain and right brain that affect how we learn? Educators have often taught students that there is a difference between the right brain and left brain, with one side being more creative and the other more analytical. This idea is not supported by current brain research that shows that **both sides of the brain work together**. New findings show that the right side of the brain tends to remember the main ideas and the left side remembers the details, but every brain is unique.[2] It is suggested that to improve memory, it is important to begin with the main idea (right brain) and then remember the details (left brain).

Visual Learning Strategies

Some scientists have found that vision is the best tool for learning anything. The more visual the input, the more likely it is to be remembered. It was found that 72 hours after learning something, people recalled only 10% of material presented orally versus 65% recollection when a picture was added.[3] When we animate the pictures, learning is further improved. It is important to use visualization as an aid to studying and remembering. Make a visual picture of what you need to remember. If you can make a mental video, recall is further enhanced.

Here are some visual learning strategies. Highlight or place a checkmark in front of the learning strategies that you can use:

_____Make a visual image of what you are learning. For example, while reading history, picture in your mind's eye what it would be like to live in that historical period. Even better, make a video.

_____If you are having difficulties understanding a concept, find an online video that explains it.

_____Use color to highlight the important points in the text while reading. Review the important points by looking at the highlighted passages again.

_____Take notes and use underlining and highlighting in different colors to highlight the important points. Include flow charts, graphs, and pictures in your notes.

_____Make summary sheets or mind maps to summarize and review your notes.

_____Use pictures, diagrams, flow charts, maps, graphs, time lines, videos, and multimedia to aid in learning and preparing for exams.

_____Use flash cards to remember the details.

_____Sit in front of the class so you can carefully observe the professor. Copy what is written on the board or use your cell phone to photograph it.

_____Create visual reminders to keep on track. Make lists on note pads or use sticky notes as reminders.

_____Before answering an essay question, picture the answer in your mind and then make an outline or mind map.

_____Use mind maps and outlines to review for exams.

_____When learning new material, begin with visual learning strategies and then reinforce them with audio, kinesthetic, tactile, or olfactory strategies.

Audio Learning Strategies

Audio learning strategies involve using the sense of hearing to learn new information. Use these techniques to reinforce visual learning. Highlight or place a checkmark next to the strategies you can use.

_____As you are reading, ask questions or say out loud what you think will be important to remember.

_____Make it a priority to attend lectures and participate in classroom discussions.

_____To prepare for exams, rehearse or say the information verbally. For example, while studying math, say the equations out loud.

_____Discuss what you are learning with other students or friends. Form a study group.

_____Use memory devices, rhymes, poems, rhythms, or music to remember what you are studying. For example, turn facts into a rap song or musical jingle to aid in recall.

_____Memorize key concepts by repeating them aloud.

_____If you are having problems reading your textbook or understanding the directions, read them out loud.

_____Some students can study better with music. However, if your attention shifts to the music, you are multi-tasking and it will take longer to complete your work. On the other hand, some students use music for relaxation, which can be beneficial to studying. Experiment to see if you can be more efficient with the music on or off.

Tactile Learning Techniques

You can increase your learning by using your sense of touch to learn new information. Here are some tactile learning strategies: highlight or place a checkmark next to the ones you can use:

_____Writing is one of the best tactile learning strategies. Take notes, write a journal, list key ideas, make an outline, or create a mind map.

_____Use real objects to help you learn. For example, in a physics course, if you are studying levers, make a simple lever and observe how it works. If you are studying geography, use a globe or map to aid in studying.

_____Use flash cards to review the key ideas as well as the details.

Kinesthetic Learning Strategies

These strategies involve moving around while studying. Highlight or place a checkmark in front of the strategies that you can use.

_____Move while studying. For example, review material while on your exercise bike or stair stepper.

_____Participate in kinesthetic learning experiences such as drama, building, designing, visiting, interviewing, and going on field trips.

_____Take frequent breaks and study in different locations.

_____Use a study group to teach the material to someone else.

Olfactory Learning Strategies

Olfactory refers to our sense of smell and is strongly associated with learning and memory. Marketing companies are using this sense to increase sales. For example, bakeries often distribute the smells from baking outside as a way of drawing in customers. Perfumes and body sprays are often advertised as a way to attract the opposite sex. Researchers had two groups watch a movie and tested them for recall. One group was tested without smell, and one was tested with the smell of popcorn in the room. The group with the popcorn smell had significantly increased recall.[4] Smells are powerful because they are often connected to emotions. In our previous example, movies and popcorn are positive experiences. Can you think of creative ways to use smell to increase memory? When creating that visual picture or video to enhance memory, include the sense of smell. Make it a four-dimensional movie (visual, audio, kinesthetic and olfactory!). You can use smells to create a positive learning environment.

Gustatory Learning Strategies

Gustatory refers to our sense of taste and can be used to enhance recall. You can eat your favorite piece of candy or chewing gum when trying to remember something that is difficult or seems uninteresting to you. Your sense of taste can be used to stimulate the reward center of the brain which regulates motivation, learning, memory, and goal-directed behavior. A caution on this technique is to avoid overeating and the resultant weight gain. One piece of candy or sugarless gum will do!

Journal Entry #1

Neuroscientists have discovered that learning is increased by using and integrating all the senses. How would you study a chapter in history, biology, or one of your current courses by using all your senses?

Applying Memory Strategies to Reading

You can apply memory strategies to store information from reading in your long-term memory.

A Study System for Reading a College Textbook: SQ4R

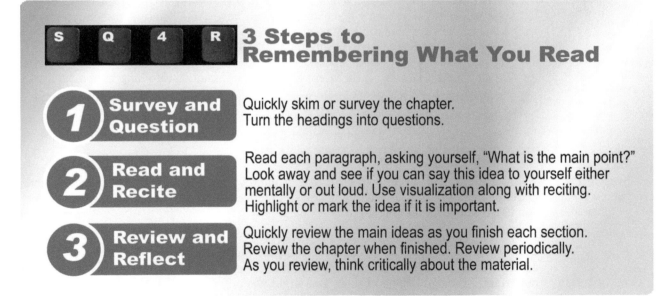

Figure 7.1 The SQ4R System for reading a college textbook.
Courtesy of Charlotte Moore. © Kendall Hunt Publishing Company.

Many students spend time reading their college textbooks with little benefit. Often students say that they cannot remember the material they have just read. The reason for this problem is not lack of intelligence, but rather a simple lack of rehearsal. If you are just reading the material, you are placing it in short-term memory, which quickly disappears. Effective study systems for reading a college textbook include techniques for storing information in long-term memory including recognizing major points, organizing the material to be learned, reviewing, intending to remember, and critical thinking about reading. It helps to think positively about the material and look for something interesting or meaningful in it. The essential point is that you must repeat or rehearse the material to transfer it to long-term memory. The **SQ4R system** (**Survey**, **Question**, **Read**, **Recite**, **Review**, and **Reflect**) is a simple and effective way to store information in long-term memory. This system can be broken down into three steps.

Step 1: Survey and Question. Finding the important points and understanding the organization of the reading is essential for learning and recall. The typical pattern of a college text is title, subtitle, paragraph, and topic sentence. **Learn to focus on the pattern and major points and then add the details.** This is accomplished by surveying and questioning the chapter before you begin reading it in detail. Read the title and first paragraph or introduction to the chapter and then look quickly through the chapter, letting your eyes glide across bold headings, diagrams, illustrations, and photos. Read the last paragraph or summary of the chapter. This process should take five minutes or less for a typical chapter in a college textbook. It is time well spent for transferring the information to your long-term memory.

While you are surveying the chapter, ask yourself questions. Take each major heading in the chapter and turn it into a question. For example, in this section of the book you might ask: What is a system for reading a college text? Why do I need a system? What is SQ4R? What is the first step of SQ4R? You can also ask some general questions as you survey the chapter: What is the main point? What will I learn? Do I know something about this? Can I find something that interests me? How can I use this? Does this relate to something said in class? What does this mean? Is this a possible test question? Asking questions will help you to become an active reader and to find some personal meaning in the content that will help you remember it. If you at least survey and question the relevant textbook material before you go to class, you will have the advantage of being familiar with some of the key ideas to be discussed.

There are several benefits to taking this first step:

- This is the first step in rehearsal for storage of information into long-term memory.
- The quick survey is a warmup for the brain, similar to an athlete's warmup before exercise.
- A survey step is also good practice for improving your reading speed.
- Reading to answer questions increases comprehension, sparks interest, and has the added bonus of keeping you awake while reading.

> "The important thing is to not stop questioning."
> Albert Einstein

If you want to be able to read faster, improve your reading comprehension, and increase retention of your reading material, practice the survey and question step before you begin your detailed reading.

Step 2: Read and recite. The second step in reading a text is to read and recite. Read each paragraph and look for the most important point or topic sentence. If the point is important, highlight or underline it. You might use different colors to organize the ideas. You can also make a notation or outline in the margin of the text if the point is especially significant, meaningful, useful, or likely to appear on an exam. A picture, diagram, or chart drawn in the margin is a great way to use visualization to improve retention of the material. If you are reading online, take notes on the important points or use cut and paste to collect the main ideas in a separate document.

Next, look away and see if you can say the main point to yourself either silently or out loud. Reciting is even more powerful if you combine it with visualization. Make a video in your head to illustrate what you are learning. Include color, movement, and sound if possible. Reciting is crucial to long-term memory storage. It will also keep you awake. Beginning college students will find this step a challenge, but practice makes it a habit that becomes easier and easier.

© George Dolgikh/Shutterstock.com

If you read a paragraph or section and do not understand the main point, try these techniques:

1. **Notice any vocabulary or technical terms that are unfamiliar.** Look up these words in a dictionary or in the glossary at the back of the book. Use index cards; write the words on one side and the definition on the other side. Use the SAFMEDS technique (Say All Fast in one Minute Each Day Shuffle) discussed earlier in this textbook. You are likely to see these vocabulary words on quizzes and exams.

2. **Read the paragraph again.** Until you get into the habit of searching for the main point, you may need to reread a paragraph until you understand. If this does not work, reread the paragraphs before and after the one you do not understand.

3. **Write a question in the margin and ask your instructor or tutor to explain.** College instructors have office hours set aside to assist students with questions, and faculty are generally favorably impressed with students who care enough to ask questions. Most colleges offer tutoring free of charge.

4. **If you are really frustrated, put your reading away and come back to it later.** You may be able to relax and gain some insight about the material.

5. **Make sure you have the proper background for the course.** Take the introductory course first.

6. **Assess your reading skills.** Colleges offer reading assessments, and counselors can help you understand your skill level and suggest appropriate courses. Most colleges offer reading courses that can help you to be successful in college.

7. **If you have always had a problem with reading, you may have a learning disability.** A person with a learning disability is of average or higher-than-average intelligence, but has a problem that interferes with learning. Most colleges offer assessment that can help you understand your learning disability and tutoring that is designed to help you to compensate for the disability.

Step 3: Review and reflect. The last step in reading is to review and reflect. After each section, quickly review what you have highlighted or underlined. Again, ask questions. How can I use this information? How does it relate to what I already know? What is most important? What is likely to be on the exam? Is it true? Learn to think critically about the material you have learned.

When you finish the chapter, quickly (in a couple of minutes) look over the highlights again. This last step, review and reflect, is another opportunity for rehearsal. At this point, you have stored the information in long-term memory and want to make sure that you can access the information again in the future. Think of this last step as a creative step in which you put the pieces together, gain an understanding, and begin to think of how you can apply your new knowledge to your personal life. This is the true reward of studying.

Review is faster, easier, and more effective if done immediately. As discussed previously, most forgetting occurs in the first 20 minutes after exposure to new information. If you wait 24 hours to review, you will probably have forgotten 80 percent of the material and will have to spend a longer time in review. Review periodically to make sure that you can access the material easily in the future, and review again right before the test.

As you read about the above steps, you may think that this process takes a lot of time. Remember that it is not how much you read, but how you read that is important. In reality, the SQ4R technique is a time-saver in that you do not have to reread all the material before the test. You just need to quickly review information that is stored in long-term memory. Rereading can be purely mechanical and consume your time with little payoff. Rather than rereading, spend your time reciting the important points. With proper review, you can remember 80 to 90 percent of the material.

Research has shown that you can retain 88% of the material you study using the following review schedule.[5] The rate of retention using this schedule is four times better.

1. Review immediately within 30 seconds.

2. Review after a few minutes.

3. Review after one hour.

4. Review a day later after an overnight rest.

5. Review after a week.

6. Review after one month.

Suggestions for review schedules vary, but the key point is that review is most effective when it is done in short sessions spaced out over time. The review can be done quickly; it is probably the most important investment you can make in remembering what you have read.

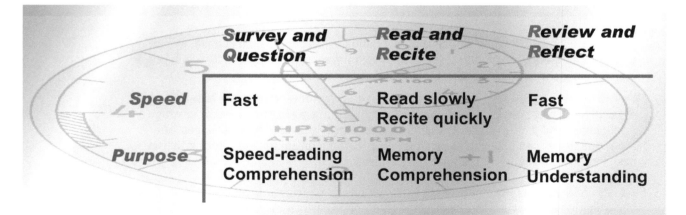

Figure 7.2 This chart summarizes the speed and purpose of each SQ4R step.

What to Do If Your Reading Goes in One Ear and Out the Other

1. **Silence your inner critic.**
   If you have always told yourself that you are a poor reader or hate reading, these thoughts make it difficult to read. Think positively and tell yourself that with some effort, you can read and understand. Focus on what you can do, rather than what you can't do.

2. Look for the key ideas and underline them.

3. **Try visualization.**
   Make a mental picture or video with the material you are reading.

4. **Look for personal meaning.**
   Can you relate the material to your life in any way?

5. Do a quick scan of the material to find some major points and then reread the material closely.

6. Try talking to the text as you read it. Ask questions. Why is this important? Do you know anything about this? Do you agree or disagree? Do you think it is a good or bad idea? Can you use this information in the future? Can you find something interesting in the text? Challenge the material and think critically about it. Make humorous remarks. Imagine yourself in the situation. What would it be like and what would you do? You can write your comments in the text or do this silently in your head.

© wavebreakmedia/Shutterstock.com

Reading Strategies for Different Subjects
Math

1. Skimming the textbook can help you to decide if you are enrolled in the correct course. While skimming a math book, keep in mind that many of the topics will be unfamiliar to you. You should be able to understand the first few pages and build your knowledge from there. If you do not understand these first few pages, you may need to go back and take a review math course, especially if there has been a gap in studying math. If all the concepts are familiar to you, you may be taking a class that you do not need.

2. It is helpful to read your math textbook before you go to class so you can begin to understand key concepts and vocabulary. Make note of areas that need special attention to increase your understanding. Pre-reading or at least skimming the text will help you to understand the lecture better.

3. As you are reading, make flash cards to review important formulas, vocabulary, and definitions.

4. It is not enough to read and understand mathematical concepts. Make sure that you add practice to your study system. Practice builds self-confidence needed for success on math exams.

5. Focus on understanding math concepts rather than on memorizing problems.

Science

1. In science classes, the scientific method is used to describe the world. The scientific method relies on questioning, observing, hypothesizing, researching, and analyzing. You will learn about theories and scientific principles. Highlight or mark theories, names of scientists, definitions, concepts, and procedures.

2. Understand the scientific principles and use flash cards to remember details and formulas.

3. Study the charts, diagrams, tables, and graphs. Draw your own pictures and graphs to get a visual picture of the material.

4. Use lab time as an opportunity to practice the theories and principles that you have learned.

Social and Behavioral Sciences

1. Social and behavioral scientists focus on principles of behavior, theories, and research. Notice that there are different theories that explain the same phenomena. Highlight, underline, and summarize these theories in your own words.

2. When looking at the research, ask yourself what the point of the research was, who conducted the research, when the research was completed, what data was collected, and what conclusions were drawn.

3. Think of practical applications of theories.

4. Use flash cards to remember details.

Literature Courses

When taking a course in literature, you will be asked to understand, appreciate, interpret, evaluate, and write about the literature.

1. Underline the names of characters and write plot summaries.

2. Write notes about your evaluation of literary works.

3. Make flash cards to remember literary terms.

4. Write down important quotes or note page numbers on a separate piece of paper so that you don't have to go back and find them later when you are writing about a work.

Foreign Language Courses

Foreign language courses require memorization and practice.

1. Distribute the practice. Practice a small amount each day. It is not possible to learn everything at once.

2. Complete the exercises as a way to practice and remember.

3. Study out loud.

4. Practice speaking the language with others.

5. Use flash cards to remember vocabulary.

6. Make charts to practice verb conjugations.

7. Ask for help if you do not understand.

8. Learn to think in the foreign language. Translating from English causes confusion because the structures of languages are different.

> "Whatever the mind of man can conceive and believe, it can achieve."
> Napoleon Hill

Improving Reading Concentration

Hank Aaron said that what separates the superstar from the average ballplayer is that the superstar concentrates just a little longer. Athletes are very aware of the power of concentration in improving athletic performance. Coaches remind athletes to focus on the ball and to develop good powers of concentration and visualization. Skilled athletes, musicians, and artists don't have any trouble concentrating. Think about a time when you were totally focused on what you were doing. You were motivated to continue.

Being able to concentrate on your reading helps you to study more efficiently. You can set the stage for paying attention by focusing on your goals, getting some exercise, being well-rested, and avoiding multi-tasking. Here are some suggestions for managing the distractions and improving concentration.

Manage your external environment. Find an environment that minimizes distractions. One idea is to study in the library where there are many cues that remind you to study. There are books and learning resources and other people studying. Concentration and motivation can be increased by varying the places where you study. You may be able to set up a learning environment in your home where you can place a desk or table, your computer, and your materials for learning. Vary your routine by finding a quiet place outside to study, or any place where you can focus your attention. Avoid studying in the kitchen, in your bed, or in front of the TV where you can be distracted by food, sleep, or an interesting program on TV.

Manage your internal distractions

1. **Become an active reader.** Read to answer questions. Search for the main idea. Recite or re-say the main idea in your mind. Reflect and think critically about the material you are reading. Mark or highlight the text. Visualize what you are reading.

2. **Remind yourself of your purpose for reading.** Think of your future college and career goals.

3. **Give yourself permission to daydream once in a while.** Use daydreaming as a break from your studies. Come back to your studies with a relaxed attitude.

4. **Break the task into small parts.** If the task seems overwhelming, break it into small parts and do the first part. If you have 400 pages to read in 10 days, read 40 pages each day. Make a schedule that allows time to read each day until you have accomplished your goal. Use distributed practice in your studies. Study for a short time each day rather than holding a marathon study session just before the test.

5. **Vary the content and subjects that you are studying.** Athletes maintain concentration and motivation by including strength, speed, and skill practice in each workout. Musicians practice scales, different musical pieces, and rhythm exercises in one practice session. In your studies, you can do the same. For example, when studying a foreign language, spend some time on reading, some time on learning vocabulary, and some practice in speaking the language. Then do some problems for your math class.

6. **Be here now.** Choose where you will place your attention. Your body can be attending a lecture or be at the desk reading, but your mind can be in many different and exciting places. You can tell yourself, "Be here now." You cannot force yourself to pay attention, but when your mind wanders, notice that you have drifted off and gently return your attention to your lecture or reading. This will take some practice, since attention tends to wander often.

© Diego Cervo/Shutterstock.com

7. **The spider technique.** If you hold a tuning fork to a spider web, the web vibrates and the spider senses that it has caught some tasty food and goes looking for it. After a while the spider discovers that there is no food and learns to ignore the vibrations caused by the tuning fork. When you are sitting in the library studying and someone walks in talking and laughing, you can choose to pay attention either to the distraction or to the studying. Decide to continue to pay attention to the studying.

8. **Set up a worry time.** Many times, worries interfere with concentration. Some people have been successful in setting up a worry time. Here's how it works:

   a. Set a specific time each day for worrying.

   b. When worries distract you from your studies, remind yourself that you have set aside time for worrying.

   c. Tell yourself, "Be here now."

   d. Keep your worry appointment.

   e. During your worry time, try to find some solutions or take some steps to resolve the things that cause you to worry.

9. **Take steps to solve personal problems.** If you are bothered by personal problems, take steps to solve them. See your college counselor for assistance. Another strategy is to plan to deal with the problem later so you can study now.

10. **Use the checkmark technique.** When you find yourself distracted from a lecture or from studying, place a checkmark on a piece of paper and refocus your attention on the task at hand. You will find that your checkmarks decrease over time and your attention improves.

Journal Entry #2

Write five intention statements about improving your reading and concentration. I intend to . . .

E-Learning Strategies

Reading and studying online require some different strategies. Here are some online reading strategies and tips for succeeding in online courses.

Online Reading Strategies

© Naypong/Shutterstock.com

The amount of online reading we do is increasing, so it is important to have some online reading strategies. First, determine your purpose for reading. If you are reading for entertainment, to interact with others, or to find needed information, quickly scan the material to see if it meets your needs. Look for bulleted lists, menu bars, highlighted words, and headers. Read only what suits your purpose. Avoid getting lost on your search by using browser tools such as favorites, bookmarks, or the history menu, which is a list of the pages you have visited before. Use multiple browser windows to compare and synthesize information. To avoid eyestrain while reading online, be sure to take breaks and look away from the screen. It is important to get up and stretch periodically.

If you are studying for an online course, first scan the material for key words. Then carefully read each section and summarize what you have learned. If you cannot summarize the material, then read it again, searching for the main ideas. Take notes or highlight the important points. You can save time by opening a separate document in a new window and cutting and pasting the important points into your notes. Be sure to include the source of the material, so that you can find it again and use it in writing papers. As in reading print material, use some techniques to assure good comprehension: as you read each section, visualize what you are reading, ask questions, and think critically about the material. As in reading print materials, you will need to practice, rehearse, or repeat the material to store it in your long-term memory.

Tips for Online Learning

There are many opportunities for learning online, including online courses, professional development, or learning for your personal life. Students who are independent learners or introverts who enjoy individual learning in a quiet place may prefer online learning. Students who prefer having a professor to guide learning with immediate feedback and extraverts who are energized by social interaction may prefer traditional classroom education. Because of work, family, and time constraints, online learning might be a convenient way to complete your courses.

If you have never taken an online course, be aware of some of the myths of online learning. One of the most popular myths is that online courses are easier than traditional courses. Online courses typically involve more writing, cover the same content, and are just as rigorous as traditional face-to-face courses. However, you will save time in commuting to class and have the added convenience of working on your class at any time or place where you can access the Internet.

Here are some suggestions for a successful e-learning experience.

- The most important key to success in online learning is to **log in regularly** and complete the work in a systematic way, rather than waiting to complete assignments just before the deadline. Set goals for what you need to accomplish each week and do the work a step at a time. Get in the habit of regularly doing your online study, just as you would do in a traditional course each week.

- It is important to **carefully read the instructions** for the assignments and **ask for help** if you need it. Your online professor will not know when you need help.

- Begin your online work by getting familiar with the requirements and components of the course. Generally, online courses have reading material, quizzes, discussion boards, chat rooms, assignments, and multimedia presentations. Make sure that you **understand all the resources**, **components**, and **requirements** of the course.

- **Have a backup plan** if your computer crashes or your Internet connection is interrupted. Colleges generally have computer labs where you can do your work if you have technical problems at home.

- Remember to **participate** in the online discussions or chats. It is usually part of your grade and a good way to learn from other students and apply what you have learned. The advantage of online communication is that you have time to think about your responses.

- **Check your grades** online to make sure you are completing all the requirements. Celebrate your success as you complete each component of your online course. Online learning becomes easier with experience.

Guidelines for Marking Your Textbook

Marking your textbook can help you pick out what is important, save time, and review the material. It is a great way to reinforce your memory. In high school, you were given the command, "Thou shalt not mark in thy book!" College is different. You have paid for the book and need to use it as a tool. Even if you plan to sell your book, you can still mark it up. Here are some guidelines for marking your book:

- Underline or mark only the key ideas in your text. You don't have to underline complete sentences; just underline enough to make sense when you review your markings. If reading online, use the highlighter tool to mark the main points and then cut and paste the main points into a separate document.

> "The illiterate of the 21st Century will not be those who cannot read or write, but those who cannot learn, unlearn, and relearn."
>
> Alvin Toffler

- Aim for marking or highlighting about 20 percent of the most important material. If you mark too much of your reading, it will be difficult to review the main points.
- Read each paragraph first. Ask yourself, "What is the main point?" Highlight or mark the main point if it is important. Not every paragraph has a main point that needs to be marked.
- Use other marks to help you organize what you have read. Write in numbers or letters and use different colors to help you organize ideas.
- Most college texts have wide margins. Use these margins to write down questions, outlines, or key points to remember.
- Learn to be brief, fast, and neat in your marking or highlighting.
- If you are tempted to mark too much, use the double system of first underlining with a pencil as much as you want and then using a highlighter to pick out the most important 20 percent of the material in the chapter.

QUIZ

Learning Strategies and Reading

Test what you have learned by selecting the correct answers to the following questions.

1. For optimal learning, brain scientist believe that it is best to use

    a. your left brain.
    b. your right brain.
    c. multisensory input.

2. Brain scientists have recently found that you learn best by using

    a. your preferred learning style.
    b. all of your senses to remember.
    c. auditory techniques.

3. Most scientists believe that the most powerful strategy for learning anything is

    a. visual.
    b. auditory.
    c. kinesthetic.

4. If you have read the chapter and can't remember what you have read,

    a. read the chapter again.
    b. remember to select important points and review them.
    c. the material is stored in long-term memory.

5. When you start reading a new textbook,

    a. begin with chapter one.
    b. focus on the details you will need to remember.
    c. skim over the text to get a general idea of what you will be reading.

How did you do on the quiz? Check your answers: 1. c, 2. b, 3. a, 4. b, 5. c

Journal Entry #3

You have just read a chapter in your economics textbook and can't remember what you have just read. How can you apply the ideas in this chapter to improve your reading comprehension?

How to Be Successful in Your Math Courses

To improve math study, it is helpful to begin by realizing the importance of math. The careers with the highest salaries require math and it is a requirement for graduation from college. However, students often have math phobia and postpone taking math courses until the end of their college studies. This can result in limited choice of a college major, dropping out of college, or a delay in graduation. It is important to take math early in your college studies and to enroll in math courses each semester until your math requirement is complete.

If you struggle with math and avoid the subject, examine your thoughts about math. It is often assumed that some people are born with a talent for math and others are not. Even worse, it is sometimes assumed that men are better at math than women. It is important to understand that both men and women develop the skill to succeed in math by having a positive attitude and practicing math problems. As your skills develop, your self-confidence increases along with your success in math. Another barrier to success in math is the fear of asking questions or asking for extra help. Students often fear that asking for help is a sign of lacking the intelligence to succeed in math. Faculty appreciate students who ask questions in class or ask for extra help because it shows they are interested in learning.

Researchers have studied the variables contributing to success in math.[6] About 50% of math success depends on your previous knowledge of math skills and how fast you can learn math. For this reason, it is important to take a math placement test and start at the level that is right for you. If you have had a gap in your math studies, you may need to go back and enroll in math review courses. About 25% of success in math depends on the quality of instruction in math. You may need to find the math instructor who matches how you learn best. The remaining 25% of success depends on math study skills and personal characteristics related to success in math. Successful students:

- Think positively about their ability to succeed in math. If you have had difficulties with math in the past and believe that you may not be successful in your college math courses, you will not take the steps needed to be successful in math. If you have self-statements such as "I hate math" or "I'm not good at math," change your statement to "I can learn to be successful in math."

- Use an internal locus of control, which means taking responsibility for your own success. Rather than blaming a teacher or past bad experiences, take the steps necessary to be successful.

- Use the motivation techniques from the first chapter to increase success, especially growth mindset and grit. Realize that you can learn to be good at math. Stay positive, be gritty and don't give up.

- Prepare adequately for math courses to minimize test anxiety. This topic is covered more in depth in the test-taking chapter.

- Make it a goal to earn an A or a B in their math courses. Lower grades will make it difficult to succeed in the next level.

  Here are some tips for improving your math success:

It is estimated that you will need to spend at least 10 hours a week studying math to be successful in a college math course. College math courses go four times faster than high-school math courses and require more work outside of class.[7] Make a study schedule and plan the time needed for reading your math text, reviewing your notes, doing your homework, and practicing math problems. Invest the time and effort needed to be successful.

Make studying math a priority. Study math first and then study subjects that are easier for you. Make use of your prime time when you are most alert to study math.

Math involves practice. Unlike other courses that rely on critical thinking, memorization, and recall, math also requires the application of math concepts to solving problems. To be successful on math exams, practice solving problems until you feel comfortable with them. Make practice tests to prepare for exams. It is important to apply the concept of distributed practice to study math. Study frequently over a period of time and review what you have learned in the past. Massed study will not work in a math course. Math can be compared to success in sports or music in that they all require practice to be successful. Rehearsal and practice are needed to store math concepts in long-term memory.

Use effective review techniques. It is important to review what is learned in your math classes as soon as practical after class. Remember that most of the forgetting occurs immediately after learning something new. Review your notes right after class, review what you have read in your math text at the end of your reading session, and use small amounts of time to quickly review important concepts on flash cards. Immediate review is a powerful memory technique.

Realize that math is sequential. You must understand the first step before you can go on to the next. For this reason, start at your level, attend every class, and make it your goal to earn an A or a B on your first test. If you miss any step, see a tutor early in the semester or use online resources to fill in the gap.

Math is like a foreign language. Math uses specialized vocabulary that you must understand in order to do your math problems. Make sure to write down the definitions of math terms in your notes and review these terms. Use flash cards to review the vocabulary.

Use a study group. Choose two to six students who are serious about math success. Have each group member bring note cards with sample questions for the group to practice. Create practice tests and practice taking the tests. Sometimes it is easier learning from your peers and you may be more comfortable asking questions.

Use additional resources. Find out about tutoring in your college and use these services early in your math course. If you are stuck on a problem, use Google or You Tube to find out how to solve the problems.

Ask questions in class. As soon as you don't understand something in class, ask questions. Other students probably have the same question and may be thankful that you asked it. Faculty generally appreciate questions because it shows you are paying attention and interested in the course. Student questions help faculty to make sure students understand what they are teaching.

Use multisensory techniques to study math. Remember that learning is easier if you use all of your senses. Highlight or place a checkmark in front of the study techniques that you can use:

_____ Read important math concepts out loud.

_____Use flash cards make from note cards or virtual flashcards from Study Stacks: http://www.studystack.com/.

_____Watch YouTube videos on math concepts and solving problems.

_____Use different colors of ink to take notes on math.

_____Take pictures of the board with your cell phone.

_____Say important concepts, formulas, or definitions out loud.

_____Record important concepts and listen to them in your car.

_____Teach group members how to solve problems.

_____Use math manipulatives to understand problems. Math manipulatives are letters, numbers, magnetic boards, and other pieces that help to understand math concepts. They are available at learning stores. There are also virtual manipulative sites such as the Computing Technology for Math Excellence site at: http://www.ct4me.net/math_manipulatives_2.htm.

_____Use Facebook to post pictures of your math homework and discuss it with friends.

_____Move around while studying.

_____Rewrite or highlight your math notes.

_____Use a math app to learn how to solve problems.

Some Useful Math Apps

Search for math apps on any search engine such as Google. Here are some useful ones:

MyScript Calculator allows you to write problems on your tablet screen and the built in calculator solves the problem.

Algebra Tutor includes many different apps to solve algebra problems.

Algeo is an online graphing calculator.

Photomath allows you to take a photo of a problem and solve it with the app.

Wolfram Alpa is a collection of data and algorithms used to solve problems. It is used in Siri to calculate the answers to problems.

*A Student Perspective: How to Be Successful in Math

Personally, I had always experienced immense anxiety around the subject of mathematics since I was a young child. Just as the text suggested, I had an experience in the first grade trying to do addition with some blocks. I struggled a bit from what I can remember, and the experience altered my perceptions of mathematics for many, many years.

When I started college, I was tested on my mathematic skills for placement, and fell into the remedial math course. It was difficult at first, but I knew that to succeed I needed to put in a lot of work to get through it, and just do the best I could.

Funny enough, I have successfully completed all my math courses to include statistics with "passing" and "A" grades. This wasn't the result of luck, but the result of effort, positivity, understanding, time, patience, and learning when to ask for help.

*Courtesy of Sasha Zimmerman

Courtesy of Aaron Dressin

Because of my personal awareness of my mathematics struggles, I put in an immense amount of effort. I practiced A LOT. If I didn't understand something, I worked with tutors, sought help from co-workers, and stayed after class to work with the professors. I would also look up information on how to solve a problem on YouTube and the Khan Academy.

I would take a break when I was frustrated, remain positive during difficult times, and further, I thought of the work as little puzzles. Thinking of mathematics as puzzles to be solved versus hard work changed my perception of math. I would get excited when I solved long math equations!

Also, I attended every single class and completed all my homework for all my math classes. I knew that if failed to do just that, I would fail the class. You can't miss a class or skip your homework. It's that simple. Math will snowball on you as it is truly a class that builds off the previous ones. You can't miss a segment or you will be totally lost. It's also important to take your math courses as close to the other as possible. We tend to forget the things that we don't use often or that we don't like. So, if you wait a year or so to take a different math course, you could be lost because you forgot everything you learned in your previous math course.

All I know is that it takes a crazy amount of work, practice, and dedication to succeed in math. It's work, but in the end, you will realize that are you weren't so bad at math after all. It was just all in your head like it was mine. My math courses are my proudest accomplishments in college thus far.

QUIZ

Math Success

1. About 50% of your success in math depends on

    a. placement in the proper level of math.
    b. your attitude toward math.
    c. your math study skills.

2. The estimated time needed per week to study for a college math course is

    a. 3 hours.
    b. 10 hours.
    c. 6 hours.

3. Preparation for exams in math is different from other subjects. To be successful on math exams, the most important strategy is

    a. memorization.
    b. recall.
    c. practice.

4. The best time to review in your math class is

    a. a marathon study session just before the test.
    b. as soon as possible after learning new material.
    c. on weekends when you are relaxed.

5. Learning in math is sequential which means

    a. it is OK to miss your math class once in awhile.
    b. it is not too important to do the math homework if it is not collected.
    c. you must understand the first step before you can understand the next step.

How did you do on the quiz? Check your answers: 1. a, 2. b, 3. c, 4. b, 5. c

KEYS TO SUCCESS

Create Your Success

We are responsible for our success in college as well as what happens in our lives. We make decisions and choices that create the future. Our behavior leads to success or failure. Too often we believe that we are victims of circumstance. When looking at our lives, we often look for others to blame for how our lives are going.

- I failed math. I had a bad math teacher.

- My grandparents did it to me. I inherited these genes.

- My parents did it to me. My childhood experiences shaped who I am.

- It was my teacher's fault. He gave me a bad grade.

- My boss did it to me. She gave me a poor evaluation.

- The government did it to me. All my money goes to taxes.

- Society did it to me. I have no opportunity.

These factors are all powerful influences in our lives, but we are still left with choices. You can study independently and be successful in math in spite of your math teacher. You can ask yourself how you created your failing grade and how you can improve in the future. You can use your job evaluation as a way to improve your job performance. You can create your own opportunity.

Concentration camp survivor Viktor Frankl wrote a book, *Man's Search for Meaning*, in which he describes his experiences and how he survived his ordeal in a concentration camp. His parents, brother, and wife died in the camps. He suffered starvation and torture. Through all of his sufferings and imprisonment, he still maintained that he was a free man because he could make choices.

We who lived in concentration camps can remember the men who walked through the huts comforting others, giving away their last piece of bread. They may have been few in number, but they offer sufficient proof that everything can be taken from a man but one thing: the last of the human freedoms—to choose one's attitude in any given set of circumstances, to choose one's own way. . . . Fundamentally, therefore, any man can, even under such circumstances, decide what shall become of him— mentally and spiritually. He may retain his human dignity even in a concentration camp.[7]

Viktor Frankl could not choose his circumstance at that time, but he did choose his attitude. He decided how he would respond to the situation. He realized that he still had the freedom to make choices. He used his memory and imagination to exercise his freedom. When times were the most difficult, he would imagine that he was in the classroom lecturing to his students about psychology. He eventually did get out of the concentration camp and became a famous psychiatrist.

Hopefully, none of you will ever have to experience the circumstances faced by Viktor Frankl, but we all face challenging situations. It is empowering to think that our behavior is more a function of our decisions than of our circumstances. It is not productive to look around and find someone to blame for your problems. Psychologist Abraham Maslow says that instead of blaming, we should see how we can make the best of the situation.

One can spend a lifetime assigning blame, finding a cause, "out there" for all the troubles that exist. Contrast this with the responsible attitude of confronting the situation, bad or good, and instead of asking, "What caused the trouble? Who was to blame?" asking, "How can I handle the present situation to make the best of it?"[9]

(Continued)

Author Stephen Covey suggests that we look at the word responsibility as "response-ability."[10] It is the ability to choose responses and make decisions about the future. When you are dealing with a problem, it is useful to ask yourself what decisions you made that led to the problem. How did you create the situation? If you created the problems, you can create a solution.

At times, you may ask, "How did I create this?" and find that the answer is that you did not create the situation. We certainly do not create earthquakes or hurricanes, for example. But we do create or at least contribute to many of the things that happen to us. Even if you did not create your circumstances, you can create your reaction to the situation. In the case of an earthquake, you can decide to panic or find the best course of action at the moment.

Author Steven Covey relates this concept to careers:

> But the people who end up with the good jobs are the proactive ones who are solutions

© Anson0618/Shutterstock.com

> to problems, not problems themselves, who seize the initiative to do whatever is necessary, consistent with correct principles, to get the job done.[11]

Use your resourcefulness and initiative to create the future that you want.

Journal Entry #5

Give your thoughts on the following:

Each of us is responsible for what happens in our life. We make decisions and choices that create the future. We create our own success.

College Success 1

© Lyudmyla Kharlamova/Shutterstock.com

The College Success 1 website is continually updated with supplementary material for each chapter including Word documents of the journal entries, classroom activities, handouts, videos, links to related materials, and much more. See http://www.collegesuccess1.com/.

Notes

1. Terry Doyle and Todd Zakrajsek, *The New Science of Learning, How to Learn in Harmony with Your Brain*, (Sterling, Virginia: Stylus), 45.

2. John Medina, *Brain Rules*, (Seattle: Pear Press, 2008), 250.

3. Ibid., 233–234.

4. Ibid., 212.

5. Colin Rose, *Accelerated Learning,* (New York: Dell Publishing, 1985), 51.

6. Paul Nolting, *Winning at Math*, (Bradenton, FL: Academic Success Press, 2014), 37.

7. Ibid., 19.

8. Viktor Frankl, *Man's Search for Meaning* (New York: Pocket Books, 1963), 104–105.

9. Quoted in Rob Gilbert, ed., *Bits and Pieces*, November 4, 1999.

10. Stephen Covey, *The Seven Habits of Highly Effective People* (New York: Simon and Schuster, 1989), 71.

11. Ibid., 75

Check Your Textbook Reading Skills

Name _____   Date _____

As you read each of the following statements, mark your response using this key:

1 I seldom or never do this.

2 I occasionally do this, depending on the class.

3 I almost always or always do this.

_____ **1.** Before I read the chapter, I quickly skim through it to get main ideas.

_____ **2.** As I skim through the chapter, I form questions based on the bold printed section headings.

_____ **3.** I read with a positive attitude and look for something interesting.

_____ **4.** I read the introductory and summary paragraphs in the chapter before I begin reading.

_____ **5.** As I read each paragraph, I look for the main idea.

_____ **6.** I recite the main idea so I can remember it.

_____ **7.** I underline, highlight, or take notes on the main ideas.

_____ **8.** I write notes or outlines in the margin of the text.

_____ **9.** After reading each section, I do a quick review.

_____ **10.** I quickly review the chapter immediately after reading it.

_____ **11.** During or after reading, I reflect on how the material is useful or meaningful to me.

_____ **12.** I read or at least skim the assigned chapter before I come to class.

_____ **13.** I have planned reading time in my weekly schedule.

_____ **14.** I generally think positively about my reading assignments.

_____ **Total points**

Check your score.
42–36   You have excellent college reading skills.
35–30   You have good skills, but can improve.
29–24   Some changes are needed.
23–14   Major changes are needed.

Becoming an Efficient College Reader

Name _____ Date _____

1. Based on your responses to the reading skills checklist on the previous page, list some of your good reading habits.

2. Based on this same checklist, what are some areas you need to improve?

3. Review the material on SQ4R and reading for speed and comprehension. Write five intention statements about how you plan to improve your reading. I intend to . . .

4. Review the material on how to concentrate while reading. List some ideas that you can use.

Surveying and Questioning a Chapter

Name _____ Date _____

Using the *next chapter* assigned in this class or any other class, answer these questions. Again, challenge yourself to do this activity quickly. Can you finish the exercise in five to seven minutes? Notice your beginning and end times.

1. What is the title of the chapter? For example, the title of this chapter is "Using Brain Science to Improve Study Skills." A good question would be, "How can I use brain science to improve my study skills?"

2. Briefly list one key idea mentioned in the introduction or first paragraph.

3. Write five questions you asked yourself while surveying this chapter. Read the bold section headings in the chapter and turn them into questions. For example, one heading in this chapter is "Neuroscience and Practical Learning Strategies." This heading might prompt you to ask, "What are some new findings in neuroscience? How can this help me to improve study skills?"

4. List three topics that interest you.

5. Briefly write one key idea from the last paragraph or chapter summary.

6. How long did it take you to do this exercise? Write your time here.

7. What did you think of this exercise on surveying and questioning a chapter?

CHAPTER

Taking Notes, Writing, and Speaking

Learning Objectives

Read to answer these key questions:

- Why is it important to take notes?

- What are some good listening techniques?

- What are some tips for taking good lecture notes?

- What are some note-taking systems?

- What is the best way to take notes in math?

- What is the best way to review my notes for the test?

- What is power writing?

- How can I make a good speech?

Knowing how to listen and take good notes can make your college life easier and may help you in your future career as well. Professionals in many occupations take notes as a way of recording key ideas for later use. Whether you become a journalist, attorney, architect, engineer, or other professional, listening and taking good notes can help you to get ahead in your career.

Good writing and speaking skills are important to your success in college and in your career. In college, you will be asked to write term papers and complete other writing assignments. The writing skills you learn in college will be used later in jobs involving high responsibility and good pay; on the job, you will write reports, memos, and proposals. In college, you will probably take a speech class and give oral reports in other classes; on the job, you will present your ideas orally to your colleagues and business associates.

Why Take Notes?

The most important reason for taking notes is to remember important material for tests or for future use in your career. If you just attend class without taking notes, you will forget most of the material by the next day.

How does taking notes enhance memory?

- In college, the lecture is a way of supplementing the written material in the textbook. Without good notes, an important part of the course is missing. Note taking provides material to rehearse or recite, so that it can be stored in long-term memory.

- When you take notes and impose your own organization on them, the notes become more personally meaningful. If they are meaningful, they are easier to remember.

- Taking notes helps you to make new connections. New material is remembered by connecting it to what you already know.

- The physical act of writing the material is helpful in learning and remembering it.

- Notes provide a visual map of the material to be learned.

- Taking notes is a way to listen carefully and record information to be stored in the memory.

- Note taking helps students to concentrate, maintain focus, and stay awake.

- Attending the lectures and taking notes helps you to understand what the professor thinks is important and to know what to study for the exam.

© Monkey Business Images/Shutterstock.com

The College Lecture

You will experience many different types of lectures while in college. At larger universities, many of the beginning-level courses are taught in large lecture halls with 300 people or more. More advanced courses tend to have fewer students. In large lecture situations, it is not always possible or appropriate to ask questions. Under these circumstances, the large lecture is often supplemented by smaller discussion sessions where you can ask questions and review the lecture material. Although attendance may not be checked, it is important to attend both the lectures and the discussion sessions.

A formal college lecture is divided into four parts. Understanding these parts will help you to be a good listener and take good notes.

> "Education is not a problem. It is an opportunity."
> Lyndon B. Johnson

1. **Introduction.** The professor uses the introduction to set the stage and to introduce the topic of the lecture. Often an overview or outline of the lecture is presented. Use the introduction as a way to begin thinking about the organization of your notes and the key ideas you will need to write down.

2. **Thesis.** The thesis is the key idea in the lecture. In a one-hour lecture, there is usually one thesis statement. Listen carefully for the thesis statement and write it down in your notes. Review the thesis statement and related ideas for the exam.

3. **Body.** The body of the lecture usually consists of five or six main ideas with discussion and clarification of each idea. As a note taker, your job is to identify the main ideas, write them in your notes, and put in enough of the explanation or examples to understand the key ideas.

4. **Conclusion.** In the conclusion, the professor summarizes the key points of the lecture and sometimes asks for questions. Use the conclusion as an opportunity to check your understanding of the lecture and to ask questions to clarify the key points.

How to Be a Good Listener

Effective note taking begins with good listening. What is good listening? Sometimes students confuse listening with hearing. Hearing is done with the ears. Listening is a more active process done with the ears and the brain engaged. Good listening requires attention and concentration. Practice these ideas for good listening:

- **Be physically ready.** It is difficult to listen to a lecture if you are tired, hungry, or ill. Get enough sleep so that you can stay awake. Eat a balanced diet without too much caffeine or sugar. Take care of your health and participate in an exercise program so that you feel your best.

- **Prepare a mental framework.** Look at the course syllabus to become familiar with the topic of the lecture. Use your textbook to read, or at least survey, the material to be covered in the lecture. If you are familiar with the key concepts from the textbook, you will be able to understand the lecture and know what to write down in your notes. If the material is in your book, there is no need to write it down in your notes.

  The more complex the topic, the more important it is for you to read the text first. If you go to the lecture and have no idea what is being discussed, you may be overwhelmed and find it difficult to take notes on material that is totally new to you. Remember that it is easier to remember material if you can connect it to material you already know.

- **Find a good place to sit.** Arrive early to get a good seat. The best seats in the classroom are in the front and center of the room. If you were buying concert tickets, these would be the best and most expensive seats. Find a seat that will help you to hear and focus on the speaker. You may need to find a seat away from your friends to avoid distractions.

- **Have a positive mental attitude.** Convince yourself that the speaker has something important to say and be open to new ideas. This may require you to focus on your goals and to look past some distractions. Maybe the lecturer doesn't have the best speaking voice or you don't like his or her appearance. Focus on what you can learn from the professor rather than outward appearances.

- **Listen actively to identify the main points.** As you are listening to the lecture, ask yourself, "What is the main idea?" In your own words, write the main points down in your notes. Do not try to write down everything the professor says. This will be impossible and unnecessary. Imagine that your mind is a filter and you are actively sorting through the material to find the key ideas and write them down in your notes. Try to identify the key points that will be on the test and write them in your notes.

- **Stay awake and engaged in learning.** The best way to stay awake and focused is to listen actively and take notes. Have a mental debate with the professor. Listen for the main points and the logical connection between ideas. The physical act of writing the notes will help to keep you awake.

Tips for Good Note Taking

Here are some suggestions for taking good notes:

1. Attend all of the lectures. Because many professors do not take attendance, students are often tempted to miss class. If you do not attend the lectures, however, you will not know what the professor thinks is important and what to study for the test. There will be important points covered in the lectures that are not in the book.

2. Have the proper materials. A three-ring notebook and notebook paper are recommended. Organize notes chronologically and include any handouts given in class. You can have a small notebook for each class or a single large notebook with dividers for each class. Just take the notebook paper to class and later file it in your notebook at home. Use your laptop as an alternative to a paper notebook.

3. Begin your notes by writing the date of the lecture, so you can keep your notes in order.

4. Write notes on the front side only of each piece of paper. This will allow you to spread the pages out and see the big picture or pattern in the lectures when you are reviewing.

© Monkey Business Images/Shutterstock.com

5. Write notes neatly and legibly so you can read and review them easily.

6. Do not waste time recopying or typing your notes. Your time would be better spent reviewing your notes.

7. As a general rule, do not rely on an audio recorder for taking notes. With an audio recorder, you will have to listen to the lecture again on tape. For a semester course, this would be about 45 hours of recording! It is much faster to review carefully written notes.

8. Copy down everything written on the board and the main points from PowerPoint or other visual presentations. If it is important enough for the professor to write on the board, it is important enough to be on the test.

9. Use key words and phrases in your notes. Leave out unimportant words and don't worry about grammar.

10. Use abbreviations as long as you can read them. Entire sentences or paragraphs are not necessary and you may not have time to write them.

11. Don't loan your whole notebook to someone else because you may not get it back. If you want to share your notes, make copies.

12. If the professor talks too fast, listen carefully for the key ideas and write them down. Leave spaces in your notes to fill in later. You may be able to find the information in the text or get the information from another student.

13. Explore new uses of technology for note taking. Students are taking notes and sharing them on Facebook and GradeGuru, for example.

Journal Entry #1

Write one paragraph giving advice to a new student about taking notes in college. Use any of these questions to guide your thinking:

- Why is note taking necessary in college?
- How can you be a good listener?
- What are some tips for taking good notes?
- What are some ideas that don't work?

Note-Taking Systems

We remember by finding patterns in new information including similarities, differences, hierarchy, and relationships among items. Recognizing patterns is useful in taking good notes. There are several systems for taking notes, depending on the patterns and organization that make sense to you. The most familiar pattern is using your own words to record the important points.

> **Note-Taking Systems**
> - Cornell format
> - Outline method
> - Mind map

The Cornell Format

The Cornell format is an efficient method of taking notes and reviewing them. It appeals to students who are logical, orderly, and organized and have lectures that fit into this pattern. The Cornell format is especially helpful for thinking about key points as you review your notes.

Step 1: Prepare. To use the Cornell format, you will need a three-ring notebook with looseleaf paper. Draw or fold a vertical line 2½ inches from the left side of the paper.

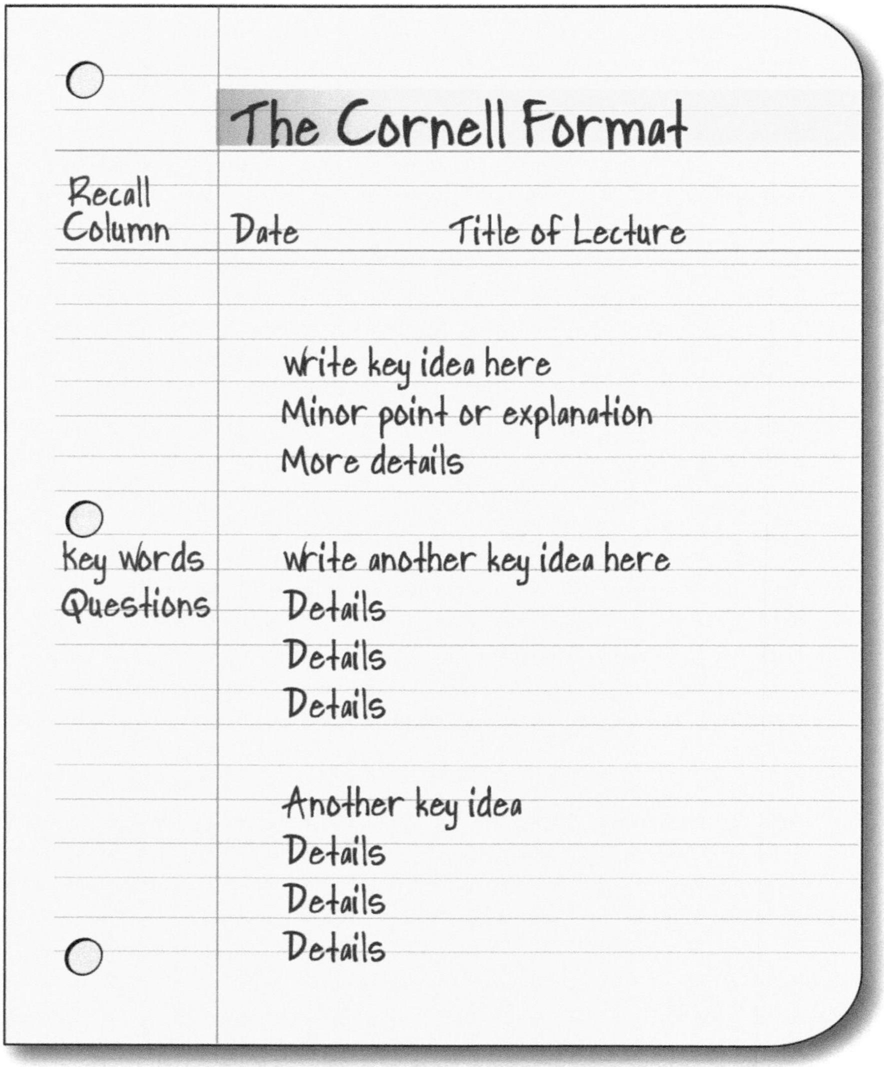

Figure 8.1 The Cornell format is an efficient way of organizing notes and reviewing them.

Courtesy of Charlotte Moore. © Kendall Hunt Publishing Company.

This is the recall column that can be used to write key ideas when reviewing. Use the remaining section of the paper for your notes. Write the date and title of the lecture at the top of the page.

Step 2: Take notes. Use the large area to the right of the recall column to take notes. Listen for key ideas and write them just to the right of the recall column line, as in the diagram above. Indent your notes for minor points and illustrative details. Then skip a space and write the next key idea. Don't worry about using numbers or letters as in an outline format. Just use the indentations and spacing to highlight and separate key ideas. Use short phrases, key words, and abbreviations. Complete sentences are not necessary, but write legibly so you can read your notes later.

Step 3: Use the recall column for review. Read over your notes and write down key words or ideas from the lecture in the recall column. Ask yourself, "What is this about?" Cover up the notes on the right-hand side and recite the key ideas of the lecture. Another variation is to write questions in the margin. Find the key ideas and then write possible exam questions in the recall column. Cover your notes and see if you can answer the questions.

The Outline Method

If the lecture is well organized, some students just take notes in outline format. Sometimes lecturers will show their outline as they speak.

- Use Roman numerals to label main topics. Then use capital letters for main ideas and Arabic numerals for related details or examples.
- You can make a free-form outline using just indentation to separate main ideas and supporting details.
- Leave spaces to fill in material later.
- Use a highlighter to review your notes as soon as possible after the lecture.

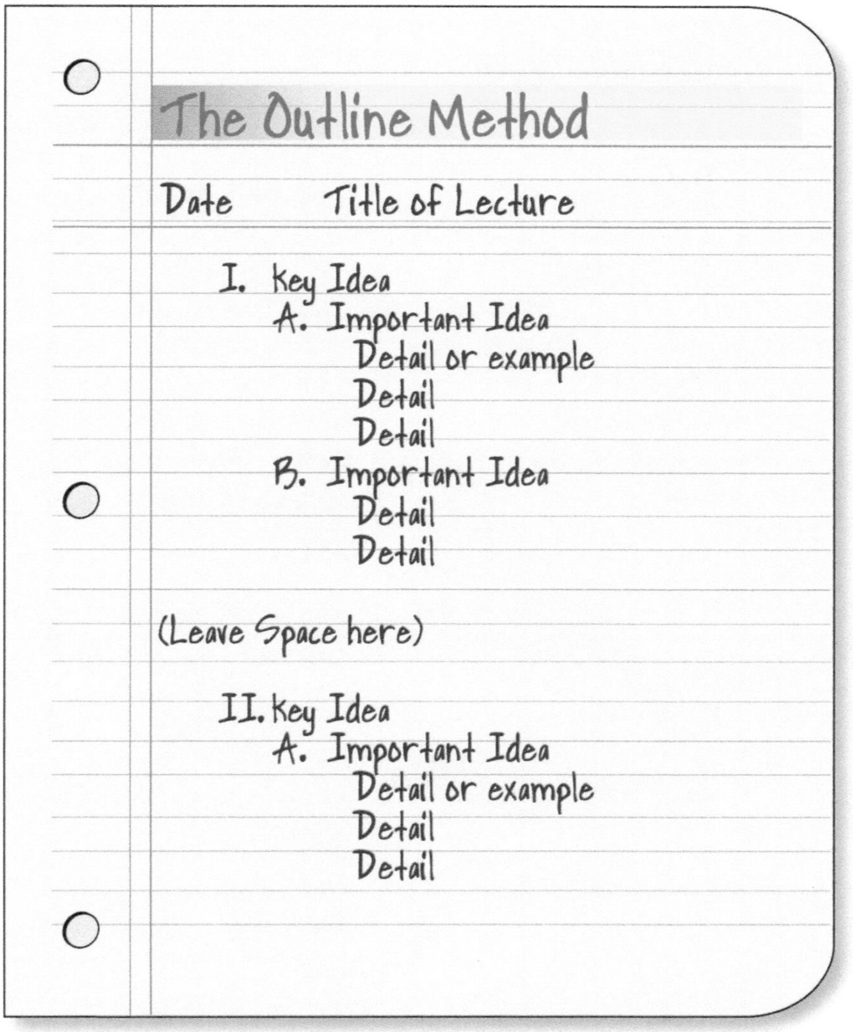

Figure 8.2 If a lecture is well organized, the outline format of taking notes works well.

Courtesy of Charlotte Moore. © Kendall Hunt Publishing Company.

The Mind Map

A mind map shows the relationship between ideas in a visual way. It is much easier to remember items that are organized and linked together in a personally meaningful way. As a result, recall and review is quicker and more effective. Mind maps can be used to show the contents of a lecture in a visual way and appeal to those who do not want to be limited to a set structure, as in the outline formats. They can also be used for lectures that are not highly structured. Here are some suggestions for using the mind-mapping technique:

- Turn your paper sideways to give you more space. Use standard-size notebook paper or consider larger sheets if possible.
- Write the main idea in the center of the page and circle it.
- Arrange ideas so that more important ideas are closer to the center and less important ideas are farther out.
- Show the relationship of the minor points to the main ideas using lines, circles, boxes, charts, and other visual devices. Here is where you can use your creativity and imagination to make a visual picture of the key ideas in the lecture.

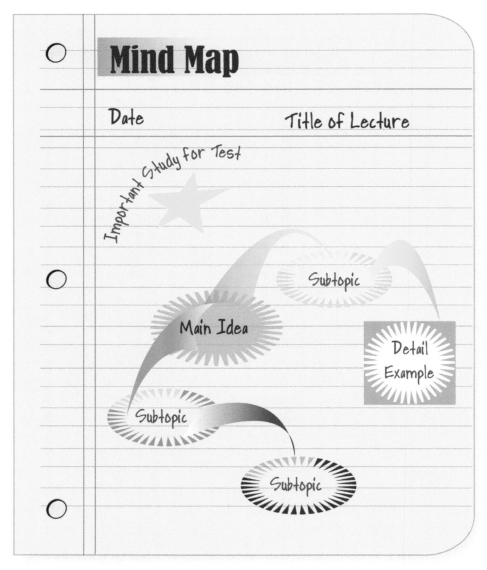

Figure 8.3 The mind map format of taking notes shows the relationship between ideas in a visual way.

Courtesy of Charlotte Moore. © Kendall Hunt Publishing Company.

- Use symbols and drawings.
- Use different colors to separate main ideas.
- When the lecturer moves to another main idea, start a new mind map.
- When you are done with the lecture, quickly review your mind maps. Add any written material that will be helpful in understanding the map later.
- A mind map can also be used as:
  - a review tool for remembering and relating the key ideas in the textbook;
  - a preparation tool for essay exams in which remembering main ideas and relationships is important; and
  - the first step in organizing ideas for a term paper.

Taking Notes in Math

Prepare for note-taking in math by prereading the chapter. This will help you to understand key ideas and areas where you need help. As you are reading, note some areas for asking questions in class. It is also a good idea to review the notes from the previous

Modified Three Column Note-Taking Method

Key words/ Rules	Examples	Explanations
Solve a linear equation	$5(x + 4) + 3(x - 4) = 2(x - 2)$	Have to get x on one side of the = and numbers on the other side of the =.
Distributive Property	$5x + 20 + 3x - 12 = 2x - 4$	Multiply numbers to the left of the () by each variable and number in the ().
Commutative Property	$5x + 3x + 20 - 12 = 2x - 4$	Regroup numbers and variables
Combine Like Terms	$8x + 8 = 2x - 4$	Add x's together and numbers together.

Adapted from *Winning at Math* by Paul Nolting. Courtesy of Charlotte Moore.
© Kendall Hunt Publishing Company.

lecture so you can build on previous knowledge. Make sure to copy down anything written on the board or use your cell phone to photograph the board and write notes later. The Modified Three Column Note-Taking Method is recommended for taking notes in a math class.[1] Once you are used to using this system, you may no longer need to label the columns.

There are three steps to using this format. Begin with writing the example in the middle of the page. Next write the explanation, and lastly, write down the key words to the left. To review the notes, cover up the examples and explanations and say the meaning of the key word or term. Then place a checkmark next to the terms you don't know so you can review them again. Make note cards or use the StudyStack website (http://www.studystack.com/ to create flashcards for review.

Improving Note-Taking Efficiency

Improve note-taking efficiency by listening for key words that signal the main ideas and supporting details. Learn to write faster by using telegraphic sentences, abbreviations, and symbols.

Telegraphic Sentences

Telegraphic sentences are short, abbreviated sentences used in note taking. They are very similar to the text messages sent on a cell phone. There are four rules for telegraphic sentences:

1. Write key words only.

2. Omit unnecessary words (*a, an, the*).

3. Ignore rules of grammar.

4. Use abbreviations and symbols.

Here is an example of a small part of a lecture followed by a student's telegraphic notes:

Heavy drinking of alcoholic beverages causes students to miss class and to fall behind in schoolwork. College students who are considered binge drinkers are at risk for many alcohol-related problems. Binge drinking is simply drinking too much alcohol at one time. Binge drinking is defined by researchers as drinking five or more drinks in a row for men or four or more drinks in a row for women. Researchers estimate that two out of five college students (40 percent) are binge drinkers.

Binge drinking—too much alcohol at one time
Men = 5 in row
Women = 4
2 out of 5 (40%) college students binge

© Lightspring Shutterstock.com

Signal Words

Signal words are clues to the patterns, structure, and content of a lecture. Recognizing signal words can help you to identify key ideas and organize them in your notes. The table on the following page lists some common signal words and their meaning.

Signal Words

Type	Examples	Meaning
Main idea words	And most important A major development The basic concept is Remember that The main idea is We will focus on The key is	Introduce the key points that need to be written in your notes.
Example words	To illustrate For example For instance	Clarify and illustrate the main ideas in the lecture. Write these examples in your notes after the main idea. If multiple examples are given, write down the ones you have time for or the ones that you understand the best.
Addition words	In addition Also Furthermore	Add more important information. Write these points down in your notes.
Enumeration words	The five steps First, second, third Next	Signal a list. Write down the list in your notes and number the items.
Time words	Before, after Formerly Subsequently Prior Meanwhile	Signal the order of events. Write down the events in the correct order in your notes.
Cause and effect words	Therefore As a result If . . ., then	Signal important concepts that might be on the exam. When you hear these words, label them "cause" and "effect" in your notes and review these ideas for the exam.
Definition words	In other words It simply means That is In essence	Provide the meanings of words or simplify complex ideas. Write these definitions or clarifications in your notes.
Swivel words	However Nevertheless Yes, but Still	Provide exceptions, qualifications, or further clarification. Write down qualifying comments in your notes.
Compare and contrast words	Similarly Likewise In contrast	Present similarities or differences. Write these similarities and differences in your notes and label them.
Summary words	In conclusion To sum up In a nutshell	Restate the important ideas of the lecture. Write the summaries in your notes.
Test words	This is important. Remember this. You'll see this again. You might want to study this for the test.	Provide a clue that the material will be on the test. Write these down in your notes and mark them in a way that stands out. Put a star or asterisk next to these items or highlight them. Each professor has his or her own test clue words.

How to Review Your Notes

Immediate review. Review your notes as soon as possible after the lecture. The most effective review is done immediately or at least within 20 minutes. If you wait until the next day to review, you may already have forgotten much of the information. During the immediate review, fill in any missing or incomplete information. Say the important points to yourself. This begins the process of rehearsal for storing the information in long-term memory.

Intermediate review. Set up some time each week for short reviews of your notes and the key points in your textbook from previous weeks. Quickly look over the notes and recite the key points in your mind. These intermediate reviews will help you to master the material and avoid test anxiety.

Test review. Complete a major review as part of your test preparation strategy. As you look through your notes, turn the key ideas into possible test questions and answer them.

Final review. The final review occurs after you have received the results of your test. Ask yourself these questions:

- What percentage of the test questions came from the lecture notes?
- Were you prepared for the exam? If so, congratulate yourself on a job well done. If not, how can you improve next time?
- Were your notes adequate? If not, what needs to be added or changed?

© Terence Shutterstock.com

Listening and Note Taking

Test what you have learned by selecting the correct answer to the following questions.

1. When taking notes on a college lecture, it is most important to
   a. write down everything you hear.
   b. write down the main ideas and enough explanation to understand them.
   c. write down names, dates, places, and numbers.

2. To be a good listener,
   a. read or skim over the material before you attend the lecture.
   b. attend the lecture first and then read the text.
   c. remember that listening is more important than note taking.

3. To stay awake during the lecture,
   a. drink lots of coffee.
   b. sit near your friends so you can make some comments on the lecture.
   c. listen actively by taking notes.

4. Since attendance is not always checked in college classes,
   a. it is not necessary to attend class if you read the textbook.
   b. it is acceptable to miss lectures as long as you show up for the exams.
   c. it is up to you to attend every class.

5. The best time to review your notes is
   a. as soon as possible after the lecture.
   b. within 24 hours.
   c. within one week.

How did you do on the quiz? Check your answers: 1. b, 2. a, 3. c, 4. c, 5. a

Journal Entry #2

Write five intention statements about improving your note-taking skills. Consider your note-taking system, how to take notes more efficiently, and the best way to review your notes. I intend to . . .

"The highest reward for a person's toil is not what they get for it, but what they become by it."
John Ruskin

Power Writing

Effective writing will help you in school, on the job, and in your personal life. Good writing will help you to create quality term papers. The writing skills that you learn in college will be used later in jobs involving high responsibility and good pay. You can become an excellent writer by learning about the steps in POWER writing: prepare, organize, write, edit, and revise.

Power Writing
- Prepare
- Organize
- Write
- Edit
- Revise

Prepare

Plan your time. The first step in writing is to plan your time so that the project can be completed by the due date. Picture this scene: It is the day that the term paper is due. A few students proudly hand in their term papers and are ready to celebrate their accomplishments. Many of the students in the class are absent, and some will never return to the class. Some of the students look as though they haven't slept the night before. They look stressed and weary. At the front of the class is a line of students wanting to talk with the instructor. The instructor has heard it all before:

- I had my paper all completed and my printer jammed.
- My hard drive crashed and I lost my paper.
- I was driving to school and my paper flew off my motorcycle.
- I had the flu.
- My children were sick.
- I had to take my dog to the vet.
- My dog ate my paper.
- My car broke down and I could not get to the library.
- My grandmother died and I had to go to the funeral.
- My roommate accidentally took my backpack to school.
- I spilled salad dressing on my paper, so I put it in the microwave to dry it out and the writing disappeared!

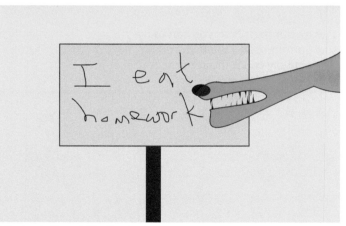

© Benjamin Howell/Shutterstock.com

To avoid being in this uncomfortable and stressful situation, plan ahead. Plan to complete your project at least one week ahead of time so that you can deal with life's emergencies. Life does not always go as planned. You or your children may get sick, or your dog may do strange things to your homework. Your computer may malfunction, leading you to believe it senses stress and malfunctions just to frustrate you even more.

To avoid stress and do your best work, start with the date that the project is due and then think about the steps needed to finish. Write these dates on your calendar or on your list of things to do. Consider all these components:

Prepare

- Plan your time
- Find space and time
- Choose general topic
- Gather information
- Write thesis statement

Project due date:

To do	By when?
1. Brainstorm ideas.	_____
2. Choose a topic.	_____
3. Gather information.	_____
4. Write a thesis statement.	_____
5. Write an outline.	_____
6. Write the introduction.	_____
7. Write the first draft.	_____
8. Prepare the bibliography.	_____
9. Edit.	_____
10. Revise.	_____
11. Print and assemble.	_____

You can also try an assignment calculator app that helps you to develop a timeline such as the one created at the University of Minnesota at https://www.lib.umn.edu/apps/ac/

Find a space and time. Find a space where you can work. Gather the materials that you will need to write. Generally, writing is best done in longer blocks of time. Determine when you will work on your paper and write the time on your schedule. Start right away to avoid panic later.

Choose a general topic. This task will be easy if your topic is already clearly defined by your instructor or your boss at work. Make sure that you have a clear idea of what is required, such as length, format, purpose, and method of citing references and topic. Many times the choice of a topic is left to you. Begin by doing some brainstorming. Think about topics that interest you. Write them down. You may want to focus your attention on brainstorming ideas for five or 10 minutes, and then put the project aside and come back to it later. Once you have started the process of thinking about the ideas, your mind will continue to work and you may have some creative inspiration. If inspiration does not come, repeat the brainstorming process.

Gather information. Go to your college library and use the Internet to gather your information. As you begin, you can see what is available, what is interesting to you, and what the current thinking is on your topic. Note the major topics of interest that might be useful to you. Once you have found some interesting material, you will feel motivated to continue your project. As you find information relevant to your topic, make sure to write down the sources of your information to use in your bibliography. The bibliography contains information about where you found your material. Write down the author, the title of the publication, the publisher, and the place and date of publication. For Internet resources, list the address of the website and the date accessed.

Write the thesis statement. The thesis statement is the key idea in your paper. It provides a direction for you to follow. It is the first step in organizing your work. To write a thesis statement, review the material you have gathered and then ask these questions:

- What is the most important idea?
- What question would I like to ask about it?
- What is my answer?

© Elena Elisseeva/Shutterstock.com

For example, if I decide to write a paper for my health class on the harmful effects of smoking, I would look at current references on the topic. I might become interested in how the tobacco companies misled the public on the dangers of smoking. I would think about my thesis statement and answer the questions stated above.

- **What is the most important idea?** Smoking is harmful to your health.
- **What question would I like to ask about it?** Did the tobacco companies mislead the public about the health hazards of smoking?
- **What is my answer?** The tobacco companies misled the public about the hazards of smoking in order to protect their business interests.
- **My thesis statement:** Tobacco companies knew that smoking was hazardous to health, but to protect their business interests, they deliberately misled the public.

The thesis statement helps to narrow the topic and provide direction for the paper. I can now focus on reference material related to my topic: research on health effects of smoking, congressional testimony relating to regulation of the tobacco industry, and how advertising influences people to smoke.

Organize

At this point you have many ideas about what to include in your paper, and you have a central focus, your thesis statement. Start to organize your paper by listing the topics that are related to your thesis statement. Here is a list of topics related to my thesis statement about smoking:

- Tobacco companies' awareness that nicotine is addictive
- Minimizing health hazards in tobacco advertisements
- How advertisements encourage people to smoke
- Money earned by the tobacco industry
- Health problems caused by smoking
- Statistics on numbers of people who have health problems or die from smoking
- Regulation of the tobacco industry
- Advertisements aimed at children

Think about the topics and arrange them in logical order. Use an outline, a mind map, a flowchart, or a drawing to think about how you will organize the important topics. Keep in mind that you will need an introduction, a body, and a conclusion.

Organize
- List related topics
- Arrange in logical order
- Have an organizational structure

Having an organizational structure will make it easier for you to write because you will not need to wonder what comes next.

Write

Write the First Sentence

Begin with the main idea.

Write the Introduction

This is the road map for the rest of the paper. The introduction includes your thesis statement and establishes the foundation of the paper. It introduces topics that will be discussed in the body of the paper. The introduction should include some interesting points that provide a "hook" to motivate the audience to read your paper. For example, for a paper on the hazards of smoking, you might begin with statistics on how many people suffer from smoking-related illnesses and premature death. Note the large profits earned by the tobacco industry. Then introduce other topics: deception, advertisements, and regulation. The introduction provides a guide or outline of what will follow in the paper.

> **Write**
> - First sentence
> - Introduction
> - Body
> - Conclusion
> - References

Write the Body of the Paper

The body of the paper is divided into paragraphs that discuss the topics that you have introduced. As you write each paragraph, include the main idea and then explain it and give examples. Here are some good tips for writing:

1. **Good writing reflects clear thinking.** Think about what you want to say and write about it so the reader can understand your point of view.

2. **Use clear and concise language.** Avoid using too many words or scholarly-sounding words that might get in the way of understanding.

3. **Don't assume that the audience knows what you are writing about.** Provide complete information.

4. **Provide examples, stories, and quotes to support your main points.** Include your own ideas and experiences.

5. **Beware of plagiarism.** Plagiarism is copying the work of others without giving them credit. It is illegal and can cause you to receive a failing grade on your project or even get you into legal trouble. Faculty regularly uses software programs that identify plagiarized material in student papers. You can avoid plagiarism by using quotation marks around an author's words and providing a reference indicating where you found the material. Another way to avoid plagiarism is by carefully reading your source material while using critical thinking to evaluate it. Then look away from the source and write about the ideas in your own words, including your critical thinking about the subject. Don't forget to include a reference for the source material in your bibliography.

Write the Conclusion

The conclusion summarizes the topics in the paper and presents your point of view. It makes reference to the introduction and answers the question posed in your thesis statement. It often makes the reader think about the significance of your point and the implications for the future. Make your conclusion interesting and powerful.

Include References

No college paper is complete without references. References may be given in footnotes, endnotes, a list of works cited, or a bibliography. You can use your computer to insert these references. There are various styles for citing references depending on your subject area.

There are computer programs that put your information into the correct style. Ask your instructor which style to use for your particular class or project. Three frequently used styles for citing references are APA, Chicago, and MLA.

1. The American Psychological Association (APA) style is used in psychology and other behavioral sciences. Consult the *Publication Manual of the American Psychological Association*, 6th ed. (Washington, DC: American Psychological Association, 2010). You can find this source online at www.apastyle.org.

2. Chicago style is used by many professional writers in a variety of fields. Consult the *Chicago Manual of Style*, 16th ed. (Chicago: University of Chicago Press, 2010). You can find this source online at www.chicagomanualofstyle.org/home.html.

3. The Modern Language Association (MLA) style is used in English, classical languages, and the humanities. Consult the *MLA Handbook for Writers of Research Papers*, 8th ed. (New York: Modern Language Association, 2016). This source is available online at www.mla.org/style.

Each of these styles uses a different format for listing sources, but all include the same information. Make sure you write down this information as you collect your reference material. If you forget this step, it is very time-consuming and difficult to find later.

- Author's name
- Title of the book or article
- Journal name
- Publisher
- City where book was published
- Publication date
- Page number (and volume and issue numbers, if available)

Save Your Work

As soon as you have written the first paragraph, save it on your computer. If your computer is not backed up by a remote server such as iCloud or Carbonite, save another copy on a flash drive. When you are finished, print your work and save a paper copy. Then, if your hard drive crashes, you will still have your work at another location. If your file becomes corrupted, you will still have the paper copy. Following these procedures can save you a lot of headaches. Any writer can tell you stories of lost work because of computer problems, lightning storms, power outages, and other unpredictable events.

Put It Away for a While

"All things are difficult before they are easy."
John Norley

The last step in writing the first draft is to take a break. Put it away for a while and come back to it later. In this way, you can relax and gain some perspective on your work. You will be able to take a more objective look at your work to begin the process of editing and revising.

Writer's Block

Many people who are anxious about writing experience "writer's block." You have writer's block if you find yourself staring at that blank piece of paper or computer screen not knowing how to begin or what to write. Here are some tips for avoiding writer's block.

- **Write freely.** Just write anything about your topic that comes to mind. Don't worry about organization or perfection at this point. Don't censure your ideas. You can

© Creativa/Shutterstock.com

always go back to organize and edit later. Free-writing helps you to overcome one of the main causes of writer's block: you think it has to be perfect from the beginning. This expectation of perfection causes anxiety. You freeze up and become unable to write. Perhaps you have past memories of writing where the teacher made many corrections on your paper. Maybe you lack confidence in your writing skills. The only way you will become a better writer is to keep writing and perfecting your writing skills. Don't worry how great it is. You can fix it later. Just begin.

- **Use brainstorming if you get stuck.** For five minutes, focus your attention on the topic and write whatever comes to mind. You don't even need to write full sentences; just jot down ideas. If you are really stuck, try working on a different topic or take a break and come back to it later.

- **Realize that it is only the first draft.** It is not the finished product and it does not have to be perfect. Just write some ideas on paper; you can revise them later.

- **Read through your reference materials.** The ideas you find can get your mind working. Also, reading can make you a better writer.

- **Break the assignment up into small parts.** If you find writing difficult, write for five minutes at a time. Do this consistently and you can get used to writing and can complete your paper.

- **Find a good place for writing.** If you are an introvert, look for a quiet place for concentration. If you are an extrovert, go to a restaurant or coffee shop and start your writing.

- **Beware of procrastination.** The more you put off writing, the more anxious you will become and the more difficult the task will be. Make a schedule and stick to it.

Tips to Overcome Writer's Block
1. Write freely
2. Use brainstorming
3. Realize it's a first draft
4. Read reference materials
5. Break up assignment
6. Find a good place to write
7. Beware of procrastination

Edit and Revise

The editing and revising stage allows you to take a critical look at what you have written. It takes some courage to do this step. Once people see their ideas in writing, they become attached to them. With careful editing and revising, you can turn in your best work and be proud of your accomplishments. Here are some tips for editing and revising:

1. **Read your paper as if you were the audience.** Pretend that you are the instructor or another person reading your paper. Does every sentence make sense? Did you say what you meant to say? Read what you have written, and the result will be a more effective paper.

© Madhourses/Shutterstock.com

2. **Read paragraph by paragraph.** Does each paragraph have a main idea and supporting details? Do the paragraphs fit logically together? Use the cut-and-paste feature on your computer to move sentences and paragraphs around if needed.

3. **Check your grammar and spelling.** Use the spell check and grammar check on your computer. These tools are helpful, but they are not thorough enough. The spell check will pick up only misspelled words. It will skip words that are spelled correctly but not the intended word—for example, if you use "of" instead of "on" or "their" instead of "there." To find such errors, you need to read your paper after doing a spell check.

4. **Check for language that is biased in terms of gender, disability, or ethnic group.** Use words that are gender neutral. If a book or paper uses only the pronoun "he" or "she," half of the population is left out. You can often avoid sexist language by using the plural forms of nouns:

(singular)   The successful student knows *his* values and sets goals for the future.

(plural)   Successful students know *their* values and set goals for the future.

After all, we are trying to make the world a better place, with opportunity for all. Here are some examples of biased language and better alternatives.

Biased Language	*Better Alternatives*
policeman	police officer
chairman	chair
fireman	firefighter
postman	mail carrier
mankind	humanity
manmade	handcrafted
housewife	homemaker

5. **Have someone else read your paper.** Ask your reader to check for clarity and meaning. After you have read your paper many times, you do not really see it anymore. If you need assistance in writing, colleges offer tutoring or writing labs where you can get help with editing and revising.

6. **Review your introduction and conclusion.** They should be clear, interesting, and concise. The introduction and conclusion are the most powerful parts of your paper.

Tips for Editing and Revising

1. Read your paper objectively
2. Read paragraph by paragraph
3. Check grammar and spelling
4. Check for biased language
5. Have someone else read your paper
6. Review the introduction and conclusion
7. Prepare final copy
8. Prepare title page

7. **Prepare the final copy.** Check your instructor's instructions on the format required. If there are no instructions, use the following format:

- Use double-spacing.
- Use 10- or 12-point font.
- Use one-inch margins on all sides.
- Use a three-inch top margin on the first page.
- Single-space footnotes and endnotes.
- Number your pages.

8. **Prepare the title page.** Center the title of your paper and place it one third of the page from the top. On the bottom third of the page, center your name, the professor's name, the name of the class, and the date.

Final Steps

Make sure you follow instructions about using a folder or cover for your paper. Generally professors dislike bulky folders or notebooks because they are difficult to carry. Imagine your professor trying to carry 50 notebooks to his or her office! Unless asked to do so, do not use plastic page protectors. Professors like to write comments on papers, and it is extremely difficult to write on papers with page protectors.

If you are submitting your paper online, check to make sure you have submitted the correct document and that is was successfully uploaded.

Turning your paper in on time is very important. Some professors do not accept late papers. Others subtract points if your paper is late. Put your paper in the car or someplace where you will have to see it before you go to class. **Then reward yourself for a job well done!**

Journal Entry #3

Write five intention statements about improving your writing. While thinking about your statements, consider the steps of POWER writing: prepare, organize, write, edit, and revise. Do you need to work on problems such as writer's block or getting your writing done on time? I intend to . . .

Effective Public Speaking

You may need to take a speech class in order to graduate from college, and many of your classes will require oral presentations. Being a good speaker can contribute to your success on the job as well. A study done at Stanford University showed that one of the top predictors of success in professional positions was the ability to be a good public speaker.[2] You will need to present information to your boss, your colleagues, and your customers or clients.

"Let us think of education as the means of developing our greatest abilities, because in each of us there is a private hope and dream which, fulfilled, can be translated into greater benefit for everyone and greater strength for our nation."
John F. Kennedy

© Sanjay Deva/Shutterstock.com

Learn to Relax

Students often panic when they find out that they have to make a speech. Good preparation can help you to feel confident about your oral presentation. Professional speaker Lilly Walters believes that you can deal with 75 percent of your anxiety by being well prepared.[3] You can deal with the remaining 25 percent by using some relaxation techniques.

- If you are anxious, admit to yourself that you are anxious. If it is appropriate, as in a beginning speech class, you can even admit to the audience that you are anxious. Once you have admitted that you are anxious, visualize yourself confidently making the speech.
- You do not have to be perfect; it is okay to make mistakes. Making mistakes just shows you are human like the rest of us.
- If you are anxious before your speech, take three to five deep breaths. Breathe in slowly and hold your breath for five seconds, and then breathe out slowly. Focus your mind on your breathing rather than your speech.
- Use positive self-talk to help you to relax. Instead of saying to yourself, "I will look like a fool up there giving the speech," tell yourself, "I can do this" or "It will be okay."
- Once you start speaking, anxiety will generally decline.
- With experience, you will gain confidence in your speaking ability and will be able to relax more easily.

Preparing and Delivering Your Speech

Write the Beginning of the Speech

The beginning includes a statement of your objective and what your speech will be about. It should prepare the audience for what comes next. You can begin your speech with a personal experience, a quote, a news article, or a joke. Jokes can be effective, but they are risky. Try out your joke with your friends to make sure that it is funny. Do not tell jokes that put down other people or groups.

Write the Main Body of the Speech

The main body of the speech consists of four or five main points. Just as in your term paper, state your main points and then provide details, examples, or stories that illustrate them. As you present the main points of your speech, consider your audience. Your speech will be different depending on whether it is made to a group of high school students, your college classmates, or a group of professionals. You can add interest to your speech by using props, pictures, charts, PowerPoint, music, or video clips. College students today are increasingly using PowerPoint software to make classroom presentations. If you are planning to enter a professional career, learning how to make PowerPoint presentations will be an asset.

Write the Conclusion

In your conclusion, summarize and review the key points of your speech. The conclusion is like the icing on a cake. It should be strong, persuasive, and interesting. Invest some time in your ending statement. It can be a call to action, a recommendation for the future, a quote, or a story.

Practice Your Speech

Practice your speech until you feel comfortable with it. Prepare a memory system or notes to help you deliver your speech. You will want to make eye contact with your audience, which is difficult if you are trying to read your speech. A memory system useful for delivering speeches is the loci system. Visualize a house, for example: the entryway is the introduction, and each room represents a main point in the speech. Visualize walking into each room and what you will say in each room. Each room can have items that remind you of what you are going to say. At the conclusion, you say good-bye at the door. Another technique is to prepare brief notes or outlines on index cards or sheets of paper. When you are practicing your speech, time it to see how long it is. Keep your speech within the time allowed. Most people tend to speak longer than necessary.

Review the Setup

If you are using props, make sure that you have them ready. If you are using equipment, make sure it is available and in working condition. Make arrangements in advance for the equipment you need and, if possible, check to see that it is running properly right before your presentation.

Deliver the Speech

Wear clothes that make you feel comfortable, but not out of place. Remember to smile and make eye contact with members of the audience. Take a few deep breaths if you are nervous. You will probably be less nervous once you begin. If you make a mistake, keep your sense of humor. I recall the famous chef Julia Child doing a live television production on how to cook a turkey. As she took the turkey out of the oven, it slipped and landed on the floor right in front of the television cameras. She calmly picked it up and said, "And remember that you are the only one that really knows what goes on in the kitchen." It was one of the shows that made her famous.

Writing and Speaking

Test what you have learned by selecting the correct answers to the following questions.

1. To make sure to get your paper done on time,

    a. have someone remind you of the deadline.
    b. write the due date on your calendar and the date for completion of each step.
    c. write your paper just before the due date to increase motivation.

2. The thesis statement is the

    a. most important sentence in each paragraph.
    b. key idea in the paper.
    c. summary of the paper.

3. If you have writer's block, it is helpful to

    a. delay writing your paper until you feel relaxed.
    b. make sure that your writing is perfect from the beginning.
    c. begin with brainstorming or free writing.

4. No college paper is complete without

    a. the references.
    b. a professional-looking cover.
    c. printing on quality paper.

5. You can deal with most of your anxiety about public speaking by

    a. striving for perfection.
    b. visualizing your anxiety.
    c. being well prepared.

How did you do on the quiz? Check your answers: 1. b, 2. b, 3. c, 4. a, 5. c

Journal Entry #4

Write one paragraph giving advice to a new college student on how to make a speech. Use any of these questions to guide your thinking:

- What are some ways to deal with anxiety about public speaking?
- How can you make your speech interesting?
- What are some steps in preparing a speech?
- What are some ideas that don't work?

KEYS TO SUCCESS

Be Selective

Psychologist and philosopher William James said, "The essence of genius is knowing what to overlook."[4] This saying has a variety of meanings. In reading, note taking, marking a college textbook, and writing, it is important to be able to pick out the main points first and then identify the supporting details. Imagine you are trying to put together a jigsaw puzzle. You bought the puzzle at a garage sale and all the pieces are there, but the lid to the box with the picture of the puzzle is missing. It will be very difficult, if not impossible, to put this puzzle together. Reading, note taking, marking, and writing are very much like putting a puzzle together. First you will need an understanding of the main ideas (the big picture) and then you can focus on the details.

How can you get the overall picture? When reading, you can get the overall picture by skimming the text. As you skim the text, you get a general outline of what the chapter contains and what you will learn. In note taking, actively listen for the main ideas and write them down in your notes. In marking your text, try to pick out about 20 percent of the most important material and underline or highlight it. In writing, think about what is most important, write your thesis statement, and then provide the supporting details.

To select what is most important, be courageous, think, and analyze.

Does this mean that you should forget about the details? No, you will need to know some details too. The supporting details help you to understand and assess the value of the main idea. They help you to understand the relationship between ideas. Being selective means getting the general idea first, and then the details will make sense to you and you will be able to remember them. The main ideas are like scaffolding or a net that holds the details in some kind of framework so you can remember them. If you focus on the details first, you will have no framework or point of reference for remembering them.

Experiment with the idea of being selective in your personal life. If your schedule is impossibly busy, be selective and choose to do the most important or most valuable activities. This takes some thinking and courage too. If your desk drawer is stuffed with odds and ends and you can never find what you are looking for, take everything out and only put back what you need. Recycle, give away, or throw away surplus items around the house. You can take steps toward being a genius by being selective and taking steps to simplify and organize your life and your work.

Journal Entry #5

How can being selective help you achieve success in college and in life? Use any of these questions to guide your thinking:

- How can being selective help you to be a better note taker, writer, or speaker?

- How can being selective help you to manage your time and your life?

- What is the meaning of this quote by William James: "The essence of genius is knowing what to overlook?"

© Lyudmyla Kharlamova/
Shutterstock.com

College Success 1

The College Success 1 website is continually updated with supplementary material for each chapter including Word documents of the journal entries, classroom activities, handouts, videos, links to related materials, and much more. See http://www.collegesuccess1.com/.

Notes

1. Paul Nolting, *Winning at Math*, (Bradenton, FL: Academic Success Press, 2014), 139.

2. T. Allesandra and P. Hunsaker, *Communicating at Work* (New York: Fireside, 1993), 169.

3. Lilly Walters, *Secrets of Successful Speakers: How You Can Motivate, Captivate, and Persuade* (New York: McGraw-Hill, 1993), 203.

4. Quoted in Rob Gilbert, ed., *Bits and Pieces*, August 12, 1999, 15.

Note-Taking Checklist

Name _____ Date _____

Place a checkmark next to the note-taking skills you have now.

_____ I attend every (or almost every) lecture in all my classes.

_____ I check the syllabus to find out what is being covered before I go to class.

_____ I read or at least skim through the reading assignment before attending the lecture.

_____ I attend lectures with a positive attitude about learning as much as possible.

_____ I am well rested so that I can focus on the lecture.

_____ I eat a light, nutritious meal before going to class.

_____ I sit in a location where I can see and hear easily.

_____ I have a laptop or a three-ring binder, looseleaf paper, and a pen for taking notes.

_____ I avoid external distractions (friends, sitting by the door).

_____ I am alert and able to concentrate on the lecture.

_____ I have a system for taking notes that works for me.

_____ I am able to determine the key ideas of the lecture and write them down in my notes.

_____ I can identify signal words that help to understand key points and organize my notes.

_____ I can write quickly using telegraphic sentences, abbreviations, and symbols.

_____ If I don't understand something in the lecture, I ask a question and get help.

_____ I write down everything written on the board or on visual materials used in the class.

_____ I review my notes immediately after class.

_____ I have intermediate review sessions to review previous notes.

_____ I use my notes to predict questions for the exam.

_____ I have clear and complete notes that help me to prepare adequately for exams.

Evaluate Your Note-Taking Skills

Name _____   Date _____

Use the note-taking checklist on the previous page to answer these questions.

1. Look at the items that you checked. What are your strengths in note taking?

2. What are some areas that you need to improve?

3. Write at least three intention statements about improving your listening and note-taking skills.

Assess Your College Writing Skills

Name _____ Date _____

Read the following statements and rate how true they are for you at the present time. Use the following scale:

5 Definitely true
4 Mostly true
3 Somewhat true
2 Seldom true
1 Never true

_____ I am generally confident in my writing skills.

_____ I have a system for reminding myself of due dates for writing projects.

_____ I start writing projects early so that I am not stressed by finishing them at the last minute.

_____ I have the proper materials and a space to write comfortably.

_____ I know how to use the library and the Internet to gather information for a term paper.

_____ I can write a thesis statement for a term paper.

_____ I know how to organize a term paper.

_____ I know how to write the introduction, body, and conclusion of a paper.

_____ I can cite references in the appropriate style for my subject.

_____ I know where to find information about citing material in APA, MLA, or Chicago style.

_____ I know what plagiarism is and know how to avoid it.

_____ I can deal with "writer's block" and get started on my writing project.

_____ I know how to edit and revise a paper.

_____ I know where I can get help with my writing.

_____ **Total**

60–70   You have excellent writing skills, but can always learn new ideas.

50–59   You have good writing skills, but there is room for improvement.

Below 50   You need to improve writing skills. The skills presented in this chapter will help. Consider taking a writing class early in your college studies.

Thinking about Writing

Name _____ Date _____

List 10 suggestions from this chapter that could help you improve your writing skills.

1.

2.

3.

4.

5.

6.

7.

8.

9.

10.

CHAPTER 9

Test Taking

Learning Objectives

Read to answer these key questions:

- What are some test preparation techniques?

- How should I review the material?

- How can I predict the test questions?

- What are some emergency test preparation techniques?

- How can I deal with test anxiety?

- How can I overcome math anxiety and be successful on math tests?

- What are some tips for taking math tests?

- What are some tips for taking objective tests?

- How can I write a good essay?

An important skill for survival in college is the ability to take tests. Passing tests is also important in careers that require licenses, certificates, or continuing education. Knowing how to prepare for and take tests with confidence will help you to accomplish your educational and career goals while maintaining your good mental health. Once you have learned some basic test-taking and relaxation techniques, you can turn your test anxiety into motivation and good test results.

Preparing for Tests

Attend Every Class

The most significant factor in poor performance in college is lack of attendance. Students who attend the lectures and complete their assignments have the best chance for success in college. Attending the lectures helps you to be involved in learning and to know what to expect on the test. College professors know that students who miss three classes in a row are not likely to return, and some professors drop students after three absences. After three absences, students can fall behind in their schoolwork and become overwhelmed with makeup work.

© Robert Kneschke/Shutterstock.com

Distribute the Practice

The key to successful test preparation is to begin early and do a little at a time. Test preparation begins the first day of class. During the first class, the professor gives an overview of the course content, requirements, tests, and grading. These items are described in writing in the class calendar and syllabus. It is very important to attend the first class to obtain this essential information. If you have to miss the first class, make sure to ask the professor for the syllabus and calendar and read it carefully.

Early test preparation helps you to take advantage of the powerful memory technique called distributed practice. In distributed practice, the material learned is broken up into small parts and reviewed frequently. Using this method can enable you to learn a large quantity of material without becoming overwhelmed. Here are some examples of using distributed practice:

- If you have a test on 50 Spanish vocabulary words in two weeks, don't wait until the day before the test to try to learn all 50 words. Waiting until the day before the test will result in difficulty remembering the words, test anxiety, and a dislike of studying

Spanish. If you have 50 Spanish vocabulary words to learn in two weeks, learn five words each day and quickly review the words you learned previously. For example, on Monday you would learn five words, and on Tuesday, you would learn five new words and review the ones learned on Monday. Give yourself the weekends off as a reward for planning ahead.

- If you have to read a history book with 400 pages, divide that number by the number of days in the semester or quarter. If there are 80 days in the semester, you will only have to read five pages per day or 10 pages every other day. This is a much easier and more efficient way to master a long assignment.

- Don't wait until the last minute to study for a midterm or final exam. Keep up with the class each week. As you read each chapter, quickly review a previous chapter. In this way you can comfortably master the material. Just before a major test, you can review the material that you already know and feel confident about your ability to get a good grade on the test.

Schedule a Time and a Place for Studying

To take advantage of distributed practice, you will need to develop a study schedule. Write down your work time and school time and other scheduled activities. Identify times that can be used for studying each day. Get in the habit of using these available times for studying each week. As a general rule, you need two hours of study time for each hour spent in a college classroom. If you cannot find enough time for studying, consider either reducing your course load or reducing work hours.

Use your study schedule or calendar to note the due dates of major projects and all test dates. Schedule enough time to complete projects and to finish major reviews for exams. Look at each due date and write in reminders to begin work or review well in advance of the due date. Give yourself plenty of time to meet the deadlines. It seems that around exam time, students are often ill or have problems that prevent them from being successful. Having some extra time scheduled will help you to cope with the many unexpected events that happen in everyday life.

Find a place to study. This can be an area of your home where you have a desk, computer, and all the necessary supplies for studying. As a general rule, do not study at the kitchen table, in front of the television, or in your bed. These places provide powerful cues for eating, watching television, or sleeping instead of studying. If you cannot find an appropriate place at home, use the college library as a place to study. The library is usually quiet and others are studying, so there are not too many distractions. Studying in different places can aid in recall.

© Alexander Raths/Shutterstock.com

"I can accept failure. Everyone fails at something. But I can't accept not trying."
Michael Jordan

Test Review Tools

There are a variety of tools you can use to review for tests. Choose the tools according to personal preference and the type of test for which you are preparing.

- **Flash cards.** Flash cards are an effective way to learn facts and details for objective tests such as true-false, multiple-choice, matching, and fill-in-the-blank. For example, if you have 100 vocabulary words to learn in biology, put each word on one side of a card and the definition on the other side. First, look at each definition and see if you can recall the word. It is helpful to visualize the word and even say it out loud. Carry the cards with you and briefly look at them as you are going about your daily activities. Make a game of studying by sorting the cards into stacks of information you know and those you still have to practice. Work with the flash cards frequently and review them quickly. Don't worry about learning all the items at once. Each day that you practice, you will recall the items more easily. You can also use online tools such as Quizlet (https://quizlet.com/) for making flashcards.

- **Summary sheets.** Summary sheets are used to record the key ideas from your lecture notes or textbook. It is important to be selective; write only the most important ideas on the summary sheets. At the end of the semester, you might have approximately 10 pages of summary sheets from the text and 10 pages from your notes.

- **Mind maps.** A mind map is a visual picture of the items you wish to remember. Start in the center of the page with a key idea and then surround it with related topics. You can use drawings, lines, circles, or colors to link and group the ideas. A mind map will help you to learn material in an organized way that will be useful when writing essay exams.

- **Study groups.** A study group is helpful in motivating yourself to learn through discussions of the material with other people. For the study group, select three to seven people who are motivated to be successful in class and can coordinate schedules. Study groups are often used in math and science classes. Groups of students work problems together and help each other understand the material. The study group is also useful in studying for exams. Give each member a part of the material to be studied. Have each person predict test questions and quiz the study group. Teaching the material to the study group can be the best way to learn it.

Reviewing Effectively

Begin your review early and break it into small parts. Remember that repetition is one of the effective ways to store information in long-term memory. Here are some types of review that help you to store information in long-term memory:

- **Immediate review.** This type of review is fast and powerful and helps to minimize forgetting. It is the first step in storing information in long-term memory. Begin the process by turning each bold-faced heading in the text into a question. Read each section to answer the question you have asked. Read your college texts with a highlighter in hand so that you can mark the key ideas for review. Some students use a variety of colors to distinguish main ideas, supporting points, and key examples, for instance. When you are finished using the highlighter, quickly review the items you have marked. As you complete each section, quickly review the main points. When you finish the chapter, immediately review the key points in the entire chapter again. As soon as you finish taking your lecture notes, take a few minutes to review them.

© wavebreakmedia/Shutterstock.com

To be most effective, immediate review needs to occur as soon as possible or at least within the first 20 minutes of learning something.

- **Intermediate review.** After you have finished reading and reviewing a new chapter in your textbook, spend a few minutes reviewing an earlier one. This step will help you to master the material and to recall it easily for the midterm or final exam. Another way to do intermediate review is to set up time periodically in your study schedule for reviewing previous chapters and classroom notes. Doing intermediate reviews helps to access the materials you have stored in long-term memory.

- **Final review.** Before a major exam, organize your notes, materials, and assignments. Estimate how long it will take you to review the material. Break the material into manageable chunks. For an essay exam, use mind maps or summary sheets to write down the main points that you need to remember and recite these ideas frequently. For objective tests, use flash cards or lists to remember details and concepts that you expect to be on the test. Here is a sample seven-day plan for reviewing 10 chapters for a final exam:

Day 1 Gather materials and study Chapters 1 and 2 by writing key points on summary sheets or mind maps. Make flash cards of details you need to remember. Review and highlight lecture notes and handouts on these chapters.

Day 2 Review Chapters 1 and 2. Study Chapters 3 and 4 and the corresponding lecture notes.

Day 3 Review Chapters 1 to 4. Study Chapters 5 and 6 and the corresponding lecture notes.

Day 4 Review Chapters 1 to 6. Study Chapters 7 and 8 along with the corresponding lecture notes.

Day 5 Review Chapters 1 to 8. Study Chapters 9 and 10 along with corresponding lecture notes.

Day 6 Review notes, summary sheets, mind maps, and flash cards for Chapters 1 to 10. Relax and get a good night's sleep. You are well prepared.

Day 7 Do one last quick review of Chapters 1 to 10 and walk into the test with the confidence that you will be successful on the exam.

Predicting Test Questions

There are many ways to predict the questions that will be on the test. Here are some ideas that might be helpful:

- Look for clues from the professor about what will be on the test. Many times professors put information about the tests on the course syllabus. During lectures, they often give hints about what will be important to know. If a professor repeats something more than once, make note of it as a possible test question. Anything written on the board is likely to be on the test. Sometimes the professor will even say, "This will be on the test." Write these important points in your notes and review them.

- College textbooks are usually written in short sections with bold headings. Turn each bold-faced heading into a question and read to answer the question. Understand and review the main idea in each section. The test questions will generally address the main ideas in the text.

- Don't forget to study and review the handouts that the professor distributes to the class. If the professor has taken the time and effort to provide extra material, it is probably important and may be on the test.

- Form a study group and divide up the material to be reviewed. Have each member of the group write some test questions based on the important points in each main section of the text. When the study group meets, take turns asking likely test questions and providing the answers.

- When the professor announces the test, make sure to ask what material is to be covered on the test and what kind of test it is. If necessary, ask the professor which concepts are most important. Know what kinds of test questions will be asked (essay, true-false, multiple-choice, matching, or short-answer). Some professors may provide sample exams or math problems.

- Use the first test to understand what is expected and how to study for future tests.

Journal Entry # 1

Write one paragraph about the ideal way to prepare for a major exam such as a midterm or final. Consider these factors while thinking about your answer: attendance, distribute the practice, time management, review tools, predicting test questions and the most efficient way to review.

Preparing for an Open-Book Test

In college, you may have some open-book tests. Open-book tests are often used in very technical subjects where specific material from the book is needed to answer questions. For example, in an engineering course, tables and formulas in the book may be needed to solve engineering problems on an exam. To study for an open-book test, focus on understanding the material and being able to locate key information for the exam. Consider making index tabs for your book so that you can locate needed information quickly. Be sure to bring your book, calculator, and other needed material to the exam.

Emergency Procedures

If it is a day or two before the test and you have not followed the above procedures, it is time for the college practice known as "cramming." There are two main problems that result from this practice. First, you cannot take advantage of distributed practice, so it

© Mike Elliott/Shutterstock.com

will be difficult to remember large amounts of material. Within a week, you are likely to forget 75% of the material you learned while cramming.[1] It requires much effort and results in little benefit. Second, it is not fun and, if done often, will result in anxiety and a dislike of education. Because of these problems, some students who rely on cramming wrongly conclude that they are not capable of finishing their education.

If you must cram for a test, here are some emergency procedures that may be helpful in getting the best grade possible under difficult circumstances:

- When cramming, **it is most important to be selective.** Try to identify the main points and recite and review them.

- Focus on reviewing and reciting the lecture notes. In this way, you will cover the main ideas the professor thinks are important.

- If you have not read the text, skim and search each chapter looking for the main points. Highlight and review these main points. Read the chapter summaries. In a math textbook, practice sample problems.

- Make summary sheets containing the main ideas from the notes and the text. Recite and review the summary sheets.

- For objective tests, focus on learning new terms and vocabulary related to the subject. These terms are likely to be on the test. Flash cards are helpful.

- For essay tests, develop an outline of major topics and review the outline so you can write an essay.

- Get enough rest. Staying up all night to review for the test can result in confusion, reduced mental ability, and test anxiety.

- Hope for the best.

- Plan ahead next time so that you can get a better grade.

If you have very little time to review for a test, you will probably experience information overload. One strategy for dealing with this problem is based on the work of George Miller of Harvard University. He found that the optimum number of chunks of information we can remember is seven plus or minus two (or five to nine chunks of information).[2] This is also known as the Magical Number Seven Theory. For this last-minute review technique, start with five sheets of paper. Next, identify five key concepts that are likely to be on the test. Write one concept on the top of each sheet of paper. Then check your notes and text to write an explanation, definition, or answer for each of these topics. If you have more time, find two to four more concepts and research them, writing the information on additional sheets. You should have no more than nine sheets of paper. Arrange the sheets in order of importance. Review and recite the key ideas on these sheets. Get a regular night's sleep before the test and do some relaxation exercises right before the test.

© YanLev/Shutterstock.com

Ideas That Don't Work

Some students do poorly on tests for the following reasons.

- Attending a party or social event the evening before a major test rather than doing the final review will adversely affect your test score. Study in advance and reward yourself with the party after the test.

- Skipping the major review before the test may cause you to forget some important material.

- Taking drugs or drinking alcohol before a test may give you the impression that you are relaxed and doing well on the test, but the results are disastrous to your success on the exam and your good health.

- Not knowing the date of the test can cause you to get a low grade because you are not prepared.

- Not checking or knowing about the final exam schedule can cause you to miss the final.

- Missing the final exam can result in a lower grade or failing the class.

- Arriving late for the exam puts you at a disadvantage if you don't have time to finish or have to rush through the test.

- Deciding not to buy or read the textbook will cause low performance or failure.

- Having a fight, disagreement, or argument with parents, friends, or significant others before the test will make it difficult to focus on the exam.

- Sacrificing sleep, exercise, or food to prepare for the exam makes it difficult to do your best.

- Cheating on an exam can cause embarrassment, a lower grade, or failure. It can even lead to expulsion from college.

- Missing the exam because you are not prepared and asking the professor to let you make up the exam later is a tactic that many students try. Most professors will not permit you to take an exam late.

- Inventing a creative excuse for missing an exam is so common that some professors have a collection of these stories that they share with colleagues. Creative excuses don't work with most professors.

- Arriving at the exam without the proper materials such as a pencil, Scantron, paper, calculator, or book (for open-book exams) can cause you to miss the exam or start the exam late.

Test Preparation

Test what you have learned by selecting the correct answers to the following questions.

1. In test preparation, it is important to use this memory technique:

   a. Distribute the practice.
   b. Read every chapter just before the test.
   c. Do most of the review right before the test to minimize forgetting.

2. To take advantage of distributed practice, it is important to develop a:

   a. summary sheet.
   b. study schedule.
   c. mind map.

3. Effective tools to learn facts and details are

   a. mind maps.
   b. summary sheets.
   c. flash cards.

4. The best way to review is

   a. to start early and break it into small parts.
   b. immediately before the test.
   c. in large blocks of time.

5. If you have to cram for an exam, it is most important to

   a. stay up all night studying for the exam
   b. focus on the lecture notes and forget about reading the text
   c. be selective and review and recite the main points

How did you do on the quiz? Check your answers: 1. a, 2. b, 3. c, 4. a, 5. c

Ten Rules for Success

Here are 10 rules for success on any test. Are there any new ideas you can put into practice?

1. **Make sure to set your alarm,** and consider having a backup in case your alarm doesn't go off. Set a second alarm or have someone call to make sure you are awake on time.

2. **Arrive a little early for your exam.** If you are taking a standardized test like the Scholastic Aptitude Test (SAT) or Graduate Record Exam (GRE), familiarize yourself with the location of the exam. If you arrive early, you can take a quick walk around the building to relax or spend a few minutes doing a review so that your brain will be tuned up and ready.

3. **Eat a light breakfast including some carbohydrates and protein.** Be careful about eating sugar and caffeine before a test, because this can contribute to greater anxiety and low blood sugar by the time you take the test. The worst breakfast would be something like a doughnut and coffee or a soda and candy bar. Examples of good breakfasts are eggs, toast, and juice or cereal with milk and fruit.

4. **Think positively about the exam.** Tell yourself that you are well prepared and the exam is an opportunity to show what you know.

5. **Make sure you have the proper materials:** Scantrons, paper, pencil or pen, calculator, books and notes (for open-book exams).

6. **Manage your time.** Know how long you have for the test and then scan the test to make a time management plan. For example, if you have one hour and there are 50 objective questions, you have about a minute for each question. Halfway through the time, you should have completed 25 questions. If there are three essay questions in an hour, you have less than 20 minutes for each question. Save some time to look over the test and make corrections.

7. **Neatness is important.** If your paper looks neat, the professor is more likely to have a positive attitude about the paper before it is even read. If the paper is hard to read, the professor will start reading your paper with a negative attitude, possibly resulting in a lower grade.

8. **Read the test directions carefully.** On essay exams, it is common for the professor to give you a choice of questions to answer. If you do not read the directions, you may try to answer all of the questions and then run out of time or give incomplete answers to them.

9. **If you get stuck on a difficult question, don't worry about it.** Just mark it and find an easier question. You may find clues on the rest of the test that will aid your recall, or you may be more relaxed later on and think of the answer.

10. **Be careful not to give any impression that you might be cheating.** Keep your eyes on your own paper. If you have memory aids or outlines memorized, write them directly on the test paper rather than a separate sheet so that you are not suspected of using cheat notes.

Journal Entry #2

Write one paragraph about the most common mistakes students make while getting ready for an exam.

Dealing with Test Anxiety

Some anxiety is a good thing. It can provide motivation to study and prepare for exams. However, it is common for college students to suffer from test anxiety. Too much anxiety can lower your performance on tests. Some symptoms of test anxiety include:

"Luck is what happens when preparation meets opportunity."

Darrell Royal

- Fear of failing a test even though you are well prepared
- Physical symptoms such as perspiring, increased heart rate, shortness of breath, upset stomach, tense muscles, or headache
- Negative thoughts about the test and your grade
- Mental blocking of material you know and remembering it once you leave the exam

You can minimize your test anxiety by being well prepared and by applying the memory strategies described in earlier chapters. Prepare for your exams by attending every class, keeping up with your reading assignments, and reviewing during the semester. These steps will help increase your self-confidence and reduce anxiety. Apply the principles of memory improvement to your studying. As you are reading, find the important points and highlight them. Review these points so that they are stored in your long-term memory. Use distributed practice and spread out learning over time rather than trying to learn it all at once. Visualize and organize what you need to remember. Trust in your abilities and intend to remember what you have studied.

If you find that you are anxious, here are some ideas you can try to cope with the anxiety. Experiment with these techniques to see which ones work best for you.

© Stuart Miles/Shutterstock.com

- **Do some physical exercise.** Physical exercise helps to use up stress hormones. Make physical activity a part of your daily routine. Arrive for your test a little early and walk briskly around campus for about 20 minutes. This exercise will help you to feel relaxed and energized.

- **Get a good night's sleep before the test.** Lack of sleep can interfere with memory and cause irritability, anxiety, and confusion.

- **Take deep breaths.** Immediately before the test, take a few deep breaths; hold them for three to five seconds and let them out slowly. These deep breaths will help you to relax and keep a sufficient supply of oxygen in your blood. Oxygen is needed for proper brain function.

- **Visualize and rehearse your success.** Begin by getting as comfortable and relaxed as possible in your favorite chair or lying down in bed. Visualize yourself walking into the exam room. Try to imagine the room in as much detail as possible. If possible, visit the exam room before the test so that you can get a good picture of it. See yourself taking the exam calmly and confidently. You know most of the answers. If you find a question you do not know, see yourself circling it and coming back to it later. Imagine that you find a clue on the test that triggers your recall of the answers to the difficult questions. Picture yourself handing in the exam with a good feeling about doing well on the test. Then imagine you are getting the test back and you get a good grade on the test. You congratulate yourself for a job well done. If you suffer from test anxiety, you may need to rehearse this scene several times. When you enter the exam room, the visual picture that you have rehearsed will help you to relax.

- **Acknowledge your anxiety.** The first step in dealing with anxiety is to admit that you are anxious rather than trying to fight it or deny it. Say to yourself, "I am feeling anxious." Take a few deep breaths and then focus your attention on the test.

- **Do the easy questions first and mark the ones that may be difficult.** This will help you to relax. Once you are relaxed, the difficult questions become more manageable.

Tips to Minimize Anxiety

- Exercise
- Sleep
- Take deep breaths
- Visualize success
- Acknowledge anxiety
- Easy questions first
- Yell, "Stop!"
- Daydream
- Practice perspective
- Give yourself time
- Get help

- **Yell, "Stop!"** Negative and frightening thoughts can cause anxiety. Here are some examples of negative thoughts:

> I'm going to fail this test.
>
> I don't know the answer to number 10!
>
> I never do well on tests.
>
> Essays! I have a hard time with those.
>
> I'll never make it through college.
>
> I was never any good in math!

These types of thoughts don't help you do better on the test, so stop saying them. They cause you to become anxious and to freeze up during the test. If you find yourself with similar thoughts, yell, "Stop!" to yourself. This will cause you to interrupt your train of thought so that you can think about the task at hand rather than becoming more anxious. Replace negative thoughts with more positive ones such as these:

> I'm doing the best I can.
>
> I am well prepared and know most of the answers.
>
> I don't know the answer to number 10, so I'll just circle it and come back to it later.
>
> I'll make an outline in the margin for the essay question.
>
> College is difficult, but I'll make it!
>
> Math is a challenge, but I can do it!

- **Daydream.** Think about being in your favorite place. Take time to think about the details. Allow yourself to be there for a while until you feel more relaxed.
- **Practice perspective.** Remember, one poor grade is not the end of the world. It does not define who you are. If you do not do well, think about how you can improve your preparation and performance the next time.
- **Give yourself time.** Test anxiety develops over a period of time. It will take some time to get over it. Learn the best ways to prepare for the exam and practice saying positive thoughts to yourself.
- **Get help.** If these techniques do not work for you, seek help from your college health or counseling center.

Journal Entry #3

You have a friend who prepares for exams, but suffers from test anxiety. Review the section on test anxiety and write a one paragraph e-mail to your friend with some ideas on dealing with test anxiety. Consider both physical and mental preparation as well as some relaxation techniques that can be helpful.

I am taking a college success course and the book has some ideas on dealing with test anxiety. The book suggests . . .

Dealing with Math Anxiety

Math anxiety is a negative physical and/or emotional reaction toward math. It can lead to avoidance of math and procrastination in doing your math homework. It is often caused by negative experiences with math in elementary school or at home with parents helping with homework. Often students were embarrassed by being asked to solve a problem on the board and not being successful. Perhaps teachers, parents, siblings, or friends made negative comments about your math ability. It is important to think about the source of your math anxiety and then move on to new possibilities.

© Creativa Images/Shutterstock.com

Math anxiety is often related to low confidence in math. To build self-confidence, begin with positive thinking. You may have had difficulty with math in the past, but with a positive attitude and the proper study techniques, you can meet the challenge. The first step to success in math is to put in the effort required. Attend class, do your homework, and get help if needed. It is important to experience success, even in small steps, and build on your success. If you put in the effort and hard work, you will gain experience in math. If you gain experience with math, you will become more confident in your ability to do math. If you have confidence, you will gain satisfaction in doing math. You may even learn to like it! If you like the subject, you can gain competence. The process looks like this:

> "Do not worry about your difficulties in mathematics. I can assure you mine are still greater."
> Albert Einstein

Hard work → Experience → Confidence → Satisfaction → Competence

If you suffer from math anxiety, you can make an appointment to talk with your instructor, advisor, or counselor to find out what resources may be available to you. Although you may have had difficulty with math in the past, you can become successful by following these steps. Your reward is self-satisfaction and increased opportunity in technical, scientific, and professional careers. Math is required for graduation too.

Math Tests

Taking a math test involves some different strategies:

<aside>

Tips for Avoiding Common Math Errors[2]

- Any quantity multiplied by zero is zero
- Any quantity raised to the zero power is one
- Any fraction multiplied by its reciprocal is one
- Only like algebraic terms may be combined
- Break down to the simplest form in algebra
- In algebra, multiply and divide before adding and subtracting
- If an algebraic expression has more than one set of parentheses, get rid of the inner parenthesis first and work outward
- Any operation performed on one side of the equation must be performed on the other side

</aside>

1. Some instructors will let you write down formulas on an index card or a small crib sheet. Prepare these notes carefully, writing down the key formulas you will need for the exam.

2. If you have to memorize formulas, review them right before the test and write them on the test immediately.

3. As a first step, quickly look over the test. Find a problem you can solve easily and do this problem first.

4. Manage your time. Find out how many problems you have to solve and how much time is available for each problem. Do the problems worth the most points first. Stay on track.

5. Try this four-step process:
   a. Understand the problem.
   b. Devise a plan to solve the problem. Write down the information that is given. Think about the skills and techniques you have learned in class that can help you to solve the problem.
   c. Carry out the plan.
   d. Look back to see if your answer is reasonable.

6. If you cannot work a problem, go on to the next question. Come back later when you are more relaxed. If you spend too much time on a problem you cannot work, you will not have time for the problems that you can work.

7. Even if you think an answer is wrong, turn it in. You may get partial credit.

8. Show all the steps in your work and label your answer. On long and complex problems, it is helpful to use short sentences to explain your steps in solving the problem.

9. Estimate your answer and see if it makes sense or is logical.

10. Write your numbers as neatly as possible to avoid mistakes and to make them legible for the professor.

11. Leave space between your answers in case you need to add to them later.

12. Check for careless errors. Forgetting a plus or a minus sign or adding or subtracting incorrectly can have a big impact on your grade. Be sure to use all the time allowed for the test. Save at least five minutes at the end of your test to read over your test.

13. Build your confidence and reinforce your memory by doing a final review of the most important concepts and formulas right before you go to sleep. Do not learn new material right before sleeping since this could cause math anxiety.

14. Get enough sleep before the math test. Remember that you are missing 30% of your IQ points if you miss sleeping the night before the test. If you are mentally sharp, the test will be easier.

Journal Entry #4

You are enrolled in a math course that is required for graduation and want to make sure that you are successful in this course. List and briefly explain five ideas that will help you to be successful in this math course.

© Ivelin Radkov/Shutterstock.com

Taking Tests

True-False Tests

Many professors use objective tests such as true-false and multiple-choice because they are easy to grade. The best way to prepare for these types of tests is to study the key points in the textbook, lecture notes, and class handouts. In the textbook, take each bold-faced topic and turn it into a question. If you can answer the questions, you will be successful on objective tests.

In addition to studying for the test, it is helpful to understand some basic test-taking techniques that will help you to determine the correct answer. Many of the techniques used to determine whether a statement is true or false can also be used to eliminate wrong answers on multiple-choice tests.

To develop strategies for success on true-false exams, it is important to understand how a teacher writes the questions. For a true-false question, the teacher identifies a key point in the book or lecture notes. Then he or she has two choices. For a true statement, the key idea is often written exactly as it appears in the text or notes. For a false statement, the key idea is changed in some way to make it false.

One way to make a statement false is to add a **qualifier** to the statement. **Absolute** qualifiers often make a statement false. **General** qualifiers are often found in true statements.

Absolute Qualifiers (false)		General Qualifiers (true)	
all	none	usually	frequently
always	never	often	sometimes
only	nobody	some	seldom
invariably	no one	many	much
best	worst	most	generally
everybody	everyone	few	ordinarily
absolutely	absolutely not	probably	a majority
certainly	certainly not	might	a few
no	every	may	apt to

Seven Tips for Success on True-False Tests

1. **Identify the key ideas in the text and class notes and review them.**

2. **Accept the question at face value.** Don't overanalyze or create wild exceptions in your mind.

3. **If you don't know the answer, assume it is true.** There are generally more true statements because we all like the truth (especially teachers) and true questions are easier to write. However, some teachers like to test students by writing all false statements.

4. **If any part of a true-false statement is false, the whole statement is false.** Carefully read each statement to determine if any part of it is false. Students sometimes assume a statement is true if most of it is true. This is not correct.

   Example: Good relaxation techniques include deep breathing, exercise, and visualizing your failure on the exam.

   This statement is false because visualizing failure can lead to test anxiety and failure.

5. **Notice any absolute or general qualifiers.** Remember that absolute qualifiers often make a statement false. General qualifiers often make a statement true.

   Example: The student who crams **always** does poorly on the exam.

   This statement is false because **some** students are successful at cramming for an exam.

   Be careful with this rule. Sometimes the answer can be absolute.

   Example: The grade point average is always calculated by dividing the number of units attempted by the grade points. (true)

6. **Notice words such as *because, therefore, consequently,* and *as a result.*** They may connect two things that are true but result in a false statement.

   Example: Martha does not have test anxiety. (true)

   Martha makes good grades on tests. (true)

   Martha does not have test anxiety and therefore makes good grades on tests.

   This statement is false because she also has to prepare for the exam. Not having test anxiety could even cause her to lack motivation to study and do poorly on a test.

7. **Watch for double negatives.** Two nos equal a yes. If you see two negatives in a sentence, read them as a positive. Be careful with negative prefixes such as un-, im-, mis-, dis-, il-, and ir-. For example, the phrase "not uncommon" actually means "common." Notice that the word "not" and the prefix "un-" when used together form a double negative that equals a positive.

   Example: Not being **un**prepared for the test is the best way to earn good grades.

   The above sentence is confusing. To make it clearer, change both of the negatives into a positive:

   Being prepared for the test is the best way to earn good grades.

Practice True-False Test

Answer the following questions by applying the tips for success in the previous section. Place a T or an F in the blanks.

_____ **1.** If a statement has an absolute qualifier, it is always false.

_____ **2.** Statements with general qualifiers are frequently true.

_____ **3.** If you don't know the answer, you should guess true.

_____ **4.** Studying the key points for true-false tests is not unimportant.

_____ **5.** Good test-taking strategies include eating a light breakfast that includes carbohydrates and protein and drinking plenty of coffee to stay alert.

_____ **6.** Ryan attended every class this semester and therefore earned an A in the class.

How did you do on the test? Answers: 1. F, 2. T, 3. T, 4. T, 5. F, 6. F

Multiple-Choice Tests

College exams often include multiple-choice questions rather than true-false questions because it is more difficult to guess the correct answer. On a true-false question, the student has a 50 percent chance of guessing the correct answer, while on a multiple-choice question, the odds of guessing correctly are only 25 percent. You can think of a multiple-choice question as four true-false questions in a row. First, read the question and try to answer it without looking at the options. This will help you to focus on the question and determine the correct answer. Look at each option and determine if it is true or false. Then choose the **best** answer.

To choose the best option, it is helpful to understand how a teacher writes a multiple-choice question. Here are the steps a teacher uses to write a multiple-choice exam:

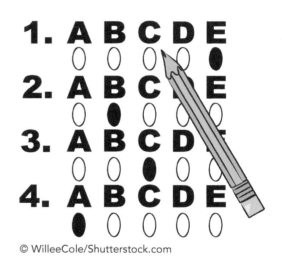

© WilleeCole/Shutterstock.com

1. Find an important point in the lecture notes, text, or handouts.

2. Write a **stem**. This is an incomplete statement or a question.

3. Write the correct answer as one of the options.

4. Write three or four plausible but incorrect options that might be chosen by students who are not prepared. These incorrect options are called **decoys**. Here is an example:

   Stem: If you are anxious about taking math tests, it is helpful to:

   a. Stay up the night before the test to review thoroughly. (**decoy**)

   b. Visualize yourself doing poorly on the test so you will be motivated to study. (**decoy**)

   c. Practice math problems regularly during the semester. (**correct answer**)

   d. Do the most difficult problem first. (**decoy**)

Courtesy of Charlotte Moore. © Kendall Hunt Publishing Company.

Being well prepared for the test is the most reliable way of recognizing the correct answer and the decoys. In addition, becoming familiar with the following rules for recognizing decoys can help you determine the correct answer or improve your chances of guessing the correct answer on an exam. If you can at least eliminate some of the wrong answers, you will improve your odds of selecting the correct answer.

Rules for recognizing a decoy or wrong answer:

1. **The decoys are all true or all false statements.** Read each option and determine which options are false and which statements are true. This will help you to find the correct answer.

   Example: To manage your time on a test, it is important to:

   a. Skip the directions and work as quickly as possible. (false)

   b. Skim through the test to see how much time you have for each section. (true)

   c. Do the most difficult sections first. (false)

   d. Just start writing as quickly as possible. (false)

   Read the stem carefully, because sometimes you will be asked to identify one false statement in a group of true statements.

2. **The decoy may contain an absolute qualifier.** The option with the absolute qualifier (e.g., always, only, every) is likely to be false because few things in life are absolute. There are generally exceptions to any rule.

3. **The decoy can be partly true.** However, if one part of the statement is false, the whole statement is false and an incorrect answer.

   Example: Memory techniques include visualization, organization, and telling yourself you won't remember.

   In this example, the first two techniques are true and the last part is false, which makes the whole statement false.

4. **The decoy may have a conjunction or other linking words that makes it false.** Watch for words and phrases such as *because, consequently, therefore,* and *as a result.*

5. **The decoy may have a double negative.** Having two negatives in a sentence makes it difficult to understand. Read the two negatives as a positive.

6. **The decoy may be a foolish option.** Writing multiple decoys is difficult, so test writers sometimes throw in foolish or humorous options.

   Example: In a multiple-choice test, a decoy is:

   a. a type of duck.

   b. an incorrect answer.

c. a type of missile used in air defense.

d. a type of fish.

The correct answer is b. Sometimes students are tempted by the foolish answers.

7. **The decoy is often a low or high number.** If you have a multiple-choice question with numbers, and you are not sure of the correct answer, choose the number in the middle range. It is often more likely to be correct.

Example: George Miller of Harvard University theorized that the optimum number of chunks of material that we can remember is:

a. 1–2 (This low number is a decoy.)

b. 5–9 (This is the correct answer.)

c. 10–12 (This is close to the correct answer.)

d. 20–25 (This high number is a decoy.)

There is an exception to this rule when the number is much higher or lower than the average person thinks is possible.

8. **The decoy may look like the correct answer.** When two options look alike, one is incorrect and the other may be the correct answer. Test writers often use words that look alike as decoys.

Example: In false statements, the qualifier is often:

a. absolute.

b. resolute.

c. general.

d. exaggerated.

The correct answer is a. Answer b is an incorrect look-alike option.

9. **Decoys are often shorter than the correct answer.** Longer answers are more likely to be correct because they are more complete. Avoid choosing the first answer that seems to be correct. There may be a better and more complete answer.

Example: Good test preparation involves:

a. doing the proper review for the test.

b. good time management.

c. a positive attitude.

d. having good attendance, studying and reviewing regularly, being able to deal with test anxiety, and having a positive mental attitude.

Option d is correct because it is the most complete and thus the best answer.

10. **Decoys may be grammatically incorrect.** The correct answer will fit the grammar of the stem. A stem ending with "a" will match an answer beginning with a consonant; stems ending with "an" will match a word beginning with a vowel. The answer will agree in gender, number, and person with the stem.

Example: In test taking, a decoy is an:

a. incorrect answer.

b. correct answer.

c. false answer.

d. true answer.

The correct answer is A. It is also the only answer that grammatically fits with the stem. Also note that decoys can be all true or all false. In standardized tests, the grammar is usually correct. On teacher-made tests, the grammar can be a clue to the correct answer.

11. **A decoy is sometimes an opposite.** When two options are opposites, one is incorrect and the other is sometimes, but not always, correct.

Example: A decoy is:

a. a right answer.

b. a wrong answer.

c. a general qualifier.

d. a true statement.

The two opposites are answers a and b. The correct answer is b.

12. **A decoy may be the same as another answer.** If two answers say the same thing in different ways, they are both decoys and incorrect.

Example: A true statement is likely to have this type of qualifier:

a. extreme

b. absolute

c. general

d. factual

Notice that answers a and b are the same and are incorrect. The correct answer is c.

Example: How much does a gallon of water weigh?

a. 8.34 pounds

b. 5.5 pounds

c. 5 pounds 8 ounces

d. 20 pounds

B and c are the same and are therefore incorrect answers. Answer d is a high number. The correct answer is a.

If you are unable to identify any decoys, these suggestions may be helpful:

- Mark the question and come back to it later. You may find the answer elsewhere on the test, or some words that help you remember the answer. After answering some easier questions, you may be able to relax and remember the answer.
- Trust your intuition and choose something that sounds familiar.
- Do not change your first answer unless you have misread the question or are sure that the answer is incorrect. Sometimes students overanalyze a question and then choose the wrong answer.
- The option "All of the above" is often correct because it is easier to write true statements rather than false ones. Options like A and B, B and D, or other combinations are also likely to be correct for the same reason.
- If you have no idea about the correct answer, guess option B or C. Most correct answers are in the middle.

© Peter Gyure/Shutterstock.com

Practice Multiple-Choice Test

Circle the letters of the correct answers. Then check your answers using the key at the end of this section.

1. The correct answer in a multiple-choice question is likely to be
   a. the shortest answer.
   b. the longest and most complete answer.
   c. the answer with an absolute qualifier.
   d. the answer that has some truth in it.

2. When guessing on a question involving numbers, it is generally best to
   a. choose the highest number.
   b. choose the lowest number.
   c. choose the mid-range number.
   d. always choose the first option.

3. If you have test anxiety, what questions should you answer first on the test?
   a. The most difficult questions
   b. The easiest questions
   c. The questions at the beginning
   d. The questions worth the least number of points

4. When taking a multiple-choice test, you should
   a. pick the first choice that is true.
   b. read all the choices and select the best one.
   c. pick the first choice that is false.
   d. choose the extreme answer.

5. A good method for guessing is to
   a. identify which choices are true and false.
   b. use the process of elimination.
   c. notice absolute qualifiers and conjunctions.
   d. all of the above.

6. The key to success when taking a multiple-choice test is
   a. cheating.
   b. good preparation.
   c. knowing how to guess.
   d. being able to recognize a qualifier.

(Continued)

7. The following rule about decoys is correct:
   a. A decoy is always absolute.
   b. A decoy can be partly true.
   c. Every decoy has a qualifier.
   d. Decoys are invariably false statements.

8. An example of an absolute qualifier is
   a. generally.
   b. never.
   c. sometimes.
   d. frequently.

9. Statements with absolute qualifiers are generally
   a. true.
   b. false.
   c. irrelevant.
   d. confusing.

10. If two multiple-choice options are the same or very similar, they are most likely
    a. a decoy and a correct answer.
    b. a correct answer.
    c. a true answer.
    d. a mistake on the test.

11. It is generally not a good idea to change your answer unless
    a. you are very anxious about the test.
    b. you do not have good intuition.
    c. you notice that your intelligent friend has a different answer.
    d. you have misread the question and you are sure that the answer is incorrect.

How did you do on the quiz? Check your answers: 1. b, 2. c, 3. b, 4. b, 5. d, 6. b, 7. b (Notice the absolute qualifiers in the decoys), 8. b, 9. b (Notice the opposites), 10. a (Notice the grammar), 11. d

Matching Tests

A matching test involves two lists of facts or definitions that must be matched together. Here are some tips to help you successfully complete a matching exam:

1. Read through both lists to discover the pattern or relationship between the lists. The lists might give words and definitions, people and accomplishments, or other paired facts.

2. Count the items on the list of answers to see if there is only one match for each item or if there are some extra answer choices.

3. Start with one list and match the items that you know. In this way, you have a better chance of guessing on the items that you do not know.

4. If you have difficulty with some of the items, leave them blank and return later. You may find the answers or clues on the rest of the test.

Practice Matching Test

Match the items in the first column with the items in the second column. Write the letter of the matching item in the blank at the left.

_____ 1.	Meaningful organization	**A.** Learn small amounts and review frequently.
_____ 2.	Visualization	**B.** The more you know, the easier it is to remember.
_____ 3.	Recitation	**C.** Tell yourself you will remember.
_____ 4.	Develop an interest	**D.** Pretend you like it.
_____ 5.	See the big picture	**E.** Make a mental picture.
_____ 6.	Intend to remember	**F.** Rehearse and review.
_____ 7.	Distribute the practice	**G.** Focus on the main points first.
_____ 8.	Create a basic background	**H.** Personal organization.

Answers: 1. H,   2. E,   3. F,   4. D,   5. G,   6. C,   7. A,   8. B

Sentence-Completion or Fill-in-the-Blank Tests

Fill-in-the-blank and sentence-completion tests are more difficult than true-false or multiple-choice tests because they require the **recall** of specific information rather than the **recognition** of the correct answer. To prepare for this type of test, focus on facts such as definitions, names, dates, and places. Using flash cards to prepare can be helpful. For example, to memorize names, place each name on one side of a card and some identifying words on the other side. Practice looking at the names on one side of the card and then recalling the identifying words on the other side of the card. Then turn the cards over and look at the identifying words to recall the names.

Sometimes the test has clues that will help you to fill in the blank. Clues can include the length of the blanks and the number of blanks. Find an answer that makes sense in the sentence and matches the grammar of the sentence. If you cannot think of an answer, write a general description and you may get partial credit. Look for clues on the rest of the test that may trigger your recall.

Practice Fill-in-the-Blank Test

Complete each sentence with the appropriate word or words.

1. Fill-in-the-blank tests are more difficult because they depend on the _____ of specific information.

2. On a true-false test, a statement is likely to be false if it contains an _____ qualifier.

3. Test review tools include _____, _____, and _____.

4. When studying for tests, visualize your _____.

Answers: 1. recall, 2. absolute, 3. flash cards, summary sheets, and mind maps (also study groups and highlighters), 4. success

Essay Tests

Many professors choose essay questions because they are the best way to show what you have learned in the class. Essay questions can be challenging because you not only have to know the material, but must be able to organize it and use good writing techniques in your answer.

© Lucky Business/Shutterstock.com

Essay questions contain key words that will guide you in writing your answer. One of the keys to success in writing answers to essay questions is to note these key words and then structure your essay accordingly. As you read through an essay question, look for these words:

Analyze	Break into separate parts and discuss, examine, or interpret each part.
Argue	State an opinion and give reasons for the opinion.
Comment	Give your opinion.
Compare	Identify two or more ideas and identify similarities and differences.
Contrast	Show how the components are the same or different.
Criticize	Give your opinion and make judgments.
Defend	State reasons.
Define	Give the meaning of the word or concept as used within the course of study.
Describe	Give a detailed account or provide information.
Demonstrate	Provide evidence.
Diagram	Make a drawing, chart, graph, sketch, or plan.
Differentiate	Tell how the ideas are the same and how they are different.
Describe	Make a picture with words. List the characteristics, qualities, and parts.
Discuss	Describe the pros and cons of the issues. Compare and contrast.
Enumerate	Make a list of ideas, events, qualities, reasons, and so on.
Explain	Make an idea clear. Show how and why.
Evaluate	Describe it and give your opinion about something.
Illustrate	Give concrete examples and explain them. Draw a diagram.
Interpret	Say what something means. Describe and then evaluate.
Justify	Prove a point. Give the reasons why.
Outline	Describe the main ideas.
Prove	Support with facts. Give evidence or reasons.
Relate	Show the connections between ideas or events.
State	Explain precisely. Provide the main points.
Summarize	Give a brief, condensed account. Draw a conclusion.
Trace	Show the order of events.

Here are some tips on writing essays:

1. To prepare for an essay test, use a mind map or summary sheet to summarize the main ideas. Organize the material in the form of an outline or mental pictures that you can use in writing.

2. The first step in writing an essay is to quickly survey the test and read the directions carefully. Many times you are offered a choice of which and how many questions to answer.

3. Manage your time. Note how many questions need to be answered and how many points each question is worth. For example, if you have three questions to answer in one hour, you will have less than 20 minutes for each question. Save some time to check over your work.

   If the questions are worth different numbers of points, divide up your time proportionately. In the above example with three questions, if one question is worth 50 points and the other two are worth 25 points, spend half the time on the 50-point question (less than 30 minutes) and divide the remaining time between the 25-point questions (less than 15 minutes each).

4. If you are anxious about the test, start with an easy question in order to relax and build your confidence. If you are confident in your test-taking abilities, start with the question that is worth the most points.

5. Get organized. Write a brief outline in the margin of your test paper. Do not write your outline on a separate sheet of paper because you may be accused of using cheat notes.

6. In the first sentence of your essay, rephrase the question and provide a direct answer. Rephrasing the question keeps you on track and a direct answer becomes the thesis statement or main idea of the essay.

   Example: (Question:) Describe a system for reading a college textbook.
   (Answer:) A system for reading a college textbook is Survey, Question, Read, Review, Recite, and Reflect (SQ4R). (Then you would go on to expand on each part of the topic.)

7. Use the principles of good composition. Start with a thesis statement or main idea. Provide supporting ideas and examples to support your thesis. Provide a brief summary at the end.

8. Write your answer clearly and neatly so it is easy to grade. Grading an essay involves an element of subjectivity. If your paper looks neat and is easy to read, the professor is likely to read your essay with a positive attitude. If your paper is difficult to read, the professor will probably read your paper with a negative attitude.

9. Determine the length of your essay by the number of points it is worth. For example, a five-point essay might be a paragraph with five key points. A 25-point essay would probably be a five-paragraph essay with at least 25 key points.

10. Save some time at the end to read over your essays. Make corrections, make sure your answers make sense, and add any key information you may have forgotten to include.

What to Do When Your Test Is Returned

When your test is returned, use it as feedback for future test preparation in the course. Look at your errors and try to determine how to prevent these errors in the future.

- Did you study correctly?
- Did you study the proper materials?
- Did you use the proper test-taking techniques?
- Was the test more difficult than you expected?
- Did you run out of time to take the test?
- Was the test focused on details and facts or on general ideas and principles?
- Did you have problems with test anxiety?

Analyzing your test performance can help you to do better in the future.

Journal Entry #5

Of course it is a good idea to be well prepared for exams, but there are times when you will have to figure out the answer or even make a guess on the correct answer. Review the section on "Taking Tests" and list five ideas for guessing that you can try in the future.

© airdone/Shutterstock.com

KEYS TO SUCCESS

Be Prepared

The key idea in this chapter is to be prepared. Good preparation is essential for success in test taking as well as in many other areas of life. Being successful begins with having a vision of the future and then taking steps to achieve your dream.

Sometimes people think of success in terms of good luck. Thomas Jefferson said, "I'm a great believer in luck, and I find the harder I work, the more I have of it." Don't depend on good luck. Work to create your success.

You can reach your dream of attaining a college education through preparation and hard work. Use the ideas in this chapter to ensure your success. Remember that preparation begins on the first day of class; it does not begin when the professor announces a test. On the first day of class, the professor provides an overview, or outline, of what you will learn. Attend every class. The main points covered in the class will be on the test. Read your assignments a little at a time starting from the first day. If you distribute your practice, you will find it easier to learn and to remember.

When it comes time to review for the test, you will already know what to expect on the test, and you will have learned the material by attending the lectures and reading your text. Reviewing for the test is just review; it is not original learning. It is a chance to strengthen what you have learned so that you can relax and do your best on the test. Review is one of the final steps in learning. With review, you will gain a sense of confidence and satisfaction in your studies.

If you are not prepared, you will need to cram for the test and you may not be as successful on the test as you could be. If you are not successful, you may get the mistaken idea that you cannot be successful in college. Cramming for the test produces stress, since you will need to learn a great deal of information in a short time. Stress can interfere with memory and cause you to freeze up on exams. It is also difficult to remember if you have to cram. The memory works best if you do a small amount of learning regularly over a period of time. Cramming is hard work and no fun. The worst problem with cramming is that it causes you to dislike education. It is difficult to continue to do something that you have learned to dislike.

Good preparation is the key to success in many areas of life. Whether you are taking a college course, playing a basketball game, going on vacation, planning a wedding, or building a house, good preparation will help to guarantee your success. Begin with your vision of the future and boldly take the first steps. The best preparation for the future is the good use of your time today.

> "The secret of getting ahead is getting started. The secret of getting started is breaking your complex, overwhelming tasks into small manageable tasks, and then starting on the first one."
>
> Mark Twain

> "The future starts today, not tomorrow."
>
> Pope John Paul II

College Success 1

The College Success 1 website is continually updated with supplementary material for each chapter including Word documents of the journal entries, classroom activities, handouts, videos, links to related materials, and much more. See http://www.collegesuccess1.com/.

© Lyudmyla Kharlamova/
Shutterstock.com

Notes

1. Terry Doyle and Todd Zakrajsek. The New Science of Learning (Sterling, Virginia: Stylus) 2013, 75.

2. G. A. Miller, "The Magical Number Seven, Plus or Minus Two: Some Limits on Our Capacity for Processing Information," *Psychological Review* 63 (March 1956): 81–97.

Test-Taking Checklist

Name _____ Date _____

Place checkmarks next to the test-taking skills you have now.

_____ Attend every class (or almost every class)

_____ Have a copy of the course syllabus with test dates

_____ Start test preparation early and study a little at a time

_____ Do not generally cram for exams

_____ Have a place to study (not the kitchen, TV room, or bedroom)

_____ Participate in a study group

_____ Review immediately after learning something

_____ Review previous notes and reading assignments on a regular basis

_____ Schedule a major review before the exam

_____ Know how to predict the test questions

_____ Get enough rest before a test

_____ Visualize my success on the exam

_____ Eat a light but nutritious meal before the exam

_____ Maintain a regular exercise program

_____ Read all my textbook assignments before the exam

_____ Review my classroom notes before the exam

_____ Skim through the test and read all directions carefully before starting the test

_____ Answer the easy questions first and return later to answer the difficult questions

_____ Check over my test before handing it in

_____ Write an outline before beginning my essay answer

_____ Manage my study time to adequately prepare for the test

_____ Review my returned tests to improve future test preparation

_____ Write the test neatly and make sure my writing is legible

_____ Avoid test anxiety by being well prepared and practicing relaxation techniques

_____ Prepare adequately for tests

Analyze Your Test-Taking Skills

Name _____ Date _____

Use the test-taking checklist on the previous page to answer the following questions.

1. My strengths in test-taking skills are

2. Some areas I need to improve are

3. Write three intention statements about improving your test-taking skills.

Math Success Checklist

Name _____ Date _____

Highlight or place a checkmark next to the items you regularly do in your math course.

_____ I spend about 10 hours a week or more studying for my math course.

_____ My goal is to make an A or a B on my first math test.

_____ I have confidence that I can succeed in my math course.

_____ If I don't understand something in my math course, I ask questions or get help.

_____ I take notes in my math course and review them as soon as possible after class.

_____ I write as neatly as possible in my math homework and exams.

_____ I make note cards on important information and review them frequently.

_____ I learn the definition of math terms in my class.

_____ I preview the chapter in my math text before the lecture.

_____ I practice math problems until I feel comfortable with them.

_____ I study math and do my math homework when I am most alert during the day.

_____ I make it a priority to attend all my math classes.

_____ I have a weekly study schedule for studying math.

_____ I know about some relaxation techniques I can use if I become anxious during the exam.

_____ I use practice tests to prepare for math exams.

_____ The night before math exams, I do a quick review and then get a good night's sleep.

_____ On math exams, I quickly survey the test and do the easy questions first.

_____ On math exams, I estimate the answer and see if it makes sense and is logical.

To improve my success in math, I intend to:

Practice with Short Essays

Name _____ Date _____

Your professor may ask you to do this as a classroom exercise. Review the section in the text on how to write a short essay. Answer the following short essay question worth five points.

1. Explain how you can improve your chances of success when preparing for exams. Include the physical, mental, and emotional preparation necessary for success.

2. Rate your essay. Did you do the following?

   _____ I read the directions and the essay question thoroughly before I began.

   _____ I organized my thoughts or made a brief outline before starting.

   _____ The first sentence was a direct answer and rephrased the question.

   _____ My thesis statement or main idea was clear.

   _____ The remaining sentences in the essay supported my main idea.

   _____ Since this is a five-point essay, I made at least five key points in the essay.

   _____ My answer was written clearly and neatly. My handwriting was legible.

   _____ I spelled the words correctly and used good grammar.

   _____ I read over my essay to make sure it made sense.

3. For essay exams, I need to work on

PART III

Lifelong Success

CHAPTER 10

Communication and Relationships

Learning Objectives

Read to answer these key questions:

- What is my personal communication style?

- What are some problems in communication?

- What are some techniques for being a good listener?

- What is the best way to communicate in a crisis situation?

- How does language affect behavior?

- What are some conflict management techniques?

- What are the qualities of a good friendship?

- How can I get along with my roommate?

- How can I improve my relationships?

- How is failure an opportunity for learning?

When you look back on your college experience, what you are most likely to remember and value are the personal relationships established while in college. These relationships can be a source of great pleasure or disappointment. What makes a good relationship? The answer to this question is complex and different for each individual. Good relationships begin with an understanding of personality differences and the components of effective communication. These skills can be useful in establishing satisfying friendships, happy marriages, effective parenting skills, and good relationships in the workplace.

Understanding Your Personal Communication Style

Becoming familiar with personality types can help you better understand yourself and others. Personality has a major impact on our style of communication. While we can make some generalizations about personality types, keep in mind that each individual is unique and may be a combination of the various types. For example, some people are a combination of introvert and extravert. The following descriptions will help you begin thinking about your own communication style and understanding others who are different. Remember that each personality type has positive and negative aspects. Knowledge of these differences can help individuals accentuate the positives and keep the negatives in perspective.

© VLADGRIN/Shutterstock.com

Introvert and Extravert Types

Extraverts are very social types who easily start conversations with strangers as well as friends. They know a lot of people and have many friends. They like going to parties and other social events and are energized by talking to people. They like to talk on the telephone and can read while watching TV, listening to music, or carrying on a conversation with someone else. They find talking easy and sometimes dominate the conversation. They find it more difficult to listen. They tend to talk first and think later, and sometimes regret that they have put their foot in their mouths.

In personal relationships, extraverts are fun to know and get along well with others. It is easy for them to make a date and do the talking. When extraverts are in conflict situations, they just talk louder and faster. They believe that the argument can be won if they can say just one more thing or provide more explanation. If there is a problem, extraverts want to talk about it right away. If they cannot talk about it, they become very frustrated.

The **introvert** is the opposite of the extravert. Introverts want to rehearse what they are going to say before they say it. They need quiet for concentration and enjoy peace and quiet. They have great powers of concentration and can focus their attention on projects for a long period of time. Because they tend to be quieter than extraverts, they are perceived as great listeners. Because they need time to think before talking, they often find it difficult to add their ideas to a conversation, especially when talking with extraverts. They often wish they could participate more in conversations. Because they are reserved and reflective, people often label the introvert as shy. In American society, introverts are the minority. There are three extraverts to every introvert. For this reason, the introvert is often pressured to act like an extravert. This can cause the introvert a great deal of anxiety.

The introvert often finds it difficult to start conversations or invite someone on a date. Introverts are often attracted to extraverts because they can relax and let the extravert do the talking. In conflict situations, the introverts are at a disadvantage. They will often withdraw from conflict because they need time to think about the situation and go over in their minds what to say. Introverts become stressed if they are faced with a conflict without advance notice.

Introverts and extraverts can improve their relationship by understanding each other and respecting their differences. The extravert can improve communication with the introvert by pausing to let the introvert have time to speak. He or she has to make a conscious effort to avoid monopolizing the conversation. Introverts can improve communication by making an effort to communicate. Introverts sometimes act like extraverts in social situations. Since this takes effort, they may need quiet time to relax and recharge after social events.

Imagine that two roommates are opposite types, extravert and introvert. The extravert enjoys talking and making noises. She will have guests, take telephone calls, and play music in the background while studying. These actions will cause the introvert to withdraw and leave the room to find a quiet place to study. These two roommates need to talk about their differences and do some compromising to get along with one another.

Sensing and Intuitive Types

Sensing types collect information through the senses. Their motto could be, "Seeing is believing." They are practical and realistic. They like communication to be exact and sequential. They want details and facts. They ask specific questions and want concrete answers. About 70 percent of the population of the United States is the sensing type.

In a dating situation, the sensing type focuses on actual experience. A sensor will describe the date in terms of what his or her companion looked like, how the food tasted, how the music sounded, and the feelings involved. During the date, sensors may talk about concrete events such as people they have known, experiences they have had, and places they have visited. Sensing types are generally on time for the date and get irritated if the other person is late. In conflict situations, sensing types argue the facts. They often don't see the big issues because they are concentrating on the accuracy of the facts.

Intuitive types gather information from the senses and immediately look for possibilities, meanings, and relationships between ideas. They are often ingenious and creative. Sensing types often describe intuitives as dreamers who have their heads in the clouds. They represent about 30 percent of the population.

In social situations such as dating, the intuitive person starts to fantasize and imagine what it is going to be like before it begins. The fantasies are often more exciting than the actual date. Conversations follow many different and creative trains of thought. Intuitive types are more likely to talk about dreams, visions, beliefs, and creative ideas, skipping from one topic to another. Sensing types sometimes have difficulty following the conversation. Intuitive types are less worried about being exactly on time. They believe that time is flexible and may not be on time for the date, much to the annoyance of sensing types. In conflict situations, intuitive types like to make broad generalizations. When sensing types remind them of the facts, they may accuse them of nitpicking.

Having both sensing and intuitive types in a relationship or business environment has many advantages, as long as these types can understand and appreciate one another. Sensing types need intuitive types to bring up new possibilities, deal with changes, and understand different perspectives. Intuitive types need sensing types to deal with facts and details.

Feeling and Thinking Types

Feeling types prefer to make decisions based on what they feel to be right or wrong based on their subjective values. They prefer harmony and are often described as tenderhearted. Other people's feelings are an important consideration in any decision they make. The majority of women (60 percent) are feeling types. In a conflict situation, feeling types take things personally. They prefer to avoid disagreements and will give in to reestablish a harmonious relationship.

Thinking types are logical, detached, analytical, and objective and make decisions based on these characteristics. They like justice and clarity. The majority of men (60 percent) are thinking types. In a conflict situation, thinking types use logical arguments. They often get frustrated with feeling types and think they are too emotional.

In a dating situation, the differences between feelers and thinkers can cause much misunderstanding and conflict. Thinking types strive to understand love and intimacy. Feeling types like to experience emotions. Thinking types process and analyze their feelings. For the thinker, love is to be analyzed. For the feeling types, love just happens.

Remember that while most women are feeling types and most men are thinking types, there are still 40 percent of women who are thinking types and 40 percent of men who are feeling types. Unfortunately, because of gender stereotyping, feeling-type men are often seen as less masculine and thinking-type women are seen as less feminine.

There is much to gain from understanding and appreciating the differences between feeling and thinking types. Feeling types need thinking types to analyze, organize, follow policy, and weigh the evidence. Thinking types need feeling types to understand how others feel and establish harmony in relationships or in a business environment.

Judging and Perceptive Types

Judging types prefer their environment to be structured, scheduled, orderly, planned, and controlled. Judging types even plan and organize their recreation time. They need events to be planned and organized in order to relax. They are quick to make decisions, and once the decisions are made, they find it difficult to change them. In the social scene, judging types schedule and plan the dates. When traveling, judging types carefully pack their suitcases using a list of essential items to make sure that nothing is forgotten. In conflict situations, judging types know that they are right. They tend to see issues in terms of right and wrong, good and bad, or black and white. It is difficult to negotiate with a judging type.

Perceptive types are very much the opposite of the judging types. They prefer the environment to be flexible and spontaneous. Perceptive types find it difficult to make a decision and stick to it because it limits their flexibility. Perceptive types like to collect information and keep the options open. After all, something better might come along and they do not want to be restricted by a plan or schedule. In a social situation, these types are playful and easygoing. They provide the fun and find it easy to relax. They often feel controlled by judging types. In a conflict situation, this type sees many options to resolve the situation. They have trouble resolving conflicts because they keep finding many possible solutions.

The preference for judging or perceiving has the most potential for conflict between individuals. Judging types can drive perceptive types crazy with their need for schedules, planning, and organization. Perceptive types drive the judging types crazy with their spontaneous and easygoing nature. In spite of these differences, judging and perceptive types are often attracted to one another. Judging types need perceptive types to encourage them to relax and have fun. Perceptive types need judging types to help them be more organized and productive. These two types need understanding and appreciation of each other to have a good relationship. They also need excellent communication skills.

It is often asked whether two people should consider personality type in establishing relationships or choosing a marriage partner. There are two theories on this. One theory is that opposites attract. If two people have opposite personality types, they will have the potential for using the strengths of both types. For example, if one marriage partner is a judging type, this person can manage the finances and keep the family organized. The perceptive type can provide the fun and help the other to relax and enjoy life. A disadvantage is that opposite types have great potential for conflict. The conflict can be resolved by understanding the other type and appreciating different strengths the opposite type brings to the relationship. The relationship cannot work if one person tries to change the other. Good communication is essential in maintaining the relationship.

Another theory is that like types attract. If you have a relationship with another person of the same type, your basic preferences are similar. However, even matching types will be different depending on the strength of each preference. Communication is easier when two people have similar views of the world. One disadvantage is that the relationship can become predictable and eventually uninteresting.

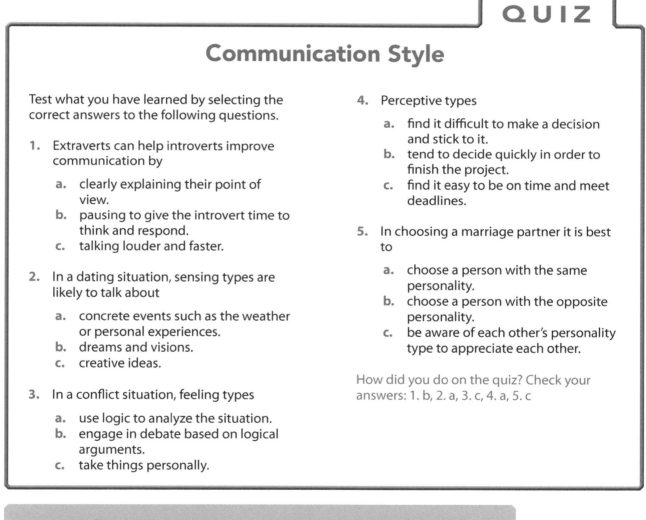

QUIZ

Communication Style

Test what you have learned by selecting the correct answers to the following questions.

1. Extraverts can help introverts improve communication by

   a. clearly explaining their point of view.
   b. pausing to give the introvert time to think and respond.
   c. talking louder and faster.

2. In a dating situation, sensing types are likely to talk about

   a. concrete events such as the weather or personal experiences.
   b. dreams and visions.
   c. creative ideas.

3. In a conflict situation, feeling types

   a. use logic to analyze the situation.
   b. engage in debate based on logical arguments.
   c. take things personally.

4. Perceptive types

   a. find it difficult to make a decision and stick to it.
   b. tend to decide quickly in order to finish the project.
   c. find it easy to be on time and meet deadlines.

5. In choosing a marriage partner it is best to

   a. choose a person with the same personality.
   b. choose a person with the opposite personality.
   c. be aware of each other's personality type to appreciate each other.

How did you do on the quiz? Check your answers: 1. b, 2. a, 3. c, 4. a, 5. c

Journal Entry #1

Consider how the following terms describe your communication style: extravert, introvert, sensing, intuitive, feeling, thinking, judging, perceptive. What is your personal communication style?

Communication for Success

To be an effective communicator, it is important to be a good listener and speaker. Practice the techniques of good listening and use language that helps you enhance your success and establish good relationships.

Problems in Communication

Effective communication involves a loop in which a sender sends a message and a receiver receives the message. Communications are disrupted when:

© mast3r/Shutterstock.com

- The receiver doesn't receive the message.
- The receiver hears the wrong message.
- The receiver doesn't care about the message.
- The receiver is more interested in talking than listening.
- The receiver only hears part of the message.
- The receiver only hears what she or he wants to hear.
- The receiver feels threatened by the sender.
- The sender didn't send the message correctly.
- The sender left out part of the message.
- The sender talks so much that nobody listens.
- The sender is not someone you want to hear.
- The sender is annoying.
- The sender was upset and did not mean to send the message.
- The sender assumes that you should know the message already.

Factors That Interfere with Good Listening

- Message overload
- Worries and anxiety
- Rapid thought
- Tired, overloaded, or distracted
- Noise and hearing problems
- Faulty assumptions

There is a joke circulating on the Internet:

A man is driving up a steep, narrow mountain road. A woman is driving down the same road. As they pass each other, the woman leans out the window and yells, "Pig!" The man replies by calling the woman a name. They each continue on their way. As the man rounds the next corner, he crashes into a pig in the middle of the road. If only people would listen!

As you can see, there are many ways to disrupt communication. Just because a message was sent does not mean that it was received. The first step in communication is to be a good listener. Many factors interfere with good listening. Do you recognize some of these reasons for not listening?

- **Message overload.** There is so much communication going on today that it is difficult to keep up with it all. There are stacks of paper, multiple email messages, text messages, television, radio, and people who want to talk to you. Introverts may find this overwhelming, while extraverts may find it exciting. Both find it challenging to keep up with all these communications and to focus on the messages.

- **Worries and anxiety.** It is difficult to listen to other people when you are preoccupied with your own thoughts. You may be thinking about an upcoming test or paper that is due or worried about a personal relationship. While others are talking, you are thinking about something else of more immediate concern to yourself.

- **Rapid thought.** People think faster than they speak. We are capable of understanding speech at about 600 words per minute, but most people talk at 100 to 150 words per minute.[1] People use the spare time to become distracted. They daydream, think about what they will do next, or think about their reply.

- **Listening is hard work.** It takes effort to listen. It requires paying attention and striving to understand. People can't listen effectively if they are tired, overloaded, or distracted.

- **Noise and hearing problems.** Our world is becoming noisier. As people get older, many suffer from hearing loss. Younger persons are suffering hearing loss from listening to loud music. It is more difficult to get your message across when people can't hear everything you are saying.

- **Faulty assumptions.** People often make faulty assumptions. They may assume that other people also know the information, and therefore they do not communicate well. Listeners may assume that they know the information already or that the information is easy, so it is not necessary for them to pay attention. Or they may assume the material is too difficult to understand and block it out.

- **Talking too much.** Since listening involves effort, people consider what they have to gain before they invest the effort in listening. They might think that there is more to gain in speaking than in listening. The speaker often feels that he or she has control. You might feel that in speaking you gain the attention or admiration of others. If you are speaking or telling a joke and everyone is listening, you feel important. Also, through speaking people release their frustration and think about their problems. They need to stop speaking in order to listen.

How to Be a Good Listener

Being a good listener takes practice and effort. Here are some tips on becoming a good listener:

- **Talk less.** It does no good to talk if no one is listening, if no one understands your message, or if your message is irrelevant to the situation. To have a better chance of communicating your message, **it is important first to listen to gain an understanding of the other person and then to speak.** In marriage counseling, a common technique is to have one person talk and express his or her point of view. Before the other person can talk, he or she has to accurately summarize what the previous person said. Too often people do not really listen; instead they are composing their own messages in their heads. It is a Native American custom that when members of the group assemble to talk about an important issue, a talking stick is used. Persons can only talk when they have the talking stick. When the person holding the talking stick is finished, it is passed to the next person who wants to talk. In this way, only one person can talk at a time, and the others listen.

> **To Be a Good Listener**
> - Talk less
> - Minimize distractions
> - Don't judge too soon
> - Look for main point
> - Ask questions
> - Feed back meaning
> - Be careful with advice

> "We have two ears and one mouth, so we should listen twice as much as we speak."
> Epictetus
>
> "Life is an echo: what you send out comes back."
> Chinese Proverb

© William Perugini/Shutterstock.com

- **Minimize distractions.** For important conversations, turn off the TV or the music. Find quiet time to focus on the communication. Manage your internal distractions as well. Focus your attention on listening first and then speaking.

- **Don't judge too soon.** Try to understand first and then evaluate. If you judge too soon, you may not have the correct information and might make a mistake. People are especially vulnerable to this problem when their ideas do not agree with those of the speaker. They focus on defending their position without really listening to the other point of view.

- **Look for the main point.** You may become distracted or impatient with people who talk too much. Try to be patient and look for the main points. In a lecture, write these points down.

- **Ask questions.** You will need to ask questions to make sure that you understand. Each person looks at the world in a different way. The picture in my mind will not match the picture in your mind. We will have a better idea of each other's pictures if we ask for more information.

- **Feed back meaning.** This communication technique involves restating the speaker's ideas in your own words to check the meaning. This is important because speakers often:
  - say one thing and mean something else.
  - say something but don't mean it, especially if emotions are involved.
  - speak in a way that causes confusion.

Feeding back meaning has two important benefits. It helps speakers to clarify their thoughts and it helps listeners make sure that they have received the correct message. Here are several ways to feed back meaning:

1. **Restate what has been said.** Sometimes this is called parroting. It is useful for clarifying information, but sometimes it annoys people if you use it too much.
   Statement: Turn right at the light.
   Feedback: Okay. So you want me to turn right at the light?

2. **Ask for clarification.**
   Statement: Take the next exit on the freeway.
   Feedback: Do you mean this exit coming up now or the next one?
   Statement: Pig! (referring to the joke about the man and woman on the mountain road)
   Feedback: What do you mean by "pig"?
   Statement: Be careful. There is a pig in the road ahead.

3. **Reword the message to check your understanding.** First, restate what you have heard and then ask for clarification. This is called active listening.
   Statement: Turn in the draft of your paper next week.
   Feedback: You want the draft next week. Does that include the outline, the draft of the entire paper, and the bibliography? Should it be typed, or is handwritten okay?
   Statement: Don't worry about your grade on this quiz.
   Feedback: You said not to worry about my grade on this quiz. Does that mean that the grade won't count or that I can make up the quiz?
   Statement: I need this project completed by Friday.
   Feedback: So this project needs to be done by Friday. What parts do you want included and how would you like me to do it?

4. **Listen for feelings.** Feelings get in the way of clear thinking. A person may say one thing and mean something else.

   Statement: Just forget about it!

   Feedback: I'm confused. You ask me to forget about it, but you sound angry.

5. **Use your own words to restate what the speaker has said.** In this way, you help the speaker to clarify his or her thoughts and hopefully to come up with some solutions.

   Statement: I wish I didn't have to work so much. I'm getting behind in school, but I have bills to pay. I have to work.

   Feedback: You seem to be caught in a bind between school and work.

   Statement: That's right. I just can't keep working so much. Maybe I should go check out financial aid and scholarships.

- **Be careful about giving advice.** Whenever possible, listen closely and be an active listener. This helps the person speaking to you to clarify his or her thoughts and think about alternatives. When you listen, it is tempting to offer advice because you may have had similar experiences. You can share your experiences and offer suggestions, but beware of giving advice for these reasons:

  - If you give advice and it turns out badly, you may be blamed.

  - If you give advice and it turns out right, the person may become dependent on you.

  - People are unique individuals with unique life situations. Something that works for one person may not work for another person at all.

Journal Entry #2

Review the section on "Communication for Success." What are three ways to improve your communication and listening skills?

I can improve my communication and listening skills by . . . .

Helpful Communication in a Crisis Situation

Most people have been in a situation where their friends or family are in distress and need immediate help. If you become aware of a dangerous or critical situation, seek professional help. Go to your college counseling center, a community service organization, your doctor, or a religious leader for help. Here are some general ideas for being a helpful listener:

- Let the person talk. Talking helps to clarify thinking.
- Paraphrase or feed back meaning.
- Avoid being critical. Comments such as "You asked for it" or "I told you so" do not help. They just make the person angry.
- Help the person analyze the situation and come up with alternatives for solving the problem.
- Share your experiences but resist giving advice.
- Ask questions to clarify the situation.
- Offer to be supportive. Say, "I'm here if you need me" or "I care about you."

© Monkey Business Images/Shutterstock.com

- Let people express their feelings. It is not helpful to say, "Don't feel sad," for example. A person may need to feel sad and deal with the situation. The emotion can be a motivation for change.
- Don't minimize the situation. Saying, "It's only a grade (job, promotion)," minimizes the situation. It might not be important to the listener, but it is causing pain for the speaker. Give him or her time to gain perspective on the problem.
- Replace pity with understanding. It is not helpful to say, "You poor thing."

The following anonymous poem summarizes some ideas on how to be a helpful listener.

When I ask you to listen to me
    and you give me advice
    you have not done what I asked.

When I ask you to listen to me
    and you begin to tell me why I shouldn't feel that way,
    you are trampling on my feelings.

When I ask you to listen to me
    and you feel you have to do something to solve my problem,
    you have failed me, strange as that may seem.

Listen! All I asked was that you listen.
    Not talk or do—just hear me.

Advice is cheap: 50 cents will get you both Dear Abby and
    Billy Graham in the same newspaper.

And I can do for myself; I'm not helpless.
    Maybe discouraged and faltering, but not helpless.

When you do something for me that I can and need to do
    for myself, you contribute to my fear and weakness.

But, when you accept as a simple fact that I do feel what I feel,
    no matter how irrational, then I can quit trying to convince

you and can get about the business of understanding what's
    behind this irrational feeling.
And when that's clear, the answers are obvious and I
    don't need advice.

Irrational feelings make sense when we understand what's
    behind them.

Perhaps that's why prayer works, sometimes, for some people
    because God is sometimes mute and doesn't give advice or
    try to fix things. He often listens and lets you
    work it out for yourself.

So please listen and hear me. And, if you want to
    talk, wait a minute for your turn; and I'll listen to you.[2]

The Language of Responsibility

The way we use language reflects our willingness to take responsibility for ourselves and affects our relationships with others. Knowing about "I" and "you" messages, as well as how we choose certain words, can help us to improve communications. We can become aware of how our thoughts influence our behavior and communication. We can choose to use cooperation in dealing with conflicts.

"I" and "You" Statements

When communicating, watch how you use the pronouns "I" and "you." For example, if you walk in and find your apartment a mess, you might say to your roommate, "Just look at this mess! You are a slob!" Your roommate will probably be angry and reply by calling you an equally offensive name. You have accomplished nothing except becoming angry and irritating your roommate. Using the pronoun "you" and calling a person a name implies that you are qualified to make a judgment about another person. Even if this is true, you will not make any friends or communicate effectively.

"You" statements label and blame. They demand a rebuttal. They cause negative emotions and escalate the situation. How would you react to these statements?

    You must be crazy.
    You are really a jerk!

You would probably get angry and think of a nasty reply in return. When you use an "I" message, you accept responsibility for yourself. You might say something like this:

    I don't understand.
    I feel angry.

There are many ways to make "I" statements. Instead of calling your roommate a slob, you could:

1. **Make an observation.** Describe the behavior.
    Your things are all over the floor.

2. **State your feelings.** Tell how you feel about the behavior.
    I get angry when I have to step over your things on the floor.

3. **Share your thoughts.** Say what you think about the situation, but beware of disguised "you" messages such as,
"I think you are a slob."
I think it is time to clean up.

4. **State what you want.**
Please pick up your things.

5. **State your intentions.** Say what you are going to do.
If you do not pick up your things, I will put them in your room.

Here are some examples of "I" statements that can be used to express various feelings:

To express anger	To express sadness
I don't like	I feel disappointed
I feel frustrated	I am sad that
I am angry that	I feel hurt
I feel annoyed	I wanted
I want	I want

To express fear	To say you are sorry
I feel worried	I feel embarrassed
I am afraid	I am sorry
I feel scared	I feel ashamed
I do not want	I didn't want
I need, I want	I want

A complete "I" message describes the other person's behavior, states your feelings, and describes the effect of the other's behavior on you. For example, "When your things are all over the floor (behavior), I feel angry (feeling) because I have to pick up after you (how it affects me)." A variation on the "I" message is the "we" message. The "we" statement assumes that both persons need to work on the problem. For example, "We need to work on this problem so that we don't have to argue."

Journal Entry #3

You are having a disagreement with a roommate, sibling, or spouse about keeping the house clean. Write three "I" statements that could help to improve the situation.

Words Are Powerful

The words that we choose have a powerful influence on behavior. One of the least powerful words is the word "should." This word is heard frequently on college campuses:

I should do my homework.
I should go to class.
I should get started on my term paper.

Figure 10.1 Ladder of Powerful Speaking.

"I promise" or "I will"

"I intend to"

"I want to"

"I might"

"I should"

Courtesy of Charlotte Moore.
© Kendall Hunt Publishing Company.

The problem with "should" is that it usually does not lead to action and may cause people to feel guilty. If you say, "I should get started on my term paper," the chances are that you will not start on it.

If you say, "I might get started on my term paper," at least you are starting to think about possibilities. You might actually get started on your term paper. If you say, "I want to get started on my term paper," the chances are getting better that you will get started. You are making a choice. If you say, "I intend to start on my term paper," you have at least expressed good intentions. The best way to get started is to make a promise to yourself that you will get started: "I will start on my term paper." The words "should," "might," "want," and "promise" or "will" represent a powerful ladder of communication. As you move up the ladder, you are more likely to accomplish what you say you will do. This ladder moves from obligation to promise, or a personal choice to act.

Next time you hear yourself saying that you "should" do something, move one more step up the ladder. Move from obligation to making a personal decision to do what is important to you. For example, if a friend wants to borrow money from you, which response is the most powerful?

- I really should pay the money back.
- Well, I might pay the money back.
- I really want to pay the money back.
- I intend to pay the money back.
- I promise to pay the money back.

Negative Self-Talk

Self-talk is what you say to yourself. It is the stream of consciousness or the little voice in your head. This self-talk affects how you communicate with others. If your self-talk is negative, you will have lower self-esteem and find it more difficult to communicate with others.

Beliefs that Lead to Negative Self-Talk

- I have to be perfect.
- I need everyone's approval.
- That's always the way it is.
- You made me feel that way.
- I'm helpless.
- If something bad can happen, it will.

© iQoncept/Shutterstock.com

There are some common irrational beliefs that lead to negative self-talk. Becoming aware of these beliefs can help you to avoid them.

- **I have to be perfect.** If you believe this, you will think that you have to be a perfect communicator and deliver flawless speeches. Since this goal is unattainable, it causes stress and anxiety. If you believe in this idea, you may try to pretend or act as if you were perfect. This takes up a lot of energy and keeps others from liking you. Everyone makes mistakes. When people stop trying to be perfect and accept themselves as they are, they can begin to relax and work on the areas needing improvement. They can write papers and make speeches knowing that they will probably make mistakes, just like the rest of the human population.

- **I need the approval of everyone.** A person who believes this finds it necessary to have the approval of almost everyone. Much energy is spent in gaining approval from others. If approval is not obtained, the person may feel nervous, embarrassed, or apologetic. It is not possible to win the approval of everyone because each individual is unique. Those who constantly seek approval will sacrifice their own values and what they think is right just to please others.

- **That's always the way it is.** People who believe this statement are making a generalization. They take a few events and use them to predict the future or exaggerate their shortcomings. Here are some examples:
  - I'm not a technical person. I can't install my computer.
  - I'm not good at numbers. I'll never to able to pass algebra.
  - Some husband (wife) I am! I forgot our anniversary.
  - You never listen to me.

Notice the absolute nature of these statements. Absolute statements are almost always false and lead to anger and negative thinking. Remember that with a positive attitude, things can change in the future. Just because it was one way in the past does not mean it has to be the same in the future. Beware of "always" and "never" statements.

- **You made me feel that way.** Your own self-talk, rather than the actions of others, is what causes emotions. No one can make you feel sad or happy. You feel sad or happy based on what you say to yourself about an event. If someone makes a negative comment about you, you can say to yourself that it is only the other person's opinion and choose how you react. Your reactions and emotions depend on how much importance you decide to attach to the event. People tend to react strongly to a comment if it is from someone they care about.

People also do not cause the emotions of others. Some people do not communicate honestly because they are afraid of causing negative emotions in the other person. They may hesitate to tell someone how they really feel. This lack of honesty leads to increasing hostility over time and difficulties in communication.

- **I'm helpless.** If you believe that what happens to you is beyond your control, you will be unlikely to do something to make the situation better. Here are some examples of helpless self-talk:

  - I'm a shy person. It is hard for me to talk to people.

  - I won't consider that career. Women are always discriminated against in that field.

  - It's difficult for me to meet people.

  Believing such statements, shy people don't attempt to talk to others, women limit their career options, and people give up trying to make friends. Believe that there is a way to change, and you can make your life better.

- **If something bad can happen, it will happen.** If you expect the worst, you may take actions that make it happen. If you expect that your speech will be a disaster, you may not prepare or you may forget your notes or props. If you believe that you will not pass the interview and will never get hired, you may not even apply for the job or attempt the interview. If you believe that your personal relationships will not get better, you will not invest the effort to make things better. There will be times when you make a poor speech, get turned down for a job, or have a relationship fail. Learn from these mistakes and do better the next time.

Barriers to Effective Communication

We all want to communicate effectively and get along with people whom we care about. We want to get along with our families, be a good parent, have friends at school, and get along with the boss and our coworkers on the job. Life is just more enjoyable when we have good communication with others. Watch for these barriers to effective communication:

© ananas/Shutterstock.com

- **Criticizing.** Making negative evaluations of others by saying, "It's your fault" or "I told you so" causes anger, which gets in the way of communication.

- **Name-calling and labeling.** If you call someone a name or put a label on them, they will attack you rather than communicate with you in any meaningful way.

- **Giving advice.** Giving advice may be viewed as talking down to a person. The person may resent your advice and you as well.

- **Ordering or commanding.** If you order someone to do something, they are likely to sabotage your request.

- **Threatening.** Trying to control someone by making threats causes resentment.

- **Moralizing.** Preaching about what a person should or should not do doesn't work because it causes resentment.

- **Diverting.** Changing the subject to talk about your own problems tells the person that you do not care about them.

- **Logical arguing.** Trying to use facts to convince without taking feelings into account is a barrier to communication. Present your facts and state your point of view, but respect the other person's feelings and different point of view.[3]

"Who among us does not choose to be a little less right to be a little less lonely?"

Robert Brault

Communication for Success

Test what you have learned by selecting the correct answer to the following questions.

1. One of the biggest problems with communication is that the message sent is not always the message that is

    a. appreciated.
    b. intended.
    c. received.

2. To be a good listener, it is important to remember that

    a. it is important to listen first, so that you can understand before speaking.
    b. it is important to talk first to make sure the other has heard your point of view.
    c. it is important to assume that the other knows what you are talking about.

3. Feeding back meaning is

    a. responding to questions.
    b. restating what has been said to check understanding.
    c. unnecessary because some people find it irritating.

4. "You" statements

    a. put the blame where it needs to be.
    b. results in anger and rebuttal.
    c. are effective communication tools.

5. Which statement is the most powerful?

    a. I should get started on my paper.
    b. I want to get started on my paper.
    c. I will get started on my paper.

How did you do on the quiz? Check your answers: 1. c, 2. a, 3. b, 4. b, 5. c

Dealing with Conflict

There are several ways to approach a conflict. In every conflict, there is the potential to be a winner or a loser.

© iQoncept/Shutterstock.com

- **Win-lose.** With this approach to conflict management, one person wins and the other loses, just as in a game or sport. Competition is part of the win-lose approach. In competition, power is important. In sports, the best and most powerful team wins.

    There are many kinds of power, however. Power may be based on authority. Examples might include your boss at work, your teacher, or even your parents. Another kind of power is based on mental ability or cleverness. Sometimes battles are not won by the strongest, but by the cleverest person. Another kind of power is majority rule. In many settings in a democratic society, the person with the most votes wins.

    In many situations, we cannot avoid the win-lose approach. Only one team can win, only one person can get the job, and only one person can marry another. In some circumstances the person you are communicating with does not want to cooperate but to compete.

The problem with this approach is that there is only one winner. What happens to the loser? The loser can feel bad, resent the winner, give up, or try again for victory. These are not always the best alternatives in personal relationships.

- **Lose-lose.** Lose-lose is another option for resolving conflicts. Both parties lose. Both parties strive to be winners, but the struggle causes damage to both sides. Wars are often lose-lose situations. In World War II, dropping an atomic bomb caused the surrender of Japan, but it contaminated the environment with radioactive material and set a dangerous precedent for nuclear war. Russia was able to stop a civil war by destroying Grozny, the capital of Chechnya. The city became nearly uninhabitable. Everyone lost. On an interpersonal level, divorce can be a lose-lose situation if the struggle becomes destructive to both parties.

© 2014, Shutterstock, Inc.

- **Compromise.** Another approach to solving conflict is compromise, where both parties to the conflict have some of their needs met. Both make some sacrifice in order to resolve the situation. For example, the buyer and seller of a used car may agree on a price somewhere between what the seller wants to get and the buyer wants to pay. As long as both parties are satisfied with the outcome, the results are satisfactory. Difficulties arise when people are asked to compromise their values. If they must compromise on something that is truly important, they may be dissatisfied with the outcome.

© 2014, Shutterstock, Inc.

- **Win-win.** In a win-win approach, both parties work together to find a solution that meets everyone's needs. There is no loser. To reach a win-win solution, set aside competition and replace it with cooperation. This is often difficult to do because emotions are involved. Put aside emotions to discuss the issue. This may mean waiting until both parties have had the opportunity to calm down. This approach can be impossible, however, when one person wants to cooperate and the other person wants to win.

© 2014, Shutterstock, Inc.

These are the steps in a win-win approach:

1. **Identify the problem.** Identify the problem as your own. If your roommate is having a party and you cannot study, it is your problem. Let your roommate know that you are unhappy about the situation, but you need to find a quiet place to study.

2. **Set a good time to discuss the issue.** When you are feeling angry is usually not a good time to discuss issues. Set a time when both parties can focus on the problem. A good rule is to wait 24 hours to let the emotions cool down and gain some perspective.

3. **Describe your problem and needs.** Use "I" messages. Resist the temptation to label and call names. Goodwill is important.

4. **Look at the other point of view.** Understand the other person's needs, and make sure the other person understands your needs.

© iQoncept/Shutterstock.com

5. **Look for alternatives that work for both parties.**

6. **Decide on the best alternative.**

7. **Take action to implement the solution.**

The win-win approach is a good tool for effective communication and maintaining good relationships.

Approaches to
Conflict

• Win-Lose
• Lose-Lose
• Compromise
• Win-Win

Journal Entry #4

Review the section on "Barriers to Effective Communication" and "Dealing with Conflict." What are some common mistakes that people make when trying to resolve problems and communicate effectively?

Friendships

College provides the opportunity to make new friends. These friends can broaden your perspective and make your life richer and more enjoyable. What do you value in a friendship? How can you establish and maintain good friendships?

ACTIVITY

Friendship

Friendship is a relationship that involves trust and support. Beyond this basic definition, we all have different ideas about what is important in a friendship. Here is a list of common qualities of friends. Highlight or place a checkmark next to those qualities that are important to you in establishing your personal friendships. A friend is a person who:

_____ can keep information confidential.	_____ spends time with me.
_____ is loyal.	_____ has a sense of humor.
_____ can be trusted.	_____ is independent.
_____ is warm and affectionate.	_____ has good communication skills.
_____ is supportive of who I am.	_____ is an educated person.
_____ is honest.	_____ is an intelligent person.
_____ is a creative person.	_____ knows how to have fun.
_____ encourages me to do my best.	_____ cares about me.

What are the top three qualities you would look for in a friend? List them below.

1. _____

2. _____

3. _____

The friends that you choose can have a big influence on your life, so it is important to choose them wisely. In college and in the workplace, you will have the opportunity to make new friends who can add a new dimension and perspective to your life. For example, if your friends have goals for the future and believe that completing college is important, you will be more likely to finish your own education. If your friends distract you with too many activities outside of school, your college performance may suffer.

Some students naturally make friends easily; others find making new friends more difficult. Here are some ideas for making new friends:

- **Be a good listener.** Spend equal time listening and talking. If you are doing all the talking, the other person is likely to feel left out of the conversation. Show interest in the other person's interests and ideas.

- **Talk about yourself.** Let others get to know you by sharing your interests, where you come from, and what is important to you. In this way, you can find mutual interests to enjoy.

- **Be supportive and caring.** We all have good days and bad ones. Help your friends to celebrate the good days and be supportive through life's challenges. Showing that you care is the basis of developing trust and friendship.

- **Be a friend.** Treat your friends the way you would like to be treated.

- **Spend time with your friends.** It is difficult to maintain relationships if you do not spend time sharing activities. Make spending time with friends a high priority.

- **Accept your friends for who they are.** Everyone has good and bad qualities. Accept the idea that you are not going to be able to change people to match your expectations.

- **Show appreciation.** Say thank you and make honest compliments. Think of something positive to say.

- **Be assertive.** This means that you ask for what you want and that you don't give in to doing something that you don't want to do. Being assertive means that you have the right to your feelings and opinions. There is a fine line, though, between being assertive and being aggressive. Aggressive behavior is domineering, rude, and intimidating. Aggressive individuals act without consideration of other people's rights and feelings.

- **Be selective.** Not everyone makes a good friend. Make friends with people you respect and admire. Stay away from people who are critical or make you feel unhappy. Avoid those who cause you to do things that you do not want to do. Choose friends that make you happy and encourage you to do your best.

> "Lots of people want to ride with you in the limo, but what you want is someone who will take the bus with you when the limo breaks down."
> Oprah Winfrey

> "Friendship is born at the moment when one person says to another, 'What! You too! I thought I was the only one.'"
> C.S. Lewis

> "When the character of a man is not clear to you, look at his friends."
> Japanese Proverb

Roommates

Getting along with a roommate can be a challenge. It can be your best or worst college experience or somewhere in between. The key to getting along with a roommate is to understand differences and to work on compromise or win-win solutions. Making a wise choice of a roommate can make the situation much easier. Below are some areas of possible disagreement for roommates:

- **Neatness.** Some students like to keep their rooms neat and others can tolerate messiness.
- **Smoking.** Some students like to smoke and others are offended by smoking.
- **Noise.** Some students need quiet for study, while others like to study with music and friends.
- **Guests.** Some students like to have guests in the room, and others do not want guests.
- **Temperature.** Some like it warm and some like it cold.
- **Studying.** Is the room a place to study or to have fun?
- **Borrowing.** Some think that borrowing is okay and some do not.
- **Sleeping.** Some go to bed early and some go to bed late. Some need quiet for sleeping.

If you have a choice of roommates, it is a good idea to discuss the above issues in advance. Even best friends can part company over some of these issues. If you are assigned a roommate, discuss the above issues to avoid conflict later on. Aim for a win-win solution or at least a compromise. If there is some conflict, following these guidelines may help.

1. Discuss problems as they arise. If you do not discuss problems, it is likely that anger and resentment will increase, causing a more serious problem at a later date.

2. Ask for what you want. Subtle hints often do not work.

3. Be nice to your roommate and treat him or her as you would want to be treated.

4. Be reasonable and overlook small problems. No one is perfect.

Relationships

A relationship starts as a friendship and then moves a step further. A relationship involves emotional attachment and interdependence. We often get our ideas about good relationships through practice and trial and error. When we make errors, the results are often painful. Although we all have different ideas about what constitutes a good relationship, at a minimum it includes these components:

- Love and caring
- Honesty
- Trust
- Loyalty
- Mutual support
- Acceptance of differences

Relationships between Men and Women

According to John Gray, popular author of *Men Are from Mars, Women Are from Venus,* men and women have such different values and needs in a relationship, it is as if they came from different planets.[4] He states that men generally value power, competency, efficiency, and achievement. He says, "A man's sense of self is defined through his ability to achieve results." While women are fantasizing about romance, a man is fantasizing about "powerful cars, faster computers, gadgets, gizmos, and new and more powerful technology."[5] The worst thing that women can do to men, according to Gray, is to offer unsolicited advice or to try to change them. These actions conflict with men's needs for power and competence and imply that they don't know what to do or can't do it on their own. We can communicate

© Aleutie/Shutterstock.com

our honest feelings about our partner's behavior and ask for what we want and need. However, we should not use our feelings and requests to manipulate another person to change. Gray identifies the most important needs for men as trust, acceptance, appreciation, admiration, approval, and encouragement.

Gray says that women generally value love, communication, beauty, and relationships. Their sense of self-worth is defined through their feelings and the quality of their relationships. The worst thing that men can do to women is to offer solutions too quickly when women are talking about their feelings, rather than listening and understanding those feelings. When this happens, women get frustrated and feel a lack of intimacy. It is possible to listen carefully and understand these feelings without necessarily agreeing with them. The most important needs for women are caring, understanding, respect, devotion, validation, and reassurance.

Gray's ideas about men and women parallel the thinking and feeling dimensions of personality presented earlier. Men are 60 percent thinking types and women are 60 percent feeling types. His ideas are interesting for discussion and apply in many relationships, but it is important to be aware of gender stereotypes. Remember that 40 percent of women are thinking types and 40 percent of men are feeling types, so not all individuals will fit into the same categories that Gray describes.

Although Gray proposes that men and women generally differ in what they consider most important, he lists the following 12 components of love.[6] Men and women can improve their relationships when they demonstrate the following:

1. **Caring.** Show that you are interested and concerned about each other.

2. **Trust.** Have a positive belief in the intentions and abilities of each other.

3. **Understanding.** Listen without judgment and without presuming that you understand the feelings of the other person. In this way, both men and women can feel free to discuss what is important to them.

4. **Acceptance.** It is probably not a good idea to marry a person if you think you can change him or her into the ideal person you have in mind. Love your partner without trying to change him or her. No one is perfect; we are each a work in progress. The key is to trust the people we love to make their own improvements.

5. **Respect.** Have consideration for the thoughts and feelings of each other.

6. **Appreciation.** Acknowledge the behavior and efforts of your partner. Appreciation can be in the form of a simple "Thank you" or sending cards or flowers.

7. **Devotion.** Give priority to the relationship so that the other person feels important.

8. **Admiration.** Show approval for the unique gifts and talents of your partner.

9. **Validation.** Do not argue with feelings. Each person has a right to his or her own feelings. We can acknowledge, try to understand, and respect the feelings of another without necessarily agreeing with them.

10. **Approval.** Show approval by acknowledging the goodness and satisfaction you have with each other.

11. **Reassurance.** Show reassurance by repeatedly showing that you care, understand, and respect each other.

12. **Encouragement.** Notice the good characteristics of each other and provide encouragement and support.

How to Survive the Loss of a Relationship

Relationships require work and good communication to keep them going strong. Relationships also change over time as people grow and change. As we search for our soul mates, we may need to end some relationships and start new ones. This process can be very painful. Following the breakup of a relationship, people generally go through three predictable stages:

1. Shock or denial

2. Anger or depression

3. Understanding or acceptance[7]

Dealing with pain is a necessary part of life. Whether the pain is a result of the loss of a relationship or the death of someone important to you, there are some positive steps you can take along the road to acceptance and understanding.

- Recognize that a loss has taken place and give yourself time to adjust to this situation. The greater the loss, the more time it will take to feel better. In the meantime, try to keep up with daily routines. It is possible to feel sad and to go to work and to school. Daily routines may even take your mind off your troubles for a while.
- It is healthy to feel sad and cry. You will need to experience the pain to get over it. It is not helpful to deny pain, cover it up, or run away from it, because it will take longer to feel better.
- Talk to a friend or a counselor. Talking about how you feel will help you to understand and accept the loss.
- Don't punish yourself with thoughts that begin "If only I had . . ."
- Realize that there is a beginning and an end to pain.
- Get plenty of rest and eat well.
- Accept understanding and support from friends and family.
- Ask for help if you need it.
- Don't try to get the old relationship going again. It will just prolong the pain.
- Anticipate a positive outcome. You will feel better in the future.
- Beware of the rebound. It is not a good idea to jump into a new relationship right away.
- Beware of addictive activities such as alcohol, drugs, smoking, or overeating.
- Take time to relax and be kind to yourself.
- Use exercise as a way to deal with stress and feel better.
- Keep a journal to help deal with your emotions and learn from the situation.[8]

© sibgat/Shutterstock.com

KEYS TO SUCCESS

Failure Is an Opportunity for Learning

Everyone makes mistakes and experiences failure. This is the human condition. There is also a saying that falling down is not failure, but not getting up is. If you can view failure as an opportunity for learning, you can put it into perspective and continue making progress toward your goals. It has been said that the famous inventor Thomas Edison tried 9,999 times to invent the light bulb. When asked if he was going to fail 10,000 times, he answered, "I didn't fail. I just discovered another way not to invent the light bulb." Failure allows you to collect feedback about how you are doing.

Imagine that your life is like a ship heading toward a destination. Sometimes the sailing is smooth, and sometimes the water is choppy and dangerous and knocks you off course. Failure acts like the rudder of the ship. It helps you to make adjustments so that you stay on course. Too often we do not learn from failure because shame and blame get in the way. Gerard Nierenberg, author of *Do It Right the First Time*, advocates the "no shame, no blame" approach to dealing with errors, mistakes, or failure.[9] The first step is to identify the mistake that has been made. What went wrong? Then you look at how much damage has been done. The next step is to take an honest look at what caused the problem. The last step is to figure out a way to fix the problem and see that it does not happen again. There is no shame or blame in the process. Following this approach results in fewer errors and failures.

Harold Kushner has another view about failure:

Life is not a spelling bee, where no matter how many words you have gotten right, if you make one mistake you are disqualified. Life is more like a baseball season, where even the best team loses one-third of its games and even the worst team has its days of brilliance. Our goal is not to go all year without ever losing a game. Our goal is to win more than we lose, and if we can do that consistently enough, then when the end comes, we will have won it all.[10]

Like a baseball player, if you lose a game, analyze what went wrong and keep on practicing. Remember that you will eventually be a winner. Everyone remembers that Babe Ruth was a great baseball player and that he had 714 home runs. People do not remember that he also struck out 1,330 times. If you can look honestly at your mistakes and learn from them, you can have many winning seasons.

© Snap2Art/Shutterstock.com

Journal Entry #5

Describe a situation in which you have been disappointed, such as a poor grade or the loss of a job or a relationship. Was there an opportunity to learn from the situation?

> "Work as hard as you ask others to. Strive for what you believe is right, no matter the odds. Learn that mistakes can be the best teacher."
> George Steinbrenner

College Success 1

The College Success 1 website is continually updated with supplementary material for each chapter including Word documents of the journal entries, classroom activities, handouts, videos, links to related materials, and much more. See http://www.collegesuccess1.com/.

© Lyudmyla Kharlamova/ Shutterstock.com

> "Success is walking from failure to failure with no lack of enthusiasm."
> Winston Churchill

Notes

1. A. Wolvin and C. G. Coakley, *Listening*, 3rd ed. (Dubuque, IA: W. C. Brown, 1988), 208.

2. *Care of the Mentally Ill* (F.A. Davis, 1977).

3. T. Gordon, *Parent Effectiveness Training* (New York: McGraw-Hill, 1970).

4. John Gray, *Men Are from Mars, Women Are from Venus* (New York: HarperCollins, 1992).

5. Ibid., 16.

6. Ibid., 133–37.

7. Melba Colgrove, Harold Bloomfield, and Peter McWilliams, *How to Survive the Loss of a Love* (New York: Bantam Books, 1988).

8. Adapted from Colgrove, Bloomfield, and McWilliams, *How to Survive the Loss of a Love.*

9. Gerard Nierenberg, *Doing It Right the First Time* (New York: John Wiley and Sons, 1996).

10. Harold Kushner, *Becoming Aware* (Dubuque, IA: Kendall Hunt).

Communication Scenarios

Name _____ Date _____

In the following scenarios, think about how personality type influences communication style. Knowing about your personality type and understanding opposite types can help to improve your communication. Your instructor may want to do this as a group activity in the classroom.

1. An introvert and an extravert are having an argument.

   How is the introvert likely to act?

   How is the extravert likely to act?

   How can the extravert improve communication?

   How can the introvert improve communication?

2. A sensing and an intuitive type are on a date.

   What is the sensing person likely to talk about?

   What is the intuitive type likely to talk about?

3. A thinking type and a feeling type are dating.

   When there are problems in the relationship, how is the thinking type likely to approach the problem?

   How will the feeling type approach the problem?

   How can the thinking type improve communication?

   How can the feeling type improve communications?

4. A judging type and a perceptive type are married. The judging type likes to keep the house neat and orderly. The perceptive type likes creative disorder. How can they resolve this conflict?

Communication Exercise

Name _____ Date _____

List 10 ideas from this chapter that will help you to improve communication with others who are important to you.

1.

2.

3.

4.

5.

6.

7.

8.

9.

10.

CHAPTER 11

Thinking Critically and Creatively

Learning Objectives

Read to answer these key questions:

- What is critical thinking?

- What are fallacies in reasoning?

- What is moral reasoning?

- What are some techniques for critical thinking?

- What is creativity?

- How can I improve my creativity?

- How is laughter a key to success?

Your college experience will help you to develop critical thinking, moral reasoning, and creative thinking skills. Critical thinking involves analyzing data, generating alternatives, and solving problems. Moral reasoning guides thought and action to help you live an ethical life. Creative thinking helps you to find new ideas to solve problems in your personal and professional life.

Critical Thinking

© art4all/Shutterstock.com

Critical thinking involves questioning established ideas, creating new ideas, and using information to solve problems. In critical thinking, reasoning is used in the pursuit of truth. Part of obtaining a college education is learning to think critically. Understanding the concepts of critical thinking will help you succeed in college courses in which critical thinking is used.

Beyond college, critical thinking is helpful in being a good citizen and a productive member of society. Throughout history, critical thinkers have helped to advance civilization. Thoughts that were once widely accepted were questioned, and newer and more useful ideas were introduced. For example, it was once assumed that bloodsucking leeches were helpful in curing diseases. Some critical thinkers questioned this practice, and the science of medicine was advanced. It was not so long ago that women were not allowed to vote. Critical thinkers questioned this practice so that women could participate in a democratic society.

A lack of critical thinking can lead to great tragedy. In his memoirs, Adolf Eichmann, who played a central role in the Nazis' killing of six million Jews during World War II, wrote:

"From my childhood, obedience was something I could not get out of my system. When I entered the armed services at the age of 27, I found being obedient not a bit more difficult than it had been during my life at that point. It was unthinkable that I would not follow orders. Now that I look back, I realize that a life predicated on being obedient and taking orders is a very comfortable life indeed. Living in such a way reduces to a minimum one's own need to think. "[1]

Critical and creative thinking are closely related. If you can think critically, you have the freedom to be creative and generate new ideas. The great American jurist and philosopher Oliver Wendell Holmes noted:

"There are one-story intellects, two-story intellects, and three-story intellects with skylights. All fact-collectors who have no aim beyond their facts are one-story men. Two-story men compare, reason, generalize, using the labor of the fact-collectors as their own. Three-story men idealize, imagine, predict—their best illumination comes from above through skylights."

Use the information in this chapter to become a three-story intellect with skylights. And by the way, even though Oliver Wendell Holmes talked about men, women can be three-story intellects too.

> "A person's mind stretched to a new idea never goes back to its original dimensions."
> Oliver Wendell Holmes
>
> "I think, therefore I am (*Cogito, ergo sum*)."
> Descartes

Fallacies in Reasoning

To think critically, you need to be able to recognize fallacies in reasoning.[2] Fallacies are patterns of incorrect reasoning. Recognizing these fallacies can help you to avoid them in your thinking and writing. You can also become aware of when others are using these fallacies to persuade you. They may use these fallacies for their own purpose, such as power or financial gain. As you read through these fallacies in reasoning, think about examples you have experienced in your personal life.

- **Appeal to authority.** It is best to make decisions by reviewing the information and arguments and reaching our own conclusions. Sometimes we are encouraged to rely on experts for a recommendation because they have specialized information. Obviously, we need to have trust in the experts to accept their conclusions. However, when we cite some person as an authority in a certain area when they are not, we make an appeal to a questionable authority. For example, when a company uses famous sports figures to endorse a product, a particular brand of athletic shoes or breakfast cereal, they are appealing to a questionable authority. Just because the athletes are famous does not mean they are experts on the product they are endorsing. They are endorsing the product to earn money. Many commercials you see on TV use appeals to a questionable authority.

- **Jumping to conclusions.** When we jump to conclusions, we make hasty generalizations. For example, if a college student borrows money from a bank and does not pay it back, the manager of the bank might conclude that all college students are poor risks and refuse to give loans to other college students.

- **Making generalizations.** We make generalizations when we say that all members of a group are the same, as in:

    All lawyers are greedy.
    All blondes are airheads.

Of course, your occupation does not determine whether or not you are greedy, and the color of your hair does not determine your intelligence. Such thinking leads to harmful stereotypes and fallacies in reasoning. Instead of generalizing, think of people as unique individuals.

- **Attacking the person rather than discussing the issues.** To distract attention from the issues, we often attack the person. Political candidates today are routinely asked about personal issues such as extramarital affairs and drug use. Of course personal integrity in politicians is important, but attacking the person can serve as a smokescreen to direct attention away from important political issues. Critical thinkers avoid reacting emotionally to personalities and use logical thinking to analyze the issues.

- **Appeal to common belief.** Just because something is a common belief does not mean that it is true. At one time people believed that the world was flat and that when you got to the edge of the earth, you would fall off. If you were to survey the people who lived in that period in history, the majority would have agreed that the earth was flat. A survey just tells us what people believe. The survey does not tell us what is true and accurate.

- **Appeal to common practice.** Appealing to common practice is the "everyone else is doing it" argument. Just because everyone else does it doesn't mean that it is right. Here are some common examples of this fallacy:

    It is okay to cheat in school. Everyone else does it.
    It is okay to speed on the freeway. Everyone else does it.
    It is okay to cheat on your taxes. Everyone else does it.

- **Appeal to tradition.** Appeal to tradition is a variation of the "everyone else is doing it" argument. The appeal to tradition is "we've always done it that way." Just because that is the way it has always been done doesn't mean it is the best way to do it. With this attitude, it is very difficult to make changes and improve our ways of doing things. While tradition is very important, it is open to question. For example, construction and automotive technology have traditionally been career choices for men, but not for women. When women tried to enter or work in these careers, there was resistance from those who did not want to change traditions. This resistance limited options for women.

> "The function of education is to teach one to think intensively and to think critically. Intelligence plus character—that is the goal of true education."
> Martin Luther King, Jr.

Fallacies in Reasoning

- Appeal to authority
- Jumping to conclusions
- Making generalizations
- Attacking the person
- Appeal to common belief
- Appeal to common practice
- Appeal to tradition
- Two wrongs
- Domino theory
- Wishful thinking
- Scare tactics
- Appeal to pity
- Appeal to loyalty
- Appeal to prejudice
- Appeal to vanity
- False causes
- Straw man/woman
- Cult behavior

- **Two wrongs.** In this fallacy, it is assumed that it is acceptable to do something because other people are doing something just as bad. For example, if someone cuts you off on the freeway, you may assume that it is acceptable to zoom ahead and cut in front of his or her car. The "two wrongs" fallacy has an element of retribution, or getting back at the other person. The old saying, "Two wrongs do not make a right," applies in this situation.

- **The slippery slope or domino theory.** The slippery slope or domino theory is best explained with an example. A student might think: If I fail the test, I will fail this class. If I fail this class, I will drop out of college. My parents will disown me and I will lose the respect of my friends. I will not be able to get a good job. I will start drinking and end up homeless. In this fallacy, the negative consequences of our actions are only remotely possible, but are assumed to be certain. These dire consequences influence people's decisions and change behavior. In this situation, it is important to evaluate these consequences. One does not necessarily lead to the other. If you fail the test, you could study and pass the next test. As a child you were probably cautioned about many slippery slopes in life:

  Brush your teeth or your teeth will fall out.
  Do your homework or you will never get into college and get a good job.

ACTIVITY

Practice Matching Fallacies in Reasoning, Part I

The column on the left contains examples of fallacies in reasoning. Match each example with the name of the fallacy on the right.

Example:

_____ 1. Women should not be automotive mechanics.

_____ 2. The best sports shoes are those endorsed by famous athletes.

_____ 3. It is OK for athletes to take drugs to enhance their performance. They all do it.

_____ 4. All women with red hair get angry easily.

_____ 5. If you fail the test, you are a failure for life.

_____ 6. To defeat a politician, research his personal background and let the public know of any past mistakes.

_____ 7. Since some children steal, children should not be allowed into the store without their parents.

_____ 8. All sharks are dangerous and should be killed.

_____ 9. If someone insults you, you should insult them back.

Fallacy:

A. Appeal to authority

B. Appeal to tradition

C. Common practice

D. Two wrongs

E. Attack the person

F. Making generalizations

G. Appeal to a common belief

H. Slippery slope

I. Jumping to conclusions

Answers: 1. B, 2. A, 3. C, 4. F, 5. H, 6. E, 7. I, 8. G, 9. D

- **Wishful thinking.** In wishful thinking, an extremely positive outcome, however remote, is proposed as a distraction from logical thinking. For example, a new sports stadium may be proposed. Extremely positive outcomes may be presented, such as downtown redevelopment, the attraction of professional sports teams, increased revenue, and the creation of jobs. Opponents, on the other hand, might foresee increased taxes, lack of parking, and neglect of other important social priorities such as education and shelter for the homeless. Neither position is correct if we assume that the outcomes are certain and automatic. Outcomes need to be evaluated realistically.

  Wishful thinking is often used in commercials to sell products. Here are a few examples:

  > Eat what you want and lose weight.
  > Use this cream and look younger.
  > Use this cologne and women will be attracted to you.
  > Invest your money and get rich quick.

- **Appeal to fear or scare tactics.** Sometimes people appeal to fear as a way of blocking rational thinking. For example, a political commercial showed wolves chasing a person through the forest. It was clearly designed to evoke fear. The message was to vote against a proposition to limit lawyers' fees. The idea was that if lawyers' fees were limited, the poor client would be a victim of limited legal services.

  This commercial used scare tactics to interfere with rational thinking about the issue.

- **Appeal to pity.** In an appeal to pity, emotion is used to replace logic. It is what is known as a "sob story." Appeals to pity may be legitimate when used to foster charity and empathy. However, the sob story uses emotion in place of reason to persuade and is often exaggerated. College faculties often hear sob stories from students having academic difficulties:

  > Please don't disqualify me from college. I failed all my classes because I was emotionally upset when my grandmother died.

  > Please don't fail me in this class. If you fail me, my parents will kick me out of the house and I will not be able to get health insurance.

  > If you fail me in this class, I won't be eligible to play football and my future as a professional will be ruined.

- **Appeal to loyalty.** Human beings are social creatures who enjoy being attached to a group. We feel loyalty to our friends, families, schools, communities, teams, and favorite musicians. Appeals to loyalty ask you to act according to a group's best interests without considering whether the actions are right or wrong. Critical thinkers, however, do not support an idea just to show support for a group with which they identify.

  Peer pressure is related to the loyalty fallacy. With peer pressure, members of a group may feel obliged to act in a certain way because they think members of the group act that way. Another variation of the loyalty fallacy is called the bandwagon argument. It involves supporting a certain idea just to be part of the group. This tendency is powerful when the group is perceived to be powerful or "cool." In elections, people often vote for the candidate that is perceived to be the most popular. If everyone else is voting for the candidate, they assume the candidate must be the best. This is not necessarily true.

- **Appeal to prejudice.** A prejudice is judging a group of people or things positively or negatively, even if the facts do not agree with the judgment. A prejudice is based on a stereotype in which all members of a group are judged to be the same. Speakers sometimes appeal to prejudice to gain support for their causes. Listen for the appeal to prejudice in hate speeches or literature directed against different ethnicities, genders, or sexual orientations.

- **Appeal to vanity.** The appeal to vanity is also known as "apple polishing." The goal of this strategy is to get agreement by paying compliments. Students who pay compliments to teachers and then ask for special treatment are engaging in apple polishing.

- **Post hoc reasoning, or false causes.** Post hoc reasoning has to do with cause and effect. It explains many superstitions. If I play a good game of golf whenever I wear a certain hat, I might conclude that the hat causes me to play a good golf game. The hat, however, is a false cause of playing a good game of golf. I may feel more comfortable wearing my lucky hat, but it is a secondary reason for playing well. I play well because I practice my golf skills and develop my self-confidence. In scientific research, care is taken to test for false causes. Just because an event regularly follows another event does not mean that the first event caused the second event. For example, when the barometer falls, it rains. The falling barometer does not cause the rain; a drop in atmospheric pressure causes the rain. If falling barometers caused the rain, we could all be rainmakers by adjusting our barometers.

- **Straw man or woman.** Watch for this fallacy during election time. Using this strategy, a politician creates a misleading image of someone else's statements, ideas, or beliefs to make them easy to attack. For example, politicians might accuse their opponents of raising taxes. That may only be part of the story, however. Maybe their opponents also voted for many tax-saving measures. When politicians or anyone else use the straw man fallacy, they are falsifying or oversimplifying. Use your critical thinking to identify the straw man or woman (political opponent) in the next election. Of course you don't have to be a politician to use this strategy. People use this strategy when they spread gossip or rumors about someone they want to discredit.

- **Cult behavior.** Cults and doomsday forecasters spread unorthodox and sometimes harmful beliefs with great fervor. These thoughts are perpetuated through mind-control techniques. With mind control, members of a group are taught to suppress natural emotions and accept the ideas of the group in exchange for a sense of belonging. These groups do not allow members to think critically or question the belief system. Mind control is the opposite of critical thinking. It is important to use critical thinking when you encounter beliefs for which there is no hard evidence. An example is the Heaven's Gate cult:

  > It all seems perfectly ludicrous: 39 people don their new sneakers, pack their flight bags and poison themselves in the solemn belief that a passing UFO will whisk them off to Wonderland.

© elder nurkovic/Shutterstock.com

Practice Matching Fallacies in Reasoning, Part II

The column on the left contains examples of fallacies in reasoning. Match each example with the name of the fallacy on the right.

Example:

_____1. You look really nice today. Can I ask you a favor?

_____2. I'll vote for a woman because I am a woman.

_____3. Earn $10,000 a month by working part time at home.

_____4. If you fail me on this test, the coach will not let me play next week.

_____5. I'm more likely to win if I wear my lucky socks.

_____6. If you vote for this politician, she will raise taxes.

_____7. If you don't buy this car, you are putting your family at risk.

_____8. All large dogs are dangerous.

_____9. The leader knows what is best for me.

Fallacy:

A. Wishful thinking

B. Scare tactics

C. Appeal to pity

D. Appeal to loyalty

E. Appeal to prejudice

F. Appeal to vanity

G. Post hoc reasoning

H. Straw man or woman

I. Cult behavior

Answers: 1. F, 2. D, 3. A, 4. C, 5. G, 6. H, 7. B, 8. E, 9. I

Journal Entry #1

Fallacies in reasoning are frequently used in advertisements and politics. From your personal experience, describe an example of a fallacy in reasoning.

How to Become a Critical Thinker

The Critical Thinking Process

When thinking about a complex problem, use these steps in the critical thinking process:

1. **State the problem in a clear and simple way.** Sometimes the message is unclear or obscured by appeals to emotion. Stating the problem clearly brings it into focus so that you can identify the issue and begin to work on it.

2. **Identify the alternative views.** In looking at different views, you open your mind to a wider range of options. The diagram entitled "Alternative Views" below gives a perspective on point of view. For every issue, there are many points of view.

The larger circle represents these many points of view. The individual point of view is represented by a dot on the larger circle. Experience, values, beliefs, culture, and knowledge influence an individual's point of view.

Figure 11.1 Alternative Views
© Kendall Hunt Publishing Company

3. **Watch for fallacies** in reasoning when looking at alternative views.

4. **Find at least three different answers.** In searching for these different answers, you force yourself to look at all the possibilities before you decide on the best answer.

5. **Construct your own reasonable view.** After looking at the alternatives and considering different answers to the problem, construct your own reasonable view. Practice this process using the critical thinking exercises at the end of this chapter.

Tips for Critical Thinking

1. **Be aware of your mindset.** A mindset is a pattern of thought that you use out of habit. You develop patterns of thinking based on your personal experiences, culture, and environment. When the situation changes, your old mindset may need to change as well.

2. **Be willing to say, "I don't know."** With this attitude you are open to exploring new ideas. In today's rapidly changing world, it is not possible to know everything. Rather than trying to know everything, it is more important to be able to find the information you need.

3. **Practice tolerance for other people's ideas.** We all have different views of the world based on our own experiences and can benefit from an open exchange of information.

4. **Try to look for several answers and understand many points of view.** The world is not either-or or black-and-white. Looking at all the possibilities is the first step in finding a creative solution.

5. **Understand before criticizing.** Life is not about justifying your point of view. It is important to understand and then offer your suggestions.

6. **Realize that your emotions can get in the way of clear thinking.** We all have beliefs that are important to us. It is difficult to listen to a different point of view when someone questions your personal beliefs. Open your mind to see all the alternatives. Then construct your reasonable view.

7. **Notice the source of the information you are analyzing.** Political announcements are required to include information about the person or organization paying for the ad. Knowing who paid for an advertisement can help you understand and evaluate the point of view that is being promoted.

8. **Ask the question, "What makes the author think so?"** In this way, you can discover what premises the author is using to justify his or her position.

9. **Ask the question, "So what?"** Ask this question to determine what is important and how the author reached the conclusion.

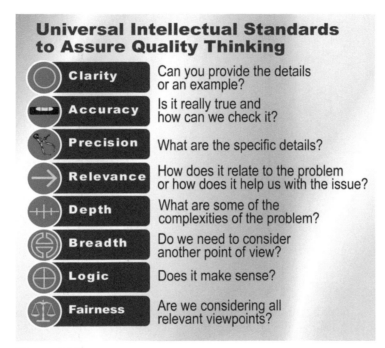

Figure 11.2
Adapted from *The Miniature Guide to Critical Thinking*, by Richard Paul and Linda Elder. Courtesy of Charlotte Moore.
© Kendall Hunt Publishing Company.

Critical Thinking over the Internet

The Internet is revolutionizing the way we access and retrieve information today. Through the use of search engines, websites, electronic periodicals, and online reference materials, it is possible to find just about any information you need. The Internet is also full of scams, rumors, gossip, hoaxes, exaggerations, and illegal activity. Anyone can put anything on the Internet. You will need to apply critical thinking to the information that you find on the Internet. Author Reid Goldsborough offers these suggestions for thinking critically about material on the Internet:

- **Don't be fooled by appearances.** It is easy to create a flashy and professional-looking website. Some products and services are legitimate, but some are scams.

- **Find out about the person or organization providing the information.** There should be links to a home page that lists the author's background and credentials. You need to be skeptical if the author is not identified. If you cannot identify the person who authored the website, find out what organization sponsored the site. Most of the Internet resources cited in this text are provided by educational or government sources. It is the goal of these organizations to provide the public with information.

Critical Thinking Tips
- Be aware of your mindset.
- Say "I don't know."
- Be tolerant.
- Look for several answers.
- Understand.
- Recognize emotions.
- Examine the source.
- Ask, "Why?"
- Ask, "So what?"

- **Look for the reason the information was posted.** What is the agenda? Keep this in mind when evaluating the information. Many websites exist to sell a product or influence public opinion.
- **Look for the date that the information was created or revised.** A good website posts the date of creation or revision.
- **Try to verify the information elsewhere,** especially if the information is at odds with common sense or what you believe to be true. Verify the information through other websites or your local library.[4]

© Sam72/Shutterstock.com

How to Recognize a Scam

Use your critical thinking skills to recognize a scam or hoax. How can you recognize a scam? Here are some signs to watch for:

- **Be aware of big promises.** If something sounds too good to be true, it probably is a hoax. If you are promised $5,000 a month for working part time out of your home, be careful. If you are offered a new TV in a box for $50, the box may contain stolen goods or even rocks!
- **The word "free" is often used to catch your attention to make a sale.** Few things in life are free.
- **A similar tactic is to offer money or a prize.** The scam goes like this: "Congratulations! You have just won a . . ." Be especially careful if you have to pay money to claim your prize.
- **Beware of high-pressure tactics.** A common scam is to ask you to pay money now or the price will go up. Take your time to think carefully about your expenditures. If the deal is legitimate, it will be there tomorrow.
- **To avoid identity theft, be careful about disclosing personal information** such as Social Security numbers and credit card numbers. Disclose this information only to people and organizations you know and trust.
- **If you suspect a scam, research the offer on the Internet.** Use a search engine such as yahoo.com or google.com and type in the word "scam." You can find descriptions of many different types of scams. You can also find information on the latest scams or file a complaint at the Federal Trade Commission website at www.ftc.gov.

Critical Thinking

Test what you have learned by selecting the correct answers to the following questions.

1. Critical thinking involves

    a. being critical of others' opinions.
    b. identifying alternative views.
    c. finding only one correct answer.

2. To be a critical thinker it is important to

    a. understand before criticizing.
    b. justify your point of view.
    c. tell yourself that you know the answer.

3. Construct your reasonable view by

    a. advocating for your point of view.
    b. always defending your mindset.
    c. first considering different answers.

4. An Internet site is legitimate if it

    a. looks professional.
    b. has useful information.
    c. has an identifiable and reputable source.

5. If you are offered something that is too good to be true,

    a. be thankful for your good fortune.
    b. suspect that it could be a scam.
    c. it could be a good investment.

How did you do on the quiz? Check your answers: 1. b, 2. a, 3. c, 4. c, 5. b

Journal Entry #2

List five ideas you can use to increase critical thinking.

Critical Thinking and Moral Reasoning

Beyond recognizing fallacies in reasoning, critical thinking involves rationally deciding what to believe, how to act, and what is right or wrong. It involves assessing personal views and the views of others in order to make good decisions about living your life in an ethical manner. Psychologist Lawrence Kohlberg studied stages of moral reasoning by investigating the reactions of individuals to moral dilemmas. Here is an example of Kohlberg's most famous dilemma:

Heinz Steals the Drug

In Europe, a woman was near death from a special kind of cancer. There was one drug that the doctors thought might save her. It was a form of radium that a druggist in the same town had recently discovered. The drug was expensive to make, but the druggist was charging 10 times what the drug cost him to make. He paid $200 for the radium and charged $2,000 for a small dose of the drug.

"It is the mark of an educated mind to be able to entertain a thought without accepting it."
Aristotle

"Education's purpose is to replace an empty mind with an open one."
Malcolm Forbes

© Lorelyn Medina/Shutterstock.com

The sick woman's husband, Heinz, went to everyone he knew to borrow the money, but he could only get together about $1,000 which was half of what it cost. He told the druggist that his wife was dying and asked him to sell it cheaper or let him pay later. But the druggist said, "No, I discovered the drug and I'm going to make money from it." So Heinz got desperate and broke into the man's store to steal the drug for his wife. Should the husband have done that?[5]

Kohlberg was not interested in the question of whether what Heinz did what was right or wrong, but the reasoning used in reaching a decision. He found that children moved through different levels and stages of moral reasoning, from an egocentric view of the world in which they made decisions based on what was good for the individual, to a more socially responsible view of the world in which decisions were made based on what was good for society, and finally to decisions based on the universal principles of fairness and justice. Individuals progress through these stages as they gain experience thinking about moral problems.

Level 1. Pre-Conventional Morality

This stage of reasoning is common in children, but is sometimes used by adults. At this level, morality is determined by consequences to the individual involved.

Stage 1: Obedience and Punishment

At this stage, children obey the rules to avoid punishment. In the case of the Heinz dilemma, here are possible actions:
- Heinz should not steal the drug because it is against the law.
- Heinz should steal the drug because the pharmacist is asking too much money for it.

Stage 2: Individualism and Exchange

At this stage, children make decisions based on how it will best serve their needs as an individual: "How will it affect me?"
- Heinz should not steal the drug because he will be unhappy if he goes to prison.
- Heinz should steal the drug because he will be happier if he can save his wife.

© Ivelin Radkov/Shutterstock.com

Level 2. Conventional Morality

Conventional morality is more typical of adolescents and adults. People take into consideration society's views and expectations in making decisions about moral behavior. The individual follows society's conventions about what is right or wrong without questioning the fairness or appropriateness of the rule.

Stage 3: Interpersonal Relationships

At this stage, individuals attempt to live up to societal expectations and are concerned about others. The child attempts to be a "good boy" or a "good girl." Adults attempt to "be nice" or conform to the rules of society.

- Heinz should not steal the drug because stealing is bad and he is not a criminal.
- Heinz should steal the drug because he is a good husband and wants to take care of his wife.

Stage 4: Maintaining Social Order

At this stage it is important to do one's duty, respect authority, and follow the rules to maintain law and order. If one person violates a law, others will do it also and society will cease to function in an orderly way.

- Heinz should not steal the drug because the law prohibits stealing. If everyone broke the law, there would be no order in society.
- Heinz should steal the drug, but be prepared to accept the punishment for his actions and to repay the druggist.

Level 3. Post-Conventional Morality

In this level of morality, individuals are seen as separate entities from society and live by the highest principles based on basic human rights such as life, liberty, and justice. Rules are viewed as useful, but changeable in order to protect human rights and maintain social order. Rules and laws are not absolute dictates that must be obeyed without question. A totalitarian society where everyone followed the rules would be well organized, but unjust.

Stage 5: Social Contract and Individual Rights

Rules are important for maintaining a society, but there are differing values, opinions, and beliefs about what is right and wrong. Laws are regarded as social contracts, and individuals should agree on them. If laws do not promote the general welfare, they should be changed to promote what is best for most people. It is important to protect human rights and resolve differences through democratic processes.

- Heinz should not steal the drug because a scientist has a right to fair compensation for the discovery. Fair compensation encourages further drug development.
- Heinz should steal the drug because everyone has the right to life, regardless of the law.

Stage 6: Universal Principles

Democratic processes do not always work as when the majority votes for laws that harm the minority. Laws are only valid if they result in justice and respect for all people; people should disobey unjust laws. The individual acts because it is right, not because is expected, legal, or agreed upon by the majority. Examples of individuals who operated at this level include Gandhi, Martin Luther King, and Cesar Chavez, who all used civil disobedience to achieve just laws. Kohlberg found it difficult to find people who consistently operated at this level.

- Heinz should not steal the drug because others may need the drug just as badly and all lives are equally important.
- Heinz should steal the drug because saving a human life is more important than property rights.

At this stage, Kohlberg suggests that we reach decisions by taking an impartial look at the situation through one another's eyes. When the druggist looks at the situation from Heinz's perspective, he might realize that human life is more important than property rights and agree to accept payments for the drug. When Heinz looks at the situation from the druggist's perspective, he might agree to make payments for the drug. This would be a fair and just solution in which everyone is given full and equal respect.

> "You must be the change you want to see in the world."
> Mahatma Gandhi

> "In the end we will remember not the words of our enemies, but the silence of our friends."
> Martin Luther King

Journal Entry #3

What would you do in the Heinz dilemma? Would you steal the drug? Why?

© Hermin/Shutterstock.com

What Is Creativity?

To see creativity in action, all we need to do is to look at young children. Movie producer Steven Spielberg describes their creativity:

"The greatest quality that we can possess is curiosity, a genuine interest in the world around us. The most used word—and I have five kids, so I know what I'm talking about—the most used word in a child's vocabulary is 'why.' A child doesn't blindly accept things as they are, doesn't blindly believe in limits, doesn't blindly believe in the words spoken by some authority figure like me."[6]

Creativity involves both divergent and convergent thinking. **Divergent thinking** is the ability to discover many alternatives. The creative individual looks for problems, asks why, and comes up with many different answers. J. P. Guilford, a researcher on creativity, said that "the person who is capable of producing a large number of ideas per unit of time, other things being equal, has a greater chance of having significant ideas."[7] After many ideas are created, **convergent thinking** is used to combine the ideas to find new and creative solutions. These creative ideas are used to make a new plan of action.

Creative thinking is useful in fields such as the arts, science, and business. Creativity helps in the enjoyment of outside activities, such as hobbies, that help us to lead satisfying lives. Creativity is important in generating alternatives necessary for effective problem solving and coming up with creative solutions to the challenges we all face in life. Creative individuals are motivated, engaged, and open to new ideas. Guilford defines creative behavior as follows:

"The individual who behaves creatively is oriented toward selecting and solving meaningful problems, using an inner drive to recombine his or her storehouse of experiences in new ways. In attacking problems, he or she does not act as a conformist; instead, he or she pioneers often, is not afraid to fail frequently, but is productive in the long run."[8]

> "Questions are the creative acts of intelligence."
> Frank Kingdon

> "Happiness lies in the joy of achievement and the thrill of creative effort."
> Franklin Roosevelt

> "The real voyage of discovery consists not in making new landscapes but in having new eyes."
> Marcel Proust

The Three S's of Creativity: Sensitivity, Synergy, and Serendipity

The creative process involves sensitivity, synergy, and serendipity. Creative persons use their **sensitivity** to discover the world and spot problems, deficiencies, and incongruities. A person who is sensitive asks, "Why does this happen?" Sensitive persons are also inventive and ask the question, "How can I do this?" They are problem finders as well as problem solvers.

Synergy occurs when two or more elements are associated in a new way and the result is greater than the sum of the parts. For example, imagine a machine that combines the telephone, the computer, the television, and a music player. The combining of these familiar devices into one machine is changing the way we live. Another example of synergy is the old saying, "Two heads are better than one." When two or more people work together and share ideas, the result is often greater than what one person could produce alone. This is the essence of creativity.

The word **serendipity** is attributed to Horace Walpole, who wrote a story about the Persian princes of Serendip. The princes made unexpected discoveries while they were looking for something else. Serendipity is finding something by a lucky accident. You can only take advantage of a lucky accident if you look around and find new meaning and opportunity in the event. An example of serendipity comes from a story about the famous musician Duke Ellington. He was playing at an outdoor concert when a noisy plane flew over the stage. He changed the tempo of the music to go with the sounds of the airplane and directed the plane along with the orchestra. Another example of serendipity is Alexander Fleming's discovery of penicillin. He was growing bacteria in his lab when a spore of *penicillium notatum* blew in the window, landed on the bacteria, and killed it. Instead of throwing away a ruined experiment, he discovered the antibiotic penicillin, one of the most important medical discoveries ever made. Serendipitous people are flexible and open to possibilities as well as fearless in trying something new. They learn to seize the opportunities that just happen in life.

> "Nothing is impossible, the word itself says 'I'm possible'!"
> Audrey Hepburn

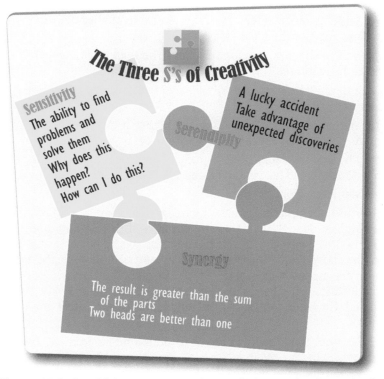

Figure 11.3 Sensitivity, synergy, and serendipity are the three S's of creativity.

Courtesy of Charlotte Moore. © Kendall Hunt Publishing Company.

Creative Thinking Techniques

- **Brainstorming.** One of the most important components of creativity is the ability to use divergent thinking to generate many ideas or alternatives. Brainstorming is one of the most frequently used techniques to develop divergent thinking. The key to brainstorming is to delay critical judgment to allow for the spontaneous flow of ideas. Critical judgment about the merit of ideas can hinder the creative process if it is applied too early. Here are the rules of brainstorming:

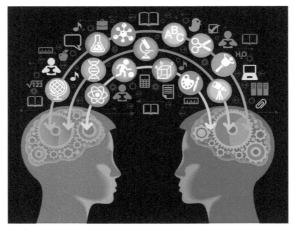

© VLADGRIN/Shutterstock.com

- Generate a large quantity of ideas without regard to quality. This increases the likelihood that some of the ideas will be good or useful.
- Set a time limit to encourage quick thinking. The time limit is generally short, from three to five minutes.
- Set a goal or quota for the number of ideas you want to generate. The goal serves as a motivator.
- The wilder and more unusual the ideas, the better. It is easier to tame down crazy ideas than to think up new ideas.
- Use synergy by brainstorming with a group of people. Build on other people's ideas. Sometimes two ideas combined can make one better idea.
- Select the best ideas from the list.

- **Relaxed attention.** Can you imagine being relaxed and paying attention at the same time? Robert McKim describes this as the paradox of the Ho-hum and the Aha![8] To be creative, it is first necessary to relax. The brain works better when it is relaxed. By relaxing, the individual releases full energy and attention to the task at hand. Athletes and entertainers must master the art of relaxation before they can excel in athletics or entertainment. If the muscles are too tense, blood flow is restricted and energy is wasted. However, totally relaxed individuals cannot think at all. They might even be asleep!

Some tension, but not too much, is needed to think and be creative; hence the term "relaxed attention." In the creative process, the person first thinks about a task, problem, or creation and then relaxes to let the ideas incubate. During this incubation period, the person often gets a flash of insight or feeling of "Aha!" Famous artist Pablo Picasso described this process:

> "For me creation first starts with contemplation, and I need long, idle hours of meditation. It is then that I work most. I look at flies, at flowers, at leaves and trees around me. I let my mind drift at ease, just like a boat in the current. Sooner or later, it is caught by something. It gets precise. It takes shape . . . my next painting motif is decided."[9]

As a student you can apply the principle of relaxed attention to improve your creativity. If you are thinking about a problem and get stuck, relax and come back to it later. Take a break, do something else, or even sleep on it. You are likely to come up with creative inspiration while you are relaxing. Then get back to solving the problem and pay attention to it.

- **Use idea files.** Keep files of ideas that you find interesting. People in advertising call these "swipe files." No one creates in a vacuum. Some of the best creative ideas

Creative Thinking Techniques

- Brainstorming
- Relaxed attention
- Idea files
- Visualization and imagination
- Read
- Keep a journal
- Think critically

involve recombining or building on the ideas of others or looking at them from a different perspective. This is different from copying other people's ideas; it is using them as the fertilizer for creative thinking.

As a college student, you might keep files of the following:

- Interesting ideas and their sources for use in writing term papers
- Information about careers
- Information for your resume
- Information that you can use to apply for scholarships

- **Practice using visualization and imagination.** Visualizing and imagining are important in the creative process. Young children are naturally good at these two skills. What happens as we grow older? As we grow older, we learn to follow the rules and color between the lines. We need rules to have an orderly society, yet we need visualization and imagination to move forward and create new ideas.

  Visualization and imagination can be fun and interesting activities to help you relax. We have often been told not to daydream, but daydreams can be a tool for relaxation as well as creativity. It is important to come back to reality once we are finished daydreaming. The last step in the creative process is doing something with the best of our creative ideas.

- **Read.** One of the best ways to trigger your creativity is to read a wide variety of materials, including newspapers, magazines, novels, nonfiction books, and articles on the Internet. The ideas that you discover will provide background information, helping you gain perspective on the world, and give you ideas for making your own contributions. When you read, you expose your mind to the greatest people who have ever lived. Make reading a habit.

- **Keep a journal.** Keep a journal of your creative ideas, thoughts, and problems. Writing often will help you think clearly. When you write about your problems, it is almost like having your own private therapist. In college, your journal can be a source of creative ideas for writing term papers and completing assignments.

- **Think critically.** Approach learning with a sense of awe, excitement, and skepticism. Here is another paradox! Creative and critical thinkers have much in common. Both ask questions, look at the world from different perspectives, and generate new alternatives.

Acquiring Wisdom and Knowledge

Positive psychologist Christopher Peterson describes wisdom and knowledge as a character strength that includes the **acquisition and use of knowledge for the general good.** Wisdom and knowledge include these components:[10]

- **Creativity** which includes new ways of thinking about things.
- **Curiosity** which includes taking an interest, exploring and discovering throughout life.
- **Love of learning** which includes the motivation to learn new things over a lifetime.
- **Open-mindedness** which includes looking at issues from all sides, weighing the evidence and being willing to change one's mind.
- **Perspective** which involves understanding different points of view.

Use the information about critical thinking and creativity in this chapter to acquire wisdom as well as knowledge.

© iQoncept/Shutterstock.com

Creative Thinking

Test what you have learned by selecting the correct answers to the following questions.

1. Divergent thinking is a creative thinking technique that involves:

    a. defending the correct answer.
    b. selecting the one best alternative.
    c. the ability to discover many different alternatives.

2. The following saying is a good definition for synergy:

    a. Seeing is believing.
    b. Two heads are better than one.
    c. Practice makes perfect.

3. Serendipity is:

    a. finding something by a lucky accident.
    b. finding something humorous in the situation.
    c. improvising while playing music.

4. When using relaxed attention as a creative process,

    a. the creative person is totally relaxed.
    b. the creative person is focusing attention.
    c. the creative person first thinks about the problem and then relaxes.

5. For brainstorming, it is important to:

    a. select the best ideas as a last step.
    b. consider only the good ideas.
    c. consider only the workable ideas.

How did you do on the quiz? Check your answers: 1. c, 2. b, 3. a, 4. c, 5. a

"Laugh at yourself first, before anyone else can."
Elsa Maxwell

"If we couldn't laugh, we would all go insane."
Jimmy Buffett

Journal Entry #4

Describe at least two creativity techniques that you use or are willing to try. Creativity techniques include brainstorming, using relaxed attention, idea files, visualization, imagination, reading, keeping a journal, and thinking critically.

KEYS TO SUCCESS

Learn to Laugh at Life

"Have a laugh at life and look around you for happiness instead of sadness. Laughter has always brought me out of unhappy situations. Even in your darkest moment, you usually can find something to laugh about if you try hard enough." Red Skelton

All of us face difficult times in life; but if we can learn the gift of laughter and have a good sense of humor, it is easier to deal with the difficulties.

Laughter has important physical as well as emotional benefits. Laughter relaxes the body, boosts the immune system, and even improves the function of blood vessels and increases blood flow, which can protect the heart. It adds joy and zest to life, reduces anxiety, relieves stress, improves mood, and enhances resilience. Being more relaxed can help you to shift perspective, solve problems, and be more creative.

If you do not feel happy, smile and pretend to feel happy. Neurophysicist Richard Hamilton says that if you pretend to be happy, you actually feel better because positive thoughts and behavior impact the biochemistry of the brain. Positive thinking helps the brain produce serotonin, a neurotransmitter linked with feelings of happiness.[11]

Humor has several components. Humor involves looking at the incongruities of life and laughing at them. It is looking at adversity and finding the humor in the situation. It is a playful attitude and the ability to make other people smile. Most children are playful, but socialization reduces their playfulness. You can develop your sense of humor by taking yourself less seriously and being grateful for the good things in your life. Learn to laugh at yourself by sharing your embarrassing moments and laughing at them. Be careful not to use humor that puts down other people or groups. Surround yourself with people who enjoy humor and laughter. Look for the humor in difficult situations. Life is full of irony and absurdity, and laughing about it unites people during difficult times. By laughing at the situation, you will be in a better position to deal with it. Keep a positive perspective by focusing on the good things that are happening in your life rather than dwelling on the negatives.

The author Mark Twain was a good example of using humor in life. Mark Twain said that he had never worked a day in his life. He said, "What I have done I have done because it has been play. If it had been work, I shouldn't have done it." He used humor throughout his life despite facing many adversities. His father died when he was 11 years old and he started work at age 12 as a printer's apprentice. He was constantly in trouble and spent some time in jail. He served in the Civil War. His wife died at an early age, and three out of four of his children died before he did.

As a child, Twain enjoyed playing pranks on his mother, and she responded with a sense of humor. After he played a prank on his mother, she told him that he gave her more trouble than all the other children. He replied, "I suppose you were afraid I wouldn't live," and she responded, "No, afraid you would." When Mark Train almost drowned in the river, she pulled him out and said, "I guess there wasn't much danger. People born to be hanged are safe in water." Mark Twain's children described him as "a very good man, and a very funny one . . . He does tell perfectly delightful stories." He started every day by making jokes at the breakfast table, and his humor is reflected in his famous books, including *Huckleberry Finn* and *Tom Sawyer.* He wrote that "humor is a great thing . . . the saving thing after all. The minute it crops up, all our hardnesses yield, all our irritations, and resentments flit away, and a sunny spirit takes their place."[12]

The path to achieving your goals is much smoother if you choose to be happy. So relax, smile, and be happy. Then work on making positive changes in your life.

College Success 1

The College Success 1 website is continually updated with supplementary material for each chapter including Word documents of the journal entries, classroom activities, handouts, videos, links to related materials, and much more. See http://www.collegesuccess1.com/.

© Lyudmyla Kharlamova/
Shutterstock.com

Notes

1. Roger Cohen, "Nazi Leader's Notes Cite 'Obedience' as Reason for His Genocidal Actions," *San Diego Union Tribune,* 13 August 1999.

2. Information in this section is adapted from the Institute for Teaching and Learning website Mission Critical, http://www.sjsu.edu/depts/itl/index.html.

3. Richard Paul and Linda Elder, "The Miniature Guide to Critical Thinking," The Foundation for Critical Thinking, http://www.criticalthinking.org.

4. Reid Goldsborough, "Teaching Healthy Skepticism about Information on the Internet," *Technology and Learning,* January 1998.

5. W.C. Crain, *Theories of Development* (New York: Prentice-Hall, 1985), 118–136, http://faculty.plts.edu/gpence/html/kohlberg.htm.

6. Steven Spielberg, commencement address at the University of Southern California, 1994.

7. Sidney Parnes, Ruth Noller, and Angelo Biondi, *Guide to Creative Action* (New York: Charles Scribner's Sons, 1977), 52.

8. Ibid., 9.

9. Robert McKim, *Experiences in Visual Thinking* (Monterey, CA: Brooks/Cole, 1972).

10. Christopher Peterson, *A Primer in Positive Psychology* (Oxford: University Press, 2006), 142.

11. Ibid.

12. Christopher Peterson and Martin Seligman, *Character Strengths and Virtues: A Handbook and Classification* (Oxford: University Press, 2004), 583–584.

Crime and Punishment

Name _____   Date _____

In 1974, at the age of 19, Doris Drugdealer was arrested for selling $200 worth of heroin to an undercover police officer in Michigan. She received a 10- to 20-year prison sentence for this crime. After serving about eight months of her sentence, she decided that she could not tolerate prison, and with the help of her grandfather, plotted an escape. She used a work pass to walk away from prison. In May 2008, after 34 years, Doris was captured again by detectives who matched fingerprints from her driver's license to her prison records.

Doris said that in 1974, she was a "stupid little . . . hippie-ish girl . . . a pothead." During the 34 years that Doris evaded prison, she worried every day that she would be caught. While looking at a sunset, she would marvel at her freedom and wonder if the past would catch up with her. She was very careful to lead the life of a model citizen and even volunteered for Common Cause, an organization that promotes government ethics and accountability. She married an executive and had three children and lived a comfortable life in an upper-middle-class neighborhood in California. She never told her family about her past. Her husband of 23 years stated that he loved his wife as much as he had the day they were married and that she was a "person of the highest integrity and compassion" and had dedicated her life to raising her children. She taught her children to be responsible citizens and to avoid drugs. Her husband said that the arrest "was the next worst thing to having a death in the family." Doris worried about the effect of her arrest on her son, who had just graduated from high school and her older daughters. A neighbor commented that it would not be useful to society to send Doris back to prison.

Undercover drug officers believed that Doris had connections to "higher-ups" in the drug world and was a teenage leader in a 1970s drug ring. They had found $600, paraphernalia for cutting heroin, and pictures of her with other drug dealers in her apartment. Doris described herself as a recent high school graduate who was strapped for cash, working at a minimum-wage job, and driving a $400 car. She said that every day of her life she regretted getting herself into this situation. She was extradited back to Michigan to serve her original prison term. Her family and friends submitted a plea for clemency to the governor of Michigan. Should the governor grant her clemency?

Use your critical thinking to analyze this situation. Your professor may use this exercise as a group discussion. Use the Critical Thinking Worksheet that follows for your analysis.

This exercise is based on excerpts from "Former Fugitive Drawing Sympathy" and "Captured Fugitive Now Waiting for Extradition, and to Learn Fate" from the *San Diego Union Tribune*, May 1 and 2, 2008.

Critical Thinking Worksheet: Crime and Punishment

Name _____ Date _____

Use the summary of the news article on crime and punishment to answer the questions below. Discuss the issues with a group of students in your class and then write your reasonable point of view.

1. State the problem as simply and clearly as you can.

2. Describe the values and point of view of Doris Drugdealer.

3. Describe the values and point of view of her husband.

4. Describe the values and point of view of her children.

5. Describe the values and point of view of her neighbors.

6. Describe the legal and societal issues.

7. After discussing the issues and looking at different points of view, what is your reasonable point of view? Why? Include a brief description of your values.

A Moral Dilemma

Name _____ Date _____

Mr. Allen's son was seriously injured, but he had no car to take him to the hospital. He approached a stranger and asked to borrow his car, but the stranger refused, saying that he had to go to an important appointment. Mr. Allen stole the car by force to take his son to the hospital. Was it right for Mr. Allen to steal the car?

Assume you are Mr. Allen. Explain why it was right for him to steal the car.

Assume you are the stranger. Explain why it was right to refuse to lend your car.

Can you provide an answer for each of Kohlberg's stages of moral development? You may want to do this exercise as a group activity in your classroom.

Stage 1: What is the reward or punishment for both Mr. Allen and the stranger?

Stage 2: What is in the best interest of Mr. Allen? Of the stranger?

Stage 3: What would a nice person do?

Stage 4: What would a good citizen do?

Stage 5: What is the greatest good?

Stage 6: What universal ethical principles are involved?

What is Kohlberg's suggestion for resolving the issue?

Maintaining a Healthy Lifestyle

Learning Objectives

Read to answer these key questions:

- How long can I expect to live in the new millennium?

- What are the best ideas on nutrition for maintaining optimum health?

- What are the dangers of smoking, alcohol abuse, and other drugs?

- How can I protect others and myself from HIV/AIDS and other sexually transmitted diseases?

- Why is it important to get enough sleep?

- What is stress and how can I deal with it?

- What are some relaxation techniques?

- How can I make positive changes in my life?

Getting a college education is an investment in the quality of your life in the future. Enjoying this increased quality of life depends on maintaining your good health. What you do every day affects your future health. The ordinary choices you make, such as what you eat and how much you exercise, avoiding harmful substances, protecting the body, relaxing, getting enough sleep, and thinking positively, will have a big effect on how long you will enjoy good health and reap the benefits of your education.

Life Expectancy

How long can you expect to live in the new millennium? Since life expectancy is increasing, it is possible that you might live to be 100 years old or older. Life expectancy depends on heredity, environment, and lifestyle. Heredity cannot be changed, but environment and lifestyle depend on personal choice. The choices made at a young age can have a major impact on health in later life.

U.S. Life Expectancy

Year	Male	Female
1900	48.2	51.1
1940	60.8	65.2
1950	65.6	71.1
1960	66.6	73.3
1970	67.1	74.7
1980	70.0	77.4
1990	71.8	78.8
2000	74.1	79.5
2020	77.1	81.9

Source: National Center for Health Statistics[1]

Scientists have been studying centenarians around the world to identify the secrets of longevity.[2] It has been found that 90 percent of centenarians remain functionally independent until age 92. From studies of identical twins that were separated at birth and reared apart, it has been determined that 20 to 30 percent of longevity is genetically determined. The most important factor in longevity is lifestyle. One group that has been studied is the Seventh-Day Adventists in Utah. They avoid alcohol, caffeine, and tobacco and live an average of eight years longer than the average American.

Another group that has been studied is centenarians who live in Okinawa, Japan. These centenarians get plenty of physical and mental exercise. Their diet is rich in fruits and vegetables containing fiber and antioxidants that protect against cancer, heart disease, and stroke. Their diets are low in fat and salt, and they eat more soy than any other population on earth. Soy contains flavonoids that protect against cancer. They practice a dietary philosophy called hara hachi bu, which means eating until 80 percent full. Seiryu Toguchi of Okinawa was a centenarian who lived to be 105 years old. Here is a description of a typical day for him:[3]

. . . He wakes at 6 A.M., in the house in which he was born, and opens the shutters. "It's a sign to my neighbors," he says, "that I am still alive." He does stretching exercises along with a radio broadcast, then eats breakfast: whole-grain rice and miso soup with vegetables. He puts in two hours of picking weeds in his 1,000 sq. ft. field. . . . A fellow has to make a living, so Toguchi buys rice and meat with the profits from his produce. At 12:30 Toguchi eats lunch: goya stir fry with egg and tofu. He naps for an hour or so, then spends two more hours in his field. After dinner he plays traditional songs—a favorite is Spring When I Was 19—on the three-stringed sanchin and makes an entry in his diary as he has done every night for the past decade. "This way," he says, "I won't forget my Chinese characters. It's fun. It keeps my mind sharp."

There are almost 100,000 centenarians in the United States and the population is increasing rapidly. Daisy McFadden of the Bronx in New York is a good example of a centenarian who eats sensibly, exercises, and stays mentally active. For breakfast she has oatmeal, cranberry juice, and a banana. For lunch she has a salad with beets, cucumbers, tomatoes, and either chicken or fish. Dinner is a plate of steamed vegetables and lean meat. She does not drink soda, but occasionally indulges in chocolate chip cookies. McFadden enjoys regular exercise walking to the senior center at least three times a week to use a treadmill, bicycle, or rowing machine. To stay mentally active, she reads the newspaper daily and does the crossword puzzles.[4]

The best advice for living a long and healthy life is to eat sensibly, exercise, and find activities that keep you mentally alert.

> "Life expectancy would grow by leaps and bounds if green vegetables smelled as good as bacon."
> Doug Larson

© ruigsantos/Shutterstock.com

Balance Nutrition and Exercise for Good Health

Balancing good nutrition with exercise contributes to a long and healthy life. A good diet helps you to enjoy life and feel your best. Being informed about the basic principles of nutrition can help you to make healthful choices. The federal government has proposed dietary guidelines that take into account age, gender, and level of exercise.[5]

Aim for a healthy weight. Maintaining a healthy weight is one of the keys to a long and healthy life. Being overweight increases the risk of high blood pressure, high blood cholesterol, heart disease, stroke, diabetes, cancer, arthritis, and breathing problems. The problem of overweight children and adults is a major health concern today. The best way to lose weight is by establishing patterns of healthy eating and exercise.

> "We don't stop playing because we grow old, we grow old because we stop playing."
> George Bernard Shaw

Americans are struggling with how to maintain a healthy weight. Some are turning to crash diets that severely restrict calories and food choices. Crash diets are not recommended because the weight loss is temporary and the body can be deprived of important nutrients. Another serious problem is eating disorders such as anorexia, which can lead to serious health problems and even death in severe cases. Symptoms of an eating disorder include a preoccupation with food or body weight, dramatic weight loss, excessive exercise, self-induced vomiting, and abuse of laxatives. Anyone with these symptoms should consult a health care provider.

Body Mass Index

The Body Mass Index (BMI) is a commonly used method of evaluating a person's weight. It is based on the ratio of weight to height. To calculate your BMI, first answer these two questions:

1. What is your height in inches? _____

2. What is your weight in pounds? _____

Calculate your BMI using the following formula:

$$\text{BMI} = (705 \times \text{body weight}) \div (\text{height} \times \text{height})$$

Example: A person who is 66 inches tall and weighs 155 pounds:

$$\text{BMI} = (705 \times 155) \div (66 \times 66) = 25$$

Calculate your BMI here. To evaluate your weight, locate your BMI in the chart below.

My BMI = (705 × my weight ____) ÷ (my height in inches____ × my height in inches _____) = _____

Body Mass Index Categories[6]

BMI	Weight
Less than 18.5	Underweight
18.5–24.9	Normal weight
25–29.9	Overweight
30 and above	Obese

There are some exceptions to consider when using BMI to evaluate weight:

- Bodybuilders and other athletes may have a higher BMI because muscle weighs more than fat.
- For the elderly, a BMI between 25 and 27 may be healthier and protect against osteoporosis.
- The BMI is not designed to be used with children.

Another way to evaluate your weight is to simply measure around your waist. A measurement of over 35 inches for women or 40 inches for men places a person at greater risk of health problems. If your BMI is over 25 or your waist measurement increases, reduce calories and increase activity.

Journal Entry #1

Calculate your BMI. Based on your BMI, do you need to maintain, lose, or gain weight?

My BMI is . . .

Based on my BMI, I need to . . .

Here are some suggestions for managing your weight:

- Be physically active.
- Choose healthy foods.
- Choose foods low in fat and sugars.
- Eat sensible portions.
- Lose weight slowly.

Be physically active each day. There are many benefits to regular physical activity:

- Increases your fitness, endurance, and strength
- Maintains healthy bones, muscles, and joints
- Helps in managing weight
- Lowers risk of cardiovascular disease, colon cancer, and Type 2 diabetes
- Promotes psychological well-being
- Reduces depression and anxiety

© Monkey Business Images/Shutterstock.com

> "Walking is the best possible exercise. Habituate yourself to walk very far."
>
> Thomas Jefferson

Two kinds of physical activity are recommended. Aerobic activity speeds up your heart rate and breathing and increases cardiovascular fitness. Strength and flexibility exercises such as lifting weights and stretching help to maintain strong bones. Choose activities that you enjoy and include them in your daily routine. It is important to remain active throughout your life.

New federal guidelines suggest the need for 30 to 60 minutes of moderately intense physical activity each day. These activities could include an hour of walking, slow swimming, leisurely bicycle riding, or golfing without a cart. More intense exercise such as jogging can provide needed exercise in a shorter time.[7]

Eat healthy. A good diet helps you to enjoy life and feel your best. Use the government dietary guidelines at http://www. choosemyplate.gov/ to make good nutritional choices. At this site you can enter your personal information for a customized recommendation of the types and amounts of food to eat for

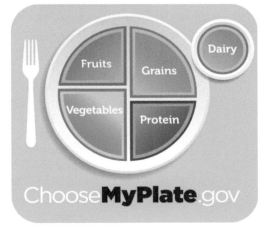

optimal health. The plate icon on the previous page provides a visual of the five different food groups with half of the plate filled with fruits and vegetables and the other half filled with whole grains and proteins.

Here are some examples of recommended food consumption based on age, gender, and activity levels. In these examples, 30 to 60 minutes of physical activity are assumed:

	Female Age 6	Female Age 18	Male Age 18	Male Age 50
Grains	5 oz	6 oz	10 oz	8 oz
Vegetables	1.5 cups	2.5 cups	3.5 cups	3 cups
Fruits	1.5 cups	2 cups	2.5 cups	2 cups
Oils	4 tsp	6 tsp	8 tsp	7 tsp
Milk	2 cups	3 cups	3 cups	3 cups
Meat/Beans	4 oz	5.5 oz	7 oz	6.5 oz
Extra Calories from Fat and Sugar	170	265	425	360
Total Calories	1400	2000	2800	2400

Here are some suggestions for making healthy food choices:

- In establishing a pattern of healthy eating, it is recommended that plant foods form the foundation of a good diet. Two-thirds of the dinner plate should be covered with fruits, vegetables, whole grains, and beans. Use meats and dairy products in moderation and use fats and sweets sparingly. This type of diet is helpful in controlling weight as well as reducing your risk of cancer.[8]

- Eat a variety of grains daily, especially whole grains. Whole grains include brown rice, cracked wheat, graham flour, whole-grain corn, oatmeal, popcorn, barley, whole rye, and whole wheat. Whole grains provide vitamins, minerals, and fiber, which helps you to feel full with fewer calories.

- Eat a variety of fruits and vegetables daily. Eating many kinds and colors of fruits and vegetables provides important vitamins and minerals. Enjoy five servings of fruits and vegetables each day with at least two servings of fruit and three servings of vegetables.

- Limit the use of solid fats such as butter, lard, margarines, and partially hydrogenated shortenings. Solid fats raise blood cholesterol and increase your chances of coronary heart disease. Use vegetable oils instead. Aim for a fat intake of no more that 30 percent of your calories.

- Moderate your intake of sugar. Foods containing added sugars have added calories and little nutritional value. The number one source of added sugar is soft drinks. Drink water instead of or in addition to soft drinks. Sweets, candies, pies, cakes, cookies, and fruit drinks are also major sources of added sugars. Eating too many foods with added sugar contributes to weight gain or eating less of the nutritious foods. Added sugar also contributes to tooth decay.

- Choose and prepare foods with less salt. Eating too much salt can increase your chances of having high blood pressure. High salt intake causes the body to secrete calcium, which is necessary for healthy bones. Only small amounts of salt occur naturally in foods. Most salt is added during food processing. Eat fresh fruits and vegetables to avoid eating too much salt.

How to Lose Weight

If you need to lose weight, you are not alone! Increasing numbers of adults in the United States are struggling with being overweight or obese. The Centers for Disease Control report that approximately 33 percent of adults are overweight and another 33 percent are obese.[9] Being overweight is defined as having a BMI between 25 and 29.9. Obesity is defined as having a BMI of 30 or above. For example, a woman who is five feet four inches tall and weighs 180 pounds is considered obese. Maintaining your ideal weight is a matter of balancing calories in from food and beverages with calories expended through physical activity.

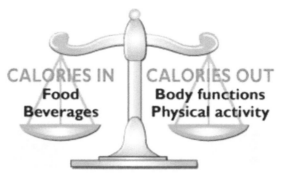

Source: From the U.S. Center for Disease Control, 2010.

Here are some practical suggestions for losing weight if your BMI is over 25 and you are not an athlete:

- Stop drinking sodas. One out of every five calories consumed in the United States is from sodas, and they are the biggest contributors to obesity.[10] Instead of drinking sodas, substitute water or unsweetened tea. Flavor your water with lemons, oranges, limes, strawberries, or mint. Be careful not to substitute sugary fruit juice, coffee, or tea for the sodas, since these drinks are often higher in calories.
- Exercise at least an hour to an hour and a half daily. Exercise is needed to burn the excess calories.
- Use the information at www.choosemyplate.gov/ to determine the number of calories needed to maintain your ideal weight. For example, the average 18-year-old female needs 2,000 calories a day. To lose weight, subtract 300 to 500 calories a day from this total.
- Eat five servings of fruits and vegetables a day. Use these fruits and vegetables as snacks.
- To control hunger, eat several small meals of 300 to 400 calories each.
- Make sure to eat breakfast. Eating breakfast helps to provide energy and avoid hunger, which leads to overeating.
- Eat smaller portions. Use a salad plate instead of a dinner plate. When you eat out, save half of your food for another meal.
- Minimize eating out at fast-food restaurants, since it is difficult to make good food choices there.
- If you are sad or anxious, try exercise instead of eating to relieve these symptoms. Practice stress reduction techniques.

"Acorns or chocolate cake?"
© Cartoonresource/Shutterstock.com

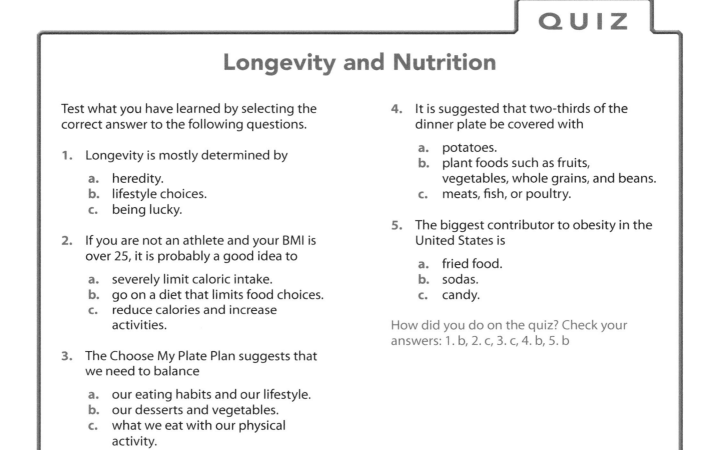

QUIZ

Longevity and Nutrition

Test what you have learned by selecting the correct answer to the following questions.

1. Longevity is mostly determined by

   a. heredity.
   b. lifestyle choices.
   c. being lucky.

2. If you are not an athlete and your BMI is over 25, it is probably a good idea to

   a. severely limit caloric intake.
   b. go on a diet that limits food choices.
   c. reduce calories and increase activities.

3. The Choose My Plate Plan suggests that we need to balance

   a. our eating habits and our lifestyle.
   b. our desserts and vegetables.
   c. what we eat with our physical activity.

4. It is suggested that two-thirds of the dinner plate be covered with

   a. potatoes.
   b. plant foods such as fruits, vegetables, whole grains, and beans.
   c. meats, fish, or poultry.

5. The biggest contributor to obesity in the United States is

   a. fried food.
   b. sodas.
   c. candy.

How did you do on the quiz? Check your answers: 1. b, 2. c, 3. c, 4. b, 5. b

---

"It's never too late to be what you might have been."

George Elliot

"The greatest wealth is health."

Virgil

Avoiding Addictions to Smoking, Alcohol, and Other Drugs

Smoking, abusing alcohol, or using illegal drugs can interfere with your success in college, on the job, and in life. These addictions can cause illness and a shortened life expectancy. Knowledge in these areas will help you make the best choices to maintain your quality of life.

Smoking Tobacco: A Leading Cause of Preventable Illness and Death

Smoking is widespread in our society. Despite a gradual decrease in the rate of smoking, about one out of every five adults is still smoking. Tobacco use is the leading cause of preventable illness and death in the United States and one out of every five deaths in the

United States is related to smoking. Each year, 480,000 Americans die too young as a result of smoking-related illnesses.[11] Imagine that three jumbo jets carrying 400 people each crashed every day of the year. This would be similar to the number of people who die each year from smoking.

Smoking is related to a variety of illnesses:

- Smoking damages and irritates the respiratory system. Smoking a package of cigarettes a day is like smearing a cup of tar over the respiratory tract. Smoking causes lung cancer, emphysema, and chronic bronchitis.

- Smoking affects the heart and circulatory system. Smoking causes premature coronary heart disease and several types of blood-vessel diseases.

- Smoking increases the probability of having strokes, which damage the brain and often leave a person with permanent disabilities.

- Smoking affects the eyes and vision. It is speculated that smoking causes vision loss by restricting blood flow to the eyes. Recent studies have connected smoking with macular degeneration, an irreversible form of blindness. Cataracts, or clouding of the lenses of the eyes, are also associated with smoking.

- Smoking irritates the eyes, nose, throat, and gums and can lead to cancer of the mouth, throat, or esophagus.

- Smoking is associated with osteoporosis, the thinning of bones due to mineral loss.

- During pregnancy, smoking damages the developing fetus, causing miscarriages, low birth weight, developmental problems, and impaired lung function at birth.

- Smoking causes premature facial wrinkling due to vasoconstriction of the capillaries of the face.[12]

Why is smoking such a major health problem? It is because smoking is an addiction that is difficult to overcome. Only 20 percent of smokers who decide to quit smoking are successful on a long-term basis.[13] For those who are successful in quitting, tobacco-related health risks are improved over time. Although smoking cessation is difficult, it is worth the investment in improved healthy living. Refraining from smoking, along with a healthy diet and exercise, can increase your life span by as much as 10 years.[14] For help with smoking cessation, visit your physician or college health office. The resources on the College Success1 website provide helpful hints for giving up smoking.

Alcohol

Each year, many college students die as a result of excessive drinking. Some students drink and drive and die in car accidents. Others die from alcohol poisoning or alcohol-related accidents. Excessive drinking is a factor in poor college performance and high dropout rates. Studies have shown that heavy drinking causes brain damage and interferes with memory.[15] Having some knowledge about alcohol use can help you to make choices to ensure your future quality of life.

Alcohol Abuse Quiz

Read each statement and decide if it is true or false. Place a checkmark in the appropriate column.

True	False	
		Alcohol abuse is the third leading health problem in the United States, behind heart disease and cancer.
		Thirteen percent of people in the United States have a problem with alcohol dependency.
		Alcohol is the most abused drug worldwide.
		Alcohol use or dependency reduces one's lifespan by 10 years.
		Alcohol is involved in 50 percent of all traffic fatalities and homicides.
		Alcohol is involved in two-thirds of college student suicides.
		Alcohol is a major factor in HIV infection.
		Alcohol is involved in 90 percent of college rapes.
		Women are at higher risk than men of serious medical conditions related to alcohol use.
		The age span 18 to 21 is the period of heaviest alcohol consumption for most drinkers in the United States.
		Each year college students spend about $5.5 billion on alcohol, mostly beer.
		College students drink enough beer each year to fill an Olympic-size swimming pool on every campus in the United States.
		Students spend more money on beer than they do on books, soda, coffee, juice, and milk combined.
		Excessive alcohol use leads to memory loss and neurological problems.
		More students drink than use cocaine, marijuana, or cigarettes combined.

How did you do on the quiz? All of the above statements are true. The fact that all of the above statements are true points to the serious nature of alcohol abuse on college campuses and in society in general.[16]

Binge Drinking

Heavy drinking causes students to miss class and fall behind in schoolwork. College students who are considered binge drinkers are at risk of many alcohol-related problems. Binge drinking is simply drinking too much alcohol at one time. In men, binge drinking is defined by researchers as drinking five or more drinks in a row. In women, it is drinking four or more drinks in a row.[17] It takes about one hour to metabolize one drink, so it would take five hours to metabolize five drinks. Researchers estimate that two out of five college students (44 percent) are binge drinkers.[18] Students who are binge drinkers are 21 times more likely to:

© advent/Shutterstock.com

- Be hurt or injured
- Drive a car after drinking
- Get in trouble with campus or local police
- Engage in unprotected sex
- Engage in unplanned sexual activity
- Damage property
- Fall behind in schoolwork
- Miss class[19]

It is particularly significant that there is a connection between binge drinking and driving. Among frequent binge drinkers, 62 percent of men and 49 percent of women said that they had driven a car after drinking. About half of the students in this study reported being a passenger in a car in which the driver was high or drunk.[20] A drink is defined as:

- A 12-ounce beer
- A four-ounce glass of wine
- A shot of liquor (1.5 ounces of 80-proof distilled spirits) straight or in a mixed drink

Because women absorb and metabolize alcohol differently than men do, they are at greater risk of alcohol-related problems. Women have less body water than men and achieve a higher concentration of alcohol in the blood after drinking the same amount as men. Women are more likely to develop liver, brain, and heart damage from excessive drinking. When alcohol is being consumed, women are at higher risk for becoming the victims of violent crime.

National studies on alcohol consumption in colleges find that students are less likely to participate in binge drinking when they put a high priority on studying, have special interests or hobbies, and participate in volunteer activities. The majority of college students (56 percent nationally) either abstain from drinking or drink in moderation. Students least likely to be binge drinkers are African American, Asian, 24 years or older, or married. Students at highest risk for binge drinking include intercollegiate athletes and members of fraternities and sororities. Students most likely to be binge drinkers are white, male, and under 24 years of age.[21]

Blood Alcohol Content (BAC)

The amount of alcohol in your blood is referred to as blood alcohol content (BAC). It is recorded in milligrams of alcohol per 100 milliliters of blood. For example, a BAC of .10 means that 1/10 of 1 percent or 1/1,000 of your total blood is alcohol. BAC depends on the amount of blood in your body, which varies with your weight, and the amount of alcohol consumed over time. The liver can only process one drink per hour. The rest builds up in the bloodstream. Below are listed the effects of increasing BAC:

.02   Mellow feeling, slight body warmth, less inhibited

.05   Noticeable relaxation, less alert, less self-focused, coordination impairment begins, most people reach this level with one or two drinks

.08   Drunk driving limit, definite impairment in coordination and judgment

.10   Noisy, possible embarrassing behavior, mood swings, reduction in reaction times

.15   Impaired balance and movement, clearly drunk

.30   Many lose consciousness

.40   Most lose consciousness, some die

.50   Breathing stops, many die[22]

The above figures point out some important facts for college students. It does not take many drinks to reach the drunk driving limit. Most people reach the drunk driving limit if they have one to three drinks, depending on weight and time since the last drink. BAC increases if you are lighter weight or if you have just had a drink. As the BAC increases, more serious effects occur. Tragically, each year college students die from alcohol poisoning, which occurs when large quantities of alcohol are consumed in a short period of time. This sometimes occurs during the hazing periods in college fraternities and sororities. Colleges are taking steps to stop hazing on college campuses nationwide.

What Is Moderate Drinking?

If adults choose to drink alcohol, it is recommended that they drink in moderation.[23] Moderation is defined as no more than one drink per day for women or two drinks per day for men. Drinking more than this can increase the risks for car accidents, high blood pressure, stroke, violence, suicide, and certain types of cancer. Women who drink during pregnancy increase the risk of birth defects. Too much alcohol causes social and psychological problems, cirrhosis of the liver, inflammation of the pancreas, and damage to the brain and heart. Heavy drinkers are also at risk for malnutrition, since alcohol contains calories that may be substituted for more nutritional foods.

It has been found that drinking in moderation may lower the risk of coronary heart disease in men over the age of 45 and women over the age of 55. However, there are other factors contributing to a healthy heart, including a healthy diet, exercise, avoidance of smoking, and maintaining a healthy weight.

There are certain people who should not drink:

- Children and adolescents
- Individuals of any age who cannot restrict their drinking to moderate levels
- Women who are pregnant or who are likely to become pregnant
- Individuals who drive or operate machinery that requires skill, attention, or coordination
- Individuals taking over-the-counter or prescription drugs that interact with alcohol

Warning Signs of Alcoholism

Alcoholics Anonymous has published 12 questions to determine if alcohol is a problem in your life. Answer these questions honestly:

1. Have you ever decided to stop drinking for a week or so but could only stop for a couple of days?

2. Do you wish people would mind their own business about your drinking and stop telling you what to do?

3. Have you ever switched from one kind of drink to another in the hope that this would keep you from getting drunk?

4. Have you ever had to have a drink upon awakening during the past year? Do you need a drink to get started or to stop shaking?

5. Do you envy people who can drink without getting into trouble?

6. Have you had problems connected with drinking during the past year?

7. Has your drinking caused problems at home?

8. Do you ever try to get extra drinks at a party because you do not get enough?

9. Do you tell yourself you can stop drinking any time you want to, even though you keep getting drunk when you don't mean to?

10. Have you missed days of work or school because of drinking?

11. Do you ever have blackouts from drinking, when you cannot remember what happened?

12. Have you ever felt that your life would be better if you did not drink?

If you answered yes to four of the above questions, it is likely that you have a problem with alcohol.

© iQoncept/Shutterstock.com

Other Drugs

While alcohol is the most commonly used drug, street drugs such as marijuana, cocaine, LSD, methamphetamines, rohypnol (the "date rape drug"), ecstasy, ketamine (a PCP-like anesthetic), and heroin interfere with the accomplishment of life goals. Clark Carr, President of Narconon, describes the following impact of illegal drug usage:

"One of the worst impacts of street drugs is their impact on ambition. Drugs have insidious yet devastating effects upon children and their ability to envision hopes and dreams. Ambition enables a person to learn to enjoy life and to pursue happiness without drugs, but it can be destroyed through drug use. When a person is intoxicated by drugs, important functions are adversely affected, including concentration, recording, and recalling. These tools are essential to learning, and without them education is impaired. Addiction becomes the all-consuming focus of activities aimed at procuring more drugs. Education, careers, relationships, and life itself take a back seat."[24]

People take drugs in order to feel better. However the high from taking drugs is followed by a low that is relieved by taking more drugs, leading to addiction. With increased drug use, the lows get lower and it becomes more difficult to reach a high. Drugs have varying levels of toxicity, but they all stress the body's nervous, digestive, respiratory, circulatory, and reproductive systems. The problem is that drugs can become life-destroying. Anyone contemplating taking drugs should ask these four questions:

1. Are the benefits going to outweigh the liabilities?
2. Will I experience more pleasure than pain, or more pain than pleasure?
3. Will the pleasure be temporary? How will I feel tomorrow?
4. Will the drug do more harm than good?

Answering these questions honestly can help you to make the right choices. An addiction to smoking, alcohol, or illegal drugs can be difficult to control. If you need help with problems caused by drug or alcohol addiction, see your physician or contact your college health office. The *College Success1 Website* contains useful links to help you to cope with addictive behavior and make some positive changes in your life.

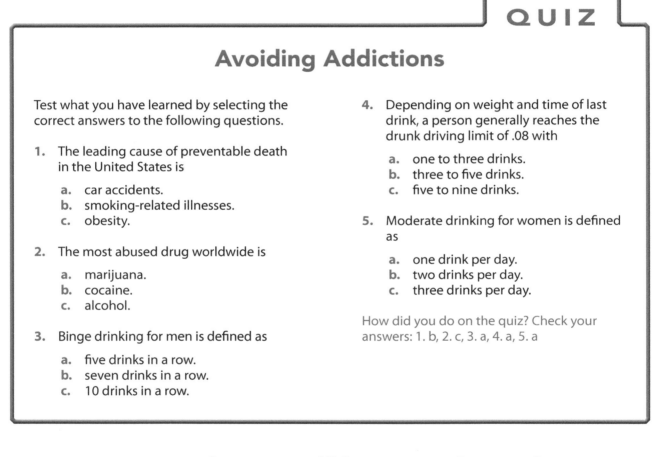

QUIZ

Avoiding Addictions

Test what you have learned by selecting the correct answers to the following questions.

1. The leading cause of preventable death in the United States is

   a. car accidents.
   b. smoking-related illnesses.
   c. obesity.

2. The most abused drug worldwide is

   a. marijuana.
   b. cocaine.
   c. alcohol.

3. Binge drinking for men is defined as

   a. five drinks in a row.
   b. seven drinks in a row.
   c. 10 drinks in a row.

4. Depending on weight and time of last drink, a person generally reaches the drunk driving limit of .08 with

   a. one to three drinks.
   b. three to five drinks.
   c. five to nine drinks.

5. Moderate drinking for women is defined as

   a. one drink per day.
   b. two drinks per day.
   c. three drinks per day.

How did you do on the quiz? Check your answers: 1. b, 2. c, 3. a, 4. a, 5. a

Protecting Yourself from Sexual Assault

Sexual assault continues to be a serious problem on college campuses and can result in suspension or expulsion from the university as well as criminal charges for the perpetrator. For the victim, sexual assault can have major consequences including physical injury, depression, low self-esteem, anxiety disorders, and lower academic achievement.

What you should know about sexual assault:[25]

- Between 20% and 25% of college women and 4% of college men report having been sexually assaulted in college.
- Estimates of dating violence range from 10% to 50%.

- Most assaults are committed by people the victim knows.
- Women 18–24 years old are at the greatest risk from partner violence.
- The perpetrators are often serial offenders.
- College rapists target victims who are drugged, drunk, passed out, or incapacitated.
- Sexual assaults on college campuses are underreported because victims fear repercussions.
- Rape is a criminal offense requiring medical attention.
- Rape victims are at risk for pregnancy and sexually transmitted diseases (STDs), including HIV.

What can students do to reduce the incidence of sexual assault? Alcohol and drugs are major risk factors for rape. Women who reported that "they sometimes or often drink more than they should are twice as likely to be victims of completed, attempted, or suspected assault compared with those who rarely or never do." Another risk factor is "hooking up" or casual sexual relationships. Sixteen percent of women who were "hooking up from time to time" were more likely to be sexually assaulted than those in more long-term relationships.[26] Men are working to reduce sexual assault by forming organizations such as "Men Can Stop Rape" in which the central message is that men can be strong without being violent.[27]

Protecting Yourself from HIV/AIDS and Other Sexually Transmitted Infections

Human immunodeficiency virus (HIV) and acquired immune deficiency syndrome (AIDS) have been described as the worst plague in modern history. AIDS is the fourth leading cause of death in the world. It is estimated that by 2020, the number of people dying from AIDS will be approximately equal to all people killed in wars in the 20th century.[28] New drugs have been developed that inhibit the growth of the virus that leads to AIDS, but there is still no cure for AIDS. These new medications are extending the healthy life of infected patients.[29] Since AIDS continues to be a leading cause of death among Americans ages 25 to 44, knowing how to protect yourself from HIV/AIDS and other sexually transmitted diseases is an important survival skill.[30] The U.S. Centers for Disease Control and Prevention provide some helpful information to minimize your risk of infection.[31]

© Amir Ridhwan/Shutterstock.com

What is HIV? HIV is the human immunodeficiency virus that causes AIDS. The virus kills the "CD4" cells that help your body fight off infection.

What is AIDS? AIDS is the acquired immunodeficiency syndrome. It is the disease you get when HIV destroys the body's immune system. Normally your immune system helps to fight off illness. When the immune system is destroyed, you can become very sick and die.

How is HIV acquired? HIV is acquired in the following ways:

- It is acquired by having unprotected sex (sex without a condom) with someone who has HIV. The virus can be in an infected person's blood, semen, or vaginal secretions. It can enter the body through tiny cuts or sores on the skin, or the lining of the vagina, penis, rectum, or mouth.
- It is acquired by sharing a needle and syringe to inject drugs or by sharing equipment used to prepare drugs for injection with someone who has HIV.

- Babies born to women who are HIV-positive can become infected during pregnancy, birth, or breastfeeding.

You cannot get HIV from the following:

- Working with or being around someone who has HIV
- Sweat, tears, spit, clothes, drinking fountains, phones, or toilet seats
- Insect bites or stings
- Donating blood
- A closed-mouth kiss

What are the best ways to protect yourself? Here are some guidelines:

- Don't share needles or syringes for injecting drugs, steroids, or vitamins, or for tattooing or body piercing. Germs from an infected person can stay in the needle and then be injected into the next person using the needle.
- Don't have sex. This is truly "safe sex."
- If you choose to have sex, have sex with only one partner that you know doesn't have HIV and is only having sex with you.
- Use a latex condom every time you have sex. This is referred to as "safer sex."
- Don't share razors or toothbrushes because of the possibility of contact with blood.
- If you are pregnant, get tested for HIV. Drug treatments are available to reduce the chances of your baby being infected with HIV.

How do I know if I have HIV or AIDS? A person can have HIV or AIDS and feel perfectly healthy. The only way to know is to get tested. Most college health offices and your local health department offer confidential testing.

What other infections are spread through sexual activity? There are more than 25 different infections spread through sexual activity. There are 19 million new cases of sexually transmitted infections (STIs) each year, half of them in young people ages 15–24.[32] According to the Centers for Disease Control and Prevention, these infections can "result in severe health consequences, cancer, impaired fertility, premature birth, infant death and disability."[33] The increase in STIs has paralleled the AIDS epidemic. The guidelines for protecting against HIV apply to other STIs as well.

The most common STIs in the United States include chlamydia, gonorrhea, syphilis, genital herpes, human papillomavirus (HPV), hepatitis B, trichomoniasis, and bacterial vaginosis. Bacterial infections such as gonorrhea, syphilis, and chlamydia can be cured with antibiotics. Viral infections such as herpes, and genital warts can be treated but not cured. New vaccines are now available to prevent hepatitis A and B which can cause serious liver damage and for HPV that causes genital warts and can lead to cancer. New drugs are now available to treat hepatitis C, D, and E, but they are expensive. It is recommended that college students (both men and women) keep their immunizations up to date and include these newer vaccinations.

Women suffer the most from STIs because they have more frequent and serious complications from them than men do. Many STIs can be passed to the fetus, newborn, or infant before, during, or after birth. Chlamydia and gonorrhea can lead to pelvic inflammatory disease (PID), which can cause chronic pelvic pain, infertility, or potentially fatal ectopic pregnancies. The human papilloma virus (HPV) can increase the risk of cervical cancer in women.

> "Sleep is a golden chain that ties our health and our bodies together."
> Thomas Dekker
>
> "A good laugh and a long sleep are the best cures in the doctor's book."
> Irish Proverb

Getting Enough Sleep

College students often miss out on sleep while cramming for exams, enjoying an active social life, and trying to balance work and school. We have seen in previous chapters that missing one night of sleep results in a 30% decline in mental abilities since sleep is needed for long-term memory formation. Lack of sleep has other detrimental effects on health:

- The ability to utilize food declines by 30% resulting in weight gain and the growth of fat instead of muscle.
- The level of stress hormones increases.
- The aging process is accelerated.
- Lack of sleep can make you less energetic, increase irritability, cause depression, and make you accident prone.
- The immune system is weakened making you more susceptible to illness.

© Andrey_Kuzmin/Shutterstock.com

Journal Entry #3

Are you getting enough sleep for optimum performance in school and to maintain good health? If not, what is your plan to get more sleep?

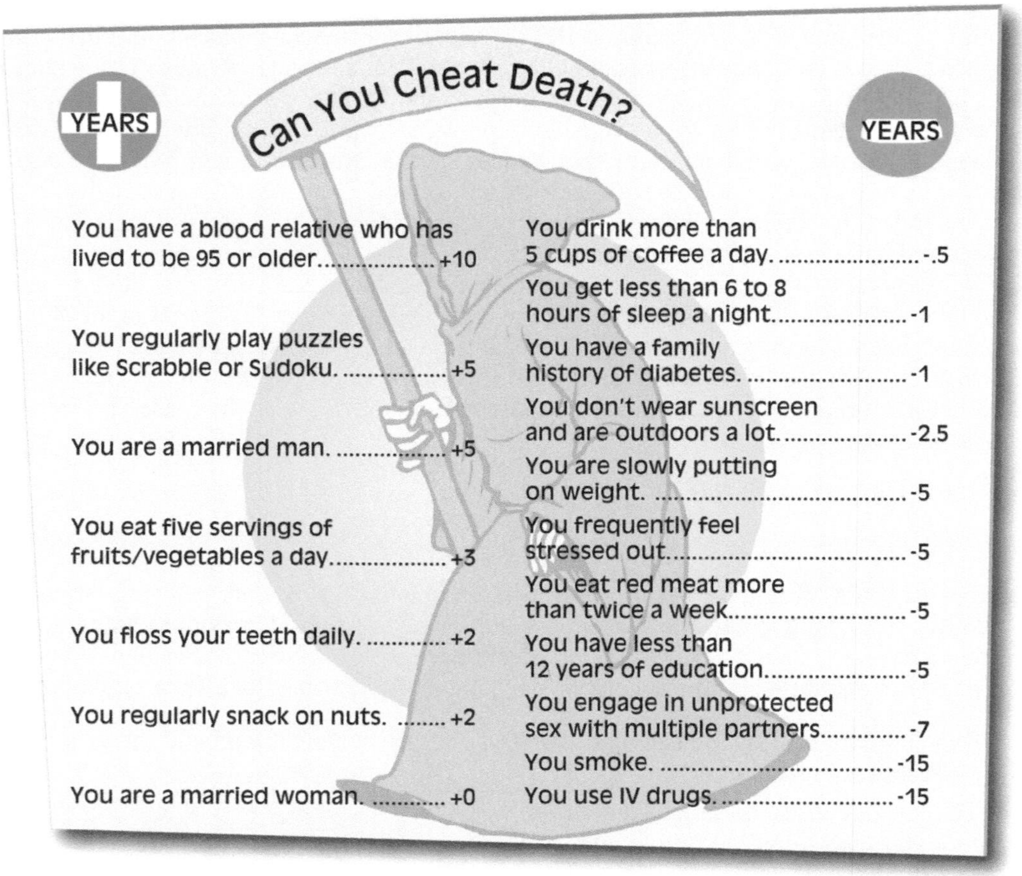

Figure 12.1 Steps to increase longevity.

Courtesy of Charlotte Moore. © Kendall Hunt Publishing Company.

Stress and Relaxation

One of the major challenges in life is dealing with stress and being able to relax. For college students, it is important to realize that too much stress interferes with memory, concentration, and learning. After graduation, it is important to be able to deal with stress on the job.

What Is Stress?

Imagine a world where there is absolutely no stress. While the thought is intriguing, it would probably be very boring. Some stress is positive and essential for well-being. For example, when we run a race, play a game of football, or act in a play, we experience stress, but it provides excitement and motivation. When a teacher announces a test, a little stress can cause the student to study for the test. Hans Selye, a famous researcher on stress, called this positive type of stress "eustress." He even went so far as to suggest, "Without stress, there could be no life."[34]

Hans Selye described negative stress as "distress." Distress has several physical symptoms that are uncomfortable and detract from good health. These symptoms can range from headaches, stomachaches, and sleeplessness to serious health problems such as high blood pressure, heart disease, and stroke. It is helpful to know some relaxation techniques to deal with the distress.

"Slow down and everything you are chasing will come around and catch you."

John De Paola

"Tension is who you think you should be. Relaxation is who you are."

Chinese Proverb

Get Aerobic Exercise

Aerobic exercise is simply exercise that raises your heart rate and exercises your heart. It includes activities such as walking, running, swimming, dancing, and playing sports. It is recommended that people do some type of aerobic exercise three to five times a week. In addition to strengthening the heart, aerobic exercise burns up stress hormones and allows us to relax.

One of the best relaxation techniques is to find some physical activities that you enjoy and participate in them often. It often requires some planning to fit these activities into our busy schedules. It is important to see these activities as a priority and to take time to enjoy them.

Practice Stress-Reducing Thoughts

When you are trying to deal with a stressful situation, listen to your self-statements. What are you saying to yourself? If these statements are negative, you will have negative emotions and will be stressed out. Think of some positive, stress-reducing thoughts that you can use in stressful situations. Here are some examples, but you will be better off to think up some of your own:

- That's the way it goes. No use getting upset.
- It's not the end of the world.
- Keep cool.
- It's no big deal.
- Relax.
- Life's too short to let this bother me.
- It's their problem.
- Life's like that.
- Be happy.
- I'll just do the best I can.
- No need to worry.

Take Action to Resolve Your Problems

If you have problems that are causing stress, take action to resolve them. Here are some steps you can take to solve problems and reduce stress:

- Concentrate your efforts on doing something about the problem.
- Seek information on how to solve the problem. This step may involve doing research or speaking to others.
- Make a plan of action.
- Make it a priority to solve the problem.
- Do what needs to be done to solve the problem, one step at a time.

Using Mindfulness to Relax

Mindfulness is a relaxation technique that involves **being aware of what is going on in a particular moment** and can be used as a quick break when you are feeling stressed and overwhelmed. It is effective because it temporarily takes your mind away from the everyday stresses of life. Living in the moment can be invigorating and help you to stay on task, as well as increasing focus and engagement. It can be as simple as stopping for a few moments to pay attention to your breathing. Here are a few ideas for taking a quick break by using mindfulness:[35]

- Focus on your breathing. When your attention wanders to your worries, bring it back to your breathing. Focus on your breathing for at least two minutes.

© Gustavo Frazao/Shutterstock.com

- Notice your surroundings. Look around and focus on the details in your surroundings.
- Practice savoring the moment. Take a piece of chocolate and unwrap it carefully. Feel the texture and notice the smell. Take a small bite and savor it as it melts on your tongue. Practice enjoying the present moment.
- Make it new. Whether working on a term paper, doing a presentation, or working on a project, think about how you can do it differently and make it new. This will increase the enjoyment and quality of the project.
- Mind the gap. Instead of being impatient at a red light or any other times when you have to wait, use the time as a break from stress. Breathe in and out. Savor the moment.
- Focus on the soles of your feet. Move your toes, feel your socks and shoes, and breathe naturally until you feel calm.
- Focus on your senses. Carefully observe your surroundings in detail including sounds and smell. Make a mental photograph. Close your eyes and see if you can remember all the details. Open your eyes and see what you missed. Mentally list the things you can appreciate in your surroundings.
- Imagine yourself in a pleasant place. When you are actually in a beautiful place, take the time to make a mental photograph. Memorize each detail so that you can return to this place in your mind when you feel stressed. Some people visualize the mountains, the beach, the ocean, a mountain stream, waterfalls, a tropical garden, or a desert scene. Choose a scene that works for you.
- Take a short walk. Pay attention to your breathing, the sensation of wind on your skin, and what you can see and hear.

Psychological Hardiness

Psychologists have studied people who are psychologically hardy.[44] These individuals are able to deal with stress in a positive way and avoid the negative consequences of stress. How do they stay healthy in spite of high-powered jobs and constant challenges? People who are stress-resistant have a positive attitude toward life and the challenges it presents. Psychologically hardy individuals have the following qualities:

- They are open to change. They view change as a challenge rather than a threat.
- They have a feeling of involvement in whatever they are doing. They are committed to their occupations and endeavors.

- They have a sense of control over events rather than a feeling of powerlessness. Having a sense of control is essential to good mental health.

Some of the hardiest individuals were those who survived the concentration camps during World War II. In spite of enduring extreme hardships, some found the strength to survive their ordeal and to live well-adapted lives. Scientists studying these survivors discovered that they used several resources for survival. Knowledge and intelligence was one resource. With knowledge and intelligence, these people could see many ways of dealing with the situation and were able to choose the best alternative. These survivors also had a strong sense of identity. They were confident and powerful individuals. Another important resource was a strong social network that gave people the collective strength to survive.

© Tatiana Popova/Shutterstock.com

Other Relaxation Techniques

Another way to deal with stress is to practice some physical and mental relaxation techniques. Here are a few suggestions:

- Listen to soothing music. Choose music that has a beat that is slower than your heart rate. Classical or New Age music can be very relaxing.
- Lie down in a comfortable place and tense and relax your muscles. Start with the muscles in your head and work your way down to your toes. Tense each muscle for five to 10 seconds and then release the tension completely.
- Use positive thinking. Look for the good things in life and take the time to appreciate them.
- Maintain a healthy diet and get enough exercise.
- Practice yoga or tai chi.
- Keep things in perspective. Ask yourself, "Will it be important in 10 years?" If so, do something about it. If not, just relax.
- Focus on the positives. What have you learned from dealing with this problem? Has the problem provided an opportunity for personal growth?
- Discuss your feelings with a friend who is a good listener or get professional counseling.
- Keep your sense of humor. Laughter actually reduces the stress hormones.
- Maintain a support network of friends and loved ones.
- Get a massage or give one to someone else.

Journal Entry # 4

Comment on your level of stress. What stress management techniques work best for you?

Making Positive Changes in Your Life

You are probably aware of the importance of implementing many of the ideas in this chapter. However, actually making some positive changes is difficult. Dr. James Prochaska has studied the process of change and identifies the six stages:[37]

1. **Precontemplation.** In this stage, a person denies that there is a problem and is not ready to change. If the habit causes difficulties, the person may blame the problems on others, especially those who are pressuring for change. There are two ways to move out of this stage. One way is through an increasing awareness or knowledge of the problem. Another way is through emotional arousal. For example, a person may see another dying of lung cancer and decide that it is time to quit smoking.

2. **Contemplation.** In this stage, a person begins to be aware of a problem and thinks seriously about taking some action. He or she weighs the pros and cons, the benefits and sacrifices, and thinks about the difficulty of change. People can only move to the next stage when they develop the self-confidence to believe that they can make a change. In the example of smoking cessation, at this stage a person would begin to look at the negative consequences of smoking but would consider change difficult.

3. **Preparation.** During this stage, people develop a strategy for change. They realize that change is necessary and desire to make the change. They discuss the change with friends and find the needed resources to make the change. They set an actual date to take action. In our smoking example, a person would start talking with friends and family members about quitting smoking and would set a time to stop smoking.

4. **Action.** This is the "just do it" stage. Without action, the goal cannot be accomplished. This stage requires some commitment. A person trying to quit smoking might just stop smoking "cold turkey" or cut down on daily smoking by a specific amount.

5. **Maintenance.** Once you have reached your goal, maintenance is the next step. This stage is the most difficult one as people struggle with the impulse to return to old patterns. Once a person has stopped smoking, the real test is maintaining the behavior.

© phloxii/Shutterstock.com

6. **Termination.** This is permanent change. It is a time when temptations stop. Many people find it difficult to reach this stage.

Six Stages of Change

1. Precontemplation
2. Contemplation
3. Preparation
4. Action
5. Maintenance
6. Termination

What is important to realize about Prochaska's model is that change is a process and that there will be slip-ups along the way. His research shows that successful changers experience some failures along the way. However, he suggests that action that fails is better than no action at all. His research shows that those who tried to act and failed were more likely to succeed in the future. In one study of 200 people who made New Year's resolutions and were still keeping them two years later, the subjects had an average of 14 lapses before they were successful in keeping their resolutions.

Setbacks in the process of change are natural, and it is important not to give up. The process of change is difficult, but rewarding when you can follow through. When you are successful, you enjoy better health and gain confidence in your ability to make positive changes.

KEYS TO SUCCESS

Live to Be 100

It is possible that you could live to be 100 years old. Of course, if you live to be 100, you will want to be healthy and capable of enjoying your life. Many people are doing this already.

John Glenn, the world's oldest astronaut at age 77, returned from space in 1998. Dr. John Charles joked that "he did pretty good for a 40-year-old guy."[38] He suffered no more bone or muscle loss than the younger astronauts on the mission, and his heart rate was slightly better than those of the younger astronauts. Doctors were so impressed with John Glenn's physical condition that they decided to take better care of their own health. How did John Glenn stay fit? He took care of himself over his lifetime. He walked several miles a day, did some light weight training, and ate a balanced diet. He challenged the notion that seniors were frail individuals. Glenn enjoyed the ride and encouraged NASA to send more senior citizens into orbit. He lived to be 95 years old.

Sarah "Sadie" Delaney wrote a bestselling novel with her sister Bessie at age 104. It contained their reminiscences of a century of achievement of African American women. They shared memories of slavery, segregation, and racism that they had experienced during their lives. Sadie lived to be 109 years old and Bessie died at age 104. They were from a family of 10 children, all of whom went to college. Their mother was a teacher and taught the children self-discipline, compassion, and confidence. When Bessie and Sadie were asked how they had lived so long, Bessie said, "Honey, we never married; we never had husbands to worry us to death." Sadie added, "Don't get married just because he looks pretty. He's got to have good genes and have some sense."[39]

> "Nobody grows old by merely living a number of years. We grow old by deserting our ideals. Years may wrinkle the skin, but to give up enthusiasm wrinkles the soul."
>
> Samuel Ullman

> "Wrinkles should merely indicate where smiles have been."
>
> Mark Twain

> "Anyone who stops learning is old, whether at twenty or eighty."
>
> Henry Ford

Mae Laborde became an actress at age 93. She played the role of Vanna White (40 years in the future), appeared on *MADtv*, and faced down the Grim Reaper in a commercial about the elderly without health insurance. She was always smiling, had a positive attitude, and was ready to take

(Continued)

on the world. She said that it was never too late to follow your dreams. She lived to be 102 years old.

Jerry Bloch at age 81 became the oldest man to climb El Capitan Mountain in Yosemite National Park. He chose the toughest and most challenging route up the mountain because he felt it might be his last mountain-climbing adventure because he was getting older.

Jeanne Calment passed away in 1997 at the age of 122. She was the oldest living person at that time. She was quite active into her old age. She took up fencing at age 85, rode a bicycle at age 100, and produced a rap CD at age 121.

During her younger life she engaged in activities such as playing the piano, tennis, roller-skating, bicycling, swimming, hunting, and going to the opera. She was never bored, and remained spirited and mentally sharp until the end. She became known for her wit and humor. One of her sayings was, "I've never had but one wrinkle, and I'm sitting on it."

Since you may live to be 100, take some advice from the experts: exercise to stay physically fit, be careful about whom you marry, stay active, have a positive attitude, and maintain your sense of humor.

© Tutti Fruitti/Shutterstock.com

Journal Entry #5

Write at least five intention statements about improving your health. Think about nutrition, exercise, avoiding addictions, preventing disease and relaxation, or other factors influencing your health. I intend to . . . .

© Lyudmyla Kharlamova/
Shutterstock.com

College Success 1

The College Success 1 website is continually updated with supplementary material for each chapter including Word documents of the journal entries, classroom activities, handouts, videos, links to related materials, and much more. See http://www.collegesuccess1.com/.

Notes

1. U.S. Department of Health and Human Services, Centers for Disease Control and Prevention, National Center for Health Statistics, "Deaths, Preliminary Data for 2011," http://www.cdc.gov/nchs/data/nvsr/nvsr61/nvsr61_06.pdf

2. Richard Corliss and Michael Lemonick, "How to Live to be 100," *Time*, August 30, 2004.

3. Ibid.

4. Jenna Goudreau, "How to Live to Be 101," MSN Health and Fitness, accessed July 2010, http://health.msn.com.

5. U.S. Department of Agriculture, www.choosemyplate.gov/

6. U.S. Department of Agriculture, *Body Mass Index and Health*, March 2000.

7. U.S. Department of Agriculture, www.choosemyplate.gov/

8. Associated Press, "Proper Diet Urged to Fight Cancer, Not Supplements," *San Diego Union Tribune*, September 5, 2000.

9. U.S. Centers for Disease Control and Prevention, "Overweight and Obesity,"accessed August 3, 2010, http://www.cdc.gov/obesity/causes/index.html.

10. Marilyn Marchione, "Soda Causes Obesity, Researchers Report," *San Diego Union Tribune*, March 5, 2006.

11. Centers for Disease Control and Prevention, "Fast Facts," from http://www.cdc.gov/tobacco/data_statistics/fact_sheets/fast_facts/index.htm, 2015.

12. Ibid.

13. Ibid.

14. Gary Fraser and David Shavlik, "Ten Years of Life," *Archives of Internal Medicine* 161, no. 13 (9 July 2001).

15. "Binge Drinking Affects Brain, memory," from http://alcoholism.about.com.

16. Samuel Autman, "CSU Panel Urges Offensive against Alcohol Abuse," *San Diego Union Tribune*, May 8, 2001. Lewis Eigan, *Alcohol Practices, Policies and Potentials of American Colleges and Universities*, U.S. Department of Health and Human Services, 1991. National Institute on Alcohol Abuse and Alcoholism, U.S. Department of Health and Human Services, *Are Women More Vulnerable to Alcohol's Effects?*, 1999. Pacific Institute for Research and Evaluation, *Cost of Underage Drinking*, U.S. Department of Justice, 1999. Also from http://www.alcoholism.about.com and http://www.stopcollegebinging.com .

17. Henry Wechsler and Toben Nelson, "Binge Drinking and the American College Student: What's Five Drinks?" *Psychology of Addictive Behaviors* 15, no. 4 (2001): 287–291.

18. Henry Wechsler, *Binge Drinking on America's College Campuses: Findings from the Harvard School of Public Health College Alcohol Study*, 2000.

19. Henry Wechsler, "College Binge Drinking in the 1990s: A Continuing Problem," *Journal of American College Health* 48 (2000): 199–210.

20. Ibid.

21. Henry Wechsler, *Findings from the Harvard School of Public Health College Alcohol Study*, 2000, http://www.hsph.harvard.edu/cas.

22. From http://www.habitsmart.com/bal.html.

23. U.S. Department of *Agriculture, Dietary Guidelines for Americans*, 2000.

24. Clark Kerr, "There is No Free Ride," *Freedom* (1998).

25. The United States Department of Justice, "Responding to Campus Sexual Assault," from http://www.justice.gov/ovw/responding-campus-sexual-assault, 2015.

26. The Washington Post, "1 in 5 College Women Say They Were Violated," from http://www.washingtonpost.com/sf/local/2015/06/12/1-in-5-women-say-they-were-violated/, June 12, 2015.

27. "Men Can Stop Rape, Creating Cultures Free from Violence," from http://www.mencanstoprape.org/, 2015.

28. Lawrence Altman, "Peak of AIDS Epidemic Still to Come, U.N. says," *San Diego Union Tribune*, July 3, 2002.

29. E.J. Mundell, "Hope for AIDS Cure Remains Alive," *WashingtonPost*.com, January 5, 2007.

30. U.S. Centers for Disease Control and Prevention, *Comprehensive HIV Prevention Messages for Young People*, 2002.

31. U.S. Centers for Disease Control and Prevention, National Center for HIV, STD, and TB Prevention, Divisions of HIV/AIDS Prevention, *HIV and AIDS: Are You at Risk?*, 2000.

32. U.S. Centers for Disease Control and Prevention, "Surveillance 2006: Trends in Sexually Transmitted Diseases in the United States 2006," from http://cdc.gov/STD/trends2006.htm.

33. Cheryl Clark, "Sex Cops Help Find Those Who Spread Diseases," *San Diego Union Tribune*, March 11, 2002.

34. From http://www.stress.org, 2002.

35. *Psychology Today*, "Back to the Present: How to Live in the Moment," from https://www.psychologytoday.com/blog/brainstorm/200812/back-the-present-how-live-in-the-moment, 2008.

36. Maya Pines, "Psychological Hardiness: The Role of Challenge in Health," *Psychology Today*, December 1980.

37. James Prochaska, "What It Takes to Change," *Health Net News*, Fall 1997.

38. Katherine Rizzo, "John Glenn, 77, Handled Space Like a Young Man," *San Diego Union Tribune*, January 29, 2000.

39. Chelsea Carter, "Sarah 'Sadie' Delaney, 109, Wrote Best Seller with her Sister at 104," *San Diego Union Tribune*, 1999.

Health Assessment

Name _____ Date _____

Go to www.livingto100.com and use the Living to 100 Life Expectancy Calculator to assess your health habits.

What are your good health habits?

What are some areas you need to improve?

Based on the above list, write three intention statements for maintaining good health in the future.

1.

2.

3.

Stress-Reducing Thoughts

Name _____ Date _____

The following story is based on a news article about road rage. As you read the article, think about Mr. Road Rage and the negative thoughts he was thinking. What stress-reducing thoughts could have been used to avoid these tragic results? Then answer the questions below. You may want to do this as a group exercise with some of your classmates.

Mr. Road Rage, who shot a man as a result of a traffic-related altercation, was sentenced to 19 years in prison today. He was a quiet man with no previous criminal record. People at his place of work, where he was employed as a computer programmer, were surprised to learn what had happened. Mr. Road Rage was not a violent man. He had even tried to get out of the Navy as a conscientious objector because he hated violence.

What happened? Mr. Rage was on the way home from work when some teenagers on bicycles cut right in front of him. Mr. Rage almost hit them. He was so angry that he stopped to talk with the teenagers. They began to call each other names and exchange obscene gestures. One of the teenagers became so angry with Mr. Rage that he threw his bicycle at Mr. Rage's car, making a small dent. The teenagers quickly left the scene. Mr. Rage continued to his apartment complex where he saw one of the teenagers involved in the altercation. He went to his apartment and got an old gun and decided that he would make a citizen's arrest of the teenager. The teenager resisted; and during the scuffle that ensued, the gun went off and the teenager was killed.

During Mr. Rage's murder trial, one of his colleagues at work said that Mr. Rage's behavior was completely out of character. He never imagined that such an incident could occur.

1. List the negative thoughts that might have been going through Mr. Rage's head during this incident.

2. What stress-reducing thoughts could Mr. Rage have used to avoid this situation?

3. Make a list of stress-reducing thoughts that you can use in stressful situations.

What Is Your Stress Index?*

Name _____ Date _____

Do you frequently: Yes   No

  1. Neglect your diet?   _____   _____

  2. Try to do everything yourself?   _____   _____

  3. Blow up easily?   _____   _____

  4. Seek unrealistic goals?   _____   _____

  5. Fail to see the humor in situations others find funny? _____   _____

  6. Act rude?   _____   _____

  7. Make a big deal out of everything?   _____   _____

  8. Look to other people to make things happen?   _____   _____

  9. Have difficulty making decisions?   _____   _____

 10. Complain you are disorganized?   _____   _____

 11. Avoid people whose ideas are different from your own? _____   _____

 12. Keep everything inside?   _____   _____

 13. Neglect exercise?   _____   _____

 14. Have only a few supportive relationships?   _____   _____

 15. Use psychoactive drugs, such as sleeping pills and tranquilizers, without physician approval?   _____   _____

 16. Get too little rest?   _____   _____

 17. Get angry when you are kept waiting?   _____   _____

 18. Ignore stress symptoms?   _____   _____

 19. Procrastinate?   _____   _____

 20. Think there is only one right way to do something?   _____   _____

 21. Fail to build in relaxation time?   _____   _____

 22. Gossip?   _____   _____

 23. Race through the day?   _____   _____

 24. Spend a lot of time lamenting the past?   _____   _____

 25. Fail to get a break from noise and crowds?   _____   _____

*From Andrew Slaby, *Sixty Ways to Make Stress Work for You*.

Score 1 for each yes answer and 0 for each no. Total score: _____

1–6   There are a few hassles in your life. Make sure, though, that you aren't trying so hard to avoid problems that you shy away from challenges.

7–13   You've got your life in pretty good control. Work on the choices and habits that could still be causing some unnecessary stress in your life.

14–20   You're approaching the danger zone. You may well be suffering stress-related symptoms and your relationships could be strained. Think carefully about choices you've made and take relaxation breaks each day.

Above 20 Emergency! You must stop now, rethink how you are living, change your attitudes, and pay scrupulous attention to your diet, exercise, and relaxation programs.

Appreciating Diversity

Learning Objectives

Read to answer these key questions:

- What is diversity and why is it important?

- How can an understanding and appreciation of diversity help me to be successful in school and in work?

- What is some vocabulary useful for understanding diversity?

- What are some ideas for communicating across cultures?

- What are some myths and facts about sexual orientation?

- How can I gain an appreciation of diversity?

Our schools, our workplaces, and our nation are becoming more diverse. Gaining an understanding and appreciation of this diversity will enhance your future success. Understanding yourself and having pride in your unique characteristics is the first step in the process. Self-knowledge includes information about your personality, interests, talents, and values. Earlier in this text you had the opportunity to begin this exploration. This chapter challenges you to examine some additional characteristics that make you a unique individual and to take pride in yourself while respecting the differences of others.

© RyFlip/Shutterstock.com

Diversity Is Increasing

Another word for diversity is differences. These differences do not make one group inferior or superior. Differences are not deficits: they are just differences. Look around your classroom, your place of employment, or where you do business. You will notice people of a variety of races, ethnic groups, cultures, genders, ages, socioeconomic levels, and sexual orientations. Other differences that add to our uniqueness include religious preference, political affiliation, personality, interests, and values. It is common to take pride in who we are and to look around and find people who share our view of the world. The challenge is to be able to look at the world from the point of view of those who are different from us. These differences provide an opportunity for learning.

Our schools and communities are becoming increasingly diverse. In the United States, one in every five students has a parent born in a foreign country. Nationwide, students who are non-Latino whites make up only 56% of the population. The current school population includes 21% Latinos, 17% African Americans, 5% Asians and 1% Native Americans. There is also an increase in people who identify themselves as multiracial. About seven million people or 2.4 percent of the population identify with at least two different racial groups. California, one of the most populous states, is leading the nation in student diversity. There is no single group in the majority: 49% are latinos, 30 percent are non-latino whites, 8 percent are African Americans, and 12 percent are Asians.[1] In New Mexico, Hawaii, and the District of Columbia, non-Latino whites are also in the minority.[2] According to the latest census data, non-Hispanic whites will drop below 50% of the U.S. population by 2043.[3]

In our schools, places of work, and communities, we increasingly study, work, and socialize with people from different ethnic groups. This morning I talked with a student from Mexico and another from France. My classes have students from Mexico, Japan, Argentina, and Iraq. A colleague called on the phone and we spoke in Spanish. He invited me to a Greek café and deli where we ate Greek salad and purchased feta cheese and baklava. This diversity provides different perspectives, and products from other countries enrich our lives. It requires open-mindedness and respect for differences for it all to work.

We also live in a **global economy**. Increased international trade will result in new career opportunities that require an understanding and appreciation of cultural differences. The United States is in the center of the largest free-trade area in the world. In 1994, the North American Free Trade Agreement (NAFTA) created a free-trade area that includes Canada, the United States, and Mexico. This act resulted in a freer flow of goods among these countries and an increase in international business. The success of this international business depends on increased cooperation and problem solving among these nations. Free-trade agreements are currently being expanded worldwide.

Another major step toward the global economy was the creation of a single currency in Europe, the euro, which was successfully launched on January 1, 2002. The purpose of this largest money changeover in history was to establish a system in which people, goods, services, and capital can move freely across national borders. The European countries using the euro have made their economies more competitive by facilitating trade, travel, and investment.

International trade accounts for a quarter of all economic activity in the United States.[4] All we have to do is look around us to see that many of the foods and products we use in our daily lives come from other countries.

Last night Jessica invited friends over for dinner and made stir-fried vegetables with chicken. She used ingredients from Vietnam, Thailand, Italy, Japan and Mexico. These foods were all purchased at her local grocery store. The guests ate dinner on plates made in Malaysia and drank wine from Australia. The next morning, she got up and dressed in a shirt made in the Dominican Republic and pants made in Mexico. She then put on her walking shoes, which were made in Thailand, and listened to Jamaican music on her iPod, which was made in China. For breakfast she ate a banana grown in Honduras and drank coffee from Colombia. She drove to school in a car that was made in Japan.

Global trade brings us many new and inexpensive products and is having a major impact on the economy and careers of the future.

Changes in technology have made an awareness and appreciation of diversity more important. The world is becoming an **electronic village** connected by an array of communication and information technologies: computers, the Internet, communications satellites, cell phones, fax machines, and the myriad of electronic devices that are an integral part of our lives today. These devices make rapid communication possible all over the world and are essential for international business and trade. The Internet is like a vast information superhighway, and each computer is an onramp to the highway. Those who do not have a computer or lack computer skills will be left off the highway and have limited access to information and opportunities.

The increased use of the Internet offers both great opportunities and challenges. The Internet can help to break down barriers between people. When communicating with someone over the Internet, differences such as race, age, religion, or economic status are not obvious. The flow of information and ideas is unrestricted, and people with similar interests can communicate easily with one another. There is great potential for use as well as misuse of the Internet. Chat groups can share information about medical conditions or treatments, but hate groups can also use the Internet to promote their political agendas.

Journal Entry #1

How will the global economy and the electronic village affect your future career and lifestyle?

Why Is Diversity Important?

Our society, schools, and work environments are becoming more diverse. Having an understanding and appreciation of diversity can help you to be successful at school, at work, and in your personal life. Here are some benefits:

© maxstockphoto/Shutterstock.com

Benefits of Diversity

- Gain critical thinking skills
- Pride in self and culture
- Learn from others
- Improve interpersonal skills
- Learn flexibility
- Develop cultural awareness

- **Gain skills in critical thinking.** Critical thinking requires identifying different viewpoints, finding possible answers, and then constructing your own reasonable view. Critical thinking skills are one of the expected outcomes of higher education. Many of your college assignments are designed to teach these skills. Whether you are writing an essay in an English class, participating in a discussion in a history class, or completing a laboratory experiment, critical thinking skills will help you to complete the task successfully. Critical thinking skills are also helpful in finding good solutions to problems or challenges you might find at work. For example, for a business manager, an important task is helping employees to work together as a team. The critical thinking process results in greater understanding of others and better problem-solving skills. To stay competitive, businesses need to find creative solutions for building better products and providing good customer service. Critical thinking skills help people work together to come up with good ideas to make a business a success.

- **Have pride in yourself and your culture.** Having pride in yourself is the foundation of good mental health and success in life. Sonia Nieto did research on a group of successful students. These students had good grades, enjoyed school, had plans for the future, and described themselves as successful. Nieto found that "one of the most consistent, and least expected, outcomes to emerge from these case studies has been a resoluteness with which young people maintain pride and satisfaction in their culture and the strength they derive from it."[5] Having pride in yourself and your culture is an important part of high self-esteem and can help you to become a better student and worker. Having good self-esteem provides the confidence to accept and care for others. The best schools and workplaces provide an environment where people can value their own culture as well as others. With respect between different cultures, ideas can be freely exchanged and the door is opened to creativity and innovation.

  The world is constantly changing and we must be ready to adapt to new situations. Sometimes it is difficult to balance "fitting in" and maintaining our own cultural identity. Researchers have described a process called **transculturation,** in which a person adapts to a different culture without sacrificing individual cultural identity. One study of Native Americans showed that retention of traditional cultural heritage was an important predictor of success. A Native American student described the process this way: "When we go to school, we live a non-Indian way but we still keep our values. . . . I could put my values aside just long enough to learn what it is I want to learn but that doesn't mean I'm going to forget them. I think that is how strong they are with me."[6] Cultural identity provides strength and empowerment to be successful.

- **Gain the ability to network and learn from others.** In college, you will have the opportunity to learn from your professors and other students who are different from yourself. You may have professors with very different personality styles and teaching styles. Your success will depend on being aware of the differences and finding a way to adapt to the situation. Each student in your classes will also come from a different perspective and have valuable ideas to add to the class.

It is through networking with other people that most people find jobs. You are likely to find a job through someone you know, such as a college professor, a student in one of your classes, a community member, or a previous employer. Once you have the job, you will gain proficiency by learning from others. The best managers are open to learning from others and help different people to work together as a team. No matter how educated or experienced you become, you can always learn from others. Every person has a different view of the world and has important ideas to share.

- **Improve interpersonal skills.** A popular Native American proverb is that you cannot understand another person until you have walked a few miles in their moccasins. Being able to understand different perspectives on life will help you to improve your personal relationships. Good interpersonal skills bring joy to our personal relationships and are very valuable in the workplace. The Secretary of Labor's Commission on Achieving Necessary Skills (SCANS) identifies having good interpersonal skills as one of the five critical competencies needed in the workplace. Workers need to work effectively in teams, teach others, serve customers, exercise leadership, negotiate to arrive at a decision, and work well with cultural diversity.[7] Efficiency and profits in any industry depend on good interpersonal skills and how well workers can provide customer service.

- **Learn to be flexible and adapt to the situation.** These two qualities are necessary for dealing with the rapid change that is taking place in our society today. We learn these qualities by successfully facing personal challenges. If you are a single parent, you have learned to be flexible in managing time and resources. If you served in the military overseas, you have learned to adapt to a different culture. If you are a new college student, you are probably learning how to be independent and manage your own life. Flexibility is a valuable skill in the workplace. Today's employers want workers who can adapt, be flexible, and solve problems.

- **Develop cultural awareness.** Cultural awareness is valuable in your personal life and in the workplace. In your personal life, you can have a wider variety of satisfying personal relationships. You can enjoy people from different cultural backgrounds and travel to different countries.

In a global economy, cultural awareness is increasingly important. Tuning into cultural differences can open up business opportunities. For example, many companies are discovering that the buying power of minorities is significant. They are developing ad campaigns to sell products to Asians, Latinos, African Americans, and other groups.

Companies now understand that cultural awareness is important in international trade. American car manufacturers could not understand why the Chevy Nova was not selling well in Latin America. In Spanish, "No va" means "It doesn't go" or "It doesn't run." Kentucky Fried Chicken found out that "Finger-lickin' good" translates as "Eat your fingers off" in Chinese! Being familiar with the cultures and languages of different countries is necessary for successful international business.

Journal Entry #2

How will an understanding of diversity help you to be successful in school and work?

Vocabulary for Understanding Diversity

Knowing some basic terms will aid in your understanding of diversity.

- **Race.** Race refers to a group of people who are perceived to be physically different because of traits such as facial features, color of skin, and hair.
- **Ethnicity.** Ethnicity refers to a sense of belonging to a particular culture and sharing the group's beliefs, attitudes, skills, ceremonies, and traditions. An ethnic group usually descends from a common group of ancestors, usually from a particular country or geographic area.
- **Ethnocentrism.** Ethnocentrism is the belief that one's own ethnic, religious, or political group is superior to all others.
- **Culture.** Culture is the behavior, beliefs, and values shared by a group of people. It includes language, morals, and even food preferences. Culture includes everything that we learn from the people around us in our community.
- **Gender, sex.** Gender refers to cultural differences that distinguish males from females. Different cultures raise men and women to act in specified ways. Sex refers to anatomical differences.
- **Sexism.** Sexism is a negative attitude or perception based on sex.
- **Stereotype.** A stereotype is a generalization that expresses conventional or biased ideas about people in a certain group. Stereotypes can lead to discrimination based on these ideas. They cause us to view others in a limited way and reduce our ability to see people as individuals.
- **Prejudice.** A prejudice is a prejudgment of someone or something. Prejudices are often based on stereotypes and reflect a disrespect for others. Sometimes people who are prejudiced are insecure about their own identities.
- **Discrimination.** Discrimination happens when people are denied opportunities because of their differences. Prejudice and stereotype are often involved.
- **Racism.** Racism occurs when one race or ethnic group holds a negative attitude or perception of another group. It is prejudice based on race. Anthropologists generally accept that the human species can be categorized into races based on physical and genetic makeup. **These scientists accept the fact that there is no credible evidence that one race is superior to another.** People who believe that their own race is superior to another are called racists.
- **Cultural pluralism.** Each group celebrates the customs and traditions of their culture while participating in mainstream society.
- **Genocide.** Genocide is the deliberate and systematic destruction of a racial, political, or cultural group. It can include the destruction of the language, religion, or cultural practices of a group of people.

Understanding Diversity

There are 7.2 billion people in the world today. Statistics provided by the Population Reference Bureau and the United Nations can give us a better understanding of diversity in the world today. By geographic area, the world's population can be broken down into these percentages:[8]

- 60 Asians
- 16 Africans
- 10 Europeans
- 9 Central and South Americans
- 5 North Americans (Canada and the United States)

> "I have learned that success is to be measured not so much by the position that one has reached in life as by the obstacles which he has had to overcome while trying to succeed."
> Booker T. Washington

> "Injustice anywhere is a threat to justice everywhere."
> Martin Luther King, Jr.

> "You must be the change you want to see in the world."
> Mahatma Gandhi

If visitors from outer space were to visit the earth and report back about the most common human being found, they would probably describe someone of Asian descent. Statistics also show that approximately 50 percent of the world population suffers from malnutrition and 80 percent live in substandard housing. Moreover, 6 percent of the population living in the United States, Japan, and Germany owns half of the wealth of the world. In addition, continuous wars and fighting among the people of the earth have contributed to human suffering and the flight of many refugees.

As children, we accept the values, assumptions, and stereotypes of our culture. We use our own culture as a filter to understand the world. Because of this limited perception, people often consider their culture to be superior and other cultures to be inferior.[9] The belief that one's own culture, religious, or political group is superior to others is called **ethnocentrism.** Native Americans have argued that the celebration of Columbus Day, commemorating the discovery of the New World by Christopher Columbus, is an example of ethnocentrism. In reality, the Native Americans lived here long before Christopher Columbus arrived in 1492.

© 2014, Kendall Hunt Publishing Co.

Ethnocentrism can lead to discrimination, interpersonal conflict, and even wars between different groups of people. In extreme cases, it can even lead to **genocide**, the deliberate and systematic destruction of a racial, political, or cultural group. History is full of examples of genocide. In the United States, Native Americans were massacred and their land was confiscated in violation of treaties. In Mexico and South America, the Spanish conquerors systematically destroyed native populations. During World War II, six million Jews were killed. Pol Pot and the Khmer Rouge killed millions of Cambodians. Unfortunately, genocide continues today in various conflicts around the world.

An understanding of the harmful effects of stereotypes is necessary to improve our understanding and appreciation of diversity. A **stereotype** is an assumption that all members of a group are alike. For example, a tall African American woman in one of my classes was constantly dealing with the assumption that she must be attending college to play basketball. Actually, she was very academically oriented and not athletic at all. It is important to remember that we all have individual differences within groups of the same ethnicity or cultural background.

All of us use stereotypes to understand people different from ourselves. Why does this happen? There are many different reasons:

- It is a fast way to make sense of the world. It requires little thought.
- We tend to look for patterns to help us understand the world.
- We are often unable or unwilling to obtain all the information we need to make fair judgments about other people.
- Stereotypes can result from fear of people who are different. We often learn these fears as children.
- The media promotes stereotypes. Movies, magazines, and advertisements often present stereotypes. These stereotypes are often used as the basis of humor. For example, the media often uses people who are overweight in comedy routines.

The problem with stereotypes is that we do not get to know people as individuals. All members of a culture, ethnic group, or gender are not alike. If we make assumptions about a group, we treat everyone in the group the same. Stereotypes can lead to prejudice and discrimination. For example, a person who is overweight may find it more difficult to find a job because of stereotyping.

Psychologists and sociologists today present the idea of **cultural relativity**, in which different cultures, ethnic groups, genders, and sexual orientations are viewed as different but equally valuable and worthy of respect.[10] These differences between cultures can help us learn new ideas that can enrich our view of the world. They can also promote greater understanding and better relationships among individuals and nations.

QUIZ

Understanding Diversity, Part I

Test what you have learned by selecting the correct answers to the following questions.

1. The belief that one's own ethnic, religious, or political group is superior to all others is called
   a. cultural pluralism.
   b. cultural relativity.
   c. ethnocentrism.

2. The assumption that all members of a group are alike is
   a. discrimination.
   b. stereotype.
   c. prejudice.

3. The deliberate destruction of a racial, cultural, or political group of people is called
   a. genocide.
   b. racism.
   c. ethnocentrism.

4. Most people on the earth are
   a. North Americans.
   b. Europeans.
   c. Asians.

5. Cultural relativity is defined as
   a. the belief that one's own ethnic group is superior.
   b. groups that are viewed as different, but equally valuable.
   c. an ethnic group that descends from a common group of ancestors.

How did you do on the quiz? Check your answers: 1. c, 2. b, 3. a, 4. c, 5. b

Journal Entry # 3

Describe an incidence in which you experienced discrimination. Consider discrimination in a broad context, including ethnicity, culture, language, gender, sexual orientation, weight, height, appearance, personality type, values, politics, religion, age, experience, socioeconomic background, academic skills, or any other factor which could cause discrimination.

© Sergey Nivens/Shutterstock.com

A New Look at Diversity: The Human Genome Project

Although the people of the world represent many racial, ethnic, and cultural groups, biologists are taking a new look at diversity by learning about human genes. Genes are composed of segments of DNA that determine the transmission of hereditary traits by controlling the operation of cells. Cells are the basic building blocks of the human body.

The Human Genome Project, a multibillion-dollar and multinational government-sponsored research project to map all human genes has now been completed. This map is a catalog of all the genetic information contained in human cells. They have identified the genes and determined the sequence of the three billion chemical base pairs in human DNA. Although the project is completed, analysis of the data will continue for many years.[11] The human genome is considered a biological treasure chest that will allow scientists to discover how a body grows, ages, stays healthy, or becomes ill. This knowledge is invaluable in discovering new medications and improving health.

Results of the Human Genome Project show that we are all genetically similar while having unique individual differences. One of the interesting findings is that "as scientists have long suspected, though the world's people may look very different on the outside, genetically speaking humans are all 99.9 percent identical."[12] While we are genetically very similar, each individual can be identified by his or her genetic code. With the exception of identical twins, each individual human being is slightly different because of the unique combination of DNA letters inherited from one's parents.

Dr. Craig Venter, head of Celera Genomics Corporation, has stated that "race is a social concept, not a scientific one."[13] While it may be easy to look at people and describe them as Caucasian, African, or Asian, there is little genetic material to distinguish one race from another. Venter says, "We all evolved in the last 100,000 years from the same small number of tribes that migrated out of Africa and colonized the world."[14] Very few

> "So let us not be blind to our differences, but let us also direct attention to our common interests and to the means by which those differences can be resolved."
>
> John F. Kennedy

> "We need to help students and parents cherish and preserve the ethnic and cultural diversity that nourishes and strengthens this community and this nation."
>
> César Chavez

genes control traits that distinguish one race from another, such as skin color, eye color, and width of nose. These outward characteristics have been able to change quickly in response to environmental pressures. People who lived near the equator evolved dark skin to protect them from ultraviolet radiation. People who lived farther from the equator evolved pale skins to produce vitamin D from little sunlight. The genes responsible for these outward appearances are in the range of .01 percent of the total. Researchers on the Human Genome Project agree that **there is only one race: the human race**.

The Human Genome Project will be important for understanding the human body and will help us to find ways to prevent or cure illnesses. It may also provide new information for critical thinking about the idea of ethnocentrism and discover some basic ways in which all human beings are similar.

Communicating across Cultures

Human beings communicate through the use of symbols. A symbol is a word that stands for something else. Problems in communication arise when we assume that a symbol has only one meaning and that everyone understands the symbol in the same way. For example, we use the word "dog" to stand for a four-legged animal that barks. However, if I say the word "dog," the picture in my mind probably doesn't match the picture in your mind because there are many varieties of dogs. I might be picturing a Chihuahua while you are picturing a German shepherd. Language becomes even more complex when we have multiple meanings for one symbol. Consider the ways we use the word "dog":

- She is a dog. (She is unattractive.)
- He is a dog. (He is promiscuous.)
- He is a lucky dog. (He is fortunate.)
- It's a dog. (It is worthless.)
- Just dog it. (Just do enough to get by.)
- He went to the dogs. (He was not doing well.)
- He was in the doghouse. (He was in trouble.)
- Let sleeping dogs lie. (Leave the situation alone.)
- My dogs hurt. (My feet hurt.)
- He put on the dog. (He assumed an attitude of wealth or importance.)
- These are the dog days of summer. (These are hot days when people feel lazy.)
- The book is dog-eared. (The corners of the pages are bent.)
- He led a dog's life. (He was not happy.)

© Erik Lam/Shutterstock.com

- May I have a doggy bag? (May I have a bag for my leftovers?)
- Doggone it! (I am frustrated!)
- I am dog-tired. (I am very tired.)

Imagine how a computer would translate the above sentences. The translations would be incomprehensible, since there are so many variations in meaning depending on the context. The problem of communication becomes even more difficult for those who are learning English. People who speak a different language might not understand the word "dog" at all because they use a different symbol for the object. Even after studying the language, it is easy to misinterpret the meaning of the word "dog." A recent immigrant was horrified when he was offered a hot dog at a ball game. He thought that this was a civilized country and was surprised that we ate dogs!

Both verbal and nonverbal symbols have different meaning in different cultures. George Henderson, in his book *Cultural Diversity in the Workplace*,[15] gives the example of the common thumbs-up gesture, which we commonly interpret as "okay." In Japan the same gesture means money. In Ghana and Iran, it is a vulgar gesture similar to raising your middle finger in the United States. Another example is silence. In the United States, if a teacher asks a question and no one responds right away, the situation is uncomfortable. In Native American cultures, the person who remains silent is admired. Many Asian students listen more than they speak. According to a Zen proverb, "He who knows does not speak and he who speaks does not know." Think about how different our communications, especially business and sales techniques, would have to be in order to be effective in different cultures.

Here are some ideas to help improve your communications with people who are culturally different from you or speak a different language:

- Be sensitive to the fact that communication is difficult and that errors in understanding are likely.
- Remember that the message sent is not necessarily the message received.
- Give people time to think and respond. You do not have to fill in the silence right away.
- Check your understanding of the message. Rephrase or repeat the information to make sure it is correct. Ask questions.
- If you feel insulted by the message, remember that it is quite possible that you could be misinterpreting it. (Remember all the meanings for "dog" listed above.)
- If you are having problems communicating with someone who speaks a different language, speak slowly and clearly or use different words. Talking louder will not help.
- Remain calm and treat others with respect. Be patient.
- Find a translator if possible.
- Study a different language. This will help in understanding other cultures and the different ways that other cultures use symbols.
- Before traveling to a different country, read about the culture and learn some basic phrases in the language used. This will help you to enjoy your travel and learn about other cultures. Attempting to speak the language will show others that you care about and respect the culture.
- Sometimes nonverbal communication can help. If you are adventurous or desperate, smile and act out the message. Be aware that nonverbal communication can be misunderstood also.
- Don't forget your sense of humor.

Journal Entry # 4

What advice would you give to a person preparing to visit another country with a very different culture and language?

© David C. Rehner/Shutterstock.com

Understanding Sexual Orientation

Major causes of stereotyping and the resulting prejudice and discrimination are fear and lack of knowledge of those who are different. Prejudice and discrimination against gays and other minorities have sometimes led to hate crimes. For example, in 1998, Matthew Shepard, a gay student at the University of Wyoming, was lured from a bar, beaten, and tied to a log fence, where he was left during cold weather. He died five days later. His murderers received life sentences in prison. At Matthew's funeral, protesters held up signs saying, "God hates fags."[16] The term "faggot," which comes from the Latin word for a bundle of sticks, may refer to the time of the Inquisition when gays were actually burned at the stake along with witches.[17]

Stereotypes about sexual orientation and the resulting discrimination are common in society today and affect a great number of people. One out of four families has a gay family member and it is estimated that up to 10 percent of the population is gay or lesbian. In a class of 30 students, it is likely that three are gay men or lesbians. Many of these people are fearful of identifying themselves as gay because of potential discrimination and lack of acceptance by the general population. Think about these stereotypes as you read the following scenario:

My brother Jake was always a little different; he was not the "typical boy." Growing up he was my best friend. It was as if he were the sister I never had. He was kind and gentle and compassionate toward all creatures. He enjoyed cooking, taking care of children and growing flowers. I remember that my father tried to make a man of him by encouraging him to join in manly activities such as hunting. My father was frustrated because Jake could not kill a deer. Jake looked the deer in the eye and decided that he could not kill such a beautiful creature. I had to agree with him, but my father was disappointed. He was frustrated in all his attempts to make my brother a man and had frequent conflicts with him. At age 16, my brother ran away from home and was "adopted" by a female teacher at our high school. She encouraged my brother to go to college and he moved across the continent, eventually working his way through medical school and becoming a well-known and respected cardiologist and critical care specialist. I was happy for my brother because he could do what he loved best: helping other people. One day my father had a heart attack and Jake returned home and saved my father's life. At this point, my father was finally proud of the man he had become.

I remember having a conversation with my other brothers about whether Jake was gay or not. I acknowledged the possibility, but said that it would be awful if we asked him and it were not true, so we never asked him. He did not look or act gay; he was just different. In fact, my girlfriends were always trying to get a date with him. One day I received a call from my brother. He was saying good-bye because he was dying. He did not want the family to visit; he just wanted to say good-bye, and he died the next day at the age of 43. Against Jake's wishes, my mother and some of my brothers traveled to New York and were shocked to find that Jake was living with a man who was HIV-positive and that Jake had died of AIDS. My father told everyone that Jake died of cancer. I felt an overwhelming sense of sadness at losing my brother and that he never felt comfortable enough to tell us that he was gay. I will always wonder if I should have asked him about being gay and if I possibly could have been more a part of his life. Since I lost my opportunity to do this, I have resolved to gain a better understanding and appreciation of sexual orientation, which is sadly the only thing I can do at this point.

Becoming educated about sexual orientation can help to diminish anti-gay prejudice and help people who are struggling with their sexual identity. Here is a list of myths and facts about gay men and lesbians. The corrected information below is provided by the Parents, Families, and Friends of Lesbians and Gays (PFLAG). This organization provides information on its website, www.pflag.org. An organization called Rainbow Bridge also provides educational materials on gays and lesbians. Most college campuses have organizations that support gay, lesbian, bisexual, and transgender students. It is common that people disagree with the following facts because of common stereotypes about sexual orientation.

Myths and Facts about Gays and Lesbians

Myth: Only one percent of the world's population is gay, lesbian, or bisexual.

Fact: It is estimated that about 10 percent of the world's population is gay, lesbian, or bisexual.

Myth: Effeminate men and masculine women are always gay.

Fact: Effeminate men and masculine women can be heterosexual. Some gay persons fit this stereotype, but most look and act like individuals from the heterosexual majority.

Myth: Homosexuality is a choice, a preference, or a learned behavior.

Fact: Homosexuality is not something that one chooses to be or learns to be. As children, gay men and lesbians are not taught or influenced by others to be homosexual. Most current research cites genetic or inborn hormonal factors in homosexuality.[18]

(Continued)

Myth: You can always tell from a person's appearance if he or she is gay.

Fact: Most gay men and lesbians look and act like individuals from the heterosexual majority.

Myth: Lesbians and gay men never make good parents.

Fact: Gay men and lesbians can make good parents. Children of gay and lesbian parents are no different in any aspects of psychological, social, or sexual development from children in heterosexual families. These children tend to be more tolerant of differences.

Myth: Gay men and lesbian women are often involved in child abuse.

Fact: Gay men and lesbians are rarely involved in child abuse. In the United States, heterosexual men commit 90 percent of all sexual child abuse. The molesters are most often fathers, stepfathers, grandfathers, uncles, or boyfriends of the mothers.

Myth: The word "homosexual" is preferred over "gay" or "lesbian."

Fact: The term "gay man" or "lesbian" is preferred over the term "homosexual."

Myth: The term "gay" refers only to men.

Fact: The term "gay" refers to both men and women.

Myth: Some cultures do not have gay men and lesbians.

Fact: All cultures have gay men and lesbians.

Myth: Only gay men get AIDS and it is a death sentence.

Fact: AIDS is increasingly a heterosexual disease. Advances in the early detection and treatment of AIDS make it a chronic, controllable disease for most patients.

Myth: Being gay is an emotional or mental disorder.

Fact: The American Psychological Association does not list being gay as an emotional or mental disorder.

Myth: Through psychotherapy, a gay person can be turned into a heterosexual.

Fact: Psychotherapy has not been successful in changing a person's sexual orientation. In some states, psychotherapy aimed at changing gay men and women into heterosexuals is now illegal.

Myth: A person is either completely heterosexual or completely homosexual.

Fact: Based on Dr. Alfred Kinsey's research, few people are predominantly heterosexual or homosexual. Most people fall on a continuum between the two extremes. A person on the middle of the continuum between heterosexual and homosexual would be a bisexual. Bisexuals are attracted to both sexes.[19]

Myth: Homosexuality does not exist in nature. It is dysfunctional.

Fact: Research suggests that homosexuality is "natural." It exists among all animals and is frequent among highly developed species.[20]

Myth: Gay people should not be teachers because they will try to convert their students.

Fact: Homosexual seduction is no more common than heterosexual seduction. Most gay teachers fear they will be fired if it is found out that they are gay.[21]

How to Appreciate Diversity

Having an appreciation for diversity enriches all of us. Poet Maya Angelou has described the world as a rich tapestry and stressed that understanding this concept can enrich and improve the world:

"It is time for us to teach young people early on that in diversity there is beauty and strength. We all should know that diversity makes for a rich tapestry, and we must understand that the threads of the tapestry are equal in value, no matter their color; equal in importance, no matter their texture."[22]

Here are some ways to appreciate diversity:

- Educate yourself about other cultures and people who are different from you. Read about or take courses on the literature or history of another culture, or learn another language.
- Explore your own heritage. Learn about the cultures that are part of your family history.
- Value diversity and accept the differences of others.
- View differences as an opportunity for learning.
- Realize that you will make mistakes when dealing with people from other cultural backgrounds. Learn from the mistakes and move on to better understanding.
- Work to understand differences of opinion. You do not have to agree, but respect different points of view.
- Travel to other countries to discover new ideas and cultures.
- Think critically to avoid stereotypes and misconceptions. Treat each person as an individual.
- Avoid judgments based on physical characteristics such as color of skin, age, gender, or weight.
- Put yourself in the other person's place. How would you feel? What barriers would you face?
- Make friends with people from different countries, races, and ethnic groups.
- Find some common ground. We all have basic needs for good health, safety, economic security, and education. We all face personal challenges and interests. We all think, feel, love, and have hope for the future.
- Be responsible for your own behavior. Do not participate in or encourage discrimination.
- Do good deeds. You will be repaid with good feelings.
- Learn from history so that you do not repeat it. Value your own freedom.
- Challenge racial or homophobic remarks or jokes.
- Teach children and young people to value diversity and respect others. It is through them that we can change the world.

Journal Entry #5

Frequently we learn discrimination through our parents, our community, the media, and our environment. What would you teach your children about diversity?

© Victor Correia/Shutterstock.com

Stages of Ethical Development

After much study, Harvard University professor William Perry developed the theory that students move through stages of ethical development.[23] Students move through these patterns of thought and eventually achieve effective intercultural communication.

Stage 1: Dualism

In this stage we view the world in terms of black or white, good or bad, "we" versus "they." Role models and authorities determine what is right. The right answers exist for every problem. If we work hard, we can find the correct answers and all will be well. Decisions are often based on common stereotypes.

Stage 2: Multiplicity

At this stage we become aware that there are multiple possibilities and answers. We know that authorities can disagree on what is right and wrong. We defend our position, but acknowledge that on any given issue, everyone has a right to his or her own opinion.

Stage 3: Relativism

As we learn more about our environment and ourselves, we discover that what is right is based on our own values and culture. We weigh the evidence and try to support our opinions based on data and evidence.

Stage 4: Commitment in Relativism

At this stage, we look at our environment and ourselves and make choices. In an uncertain world, we make decisions about careers, politics, and personal relationships based on our individual values. We make certain commitments based on the way we wish to live our lives. We defend our own values but respect the values of others. There is openness to learning new information and changing one's personal point of view. This position allows for the peaceful coexistence of different points of views and perspectives. It is at this point that we become capable of communicating across cultures and appreciating diversity.

Understanding Diversity, Part II

Test what you have learned by selecting the correct answers to the following questions.

1. Results of the Human Genome Project show that humans are

   a. 80 percent identical.
   b. 50 percent identical.
   c. 99.9 percent identical.

2. Problems in communication occur when we assume that

   a. a symbol has only one meaning.
   b. words have many meanings.
   c. it is easy to match the picture in one person's mind to a picture in another person's mind.

3. The thumbs-up gesture

   a. means "okay" in Japan.
   b. is a vulgar gesture in Iran.
   c. is understood in the same way in all cultures.

4. The following statement about sexual orientation is generally accepted as true:

   a. sexual orientation is not something one chooses or can change.
   b. some cultures do not have gay men and lesbians.
   c. homosexuality is a learned behavior.

5. In the last stage of ethical development, commitment in relativism, we

   a. view the world in terms of "good" and "bad."
   b. become aware of multiple possibilities.
   c. defend our own values but respect the values of others.

How did you do on the quiz? Check your answers: 1. c, 2. a, 3. b, 4. a, 5. c

Student Perspectives on Diversity

The following are some student comments on the subject of diversity. Many students have faced incidents of discrimination and hope for a better future.

I am always faced with problems because I'm black or my hair is long or because I am a large man. I wish people could be more sensitive and love me as a person and not judge me based on what I look like.

I am frequently discriminated against because of my religion. I feel really bad when it happens and it hurts a lot.

I have always faced discrimination because of my sexual orientation and will probably continue to experience discrimination in the future. If you are part of a minority, discrimination is inevitable. The key is to not let it drag you down so that you become a second-class citizen. That can be accomplished by taking pride in who you are and then working to fight against discrimination.

I come from Japan. I noticed that people here think their culture is better than any other. I think it's not bad to love your culture, but it is important to be open to other cultures.

(Continued)

There is a story I tell my children about words being nails. When we speak, we pound our nails into the other person's spirit. We can go back and apologize for hurtful words and maybe that removes the nail, but it still leaves a hole in the spirit.

If you constantly hear people say that you are not as good as another, you eventually start to believe it.

I've been discriminated against because I am female and a blonde. When I hear blonde jokes, I've learned to laugh with people most of the time, but it still hurts my feelings.

Discrimination is passed on to the next generation because a child believes what a parent tells them. We need to teach our children tolerance for differences.

Discrimination hurts people's feelings and doesn't allow them to become successful in life because they lose confidence and self-esteem.

Because I am black, salespeople tend to follow me around in the store thinking I am going to steal something. People of different races call me "nigger."

When I was younger, I used to wear thick glasses. People would call me names such as "four eyes," "nerd," "dork," and "geek." I can look back and laugh at this now, but it made me feel inferior. Discrimination is based on ignorance and hate.

Black kids used to mistreat me because I was not as black as them.

Once when I was 10 years old, I was playing in the park. I noticed this Caucasian kid playing on the slide and he was about to fall off the slide. I went over to catch him and the mother ran over to me and told me to take my hands off of him and that she would rather have him fall than to have some "nigger" put her hands on him. I will never forget this incident!

When I was younger, my father frequently made negative comments about women. Because of his prejudice, I felt less worthy of getting equal treatment for equal education and work. Now my father is trying to overcome this mindset, and I plan to graduate from college to earn equal pay with men.

It is sad that humans can be so cruel to one another. I hope someday this will all end and we can live in peace with one another.

By celebrating diversity, all the people of the world could come together and have peace.

Diversity Is Valuable and People Are Important

In 1963, Dr. Martin Luther King, Jr., made a famous speech in which he said, "I have a dream that my four little children will one day live in a nation where they will not be judged by the color of their skin, but by the content of their character." Because of his message of brotherhood and understanding, his birthday is celebrated as a national holiday. Tragically, King was assassinated because of his strong stand against racism. We are still working toward his ideal of brotherly love.

When I ask students to describe what success means to them, they often talk about having a good career, financial stability, owning a home, and having a nice car. Some students mention family and friends and people who are important to them. Understanding diversity and appreciating other people can add to your personal success and enjoyment of life.

To gain perspective on what is important to your success, it is interesting to think about what people will say about you after you die. What will you think is important at the end of your life? If you can ponder this idea, you can gain some insight into how to live your life now. Go to the following website:

http://www.linda-ellis.com/the-dash-the-dash-poem-by-linda-ellis-.html

Read "The Dash" by Linda Ellis.

Learn to understand, respect, and appreciate the different people in your life. Take time to love those who are important to you. Focus on cooperation and teamwork on the job. Don't forget about the people you meet on your road to success; they are important too. Having an understanding and appreciation of diversity will make the world a better place in which to live.

© Lyudmyla Kharlamova/
Shutterstock.com

College Success 1

The College Success 1 website is continually updated with supplementary material for each chapter including Word documents of the journal entries, classroom activities, handouts, videos, links to related materials, and much more. See http://www.collegesuccess1.com/.

Notes

1. "Diversity in the Classroom," The New York Times, December 22, 2011 accessed at http://projects.nytimes.com/immigration/enrollment/california

2. Ibid.

3. Daily News, "U.S. Percentage of Non-Hispanic Whites Hits All-Time Low of 63%." From http://www.nydailynews.com/news/national/percentage-non-hispanic-whites-hits-all-time-63-article-1.1371772, June 2013.

4. David Broder, "Congress Wants to Shape Trade Debate," *San Diego Union Tribune*, November 7, 2001.

5. Sonia Nieto, *Affirming Diversity: The Sociopolitical Context of Multicultural Education* (New York: Longman, 1996), 283.

6. Terry Huffman, "The Transculturation of Native American College Students," in *American Mosaic: Selected Readings on America's Multicultural Heritage,* ed. Young Song and Eugene Kim (Englewood Cliffs, NJ: Prentice-Hall, 1993), 211–19.

7. Secretary's Commission of Achieving Necessary Skills (SCANS), U.S. Department of Labor, *Learning a Living: A Blueprint for High Performance*, 1991.

8. "World Population Prospects, The 2012 Revision, Highlights and Advance Tables," United Nations, New York, 2013 accessed from http://esa.un.org/unpd/wpp/Documentation/pdf/WPP2012_HIGHLIGHTS.pdf

9. H. Triandis, "Training for Diversity," paper presented at the annual meeting of the American Psychological Association, San Francisco, 1991.

10. Benjamin Lahey, *Psychology: An Introduction* (Dubuque, IA: Brown and Benchmark, 1995), 20. "Human Genome Project Information," U.S. Department of Energy Office of Science, http://www.ornl.gov/sci/techresources/Human_Genome/home.shtml, 2008.

11. "Human Genome Project Information," U.S. Department of Energy, Office of Science.

12. National Human Genome Research Institute, retrieved from https://www.genome.gov/25520489/ July, 2017.

13. Natalie Angier, "Do Races Differ? Not Really, Genes Show," *New York Times,* August 22, 2000.

14. Ibid.

15. George Henderson, *Cultural Diversity in the Workplace: Issues and Strategies* (Westport, CT: Praeger, 1994).

16. "Mourners Gather to Honor Gay Murdered in Wyoming," *Bellingham Herald,* October 17, 1998, A8.

17. California Rainbow Bridge pamphlet, 2000.

18. American Psychological Association, http://www.apa.org.pubinfo.html, 2001.

19. Ibid.

20. Ibid.

21. Ibid.

22. Maya Angelou, *Wouldn't Take Nothing for My Journey Now* (New York: Random House, 1993).

23. William G. Perry, "Cognitive and Ethical Growth: The Making of Meaning," in *The Modern American College* by Arthur Chickering and Associates (Hoboken, NJ: Jossey-Bass, 1981), 76–116.

Find Someone Who . . .

Name _____ Date _____

Walk around the classroom and find someone who fits each description. Have the person write his or her name on the appropriate line.

_____ Shares a favorite hobby

_____ Father or mother grew up in a bilingual family

_____ Parents or grandparents were born outside the United States

_____ Speaks a language besides English

_____ Is the first one in the family to attend college

_____ Enjoys the same sports

_____ Has a friend or relative who is gay, lesbian, or bisexual

_____ Has a disability they have had to overcome

_____ Is struggling financially to attend college

_____ Has children

_____ Is a single parent

_____ Has your same major

_____ Was born in the same year as yourself

_____ Attended your high school

_____ Moved here from out of state

_____ Has been in the military

_____ Has participated on an athletic team

_____ Can play a musical instrument or sing

_____ Has played in a band

Exploring Stereotypes

Name _____ Date _____

Part 1. We are all familiar with **common stereotypes** of certain groups. Think about how these groups are often portrayed in the media. Quickly complete each statement.

1. All athletes are _____

2. All lawyers are _____

3. All male hairdressers are _____

4. All construction workers are _____

5. All redheads are _____

6. All people with AIDS are _____

7. All people on welfare are _____

8. All young people are _____

9. All old people are _____

10. All men are _____

11. All women are _____

12. All A students are _____

Part 2. Your instructor will ask you to share the above stereotypes with the class. Then discuss these questions.

1. What prejudices result from such stereotypes?

2. What is the source of these prejudices?

3. What harm can come from these prejudices?

Exploring Diversity

Name _____ Date _____

Part 1. Answer the following questions about yourself. You may be asked to share these answers with a group of students in your class.

1. What is your ethnic background?

2. Where were your parents and grandparents born?

3. How much education do your parents have?

4. What languages do you speak?

5. What is your biggest challenge this semester?

6. What is one of your hopes or dreams for the future?

7. What do you enjoy most?

8. What is your most important value and why?

9. What is one thing you are proud of?

10. What is one thing people would not know about you just by looking at you?

11. Have you ever experienced discrimination because of your differences? If so, briefly describe this discrimination.

Part 2. Meet with two other students you do not know. Introduce yourself and share answers to the above questions. Your instructor will ask you to share your answers to the following questions with the class.

List three interesting things you learned about other persons in your group.

1.

2.

3.

Did you change any assumptions you had about persons in your group?

CHAPTER 14

Thinking Positively about the Future

Learning Objectives

Read to answer these key questions:

- What is my life stage?

- How does positive thinking affect my future success?

- What are some beliefs of successful people?

- What are some secrets to achieving happiness?

C ollege students begin their college education with the dream of having a better future and achieving happiness in life. This chapter includes some tools for thinking positively about your future, analyzing what happiness means, and taking the steps to achieve happiness in your life.

Thinking Positively about Your Career

You have assessed your personal strengths, interests, and values and are on your way to choosing a major and career that will achieve your goals and make you happy in life. It is interesting to note that thoughts about work often determine whether it is just a job, a career, or a calling that makes life interesting and fulfilling. For example, consider the parable of the bricklayers:

> Three bricklayers are asked: "What are you doing?"
> The first says, "I am laying bricks."
> The second says, "I am building a church."
> The third says, "I am building the house of God."[1]

The first bricklayer has a job, the second one has a career, and the third one approaches his job with a sense of purpose and optimism; he has a calling. Depending on your thoughts, any career can be a job, a career, or a calling. You can find your calling by thinking about your purpose and how your job makes the world a better place. Although purposes are unique, you can analyze your beliefs about any job in this way and look for greater satisfaction in what you are doing. If your current work is not a calling, find ways to change or improve it to match your personal strengths and purpose. People who have found their calling are consistently happier than those who have a job or even a career.

> "Hope arouses, as nothing else can arouse, a passion for the possible."
> Rev. William Coffin Jr.

> "Three grand essentials to happiness in this life are something to do, something to love, and something to hope for."
> Joseph Addison

© kentoh/Shutterstock.com

> "Learn from yesterday, hope for tomorrow. The important thing is to not to stop questioning."
> Albert Einstein

Optimism, Hope, and Future-Mindedness

You can increase your chances of success by using three powerful tools: optimism, hope, and future-mindedness. These character traits lead to achievement in athletics, academics, careers, and even politics. They also have positive mental and physical effects. They reduce anxiety and depression as well as contributing to physical well-being. In addition, they aid in problem solving and searching out resources to solve problems. A simple definition of optimism is expecting good events to happen in the future and working to make them happen. Optimism leads to continued efforts to accomplish goals, whereas pessimism leads to giving up on accomplishing goals. A person who sets no goals for the future cannot be optimistic or hopeful.

Being hopeful is another way of thinking positively about the future. Hope is the expectation that tomorrow will be better than today.[2] When you face challenges, you learn from mistakes, expect a positive outcome, and work to overcome the challenge. It is the opposite of accepting failure, expecting the worst, and giving up. In this way hope is related to the growth mindset and perseverance, or grit. One research study showed for entering college freshmen, level of hope was a better predictor of college grades than standardized tests or high school grade point average.[3] Students who have a high level of hope set higher goals and work to attain them. If they are not successful, they think about what went wrong and learn from it, or change goals and move in a new direction with a renewed sense of hope for a positive future.

Future-mindedness is thinking about the future, expecting that desired events and outcomes will occur, and then acting in a way that makes the positive outcomes come true. It involves setting goals for the future and taking action to accomplish these goals as well as being confident in accomplishing these goals. Individuals with future-mindedness are conscientious and hardworking and can delay gratification. They make to-do lists and use schedules and day planners. Individuals who are future-minded would agree with these statements:[4]

- Despite challenges, I always remain hopeful about the future.
- I always look on the bright side.
- I believe that good will always triumph over evil.
- I expect the best.
- I have a clear picture in mind about what I want to happen in the future.
- I have a plan for what I want to be doing five years from now.
- If I get a bad grade or evaluation, I focus on the next opportunity and plan to do better.

Believe in Yourself

Anthony Robbins defines belief as "any guiding principle, dictum, faith, or passion that can provide meaning and direction in life . . . Beliefs are the compass and maps that guide us toward our goals and give us the surety to know we'll get there."[5] The beliefs that we have about ourselves determine how much of our potential we will use and how successful we will be in the future. If we have positive beliefs about ourselves, we will feel confident and accomplish our goals in life. Negative beliefs get in the way of our success. Robbins reminds us that we can change our beliefs and choose new ones if necessary.

> *"The birth of excellence begins with our awareness that our beliefs are a choice. We usually do not think of it that way, but belief can be a conscious choice. You can choose beliefs that limit you, or you can choose beliefs that support you. The trick is to choose the beliefs that are conducive to success and the results you want and to discard the ones that hold you back."[6]*

"Attitude is the librarian of our past, the speaker of our present and the prophet of our future."
John Maxwell

"¡Sí, se puede!" (Yes, you can!)
César Chavez

The Self-Fulfilling Prophecy

The first step in thinking positively is to examine your beliefs about yourself, your life, and the world around you. Personal beliefs are influenced by our environment, significant events that have happened in life, what we have learned in the past, and our picture of the future. Beliefs cause us to have certain expectations about the world and ourselves. These expectations are such a powerful influence on behavior that psychologists use the term "self-fulfilling prophecy" to describe what happens when our expectations come true.

For example, if I believe that I am not good in math (my expectation), I may not try to do the assignment or may avoid taking a math class (my behavior). As a result, I am not good in math. My expectations have been fulfilled. Expectations can also have a positive effect. If I believe that I am a good student, I will take steps to enroll in college and complete my assignments. I will then become a good student. The prophecy will again come true.

"If I believe I cannot do something, it makes me incapable of doing it. But when I believe I can, then I acquire the ability to do it, even if I did not have the ability in the beginning."
Mahatma Gandhi

To think positively, it is necessary to recognize your negative beliefs and turn them into positive beliefs. Some negative beliefs commonly heard from college students include the following:

I don't have the money for college.
English was never my best subject.
I was never any good at math.

When you hear yourself saying these negative thoughts, remember that these thoughts can become self-fulfilling prophecies. First of all, notice the thought. Then see if you can change the statement into a positive statement such as:

I can find the money for college.
English has been a challenge for me in the past, but I will do better this time.
I can learn to be good at math.

If you believe that you can find money for college, you can go to the financial aid office and the scholarship office to begin your search for money to attend school. You can look for a better job or improve your money management. If you believe that you will do better in English, you will keep up with your assignments and go to the tutoring center or ask the professor for help. If you believe that you can learn to be good at math, you will attend every math class and seek tutoring when you do not understand. Your positive thoughts will help you to be successful.

> "Human beings can alter their lives by altering their attitude of mind."
> William James

Positive Self-Talk and Affirmations

Self-talk refers to the silent inner voice in our heads. This voice is often negative, especially when we are frustrated or trying to learn something new. Have you ever had thoughts about yourself that are similar to these:

How could you be so stupid!
That was dumb!
You idiot!

ACTIVITY

What do you say to yourself when you are angry or frustrated? Write several examples of your negative self-talk.

> "We are what we think. All that we are arises With our thoughts. With our thoughts we make the world."
> Buddha

Negative thoughts can actually be toxic to your body. They can cause biochemical changes that can lead to depression and negatively affect the immune system.[7] Negative self-talk causes anxiety and poor performance and is damaging to self-esteem. It can also lead to a negative self-fulfilling prophecy. Positive thoughts can help us build self-esteem, become confident in our abilities, and achieve our goals. These positive thoughts are called affirmations.

If we make the world with our thoughts, it is important to become aware of the thoughts about ourselves that are continuously running through our heads. Are your thoughts positive or negative? Negative thoughts lead to failure. What we hear over and over again shapes our beliefs. If you say over and over to yourself such things as,

"I am stupid," "I am ugly," or "I am fat," you will start to believe these things and act in a way that supports your beliefs. Positive thoughts help to build success. If you say to yourself, "I'm a good person," "I'm doing my best," or "I'm doing fine," you will begin to believe these things about yourself and act in a way that supports these beliefs. Here are some guidelines for increasing your positive self-talk and making affirmations:

1. Monitor your thoughts about yourself and become aware of them. Are they positive or negative?

2. When you notice a negative thought about yourself, imagine creating a new video with a positive message.

3. Start the positive message with "I" and use the present tense. Using an "I" statement shows you are in charge. Using the present tense shows you are ready for action now.

4. Focus on the positive. Think about what you want to achieve and what you can do rather than what you do not want to do. For example, instead of saying, "I will not eat junk food," say, "I will eat a healthy diet."

5. Make your affirmation stronger by adding an emotion to it.

6. Form a mental picture of what it is that you want to achieve. See yourself doing it successfully.

7. You may need to say the positive thoughts over and over again until you believe them and they become a habit. You can also write them down and put them in a place where you will see them often.

> "The most common way people give up their power is by thinking they don't have any."
> Alice Walker

Here are some examples of negative self-talk and contrasting positive affirmations:

Negative: I'm always broke.

Affirmation: I feel really good when I manage my finances. See yourself taking steps to manage finances. For example, a budget or savings plan.

Negative: I'm too fat. It just runs in the family.

Affirmation: I feel good about myself when I exercise and eat a healthy diet. See yourself exercising and eating a healthy diet.

Negative: I can't do this. I must be stupid.

Affirmation: I can do this. I am capable. I feel a sense of accomplishment when I accomplish something challenging. See yourself making your best attempt and taking the first step to accomplish the project.

ACTIVITY

Select one example of negative self-talk that you wrote earlier. Use the examples above to turn your negative message into a positive one and write it here.

Journal Entry #1

Write five positive statements about your future.

Visualize Your Success

© Sergey Nivens/Shutterstock.com

Visualization is a powerful tool for using your brain to improve memory, deal with stress, and think positively. Coaches and athletes study sports psychology to learn how to use visualization along with physical practice to improve athletic performance. College students can use the same techniques to enhance college success.

If you are familiar with sports or are an athlete, you can probably think of times when your coach asked you to use visualization to improve your performance. In baseball, the coach reminds players to keep their eye on the ball and visualize hitting it. In swimming, the coach asks swimmers to visualize reaching their arms out to touch the edge of the pool at the end of the race. Pole-vaulters visualize clearing the pole and sometimes even go through the motions before making the jump. Using imagery lets you practice for future events and pre-experience achieving your goals. Athletes imagine winning the race or completing the perfect jump in figure skating. In this way they prepare mentally and physically and develop confidence in their abilities. It still takes practice to excel.

Just as the athlete visualizes and then performs, the college student can do the same. It is said that we create all things twice. First we make a mental picture, and then we create the physical reality by taking action. For example, if we are building a house, first we get the idea; then we begin to design the house we want. We start with a blueprint and then build the house. The blueprint determines what kind of house we construct. The same thing happens in any project we undertake. First we have a mental picture, and then we complete the project. Visualize what you would like to accomplish in your life as if you were creating a blueprint. Then take the steps to accomplish what you want.

As a college student, you might visualize yourself in your graduation robe walking across the stage to receive your diploma. You might visualize yourself in the exam room confidently taking the exam. You might see yourself on the job enjoying your future career. You can make a mental picture of what you would like your life to be and then work toward accomplishing your goal.

> "The future first exists in imagination, then planning, then reality."
> R.A. Wilson

Successful Beliefs

Stephen Covey's book *The 7 Habits of Highly Effective People* has been described as one of the most influential books of the 20th century.[8] In 2004, he released a new book called *The 8th Habit: From Effectiveness to Greatness.*[9] These habits are based on beliefs that lead to success.

1. **Be proactive.** Being proactive means accepting responsibility for your life. Covey uses the word "response-ability" for the ability to choose responses. The quality of your life is based on the decisions and responses that you make. Proactive people make things happen through responsibility and initiative. They do not blame circumstances or conditions for their behavior.

2. **Begin with the end in mind.** Know what is important and what you wish to accomplish in your life. To be able to do this, you will need to know your values and goals in life. You will need a clear vision of what you want your life to be and where you are headed.

3. **Put first things first.** Once you have established your goals and vision for the future, you will need to manage yourself to do what is important first. Set priorities so that you can accomplish the tasks that are important to you.

4. **Think win-win.** In human interactions, seek solutions that benefit everyone. Focus on cooperation rather than competition. If everyone feels good about the decision, there is cooperation and harmony. If one person wins and the other loses, the loser becomes angry and resentful and sabotages the outcome.

5. **First seek to understand, then to be understood.** Too often in our personal communications, we try to talk first and listen later. Often we don't really listen: we

use this time to think of our reply. It is best to listen and understand before speaking. Effective communication is one of the most important skills in life.

6. **Synergize.** A simple definition of synergy is that the whole is greater than the sum of its parts. If people can cooperate and have good communication, they can work together as a team to accomplish more than each individual could do separately. Synergy is also part of the creative process.

7. **Sharpen the saw.** Covey shares the story of a man who was trying to cut down a tree with a dull saw. As he struggled to cut the tree, someone suggested that he stop and sharpen the saw. The man said that he did not have time to sharpen the saw, so he continued to struggle. Covey suggests that we need to take time to stop and sharpen the saw. We need to stop working and invest some time in ourselves by staying healthy physically, mentally, spiritually, and socially. We need to take time for self-renewal.

8. **Find your voice, and inspire others to find theirs.** Believe that you can make a positive difference in the world and inspire others to do the same. Covey says that leaders "deal with people in a way that will communicate to them their worth and potential so clearly that they will come to see it in themselves." Accomplishing this ideal begins with developing one's own voice or "unique personal significance."[10]

Successful Beliefs
• Be proactive
• Begin with the end in mind
• Put first things first
• Think win-win
• First seek to understand, then to be understood
• Synergize
• Sharpen the saw
• Find your voice, and inspire others to find theirs

Journal Entry #2

List five beliefs that will help you to be successful in the future.

QUIZ

Positive Thinking

Test what you have learned by selecting the correct answers to the following questions.

1. The self-fulfilling prophecy refers to

   a. the power of belief in determining your future.
   b. good fortune in the future.
   c. being able to foretell the future.

2. Positive self-talk results in

   a. lower self-esteem.
   b. overconfidence.
   c. higher self-esteem.

3. The statement "We create all things twice" refers to

   a. doing the task twice to make sure it is done right.
   b. creating and refining.
   c. first making a mental picture and then taking action.

4. A win-win solution means

   a. winning at any cost.
   b. seeking a solution that benefits everyone.
   c. focusing on competition.

5. The statement by Stephen Covey, "Sharpen the saw," refers to

   a. proper tool maintenance.
   b. studying hard to sharpen thinking skills.
   c. investing time to maintain physical and mental health.

How did you do on the quiz? Check your answers: 1. a, 2. c, 3. c, 4. b, 5. c

Secrets to Happiness

Checklist for Achieving Happiness

- Express gratitude.
- Be an optimist.
- Think positively.
- Use your personal strengths.
- Practice kindness.
- Increase flow activities.
- Savor life's joys.
- Accomplish your goals.
- Take care of your body.

Many of you probably have happiness on your list of lifetime goals. It sounds easy, right? But what is happiness, anyway?

Psychologist Martin Seligman says that real happiness comes from identifying, cultivating, and using your personal strengths in work, love, play, and parenting.[11] You have identified these strengths by learning about your personality type, multiple intelligences, interests, and values.

It means living the good life in the present and increasing your longevity. These factors are associated with happiness: expressing gratitude, being optimistic, being employed, having positive self-esteem, enjoying leisure activity, having good health, and enjoying friendships.[12] Happy individuals have better marriages, friendships, and mental health. They have better work performance, and higher levels of employment and income.

Seligman contrasts authentic happiness with hedonism. He states that a hedonist "wants as many good moments and as few bad moments as possible in life."[13] Hedonism is a shortcut to happiness that leaves us feeling empty. For example, we often assume that more material possessions will make us happy. However, the more material possessions we have, the greater the expectations, and we no longer appreciate what we have.

"Suppose you could be hooked up to a hypothetical 'experience machine' that, for the rest of your life, would stimulate your brain and give you any positive feelings you desire. Most people to whom I offer this imaginary choice refuse the machine. It is not just positive feelings we want, we want to be entitled to our positive feelings. Yet we have invented myriad shortcuts to feeling good: drugs, chocolate, loveless sex, shopping, masturbation, and television are all examples. (I am not, however, suggesting that you should drop these shortcuts altogether.) The belief that we can rely on shortcuts to happiness, joy, rapture, comfort, and ecstasy, rather than be entitled to these feelings by the exercise of personal strengths and virtues, leads to the legions of people who in the middle of great wealth are starving spiritually. Positive emotion alienated from the exercise of character leads to emptiness, to inauthenticity, to depression, and as we age, to the gnawing realization that we are fidgeting until we die."[14]

Most people assume that happiness is increased by having more money to buy that new car or HDTV. However, a process called hedonistic adaptation occurs that makes this type of happiness short-lived. Once you have purchased the new car or TV, you get used to it quickly. Soon you will start to think about a better car and a bigger TV to continue to feel happy. Seligman provides a formula for happiness:[15]

$$Happiness = S + C + V$$

In the formula S stands for set range. Psychologists believe that 50 percent of happiness is determined by heredity. In other words, half of your level of happiness is determined by the genes inherited from your ancestors. In good times or bad times, people generally return to their set range of happiness. Six months after receiving a piece of good fortune such as a raise or promotion or winning the lottery, unhappy people are still unhappy. Six months after a tragedy, naturally happy people return to being happy.

The letter C in the equation stands for circumstances such as money, marriage, social life, health, education, climate, race, gender, and religion. These circumstances account for 8 to 15 percent of happiness. Here is what psychologists know about how these circumstances affect happiness:

- Once basic needs are met, greater wealth does not increase happiness.
- Having a good marriage is related to increased happiness.
- Happy people are more social.
- Moderate ill health does not bring unhappiness, but severe illness does.
- Educated people are slightly happier.

- Climate, race, and gender do not affect level of happiness.
- Religious people are somewhat happier than nonreligious people.

The letter *V* in the equation stands for factors under your voluntary control. These factors account for approximately 40 percent of happiness. Factors under voluntary control include positive emotions and optimism about the future. Positive emotions include hope, faith, trust, joy, ecstasy, calm, zest, ebullience, pleasure, flow, satisfaction, contentment, fulfillment, pride, and serenity. Seligman suggests the following ideas to increase your positive emotions:

- Realize that the past does not determine your future. The future is open to new possibilities.
- Be grateful for the good events of the past and place less emphasis on the bad events.
- Build positive emotions through forgiving and forgetting.
- Work on increasing optimism and hope for the future.
- Find out what activities make you happy and engage in them. Spread these activities out over time so that you will not get tired of them.
- Take the time to savor the happy times. Make mental photographs of happy times so that you can think of them later.
- Take time to enjoy the present moment.
- Build more flow into your life. Flow is the state of gratification we feel when totally absorbed in an activity that matches our strengths.

© nasirkhan/Shutterstock.com

Are you interested in taking steps to increase your happiness? Here are some activities proposed by Sonya Lyubomirsky, a leading researcher on happiness and author of *The How of Happiness*.[16] Choose the ones that seem like a natural fit for you and vary them so that they do not become routine or boring. After putting in some effort to practice these activities, they can become a habit.

1. **Express gratitude.** Expressing gratitude is a way of thinking positively and appreciating good circumstances rather than focusing on the bad ones. It is about appreciating and thanking the people who have made positive contributions to your life. It is feeling grateful for the good things you have in life. Create a gratitude journal and at the end of each day write down things for which you are grateful or thankful. Regularly tell those

around you how grateful you are to have them in your life. You can do this in person, by phone, in a letter, or by email. Being grateful helps us to savor positive life experiences.

2. **Cultivate optimism.** Make a habit of looking at the bright side of life. If you think positively about the future, you are more likely to take the effort to reach your goals in life. Spend some time thinking or writing about your best possible future. Make a mental picture of your future goals as a first step toward achieving them. Thinking positively boosts your mood and promotes high morale. Most importantly, thinking positively can become a self-fulfilling prophecy. If you see your positive goals as attainable, you are more likely to work toward accomplishing them and invest the energy needed to deal with obstacles and setbacks along the way.

3. **Avoid overthinking and social comparison.** Overthinking is focusing on yourself and your problems endlessly, needlessly, and excessively. Examples of overthinking include "Why am I so unhappy?" "Why is life so unfair?" and "Why did he/she say that?" Overthinking increases sadness, fosters biased thinking, decreases motivation, and makes it difficult to solve problems and take action to make life better.

Social comparison is a type of overthinking. In our daily lives, we encounter people who are more intelligent, beautiful, richer, healthier, or happier. The media fosters images of people with impossibly perfect lives. Making social comparisons can lead to feelings of inferiority and loss of self-esteem.

Notice when your are overthinking or making comparisons with others and stop doing it. Use the "Yell, 'Stop!'" technique to refocus your attention. This technique involves yelling, "Stop!" to yourself or out loud to change your thinking. Another way to stop overthinking is to distract yourself with more positive thoughts or activities. Watch a funny movie, listen to music, or arrange a social activity with a friend. If these activities are not effective, try writing down your worries in a journal. Writing helps to organize thoughts and to make sense of them. Begin to take some small steps to resolve your worries and problems.

4. **Practice acts of kindness.** Doing something kind for others increases your own personal happiness and satisfies your basic need for human connection. Opportunities for helping others surround us each day. How about being courteous on the freeway, helping a child with homework, or helping your elderly neighbor with yard work? A simple act of kindness makes you feel good and often sets off a chain of events in which the person who receives the kindness does something kind for someone else.

5. **Increase flow activities.** Flow is defined as intense involvement in an activity so that you do not notice the passage of time. Musicians are in the flow when they are totally involved in their music. Athletes are in the flow when they are totally focused on their sport. Writers are in the flow when they are totally absorbed in writing down their ideas. The key to achieving flow is balancing skills and challenges. If your skills are not sufficient for the activity, you will become frustrated. If your skills are greater than what is demanded for the activity, you will become bored. Work often provides an opportunity to experience flow if you are in a situation in which your work activities are matched to your skills and talents.

As our skills increase, it becomes more difficult to maintain flow. We must be continually testing ourselves in ever more challenging activities to maintain flow. You can take some action to increase the flow in your life by learning to fully focus your attention on the activity you are doing. It is important to be open to new and different experiences. To maintain the flow in your life, make a commitment to lifelong learning.

6. **Savor life's joys.** Savoring is the repetitive replaying of the positive experiences in life and is one of the most important ingredients of happiness. Savoring happens in the past, present, and future. Think often about the good things that have happened in the past. Savor the present by relishing the present moment. Savor the future by anticipating and visualizing positive events or outcomes in the future.

There are many ways to savor life's joys. Replay in your mind happy days or events from the past. Create a photo album of your favorite people, places, and events and look at it often. This prolongs the happiness. Take a few minutes each day to appreciate ordinary activities such as taking a shower or walking to work. Engage the senses to notice your environment. Is it a sunny day? Take some time to look at the sky, the trees, and the plants. Landscape architects incorporate artwork, trees, and flowers along the freeways to help drivers to relax on the road. Notice art and objects of beauty. Be attentive to the present moment and be aware of your surroundings. Picture in your mind positive events you anticipate in the future. All of these activities will increase your "psychological bank account" of happy times and will help deal with times that are not so happy.

7. **Commit to accomplishing your goals.** Working toward a meaningful life goal is one of the most important things that you can do to have a happy life. Goals provide structure and meaning to our lives and improve self-esteem. Working on goals provides something to look forward to in the future.

   The types of goals that you pursue have an impact on your happiness. The goals that have the most potential for long-term happiness involve changing your activities rather than changing your circumstances. Examples of goals that change your circumstances are moving to the beach or buying a new stereo. These goals make you happy for a short time. Then you get used to your new circumstances and no longer feel as happy as when you made the initial change. Examples of goals that change your activities are returning to school or taking up a new sport or hobby. These activities allow you to take on new challenges that keep life interesting for a longer period of time. Choose intrinsic goals that help you to develop your competence and autonomy. These goals should match your most important values and interests.

8. **Take care of your body.** Engaging in physical activity provides many opportunities for increasing happiness. Physical activity helps to:
   - Increase longevity and improve the quality of life.
   - Improve sleep and protect the body from disease.

© Efired/Shutterstock.com

   - Keep brains healthy and avoid cognitive impairments.
   - Increase self-esteem.
   - Increase the opportunity to engage in flow.
   - Provide a distraction from worries and overthinking.

9. Take the time to think about the good things in your life. As an exercise, at the end of each day, pause to think about the good things that happened.

> "Happiness consists more in small conveniences or pleasures that occur every day, than in great pieces of good fortune that happen but seldom."
> Benjamin Franklin

> "An aim in life is the only fortune worth finding."
> Robert Louis Stevenson

Psychologists Martin Seligman and Sonya Lyubomirsky write about the secrets to happiness. List five of their ideas and tell whether you agree or disagree with them.

Just as you have made a decision to get a college degree, make a decision to be happy. Make a decision to be happy by altering your internal outlook and choosing to change your behavior. Here are some suggestions for consciously choosing happiness.

1. Find small things that make you happy and sprinkle your life with them. A glorious sunset, a pat on the back, a well-manicured yard, an unexpected gift, a round of tennis, a favorite sandwich, a fishing line cast on a quiet lake, the wagging tail of the family dog, or your child finally taking some responsibility—these are things that will help to create a continual climate of happiness.

2. Smile and stand up straight; unhappy people tend to slouch as they walk.[17]

3. Learn to think like an optimist. "Pessimists tend to complain; optimists focus on solving their problems."[18] Never use the word "try"; this word is for pessimists. Assume you will succeed.

4. Replace negative thoughts with positive ones.

5. Fill your life with things you like to do.

6. Get enough rest. If you do not get enough sleep, you will feel tired and gloomy. Sleep deprivation can lead to depression.

7. Learn from your elders. Psychologist Daniel Mroczek says that "people in their sixties and seventies who are in good health are among the happiest people in our society. . . . They may be better able to regulate their emotions, they've developed perspective, they don't get so worried about little things, and they've often achieved their goals and aren't trying to prove themselves."[19]

8. Reduce stress.

9. Take charge of your time by doing first things first.

10. Close relationships are important. Myers and Mroczek report higher levels of happiness among married men and women.[20]

11. Keep things in perspective. Will it matter in six months to a year?

12. Laugh more. Laughter produces a relaxation response.

Journal Entry # 4

Write five intention statements about increasing your future happiness. I intend to . . .

Secrets to Happiness

Test what you have learned by selecting the correct answers to the following questions.

1. Psychologist Martin Seligman says that real happiness comes from:

   a. having enough money to buy the things you want.
   b. identifying, cultivating, and using your personal strengths in work, love, play, and parenting.
   c. your circumstances in life.

2. You can increase happiness by:

   a. expressing gratitude.
   b. being realistic.
   c. comparing yourself with other successful people.

3. Psychologists have found that this factor increases happiness:

   a. great wealth.
   b. living in a good climate.
   c. being educated.

4. About 40% of happiness is due to:

   a. factors under your voluntary control such as positive emotions and optimism.
   b. your circumstances in life such as money, marriage, and climate.
   c. the career you choose.

5. The key to intense involvement or "flow" are activities that:

   a. exceed your skills.
   b. are easy.
   c. balance skills and challenges.

How did you do on the quiz: Check your answers: 1. b, 2. a, 3. c, 4. a, 5. c

KEYS TO SUCCESS

You Are What You Think

"Whether you think you can, or think you can't . . . you're right." Henry Ford

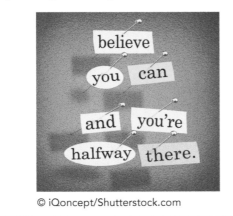

believe
you can
and you're
halfway there.

© iQoncept/Shutterstock.com

Sometimes students enter college with the fear of failure. This belief leads to anxiety and behavior that leads to failure. If you have doubts about your ability to succeed in college, you might not go to class or attempt the challenging work required in college. It is difficult to make the effort if you cannot see positive results ahead. Unfortunately, failure in college can lead to a loss of confidence and lack of success in other areas of life as well.

Henry Ford said, "What we believe is true, comes true. What we believe is possible, becomes possible." If you believe that you will succeed, you will be more likely to take actions that lead to your success. Once you have experienced some small part of success, you will have confidence in

(Continued)

your abilities and will continue on the road to success. Success leads to more success. It becomes a habit. You will be motivated to make the effort necessary to accomplish your goals. You might even become excited and energized along the way. You will use your gifts and talents to reach your potential and achieve happiness. It all begins with the thoughts you choose.

"Watch your thoughts; they become words. Watch your words; they become actions. Watch your actions; they become habits.

Watch your habits; they become character. Watch your character; it becomes your destiny."[21]

—*Frank Outlaw*

To help you choose positive beliefs, picture in your mind how you want your life to be. Imagine it is here now. See all the details and experience the feelings associated with this picture. Pretend it is true until you believe it. Then take action to make your dreams come true.

Journal Entry #5

Henry Ford said, "Whether you think you can, or think you can't . . . you're right." Based on this quote, how can your thoughts help you to be successful in college and in your career?

"You become what you believe."

Oprah Winfrey

© Lyudmyla Kharlamova/ Shutterstock.com

College Success 1

The College Success 1 website is continually updated with supplementary material for each chapter including Word documents of the journal entries, classroom activities, handouts, videos, links to related materials, and much more. See http://www.collegesuccess1.com/.

Notes

1. Angela Duckworth, Grit: The Power of Passion and Perseverance (New York: Scribner, 2016), 149.

2. Ibid.,169.

3. Daniel Goleman, "Hope Emerges as a Key to Success in Life," *New York Times*, December 24, 1991.

4. Peterson and Seligman, *Character Strengths and Virtues*, 570. Goleman "Hope Emerges as a Key to Success in Life."

5. Anthony Robbins, Unlimited Power (New York:Fawcett Columbine, 1986), 54–55.

6. Ibid., 54–55.

7. Joan Smith, "Nineteen Habits of Happy Women," *Redbook Magazine*, August 1999, 68.

8. Stephen R. Covey, *The 7 Habits of Highly Effective People* (New York: Simon and Schuster, 1989).

9. Stephen R. Covey, *The 8ᵗʰ Habit: From Effectiveness to Greatness* (New York: Free Press, 2004).

10. Ibid.

11. Christopher Peterson, A Primer in Positive Psychology (Oxford: University Press, 2006), 92.

12. Martin Seligman, Authentic Happiness: Using the New Positive Psychology to Realize Your Potential for Lasting Fulfillment (New York: The Penguin Press, 2008).

13. Ibid., 6.

14. Ibid., 8.

15. Ibid., 45.

16. Sonya Lyubomirsky, *The How of Happiness* (New York: The Penguin Press, 2008).

17. Ibid.

18. Ibid.

19. Ibid.

20. Ibid.

21. Rob Gilbert, ed., *Bits and Pieces* (Fairfield, NJ: The Economics Press), Vol. R, No. 40, p. 7, copyright 1998.

Measure Your Success

Name _____ Date _____

Now that you have finished the text, complete the following assessment to measure your improvement. Compare your results to the assessment taken at the beginning of class.

Read the following statements and rate how true they are for you at the present time.

5 Definitely true
4 Mostly true
3 Somewhat true
2 Seldom true
1 Never true

© Kenishirotie/Shutterstock.com

_____ I am motivated to be successful in college.

_____ I know the value of a college education.

_____ I know how to establish successful patterns of behavior.

_____ I avoid multi-tasking while studying.

_____ I am attending college to accomplish my own personal goals.

_____ I believe to a great extent that my actions determine my future.

_____ I am persistent in achieving my goals.

_____ **Total points for Motivation**

_____ I can describe my personality type.

_____ I can list careers that match my personality type.

_____ I can describe my personal strengths and talents based on my personality type.

_____ I understand how my personality type affects how I manage my time and money.

_____ I know what college majors are most in demand.

_____ I am confident that I have chosen the best major for myself.

_____ Courses related to my major are interesting and exciting to me.

_____ **Total points for Personality and Major**

_____ I understand the concept of multiple intelligences.

_____ I can list my multiple intelligences and matching careers.

_____ I can describe my vocational interests.

_____ I can list my top values.

_____ My personal values generally guide my actions.

_____ I can balance work, study, and leisure activities.

_____ I know the steps in making a good career decision.

_____ **Total points for Multiple Intelligences, Interests, and Values**

_____ I understand how current employment trends will affect my future.

_____ I know what work skills will be most important for the 21st century.

_____ I have an educational plan that matches my academic and career goals.

_____ I know how to use job outlook in planning my career.

_____ I have a good resume.

_____ I know how to interview for a job

_____ I know how to use up-to-date job search strategies to find a job.

_____ **Total points for Career and Education**

_____ I have a list or mental picture of my lifetime goals.

_____ I know what I would like to accomplish in the next four years.

_____ I spend my time on activities that help me accomplish my lifetime goals.

_____ I effectively use priorities in managing my time.

_____ I can balance study, work, and recreation time.

_____ I generally avoid procrastination on important tasks.

_____ I am good at managing my money.

_____ **Total points for Managing Time and Money**

_____ I understand the difference between short-term and long-term memory.

_____ I use effective study techniques for storing information in long-term memory.

_____ I can apply memory techniques to remember what I am studying.

_____ I know how to minimize forgetting.

_____ I know how to use mnemonics and other memory tricks.

_____ I know how to keep my brain healthy throughout life.

_____ I use positive thinking to be successful in my studies.

_____ **Total points for Brain Science and Memory**

_____ I understand the latest findings in brain science and can apply them to studying.

_____ I use a reading study system based on memory strategies.

_____ I am familiar with e-learning strategies for reading and learning online.

_____ I know how to effectively mark my textbook.

_____ I understand how math is different from studying other subjects.

_____ I have the math study skills needed to be successful in my math courses.

_____ I take responsibility for my own success in college and in life.

_____ **Total points for Brain Science and Study Skills**

_____ I know how to listen for the main points in a college lecture.

_____ I am familiar with note-taking systems for college lectures.

_____ I know how to review my lecture notes.

_____ I feel comfortable with writing.

_____ I know the steps in writing a college term paper.

_____ I know how to prepare a speech.

_____ I am comfortable with public speaking.

_____ **Total points for Taking Notes, Writing, and Speaking**

_____ I know how to adequately prepare for a test.

_____ I can predict the questions that are likely to be on the test.

_____ I know how to deal with test anxiety.

_____ I am successful on math exams.

_____ I know how to make a reasonable guess if I am uncertain about the answer.

_____ I am confident of my ability to take objective tests.

_____ I can write a good essay answer.

_____ **Total points for Test Taking**

_____ I understand how my personality affects my communication style.

_____ I know how to be a good listener.

_____ I can use some basic techniques for good communication.

_____ I can identify some barriers to effective communication.

_____ I know how to deal with conflict.

_____ I feel confident about making new friends in college and on the job.

_____ I am generally a good communicator.

_____ **Total points for Communication and Relationships**

_____ I have the skills to analyze data, generate alternatives, and solve problems.

_____ I can identify fallacies in reasoning.

_____ I can apply the steps of critical thinking to analyze a complex issue.

_____ I am willing to consider different points of view.

_____ I can use brainstorming to generate a variety of ideas.

_____ I am good at visualization and creative imagination.

_____ I am generally curious about the world and can spot problems and opportunities.

_____ **Total points for Critical and Creative Thinking**

_____ I understand the basics of good nutrition.

_____ I understand how to maintain my ideal body weight.

_____ I exercise regularly.

_____ I avoid addictions to smoking, alcohol, and drugs.

_____ I protect myself from sexually transmitted diseases.

_____ I generally get enough sleep.

_____ I am good at managing stress.

_____ **Total points for Health**

_____ I understand the concept of diversity and know why it is important.

_____ I understand the basics of communicating with a person from a different culture.

_____ I understand how the global economy will affect my future career.

_____ I understand how the concept of the electronic village will affect my future.

_____ I am familiar with the basic vocabulary of diversity.

_____ I try to avoid stereotypes when dealing with others who are different than me.

_____ I try to understand and appreciate those who are different from me.

_____ **Total points for Diversity**

_____ I expect good things to happen in the future and work to make them happen.

_____ Despite challenges, I always remain hopeful about the future.

_____ I have self-confidence.

_____ I use positive self-talk and affirmations.

_____ I have a visual picture of my future success.

_____ I have a clear idea of what happiness means to me.

_____ I usually practice positive thinking.

_____ **Total points for Future**

_____ I am confident of my ability to succeed in college.

_____ I am confident of my ability to succeed in my career.

_____ **Total additional points**

Total your points:

_____ Motivation

_____ Personality and Major

_____ Multiple Intelligences, Interests, and Values

_____ Career and Education

_____ Managing Time and Money

_____ Brain Science and Memory

_____ Brain Science and Study Skills

_____ Taking Notes, Writing, and Speaking

_____ Test Taking

_____ Communication and Relationships

_____ Critical and Creative Thinking

_____ Health

_____ Diversity

_____ Future

_____ Additional Points

_____ **Grand total points**

If you scored

450–500   You are very confident of your skills for success in college and your career.

400–449   You have good skills for success in college. You can always improve.

350–399   You have average skills for success in college.

Below 350   You need some help to survive in college. Visit your college counselor for further assistance or re-read some of the chapters in this text.

Use these scores to complete the exercise "Chart Your Success" as in Chapter 1. Note that the additional points are not used in the chart.

Success Wheel

Name _____ Date _____

Use your scores from "Measure Your Success" to complete the following success wheel. Use different colored markers to shade in each section of the wheel.

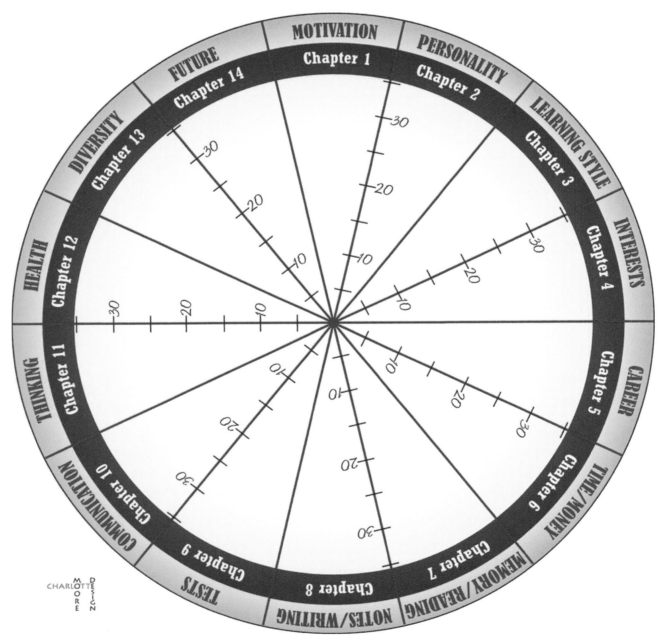

Courtesy of Charlotte Moore. © Kendall Hunt Publishing Company.

Compare your results to those on this same assessment in Chapter 1. How much did you improve?

Visualize Your Success

Name _____ Date _____

To be successful, you will need a clear mental picture of what success means to you. Take a few minutes to create a mental picture of what success means to you. Include your education, career, family life, lifestyle, finances, and anything else that is important to you. Make your picture as specific and detailed as possible. Write about this picture or draw it in the space below. You may wish to use a mind map, list, outline, or sentences to describe your picture of success.

Happiness Is . . .

Name _____ Date _____

Think of small things and big things that make you happy. List or draw them in the space below.

Intentions for the Future

Name _____ Date _____

Look over the table of contents of this book and think about what you have learned and how you will put it into practice. Write 10 intention statements about how you will use the material you have learned in this class to be successful in the future.

1.

2.

3.

4.

5.

6.

7.

8.

9.

10.

Acronym   Acronyms are short cuts in our language using the first letter of each word in the phrase to create a new word. For example, NASA stands for National Aeronautics and Space Administration.

Acrostic   This is a creative rhyme, song, poem or sentence that helps you to remember. For example, you can remember the oceans with the acrostic "I Am a Person" (Indian, Arctic, Atlantic, Pacific)

Affirmation   This is a true statement. Making positive statements increases success.

Appeal to authority   This fallacy in reasoning involves relying on a questionable expert to make a decision.

Appeal to common practice   This fallacy in reasoning involves assuming common beliefs are true.

Appeal to loyalty   In this fallacy in reasoning, loyalty is used to make decisions without considering whether they are right or wrong.

Appeal to pity   In this fallacy in reasoning, pity or emotion is used to replace logic.

Appeal to prejudice   An appeal to prejudice is a fallacy in reasoning based on a stereotype in which all members of a group are judged to be the same.

Appeal to scare tactics   In this fallacy in reasoning, fear is used as a way of blocking logical thinking.

Appeal to tradition   An example of this fallacy in reasoning is the common phrase, "Everyone else is doing it."

Appeal to vanity   This fallacy in reasoning is commonly known as "apple polishing". The goal is to get agreement by paying compliments.

Artificial Intelligence   Computers can be used to perform tasks usually performed by human beings including recognizing patterns, improving from experience, making inferences and approximating human thought.

Attacking the person   This fallacy in reasoning involves distracting attention from the issues by attacking the person.

Auditory learning strategies   This is learning through listening and talking.

Automation   Companies are using robots and automated equipment in manufacturing.

Baby boomer   This term refers to people born between 1946 and 1964.

Binge drinking   This is defined as five or more drinks in a row for men and 4 or more drinks in a row for women. Binge drinking has a negative effect on college success as well as general health.

Biomedical engineering   This new career area involves developing and testing healthcare innovations such as bionic implants, artificial limbs, eyes, ears, hearts, and kidneys.

Biotechnology   This career includes scientists who do genomic profiling, biomedical engineering, create new pharmaceuticals, and identify DNA. In the future biotechnology may be used to find cures for diabetes, arthritis, Alzheimer's disease, and heart disease.

Blood Alcohol Content (BAC)   This term refers to the amount of alcohol in your blood. In most states, the BAC limit for drunk driving is .08. Most people reach this limit with one to three drinks depending on weight and time since the last drink.

Body mass index (BMI)   This is a commonly used method of evaluating a person's weight. It uses this formula: BMI = (705 X body weight) divided by (height in inches X height in inches)

Brain science   This is another word for neuroscience which is the branch of science dealing with how the brain works, including how we learn.

Brainstorming   This is a creative thinking technique that involves first generating a quantity of ideas and then assessing their quality.

Career outlook   The career outlook refers to the availability of employment and is an important consideration in choosing a career and major.

Choose my plate   This icon is used by the federal government to help people choose foods wisely. Half of the plate is filled with fruits and vegetables, and the other half with whole grains and proteins.

Chronotype   Chronotype in this textbook refers to your time preference and when you are most alert. It is your prime time for accomplishing challenging tasks.

Communication style   This term describes your preferred way of communicating based on your personality type.

Compromise   In this approach to conflict management, both parties make a sacrifice in order to reach agreement.

Conventional   People with conventional work interests like to follow set procedures and routines. They prefer working with detail and data.

Conventional morality   This is the stage of reasoning in which people take into consideration society's views and expectations in making decisions about moral behavior.

Convergent thinking   This component of creativity is combining new ideas to find creative solutions.

Cornell format   This is a note taking system for taking organized notes consisting of a recall column and a section for taking notes.

Cramming   In college, this is the practice of waiting until the last minute to study for exams and then studying for a long period of time just before the test. This practice often leads to test anxiety and poor performance.

Critical thinking   One of the goals of higher education is learning critical thinking which includes questioning established ideas, creating new ideas, and using information to solve problems. It includes respect for the ideas of others.

Crystallizer   This is an experience that promotes the development of an intelligence.

Cult behavior   Cults use mind control to influence behavior. It is the opposite of critical thinking.

Cultural pluralism   Each group celebrates the customs and traditions of their culture while participating in mainstream society.

Culture   This is the behavior, beliefs, and values shared by a group of people.

Decoy   In this textbook, a decoy is an incorrect answer on a test. The text provides rules for recognizing a decoy, or incorrect answer.

Discrimination   Discrimination happens when people are denied opportunities because of their differences. Prejudice and stereotype are often involved.

Divergent thinking   This component of creativity is the ability to discover many different alternatives.

Diversity   This term refers to the many ways that people are different. These differences are not deficits: they are just differences. There are many advantages to appreciating diversity.

Diverting   This barrier to communication is changing the subject to talk about your own problems.

Distribute the practice   This memory technique involves learning small amounts of material and reviewing it frequently.

DNA   Deoxyribonucleic acid is the carrier of genetic information and the main constituent of chromosomes.

Dualism   This is the stage of ethical development in which we view the world as black or white, good or bad, or "we" versus "they".

E-commerce   This is the purchasing of goods, services, and information over the Internet.

Elaboration   This is a memory technique that involves adding details and connections to enhance memory. For example, you can increase elaboration by writing the material in your own words, rewriting your notes, using flash cards or creating a mind map.

E-learning strategies   These are strategies for learning or studying online.

Emotional intelligence   This is the ability to recognize, control, and evaluate your own emotions while realizing how they affect people around you. It is related to interpersonal and intrapersonal intelligences.

Environmental science   This science is developing new technology to conserve water, control pollution, create new sources of energy, manage global warming, and produce food.

Enterprising   People with enterprising work interests like to work in business.

Entrepreneurship   This term means starting your own business.

Ethnicity   Ethnicity refers to a sense of belonging to a particular culture and sharing the group's beliefs, attitudes, skills, ceremonies and traditions.

Ethnocentrism   This is the belief that one's own ethnic, religious, or political group is superior to all others.

Existential intelligence   This is one of the multiple intelligences and is defined as the capacity to ask profound questions about the meaning of life and death.

Extrinsic motivation   Extrinsic motivation comes as a result of a reward from someone else. For example, money is an extrinsic motivation for working.

Extrovert   This personality type is energized by social interaction and enjoys occupations with much social contact.

Fallacies in reasoning   These are patterns of incorrect reasoning.

Fear of failure   This is a major reason for procrastination.

Fear of success   Fear of success is not taking the last step needed to be successful because success would require major life changes. It is another reason for procrastination.

Feedback meaning   This communication technique involves restating the speaker's ideas in your own words to check understanding.

Feeling type   This personality type makes decisions based on personal values and excels at occupations dealing with people.

Fiber optics   This technology uses thin fibers of glass to transmit light and is used in telecommunication and in medicine to view inaccessible parts of the body.

Future-mindedness   This is thinking about the future, expecting that desired events and outcomes will occur, and then acting in a way that makes the positive outcomes come true.

Gender   This refers to the cultural differences that distinguish males from females. Sex refers to anatomical differences.

Generalization   This fallacy in reasoning involves treating all members of a group as if they were the same.

Generation X   This term refers to people born between 1965 and 1977.

Generation Z   This generation was born since 1995. It is also called the iGeneration, Gen Tech, Digital Natives, and the Net Gen.

Genocide   This is the deliberate and systematic destruction of a racial, political, or cultural group. It can include the destruction of the language, religion, or cultural practices of a group of people.

Globalization   Companies are increasingly doing business throughout the world.

Green jobs   These new occupations deal with the efficient use of energy, finding renewable sources of energy, and preserving the environment. It includes working with solar panels, wind turbines, biofuels, wind energy and improved food production.

Grit   This is a combination of perseverance and passion. Grittier students are more successful in college.

Gustatory learning strategies   This involves learning through taste.

Hedonist   This refers to a person who wants as many good moments and as few bad moments as possible in life.

Hedonistic adaptation   Some people assume that having more money or possessions leads to happiness, but the more you have, the more you want.

HIV/AIDS   HIV is the human immunodeficiency virus that causes the acquired immune deficiency syndrome (AIDS). Although this disease can be controlled with new medications, there is no cure for it.

Human Genome Project   This is a long-term research project to identify the 30,000 genes in human DNA. This project is helping to understand how the body works and improve medical treatment.

Interpersonal intelligence   This is one of the multiple intelligences and is defined as understanding people.

Information technology   This career includes the use of computers and related technology to store, retrieve and send information.

Intrapersonal intelligence   This is one of the multiple intelligences and is defined as the ability to understand oneself and how to best use your natural talents and abilities.

Intrinsic motivation   This means that you do an activity because you enjoy it and it has personal meaning for you. College students are more likely to be successful if they use intrinsic motivation.

Introvert   This personality type prefers more limited social contacts. They are often described as quiet or reserved. Their personal strengths are helpful in complex occupations requiring quiet for concentration.

Investigative   People with investigative work interests like work activities that have to do with thinking more than physical activity.

Immediate review   This is a powerful memory technique that involves reviewing immediately after learning something to prevent forgetting.

Intermediate review   This is a short review done periodically to minimize forgetting.

Intuitive type   This personality type focuses on possibilities, meanings and implications and enjoys creative occupations.

Jumping to conclusions   This fallacy in reasoning involves making a hasty generalization.

Judging type   This personality type is orderly and organized and often excels in business. Note that it does not mean to judge other people, as the term implies.

Kinesthetic learning strategies   This involves learning through movement, as in learning to ride a bicycle.

Laser   A laser is a device that uses a concentrated beam of light for cutting, drilling, surgery, optics and in recording and playing compact discs.

Loci systems   This is a memory technique that uses familiar places to aid in memory. For example, in a speech, imagine the entryway of a building and associate it with the introduction to the speech.

Locus of control   The locus of control is where you place the responsibility for control over your life. In other words, "Who is in control?" Students using internal locus of control believe that they are in control of their lives and take the steps needed to be successful. Students with an external locus of control blame others and may not take action to be successful.

Logical arguing   This barrier to communication is trying to use facts to convince without taking into account the feelings of others.

Long-term memory   This type of memory involves storage of memories over a long period of time as contrasted with short-term memory which quickly disappears.

Lose-lose   In this approach to conflict management, both parties lose.

Magical Number 7 Theory   George Miller of Harvard University found that the optimum number of chunks or bits of information we can hold in short-term memory is five to nine. It is frequently recommended to group information into 7 categories for the most efficient recall.

Math anxiety   You have math anxiety when you have a negative physical or emotional reaction toward math.

Millennials   This refers to the generation born between 1977 and 1995.

Mindfulness   This relaxation technique involves being aware of what is going in in a particular moment. It can be used as a quick break when you are feeling stressed.

Mind map   This is a system for taking notes that shows the relationship between ideas in a visual way.

Mindset   A mindset is a mental attitude that influences a person's responses and attitudes. A growth mindset involves positive thinking that leads a person to put in the effort needed to be successful. A fixed mindset is based on negative thinking and can be an obstacle to success.

Mnemonic   This word comes from the Greek word mneme which means to remember. Mnemonics include memory techniques such as acrostics, acronyms, and loci systems.

Modified three column note-taking method   This note-taking method is suggested for taking notes in math and includes a column for key words, examples and explanations.

Moralizing   This barrier to communication is preaching about what a person should or should not do.

Moral reasoning   This type of reasoning is a type of critical thinking that involves rationally deciding what to believe, how to act, and what is right and wrong.

Multiple Intelligences   This is the human ability to design or compose something valued in at least one culture. This definition broadens the scope of human intelligence.

Multiplicity   This is the stage of ethical development in which we realize there are multiple possibilities and answers.

Multisensory integration   This means using all the senses to learn more efficiently.

Nameplate website   This is your personal website which defines who you are and directs potential employers to your media sites.

Naturalist intelligence   This is one of the multiple intelligences and is defined as the ability to recognize, classify and analyze plants, animals, and cultural artifacts.

Negative self-talk   This is the expression of negative thoughts and feelings that are not productive and can cause increased anxiety.

Neuroscience   This is the science that deals with the structure and function of the brain, including how we learn.

New media   New media is using technology related to the Internet for communication. The definition of new media keeps changing as technology evolves.

Olfactory learning strategies   This involves learning by using the sense of smell.

Outline method   This is a system for taking notes using an outline format.

Outsourcing   Companies move jobs to other countries to reduce costs and improve profits.

Paralyzer   In this text, it refers to an experience that interferes with the development of an intelligence.

Peg systems   This is a memory device that uses words or numbers and associations to remember lists of words.

Perceptive type   This personality type likes to live life in a spontaneous and flexible way and is good at dealing with change. This type may need to work on time management to be successful.

Personal branding   Personal branding is the process by which we market ourselves to others. It is often done online.

Planful decision   A planful decision is made by carefully considering the consequences and pros and cons of each alternative before making a decision.

Positive self-talk   This means using positive thoughts that influence behavior and increase personal success.

Post-conventional morality   This is the type of moral reasoning in which basic human rights such as life, liberty and justice guide behavior.

Post hoc reasoning   This fallacy in reasoning has to do with cause and effect and explains many superstitions.

Power writing   This system for writing a college term paper includes prepare, organize, write, edit and revise.

Pre-conventional morality   This is the stage of reasoning in which morality is determined by the consequences to the individual.

Prejudice   This is a prejudgment of someone or something. Prejudices are often based on stereotypes and show disrespect for others.

Prime time   In this textbook, prime time is the time that you are most alert. Use this time to accomplish challenging academic tasks.

Procrastination   When you habitually delay or postpone doing important tasks, you are procrastinating.

Psychological hardiness   This term refers to people who are able to deal with stress in a positive way by having a positive attitude toward life.

Race   This term refers to a group of people who are perceived to be physically different because of traits such as facial features, color of skin, and hair.

Racism   Racism occurs when one race or ethnic group holds a negative attitude or perception of another group. It is prejudice based on race.

Racist   People who believe that their own race is superior are called racists.

Realistic   People with realistic job interests like work activities that include practical, hands-on problems and solutions.

Relativism   This is the stage of ethical development in which we discover what is right or wrong based on our own values and culture. Commitment in relativism is the highest stage of ethical development in which we defend our values, but respect the values of others.

Self-actualization   This is a term used by Abraham Maslow to mean knowing about and using your talents to fulfill your potential.

Self-fulfilling prophecy   Beliefs that we have about ourselves have such a powerful influence on behavior that the expectations become true.

Sensing type   This personality type learns through experience and trusts information that is concrete and observable. They excel in careers that require detailed work.

Serendipity   This creative thinking technique involves being open to unexpected discoveries.

Sexism   This is a negative attitude or perception based on sex.

Sexual orientation   This is a person's sexual identity based on the gender to which they are attracted.

Short-term memory   This is often called the working memory which is like a temporary space or desktop used to process information. Information stored in short-term memory quickly disappears.

Signal words   These words are clues to understanding the structure and content of a lecture. Some examples include: in addition, next, first, and most important.

Slippery slope   This fallacy in reasoning involves a supposed course of action that leads to disaster.

Smart goal   Smart goals are specific, measurable, achievable, realistic and timely.

Spatial intelligence   This is one of the multiple intelligences. It is defined as the ability to manipulate objects in space.

SQ4R   This study system for reading a college textbook includes survey, question, read, recite, review and reflect.

Stereotype   This is a generalization that expresses conventional or biased ideas about people in a certain group.

Straw man or woman   This fallacy in reasoning involves creating a misleading image of someone's statements, ideas, or beliefs to make them easy to attack.

Synergy   This is a creative thinking technique in which two or more elements are associated in a new way so that the result is greater than the sum of the parts.

Tactile learning strategies   This is learning through touching the material or using a "hands on" approach to learning.

Teleworking   This involves using smart phones to do business and work at home.

Telegraphic sentences   These sentences are used in note taking and are shortened and abbreviated similar to text messages.

Test anxiety   This is the fear of failing a test which can cause students to have difficulty with recall when taking tests. It is often caused by lack of proper test preparation.

Time bandit   In this textbook, the term refers to the many things that keep us from spending time on important goals.

Thinking type   This personality type prefers logical thinking and excels in scientific, business and technical occupations.

Two wrongs   In this fallacy in reasoning, it is assumed that it is acceptable to do something because other people are doing something just as bad.

Values   Values are defined as what we think is important and what we feel is right and good.

Virtual collaboration   Workers are increasingly working together by using technology such as Skype or other online software.

Visual clue   This is a memory device that involves using a memory jogger to improve memory. For example, place your keys on your books to remember to take your books to class.

Visual learning strategies   This involves learning through reading, observing or seeing things.

Win-lose   In this approach to conflict management, one person wins and the other person loses. The loser tries to get even.

Win-win   In this approach to conflict management, both parties work together to find a solution that meets everyone's needs.

Wishful thinking   In this fallacy in reasoning, an extremely positive outcome is proposed to distract from logical thinking. It is often involved in "get rich quick" scams.

Writer's block   This happens when you cannot think of what to write or how to begin. It is often caused by anxiety about writing.

Note: Page numbers followed by *f* indicate figures.

physical activity, 345
positive changes, 362–363
sexual assault, protecting from, 354–355
sleep, 357–358
stress and relaxation, 348–362
tobacco smoking, 348–349
weight losing, 347
Henderson, George, 381
Holland, John L., 79, 80
Holmes, Oliver Wendell, 318
The How of Happiness (Lyubomirsky), 403
Howe, Neil, 106
Human Genome Project, 111, 379–380
Human immunodeficiency virus (HIV), 355–357

I

Imagination, practice using, 333
Immediate review, 238
Impression, suggestions for, 124–126
Information technology, career in, 111
Intent to remember, memory techniques, 186
Interest
    artistic, 79, 82–83
    conventional, 80, 85
    developing, 183–184
    enterprising, 80, 84–85
    investigative, 79, 82
    knowing about, 6
    and lifestyle, 86–87
    Lifestyle Triangle, 87f
    O*Net Interest Profile, 79, 81–86
    realistic, 79, 81–82
    relationships between, 80f
    social, 79, 83–84
Intermediate review, 238
Internet
    critical thinking over, 325–326
    diversity, 373
Interpersonal intelligence, 69–70
Interpersonal skills, 375
Interview
    criteria in, 124
    job, 123–126
    questions, 125–126
    resume, 118–120
    worksheet, 135–136
Intrapersonal intelligence, 72–73
Intrinsic motivation, 14
Introversion, 39–41, 50, 52, 54, 292–293

Intuition, personality type, 42–43, 51, 293–294
Investigative interests, 79, 82

J

James, William, 251
Jefferson, Thomas, 283
Jobs. *See also* Career
    achievements on, 125
    developments affecting, 108–110
    interview, 123–126
    nontraditional, 109
    outsourcing, 108
    reasons for leaving, 125
    technology-related, 111
Judging, personality type, 46–47, 51–54, 294–295
Jung, Carl, 38

K

Kennedy, John F., 106
Kinesthetic learning strategies, 204
King, Martin Luther, Jr., 106, 389
Kohlberg, Lawrence, 327
Kroeger, Otto, 53
Kushner, Harold, 313

L

Lakein, Alan, 152
Language of responsibility
    "I" and "you" statements, 301–302
    negative self-talk, 303–305
    words, 302–303, 303f
Laser technologies, career in, 111
Learning
    audio, 203–204
    distributed practice, 186–187
    elaboration, 186
    failure is an opportunity for, 313
    gustatory, 204–205
    jobs and, 123–124
    kinesthetic, 204
    neuroscience and, 202–205
    olfactory, 204
    personality and, 54
    positive thinking, 183, 194
    and reading, 214
    tactile, 204
    visual, 202–203
Leonard, Frances, 159
Life decisions, values and, 87–89

Life expectancy, 342–343, 363–364
Lifestyle, 6
    interests and, 86–87, 87f
Linguistic intelligence, 72
LinkedIn, 118, 120, 122
Listening, 229–230
    factors interfere with, 296–297
    and note taking, 239
    practice and effort, 297–299
    talkers and, 64
Literature courses, 210
Loci/location systems, 190
Locus of control, 14–15
Logical-mathematical intelligence, 70
Longevity, and nutrition, 348
Long-term memory, 180–182, 260–261
Lose-lose approach, 307
Lyubomirsky, Sonya, 403

M

Magical Number Seven Theory, 184–185, 263
Major
    and career choice, 6
    choosing, 38, 56–59
    earnings and, 57–58
Management
    money, 53, 142–144
    time, 145–146, 151–154
Man's Search for Meaning (Frankl), 219
Master schedule, 149, 175–176
Matching tests, 278–279
Math
    anxiety, 269–270
    apps, 217
    improving, 215–220
    note taking in, 235–236
Math
    reading strategies for, 209
    success checklist, 287
    test strategies, 270
McKim, Robert, 332
Memory
    brain power, 192–193
    distributed practice, 186–187
    forgetting, 180–182
    improvement, 183–188
    long-term, 180–182, 260–261
    mnemonics (*see* Mnemonics)
    note taking, 228
    phenomenal, 183
    positive thinking, 183, 194
    and reading, 197–198, 205–214
    short-term, 180–182